AF646511

Anthropological Paradigm for Policy and Practice

About the Author

Prof. R.K. Mutatkar as a student of Prof. S.C. Dube, worked with Prof. Irawati Karve for ten years till she passed away in 1970. He was first Head of the Department of Anthropology, and first Professor-Director of the Interdisciplinary School of Health Sciences, University of Poona (now Savitribai Phule Pune University). He pioneered teaching of Medical Anthropology in India in 1974. He Chaired UGC Panel on Anthropology and Curriculum Development Committee which produced model anthropology curriculum for UGC in 2001. He has been Chairman of Indian National Confederation and Academy of Anthropologists (INCAA).

He established an academic institution, 'The Maharashtra Association of Anthropological Sciences' in 1976, and is the patron of 'Society for Indian Medical Anthropology'. Prof. Mutatkar initiated research on social aspects of Leprosy at WHO, Geneva in 1981. He chaired the first working group on AYUSH in Public Health for the XI Five Year Plan. He chaired the first Scientific Advisory Group of the Social-Behavioural Research Division at the ICMR. He has been a recipient of Tagore National Scholarship bestowed by Ministry of Culture (GoI), affiliated to Anthropological Survey of India.

Prof. Mutatkar has been honoured with 'International Gandhi Award for Leprosy' by Hon. Vice President of India as Chairman of International Jury Board and 'Adiwasi Sevak Puraskar' by Governor of Maharashtra.

His books "AYUSH in Public Health" (2 Volumes) (2016) "Tribal Health and Malnutrition" (2018) and "Sexuality and Sexual Behaviour—Social Science Perspectives" (2019) have been published by Concept Publishing Co. Pvt. Ltd., New Delhi.

Anthropological Paradigm for Policy and Practice

(Perspectives and Case Studies of Practicing Anthropology)

R.K. Mutatkar

CONCEPT PUBLISHING COMPANY PVT. LTD.
NEW DELHI-110059

© R.K. Mutatkar

All rights reserved. No part of this work may be reproduced, stored, adapted, or transmitted in any form or by any means, electronic, mechanical, photocopying, micro-filming recording or otherwise, or translated in any language, without the prior written permission of the copyright owner and the publisher. The book is sold subject to the condition that it shall not, by way of trade or otherwise, be lent, resold, hired out, or otherwise circulated without the prior publisher's written consent in any form of binding or cover other than that in which it is published.

The views and opinions expressed in this book are authors own and the facts reported by him have been verified to the extent possible, and the publishers and the editors are not in anyway liable for the same.

ISBN-13: 978-93-88937-52-8

First Published 2020

Published and Printed by

Concept
Since 1974

Concept Publishing Company Pvt. Ltd.
A/15-16, Commercial Block, Mohan Garden,
New Delhi-110059 (INDIA)
T : 91 11 25351460, 91 11 25351794
E : publishing@conceptpub.com *W* : www.conceptpub.com

Cataloging in Publication Data--Courtesy: D.K. Agencies (P) Ltd. <docinfo@dkagencies.com>

Mutatkar, R. K. (Ramchandra Keshav), 1936- **author.**
Anthropological paradigm for policy and practice : perspectives and case studies of practicing anthropology / R.K. Mutatkar.
pages cm
Includes bibliographical references and index.
ISBN 9789388937528

1. Tribes—India—Social conditions. 2. Tribes—India—Economic conditions. 3. Tribes—Government policy—India. 4. Rural development—India. 5. Anthropology—India. I. Title.

LCC GN17.3.I4M88 2020 | DDC 305.800954 23

DEDICATION

This book is dedicated to the memory of three Indian Anthropologists whose motivation and encouragement has resulted in the study of Anthropology, its applications and practices in my life as documented in this book.

1. Prof. Nirmal Kumar Bose, Director, Anthropological Survey of India, whose close association with Mahatma Gandhi for some time, motivated me to study Gandhian programmes focusing on Adivasi, Leprosy, Health and Nature-Cure, from anthropological perspectives.
2. Prof. Irawati Karve, a classical anthropologist whose recommendation brought me to Pune University as a faculty member. Her civilizational studies widened the scope of anthropological analysis. Her encouragement initiated development of Medical Anthropology at Pune.
3. Prof. S.C. Dube, my teacher, laid the foundations of applied anthropology in our mind. His initiative and influence positioned me at Pune University as a faculty member.

I owe deep gratitude to them.

Preface

I

This book offers a perspective about addressing the issues and concerns of people in India through an anthropological lens. The knowledge generated in classical anthropology by way of theory and method, by studying the isolated communities historically labelled as 'Primitive People', has been used to unravel the responses of lay people to programmes and processes of development, initiated in good faith by democratically elected representatives of the people.

Constitution of India is a statutory document representing the aspirations of the people, using the principle of Equity, to abolish the discrimination and deprivation amongst social groups of people. Directive Principles, Fundamental Rights and Duties, and Adult Franchise (Suffrage) are the guiding principles to uphold the human dignity and respect pluralities in the Federal structure of India.

Judiciary is expected to uphold the Constitution and direct the Executive to function as per the provisions of the Constitution. At some point of time, the Judiciary in India started entertaining Public Interest Litigation (PIL) from any citizen or citizens' groups like civil society about the issues affecting large population interests. Right to Life with Dignity, Right to Food, Right to Information etc. guaranteed by the Constitution and by subsequent legislation have become justiciable issues. Although not pointed out by anybody, Judiciary on its own, by *suo motu* injunction may ask the Executive to explain the issues affecting such Rights. Bombay High Court had thus sought explanation from the Government of Maharashtra about a large number of deaths and morbidity of tribal children supposedly due to severe malnutrition in the tribal belt of Maharashtra. Judiciary had reacted to the print and visual media reports about tribal malnutrition. There are such other issues like increasing suicides of farmers due to indebtedness, on account of crop failure, due to recurring droughts. The print and visual media discuss such public issues by conducting quick field investigations, talking to the people randomly and by organizing and reporting the view points of different political and public leaders representing various political and economic ideologies.

University system is expected to generate new knowledge of international standards. It is also expected to develop and function as the think tank about national issues. Public Universities are autonomous bodies created by the government and headed by the Governors of the States as Heads of Universities, designated as Chancellors. India as a Nation-State thus functions through the democratic interplay of all these arms. Besides, there are academic, research institutes, such as Anthropological Survey of India; in the public, private and voluntary sectors. There are also subject-specific national and regional level Associations, such as Anthropological Society, Society of Indian Medical Anthropology (SIMA), Maharashtra Association of Anthropological Sciences (MAAS), and Federation, such as Indian National Confederation and Academy of Anthropologists (INCAA), whose members deliberate regularly about the knowledge and applied aspects of their respective disciplines.

The Central and State governments have sector or line departments to govern and administer development agenda. There are Planning Commissions and Boards going down to the district level, where academicians could be invited as expert-members, or for issue-specific consultations.

Anthropology as an academic discipline is a part of the University system. Anthropology as a knowledge system claiming holistic and integrative perspective of Humanity, with conviction of Cultural Relativism, has developed as a Humanistic Science, acknowledging the bio-diversity and plural cultures. It is believed that Anthropology is more driven to stability and equilibrium, among the cultural communities, to understand and analyse natural modifications in terms of evolution and diffusion, rather than to planned and directed change, which is more visible now in decolonized countries. Classical ethnography presented the average and normal way of life of social groups and communities as existed at the point of field investigation, initiated in isolated communities, followed by the studies among peasant communities.

In the study of isolated, pre-literate communities, 'going native' was a method to understand Emic perspectives of people. The change process was very slow. The integrated whole was like a closed circle of a well in which life was lived. No doubt, the fundamental principles of human life theorized in the concepts of Culture, Cultural Relativism, Culture and Personality, concepts like Soft and Hard aspects of Culture, Status and Role, Psychic Unity of Mankind emerged out of these studies. Qualitative research methods, tools and techniques like participant observation, key informant interviews, got recognized as anthropology's contribution to social science research methodology.

However, after the Second World War, the world got changed not only due to decolonization but also due to spurt in research in science and technology. Life appears to be more easy going due to use of production, communication and transport technologies as compared to the struggles of primitive communities to collect food. However in social, economic and political aspects, life appears to be more complex. In matters of religion, there appears to be more intolerance and fundamentalism, at the global level. Pilgrimage tourism has increased as also the span of religious ceremonies and festivals. *Kumbh Mela* at Prayagraj in India, at the confluence of three rivers, one of which is believed to be mythical, as the largest religious congregation in the world is a miracle, followed by similar *Mela*, as per the signs of zodiac, at Haridwar, Nashik and Ujjain at the river-side.

In Nation-States, although prophesying democracy, significant decisions are centralized affecting the common man. Recently in India, demonetization and Goods and Service Tax (GST), accompanied with accelerating digitalization, have been the national level decisions impacting the lives of common man. Nationalization of banks, few years before, was one such major decision claiming the opening of bank credit to small entrepreneurs. Apart from such economic and financial decisions, the affirmative provisions in the Constitution are guaranteeing reservations in elected bodies to Scheduled Castes (ex-untouchables) and Scheduled Tribes (ex-primitive groups labelled as tribals) and to women. Reserved quotas are also guaranteed to 'backward classes' such as Denotified Groups (ex-criminal groups branded by British Raj), Nomadic Groups, and 'Other Backward Classes' (OBC representing the service castes from *Shudra Varna* among the caste peasantry), in educational institutions, more significantly in higher technical educational institutions and in public sector employment.

Technological advancement in agriculture, dairy, medicine etc. has brought in green and white revolutions in production and has controlled epidemics of infectious diseases. Life expectancy has increased disturbing the natural balance between fertility and mortality, leading to population explosion. There are unresolved issues about controlling Malaria, Leprosy, T.B. and Cancer or facing newer infections such as HIV and AIDS. There are more reported cases of diabetes and cancer, or cardio-vascular morbidities, labelled as life-style disorders, and mortality due to road accidents, and continuing tribal malnutrition, despite large budgetary outlays.

In a federal country like India, following the Constitution, as per the ideology of political party in power at the Centre and the States, and as per their election manifestos, schemes and programmes are designed and implemented by the bureaucracy which inherits the brand name 'Civil Services' since the British Raj in India. On the other hand, 'Civil Society' as a pillar of democratic governance has emerged from what was known as voluntary associations in the late 19th and early 20th Century in India. The common term for 'civil society' in currency is Non-Government Organization (NGO), replacing the earlier term, Voluntary Organisation. Some other terms like Community Based Organizations (CBO) like Women's groups, Youth groups and Farmers' groups, as also Self Help Groups (SHG) mainly of women, are being used to understand the interplay of democratic governance.

How does Anthropology as a knowledge system and as a university based academic discipline respond to these realities of life in a Nation-State like India, such as in linguistic states, districts, blocks or taluks; in villages, towns and cities? What is the scope and expertise of Anthropology as a Holistic study of Mankind to address the struggles and concerns of the people?

Anthropologists were commissioned in America to help the government to advise them about dealing with the 'Indians' (Natives as American Indians), through Bureau of Indian Affairs. During Second World War, several anthropologists were connected with the respective governments as consultants, such as with American Army administration in Japan. In India, Anthropology was a compulsory subject for study, at the Civil Service (ICS) examination during British Raj, to facilitate Indirect and Direct British Rule in India. Anthropology continues to be an optional subject at the Civil Services examinations, such as Indian Administrative and Allied Services.

In India, after 15 August, 1947, as a decolonized Independent country, and after 26 January, 1950, as a Sovereign Republic, anthropologists have been and are being consulted to advise about national issues such as affirmative action; about displacement due to development projects and about community participation in development and disease control programmes. Anthropologists are nervous that they are not being consulted as much as the Economists are consulted in national policy matters, and in implementation of the schemes at micro level. In fact, the early involvement of foreign and Indian anthropologists in the wake of Community Development in 1950s slipped out of their hands in favour of economists.

Anthropology is inseparably linked to tribal issues either at the research level, for adjudication about pseudo-tribal issues and about tribal development, as an off shoot of Community Development. This provided opportunities to participate in the government committees dealing with claims for Scheduled Tribe status by the non-tribal communities, to take the benefit of Art. 342 of the Constitution of India. Caste has been the much researched subject in Sociology and Anthropology. So, there are callings from the Social Welfare or Social Justice Ministry to classify the backward communities into Constitutional categories such as Scheduled Caste or as Other Backward Classes, Nomadic Groups, and De-notified groups etc.

The interaction as member of government committees has been the result of government resolutions or judicial directives to utilize the expertise of anthropology from academic institutions. Tribal Research Institute of the government or Social Welfare Department do request the university based anthropology academics to help in interpreting the Constitutional provisions about Scheduled Caste and Scheduled Tribe, and other backward communities.

Prominent mention needs to be made about an eminent Marathi intellectual and litterateur from a Scheduled Caste community, Shri Shankarrao Kharat who recommended my name to the Government of Maharashtra, to chair the Backward Classes Committee of the State Government (1992-93) with other academics as members, while Shri Sharad Pawar was the Chief Minister of Maharashtra and Shri Ramdas Athavale as the Minister of Social Welfare. Sri Kharat was earlier the Vice-Chancellor of Dr. Babasaheb Ambedkar Marathwada University. He was also President of Marathi Sahitya Sammelan (literary conference), a highest elective honour about Marathi literature (1984).

The extensions of a generalized sub-discipline such as Applied Anthropology into several sub-specialities like Medical Anthropology or Development Anthropology requires close interactions with several disciplines in social and natural sciences as also with humanities. One has to accept a collateral or subordinate position in an interdisciplinary or multi-disciplinary research or action team, to understand the roles of other colleagues to unravel the holistic perspective of anthropology, focusing about a particular issue. Anthropology as an interdisciplinary discipline has to promote networking to understand holistic reality of a situation to venture recommendations about action or intervention which is people-centric, but not populist or propagandist. The issue under scrutiny has to be analyzed in all its aspects which an anthropologist could do, due to broad vision of holism and field based investigation of ground reality.

We have to introspect about our academic preparedness and response to analyzing national issues using our holistic knowledge system. Why are we shy and withdraw our theoretical and methodological strengths, like a tortoise shrinking its legs fearing aggression? Why do we continue to prefer to live in our cocoon of ethnography of kinship or religion, or soft subjects like tobacco and smoke pollution instead of major issues of poverty, food security and self identity?

I got opportunities of being invited by medical institutions to provide exposure to them about behavioural issues relating to public health, since they have been under pressure to move from patient, disease and treatment to public health, and preventing and controlling diseases among the people at large. There have been other issues like misuse of affirmative reservations by pseudo-groups for which adjudication was required, based on scientific principles in Anthropology.

The book presents experiences of such peer interaction from across several disciplines and from various stakeholders. I am indebted to them for accepting me as a member of several teams. I hope, my anthropological insights helped them to look at issues from different perspectives and motivated them to develop humility to incorporate those insights in their policy reviews and implementation strategies.

The book does not provide literature survey of the type given in doctoral research monographs. An attempt has been made to Indianise anthropology by providing examples from the Indian field, in which I have been involved. Instead of paraphrasing the writings supporting applications of anthropology for policy planning, lengthy quotes have been provided from the writings of Western and Indian scholars.

This book entails discussion about Anthropology as a knowledge system and as an academic discipline introduced and evolved in the university system. I had a chance to be the Convener of UGC Panel on Anthropology and Nodal Person of the Curriculum Development Committee instituted by University Grants Commission (UGC) to prepare a model curriculum in anthropology for reference in the university system.

The widespread interaction and consultations with anthropology colleagues across the country through regional seminars organized for the purpose, resulted in preparing the curriculum document projecting the mix of classical anthropology with courses to confront the new challenges and opportunities, in order to respond to the vision of the Constitution (UGC: 2001).

Prof. Armaity Desai, Chairperson of University Grants Commission, who knew about my inputs in social science perspectives of leprosy, as Director of Tata Institute of Social Sciences, appointed me as Convener of Anthropology Panel and gave the responsibility of preparing a model curriculum for anthropology. Full freedom was accorded to form an all India Committee of Anthropologists, and to involve the participation of several anthropology departments by way of organizing regional meetings across the country in a workshop mode.

II

Chapter 1 discusses Anthropology as a knowledge system, evolved as classical Anthropology. Anthropology primarily developed in the West in response to quest for bio-social and cultural evolution of humanity. The studies of isolated communities with 'queer customs', without written history, led to behavioural and organizational generalizations developed into culture related theories.

Chapter 2 discusses the current position of Anthropology in India, mostly as visible in the university system, as an academic discipline. Anthropology is also visible in the academic research organizations and academic associations, as reflected in their research journals and other publications.

Chapter 3 with the title 'Practicing Anthropology' presents what is conventionally labelled as Applied Anthropology with live examples of applications in India, projecting the partnership with other disciplines, and manifesting the anthropological insights towards holistic understanding of development and governance issues.

Chapter 4 mainly presents issues about ethnic identities of groups and communities and use/misuse of affirmative action delineated in the Constitution of India, implementing the principle of Equity.

Chapter 5 discusses Rural and Tribal Development since the Government designed Community Development Programme for rural transformation and has been implementing distinct Tribal Sub-Plan (TSP), to integrate tribal areas and communities in the mainstream national plans of development.

In Chapter 6, under the general title of Medical Anthropology, specific examples have been presented about Indian systems of medicine (AYUSH) and about chronic ailments like Leprosy and HIV-AIDS due to risky sexual behaviour, having significant bio-socio-cultural and behavioural components. Primary Health Care as an aspect of Community Development is discussed in the context of National Health Policy.

Chapter 7 discusses the role of people-centric discipline of anthropology in its interaction with voluntary sector or civil society. Several social scientists including anthropologists are associated with the intervention and research programmes in collaboration with such voluntary associations, also referred as NGO.

Chapter 8 discusses research ethics and ethical issues about participation/consultation in intervention policy and implementation programmes.

The Epilogue aims to offer recommendations to the policy planners and implementers about consulting or involving trained anthropologists in addressing people-centric issues and concerns. It also projects the vision of Indian Anthropology to utilize its theoretical and methodological strengths towards Human Development.

Since the chapters are discussing plural contemporary policy planning and implementation issues where anthropological insights could make significant contributions, biographical note about initiation to those issues have been documented briefly. This might motivate young anthropologists to accept the challenge of every issue, presented by an opportunity worthy of anthropological analysis, not limiting to university classification of academic disciplines.

I hope, the book will open new vistas for debate and discussion about the strengths of anthropological paradigm for policy and practice. I hope, my colleagues and students will feel encouraged to share their experiences about such issues in subsequent publications. They will feel more confident in playing an active role, as anthropologists, in national reconstruction, following the spirit of the Constitution of India and universal human values.

III

While I joined as faculty member at the Department of Sociology and Anthropology, Poona University, located at the Deccan College

Postgraduate Research Institute, in July 1960, Anthropological Survey of India organised a two-week Summer School in Anthropology at Kodaikanal in 1961. Prof. Nirmal Kumar Bose, Director of the Anthropological Survey of India, asked for deputation of the faculty below the age of 30 years Being the youngest in a small group of senior anthropologists, I was chosen by Prof. Bose to discuss and dictate the proceedings every evening, simultaneously getting anecdotes about his interaction with Mahatma Gandhi as his Secretary for some time. My first formal publication, the summer school paper on "Changes in the caste system in a village near Gwalior, M.P." has been in the "Bulletin of the Anthropological Survey of India" publishing the proceedings of the summer school (1961, X-2; 5-9).

Since my initiation as a Masters student in Anthropology (1957-59) and later as a teacher, interacting with the students and faculty, across the country and abroad, and field trips to tribal and rural areas for academic and other work, connected with public sector calling, provided insights to crystallize the thoughts about the role of anthropology in national reconstruction.

The Masters curriculum in Anthropology (1957-59) had to follow the conventional pattern of classical anthropology introducing the students to all sub-disciplines, including laboratory training and field expedition to tribal-rural area. At Sagar University, the interaction of my teacher Prof. S.C. Dube with the Community Development Programme of rural reconstruction got into the class room as Applied Anthropology. This was extended into field based dissertation for some of us to do a monograph of a village community, emphasizing caste interactions and change process in a village. The monograph has been published as 'Caste Dimensions in a Village', the Gwalior village having been restudied by the Anthropological Survey of India, under its village restudies project. Other text book references for applications of anthropology in administration, medicine etc. were discussed, in the class room.

Joining Pune University in 1960 as faculty at the Deccan College Post Graduate Research Institute under the classical anthropologist, Prof. Irawati Karve, provided the realization that the classical anthropology as was labelled as ethnology in some quarters, could not be mastered by us, due to our training deficiency in networking Biological-Cultural-Archeological-Linguistic aspects, beyond preliminary orientation. We (with Prof. R.K. Gulati) were drafted by Prof. Irawati Karve to concentrate on structuring and implementing the distinct Masters Programme in Anthropology introduced at the University in 1963, in preference to earlier combined curriculum of Sociology and Anthropology with a Masters degree in Sociology.

Prof. Irawati Karve introduced me in 1963 to the PSM Department, Armed Forces Medical College (AFMC), Pune, as a guest faculty to deliver lectures about socio-cultural aspects of health. This led to contact with the PSM Department of B.J. Medical College (BJMC) and with Gandhi Memorial Leprosy Foundation (GMLF) as a Social Science member of the Executive Committee of GMLF. Position of guest faculty at the AFMC and BJMC was formalized through government orders from the Defence Ministry and the Government of Maharashtra respectively. Both the medical colleges were affiliated to Poona University. Medical Anthropology as a distinct course in Anthropology curriculum developed at Pune in 1974, for the first time in India, through these interactions. Amongst several public health and social work stalwarts, as members of GMLF executive committee, mention could be made of Dr. C.G. Pandit, first Director of ICMR, Dr. R.V. Wardekar, first Director of GMLF; Shri Baba Amte, eminent social worker in leprosy; Shri Devendrabhai, Member Secretary, Gandhi Memorial Trust; Dr. M.S. Gore, Chairman, ICSSR; Dr. S.D. Gokhale, Assistant Secretary General, International Council of Social Welfare; Prof. N.S. Deodhar, father-figure of Preventive and Social Medicine in India, from B.J. Medical College; and Dr. B.R. Chatterjee, an eminent leprologist. This provided opportunities, continuing now, to interact with the policy planers in the areas of health care services, and disease control programmes, focusing on leprosy, at the national and international level, including at the WHO. These also provided opportunities to apply the knowledge of Medical Anthropology in analyzing the policies, and implementation of health and disease control programmes, leading to acceptable recommendations.

Interaction with the ICMR needs special mention. Due to close interaction with Dr. C.G. Pandit who lived in the neighbourhood in his post-retirement life at Pune, I got acquainted with the visitors from ICMR such as Prof. Ramalingswami and the Directors of ICMR Institutes across the country. Dr. V.M. Katoch a leprologist, as Director General, ICMR and first Secretary, Department of Health Research, Government of India, upgraded the Social-Behavioural research unit at ICMR HQ to a full-fledged Division, with me as the first Chairman of the Scientific Advisory Group. Several anthropologists are the research scientists at ICMR headquarters and at ICMR institutes across the country.

Medical Anthropology opened flood gates for interacting with leaders dealing with Indian Systems of Medicine, more prominently with

Ayurved. Prof. Charles Leslie, an eminent medical anthropologist from U.S.A. introduced me to Pandit Shiv Sharma, doyen of post-Independence Ayurved in India and Prof. A.L. Basham, the great Indologist. This could help to develop close interactions with the world of AYUSH which led to a chapter on AYUSH in this book. Another facet of Medical Anthropology provided inputs in socio-behavioural issues dealing with sexuality in the context of HIV and AIDS. Prof. Perti Pelto another medical anthropologist from Connecticut University, U.S.A. and Dr. Moni Nag from Population Council, New York, took initiatives to rope me in this area of research. Initiatives in Medical Anthropology were identified by a pioneer agriculture-statistician Prof. P.V. Sukhatme from FAO which led to my appointment as the first Director of the U.G.C. sponsored Interdisciplinary School of Health Sciences at Pune University in the Science Faculty. Medical anthropology also helped to develop close association with luminaries in Public Health such as Dr. Banoo Coyaji, Dr. N.H. Antia and Dr. R.S. Arole, whose contributions in rural health care through their voluntary institutions (NGO) are internationally acclaimed.

My teachers, Prof. S.C. Dube and Dr. Leela Dube, as also Prof. L.P. Vidyarthi, Prof. I.P. Singh, Prof. S.C. Tiwari, Dr. K.S. Mathur, and others provided encouragement to develop anthropology at Pune University while a distinct Master's programme in Anthropology was initiated in 1963. A separate Department of Anthropology at Poona University (now Savitribai Phule Pune University) was established in 1977, seven years after the sad demise of Prof. Irawati Karve, which was earlier clubbed with Sociology, as a combined Department. I was designated as the first Head of the Department which provided me with opportunities to formally undertake networking with other disciplines within and outside the university system.

Encouragement from the then Vice-Chancellor, Prof. D.A. Dabholkar, an economist, with social consciousness, provided fillip to attract academics and tribal activists, to establish a voluntary organization, Maharashtra Association of Anthropological Sciences (MAAS) in 1976 on the University campus, with wider agenda of linking academics to people's concerns in various fields. However, his efforts to motivate other social science departments to join with us did not meet with success. Scholars from other disciplines interested basically in tribal issues such as Prof. G.B. Sardar, well known Marathi litterateur, Prof. P.V. Sukhatme, agricultural statistician earlier at FAO, Rome, Prof. A.R. Kulkarni heading History Department at Pune University and Chairman ICHR, provided guidance. Shri Janardan Valvi, a Bhil educationist and Sonu Kondu Govind (Sonu Patil), a Thakar tribal leader and social worker, hosted the maximum field training tours of Masters level anthropology students from Poona University in their respective geographical regions, as also facilitated field level workshops for social science college faculty in Maharashtra on research methodology, jointly organized by Anthropology Department and MAAS, supported by Dr. S.D. Karnik, Director, Western Regional Centre, ICSSR. MAAS became a platform of people such as social activists working on tribal issues, including government bureaucrats from forest, health and tribal development departments who aspired to receive anthropological insights to enrich their work. We could extend our concepts of 'whole' and 'totality' to understand the issues and concerns from the stakeholders' perspectives in addition to classical anthropological approach of looking at life through people's vision. Voluntary organization also provided us the freedom to experiment with organizing training workshops for college teachers, social workers and the tribal persons such as male and female *gram panchayat* members, in collaboration with the University Department of Anthropology, as an extension activity, mandated by the UGC as one of the duties of teaching, research and extension for faculty members.

All these interactions with people in the field and with bureaucrats, and academics from plural disciplines, provided opportunities to use anthropological knowledge insights for the people and understand their aspirations, about changing their lives for the better.

The initiatives taken by Anthropological Society, Kolkata in 2001 led to establishment of the Indian National Confederation and Academy of Anthropologists (INCAA) in 2004, to act as the Nodal Agency at the national level, with a mandate to hold yearly Congress. The leadership of Prof. Ajit Danda and Governing Council colleagues, brought us closer to the mainstream Anthropology, with the prospect of taking the academic discipline out of colonial research approaches, to relate to Constitutional aspirations about transforming India through participatory democratic processes.

The close association with Prof. A.K. Danda, Prof. K.K. Misra, Prof. K.K. Basa and many other colleagues such as Prof. Sarit Chaudhary, Dr. S.B. Chakravarti, Prof. P.C. Joshi, Prof. H.K. Bhat has motivated to put forward the experience of practicing anthropology in a book format. Several invited papers presented at seminars and conferences, more particularly organized and supported by Anthropological Survey of India, and IGRMS, Bhopal, and by University Departments, or INCAA, and

Anthropological Society and Asiatic Society, Kolkata, have formed the bulk of this book. I am grateful to Anthropological Survey of India for ignoring the delay in transforming and editing these papers to present them in a publishable format of a book.

The book is not a onetime activity. The title of the book emphasizing the relevance and capability of anthropology as a knowledge discipline to contribute to policy formulation and logistics of implementation at the macro and micro level in India, in tune with the spirit and directions of the Constitution of India representing "We the People of India" has evolved over the last sixty years of my apprenticeship in Anthropology. The Directors and Head of Office of the Anthropological Survey of India, and all the academic staff across the country, have been very supportive in discharging the role as Tagore Research Scholar.

I express my profound gratitude to Ms. Sharvari Nisal who provided me with excellent secretarial assistance for producing the typescript of this book, without which all the work during the last 60 years could not have been compiled and edited.

The book could not possibly be rated from the standards of classical academic scholarship, since applied aspects in the Social Sciences continue to be ignored in the University system. But the various anthropological insights which could help to develop people-centric policies and schemes, at macro and micro levels, so as to implement them basically by the people in a decentralized emic format, could be illustrative in the book. The applications have also found a place in the UGC Model Curriculum of Anthropology (2001), by way of optional courses and several Diploma and Certificate courses.

The book in a way is a case study of anthropological paradigm experienced by me in testing it in some areas about policy planning and its implementation. The book is expected to dispel the nervousness about designing and implementing intervention research about contemporary issues, with the bogey of 'value neutrality'. We owe our humanistic and ethical responsibility to use our scientific knowledge for the good of the people, by studying and recommending pro-people policies and their implementation, by involving the people as stakeholders. The universal values of plurality, co-existence and peace are the direct outcome of anthropological field studies, which have to be perennially promoted.

Acknowledgements

I express my profound gratitude to the Anthropological Survey of India, Ministry of Culture, Government of India by bestowing the Tagore National Scholarship to me, to facilitate active participation in academic activities of the Survey, across the country, which has culminated in writing of this book. I owe special gratitude to the then Director, Prof. K.K. Misra and Head of office, Dr. D.N. Pandey for being very supportive during my tenure (2012-2014) as Tagore Research Scholar.

Pune, 2 October, 2019 **R.K. Mutatkar**

Contents

Abbreviations and Glossary

Abbreviations

AFMC	:	Armed Forces Medical College
AHC	:	Ayurvedic Health Centres
AIDS	:	Acquired Immune Deficiency Syndrome
ANM	:	Auxiliary Nurse Midwife
ASHA	:	Accredited Social Health Activist
AYUSH	:	Ayurved, Yoga & Naturopathy, Unani, Siddha, Homeopathy
AUK	:	Adivasi Utthan Karyakram
ATSP	:	Additional Tribal Sub-Plan
AWW	:	Anganwadi Worker
APL	:	Above Poverty Line
AnSI	:	Anthropological Survey of India
BAIF	:	Bhartiya Agro-Industries Foundation
BAMS	:	Bachelor of Ayurvedic Medicine & Surgery
BCC	:	Behavioural Change Communication
BDO	:	Block Development Officer
BJMC	:	B.J. Medical College
BIMR	:	Birla Institute of Medical Research
BPL	:	Below Poverty Line
CBO	:	Community-Based Organization
CESS	:	Centre for Educational & Social Studies
CEO	:	Chief Executive Officer
CHV	:	Community Health Volunteer
CHC	:	Community Health Centre
CMDR	:	Centre for Multidisciplinary Development Research
CRHP	:	Comprehensive Rural Health Project
CSD	:	Centre for Social Development
CSSRL	:	Centre for Social Science Research on Leprosy
DAO	:	District Ayurved Officer
DRDA	:	District Rural Development Agencies
DT	:	Denotified Tribe
DST	:	Department of Science and Technology

EGS : Employment Guarantee Scheme
FAO : Food & Agricultural Organization
FRA : Forest Rights Act
FRHS : Foundation for Research in Health Systems
FGD : Focused Group Discussion
GDP : Gross Domestic Product
GIPE : Gokhale Institute of Politics & Economics
GMLF : Gandhi Memorial Leprosy Foundation
GNP : Gross National Product
GoM : Government of Maharashtra
GoI : Government of India
GST : Goods and Service Tax
HC : Health Centre
HDI : Human Development Index
HIV : Human Immunodeficiency Virus
IAL : Indian Association of Leprologists
IAS : Indian Administrative Service
IASTAM : International Association for the Study of Traditional Asian Medicine, India
IASTAM India : Indian Association for the Study of Traditional Asian Medicine
ICMR : Indian Council of Medical Research
ICTAM : International Congress on Traditional Asian Medicine
ICDS : Integrated Child Development Scheme
ICAR : Council of Agricultural Research
ICSSR : Indian Council of Social Science Research
ICHR : Indian Council of Historical Research
ICS : Indian Civil Service
IEC : Information, Education, Communication
IGRMS : Indira Gandhi Rashtriya Manav Sangrahalaya
IIPS : International Institute of Population Sciences
IMF : International Monetary Fund
INCAA : Indian National Confederation and Academy of Anthropologists
ISM : Indian Systems of Medicine
ISM&H : Indian Systems of Medicine and Homoeopathy
IVF : In-vitro Fertilisation
IPHS : Indian Public Health Standard
ITDP : Integrated Tribal Development Project
IUAES : International Union of Anthropological and Ethnological Sciences
JRF : Junior Research Fellow
KEMHRC : King Edward Memorial Hospital Research Centre
LBW : Low Birth Weight
LHT : Local Health Tradition
MADA : Modified Area Development Approach
MAAS : Maharashtra Association of Anthropological Sciences

MBBS : Bachelor of Medicine & Bachelor of Surgery
MDG : Millenium Development Goals
MMR : Maternal Mortality Rate
MNREGA : Mahatma Gandhi National Rural Employment Guarantee Act
MPW : Multi-purpose Worker
MPEB : Madhya Pradesh Electricity Board
MTPs : Medical Termination of Pregnancy
NABARD : National Bank for Agriculture & Rural Development
NCAER : National Council of Applied Economic Research
NEHU : North East Hill University
NFHS : National Family Health Survey
NGO : Non Governmental Organization
NHM : National Health Mission
NIRD : National Institute of Rural Development
NSSO : National Sample Survey Organisation
NSS : National Sample Survey
NT : Nomadic Tribe
NRHM : National Rural Health Mission
OBC : Other Backward Class
OPD : Out-patient Department
PDS : Public Distribution System
PESA : Panchayat Raj Extension to Scheduled Areas
PER : Protein Efficiency Ratio
PHC : Primary Health Centre
PIL : Public Interest Litigation
PO : Project Officer, Integrated Tribal Development Project
PRI : Panchayati Raj Institutions
PSM : Preventive & Social Medicine
PVTG : Particularly Vulnerable Tribal Group/Primitive Tribal Group
PQLI : Physical Quality of Life Index
RCH : Reproductive & Child Health
RUTF : Ready to Use Therapeutic Food
SBC : Special Backward Class
SC : Scheduled Caste
SEZ : Special Economic Zone
SHG : Self Help Group
ST : Scheduled Tribe
STBG : Save the Baby Girl
TBA : Traditional Birth Attendant
TDI : Taluka Development Index
TDD : Tribal Development Department
TISS : Tata Institute of Social Sciences
TRTI : Tribal Research & Training Institute
TSP : Tribal Sub Plan

UGC	:	University Grants Commission
UNESCO	:	United Nations Educational, Scientific and Cultural Organisation
UNFPA	:	United Nations Population Fund
VJ	:	Vimukta Jati
WHO	:	World Health Organization
YASHADA	:	Yashwantrao Chavan Academy of Development Administration, GoM, Pune.

Glossary

Adim Jati, Vanvasi, Girijan	:	Terms for tribe referring to primitive group, forest or hill dwellers.
Anganwadi	:	Under 5 rural child care centre in India.
Apsara	:	Heavenly nymph
Ashram School	:	Residential School in tribal India
Ayurved Gram	:	AYUSH Gram
Balutedar	:	Service caste group providing skilled work to farmers, such as carpenter, ironsmith
Baiga, Gunia, Vaidu, Bhagat, Devarshi	:	Terms used for indigenous medicine man
Bhabhi-Devar	:	Levirate relationship between a person and elder brother's wife
Brahma Hatya-Ka-Patak	:	Sin due to killing of a Brahmin
Chikki	:	Sweet cake made of amaranth seeds
Chana	:	Bengal gram
Chapati	:	Indian flat bread
Charak Samhita	:	Classic text of Ayurved written by Charak.
Chauras Ahar	:	Square Meal
Choupal, Chavdi	:	Meeting place in a village
Dal	:	Pulses cooked as curries
Dari	:	Cotton carpet
Daridranarayan	:	Poor people as images of god
Dalit	:	Refers to ex-untouchables
Deshi Dawa	:	Indian medicine (drugs)
Dev-lok	:	Heavenly habitation of god's kingdom
Dhaba	:	Refers to eateries-cum-resting places on highways
Dhoti	:	Traditional lower garment of man
Dhatu	:	Body's seven basic constituents
Dincharya	:	Ayurvedic daily routine
Doshas	:	That which vitiate the *dhatus*
Dushman-ko-maro	:	Kill the enemy (war slogan)
Ganpati	:	Hindu deity (elephant head)
Ghee	:	clarified butter

Gharelu Dawa	:	Home remedies
Gotra	:	Clan originating from common ancestor
Gram-Panchayat	:	Traditional village council of elders. Now an elected body by law
Gram Sabha	:	Traditional village council of all elders. Now village council of eligible electorate as per statutes
Gram Sevak	:	Paid Secretary of elected village council
Grameen Bank	:	Refers to voluntary banking activities of village women
Guru-Shishya	:	Teacher-Student
Haldi-kumkum	:	Sacred yellow and red powders put on the forehead of married women, as greeting
Hakim	:	Unani doctor
Holi Poornima	:	Full Moon, celebrating the Hindu New year in Hindi belt. Heralding harvest season of wheat crop.
Janbhagidar	:	Opinion leader from community involved in programmes of development and health.
Jagirdar	:	A chieftain under the king owning a territory of endowed villages.
Jati Panchayat	:	Caste council of elders
Kadha	:	Medicinal decoction of herbs
Kamsutra	:	Relating to sex behaviour and practices
Kojagiri Poornima	:	First full moon after monsoon
Kodh, Kodhi	:	Referred to leprosy and vitiligo in common usage
Kotha	:	Habitation of commercial sex workers
Kshatriya	:	Ruling 'Varna' in Hindu Social Organization
Kumbh Mela	:	Largest spiritual congregation of people by the side of designated rivers for a holy dip, to cleanse the body-spirit
Kuti	:	Cottage
Kshar-Sutra	:	Regarding anal pathological conditions
Lavni	:	Marathi belle
Mauli	:	Mother- addressed to Saint Dnyaneshwar from Maharashtra
Maharog, Kushta	:	Leprosy
Mahil Mandal	:	Women's council at village level
Mangalsutra	:	Auspicious necklace of black beeds as symbol of married woman
Mizaj	:	Body-mind equilibrium (Unani term)
Mitanin (ASHA)	:	Female village health worker
Morcha	:	Procession of people to express protest
Mukhiya	:	Village head-man (colloquial term)
Nautanki	:	Hindi belt dance-drama

Niyog	:	Insemination from a person other than husband
Ojas	:	End product of digested food as energy
Owi, Abhang, Shlok, Doha	:	Spiritual messages in poetic form
Panchayat-Samiti	:	Elected legislative body at sub-district level
Patwari/Talathi	:	Revenue clerk at village level
Panchsheel	:	Five principles for governance of tribal communities (spelt out by Nehru)
Panchmahabhoota	:	Five basic elements governing the universe
Panchkarma	:	Ayurvedic treatment regimen
Panchkanya	:	Five ideal women in Hindu mythology
Parampara	:	Tradition
Patel, Patil	:	Designation of village head-man
Peshwa	:	Brahmin Prime Minister under Maratha Rule
Prakriti	:	Body constitution or natural make up of body
Ram Rajya	:	Democratic Rule of Hindu God Rama as ideal
Rasta Roko, Rail Roko	:	Blocking public road or rail track as a protest
Rajbhavan	:	Governor's official residence
Rajpramukh	:	Prince (King) as head of state
Rasayan Chikitsa	:	Ayurvedic Treatment to promote physical and mental health
Ritucharya	:	Ayurvedic seasonal routine
Sadhu, Sanyasi	:	Monk, Mendicant
Sarpanch	:	Head of elected village council
Sattu	:	Powder of roasted gram and wheat as nutritious supplementary food
Samvidhan Din	:	Constitution Day, 26 November, celebrated especially by Dalits in Maharashtra to reinforce their rights bestowed by Dr. Babasaheb Ambedkar.
Sari, Ghagra, Odhani, Choli	:	Traditional dress of women, usually referred in Hindi belt.
Shukra	:	Semen
Shudra	:	Service castes in Varna hierarchy of Indian social structure
Shaniwarwada	:	Mansion of Brahmin Prime Ministers of Maratha Rule at Pune.
Suin (Dai)	:	Traditional birth attendant conducting labour.
Taluka/Tehsil	:	Sub-district
Vaidya	:	Ayurvedic Doctor
Vimukta Jati	:	Denotified (ex-criminal) ethnic group
Videshi Dawa	:	Western medicine (drugs)
Vipassana	:	A special type of yogic meditation
Wadi	:	Hamlet of a village
Zila Parishad	:	Elected legislative body at district level
Zamindar	:	Landlord of village lands who had authority to collect land revenue tax.

1

Anthropology: Knowledge System

"Recently a number of anthropologists and students have complained that cultural and social anthropology is failing to tackle significant problems of the modern world.... Anthropology is a child of Western imperialism. It has roots in the humanist visions of the Enlightenment, but as a university discipline and a modern science, it came into its own in the last decades of the nineteenth century and in the early twentieth century. This was the period in which western nations were making their final push to bring practically the whole pre-industrial non-Western world under their political and economic control.....Until the Second World War most of our fieldwork was carried out in societies that had been conquered by our own governments." (Gough, Kathleen, 1967: II-36, 1653-58)

Anthropology as an academic discipline in the Indian University system is about to complete the centenary. Several senior anthropologists in India had their training in Anthropology in U.K. and orientation in U.S.A. as students of pioneer anthropologists, who had their basic academic training in varied subjects, other than anthropology.

"At the turn of the century anthropology, or ethnology as it was often called, was added to the list of interests to be represented in expeditions to explore the natural history of unfamiliar parts of the world. A.C. Haddon, a zoologist, turned into an anthropologist between his 1888 and 1898 expeditions to the Torres Straits in Melanesia. On the second expedition he took along W.H.R. Rivers to "do" the natives. Rivers gave them tests of their sensory capacities and noted their customs. Though his development of the field method of recording genealogies led the way to the impressive understanding of kinship systems achieved in anthropology today, Rivers' and others' accounts of the natives observed on the Torres Straits expedition were published in a series of short papers each on some one topic; the reader sees no native life clearly as a whole....Haddon, Rivers, and Boas had their trainings respectively in zoology, psychology, and physiological optics and became anthropologists in the course of doing anthropology. They were the teachers of those first anthropologists who became such in universities. Two of these, A.R. Radcliffe-Brown and B. Malinowski, published books in 1922: The Argonauts of the Western Pacific and The Andaman Islanders. Each anthropologist had gone alone to a remote place, lived in a small and self-contained community, and come back to report a culture as a whole, and as a whole that could be understood as a system of functionally interrelated parts. (Malinowski's account was continued in a long series of publications about the Trobriands.) Attracting increasing notice as time passed, these books established clearly the model of research in social anthropology. This was what anthropologists conceived themselves as setting out to do. Each is a report, by a single investigator, of a whole that can be understood as providing for all the life's needs in some orderly way that makes sense to the people who live under it. Each is an account by a single investigator of a culture and community that stand alone, independent of others." (Redfield, 2018: 6-7)

The quotes from such pioneer teachers of anthropology as under, are meant to buttress the uniformity of thought about anthropology as a knowledge discipline about 'Man', like other scientific, academic disciplines. This is also branded as classical anthropology.

"If there is one *a priori* postulate on which all anthropologists are unanimous, it is that they wish to study men's physiques and men's cultures as other natural scientists study stars or rocks or lightning or elements or trees or animals or what goes on inside animals, Man, to every anthropologist, is an animal in the given world of nature". (Kroeber, 1948: 841)

"After all, the subject of anthropology is limited only by man. It is not restricted by time—it goes back into geology as far as man can be traced. It is not restricted by region but is world-wide in scope. It has specialized on the primitives because no other science would deal seriously with them, but it has never renounced its intent to understand the high civilizations also. Anthropology is interested in what is most exotic in mankind but equally in ourselves, here now at home. It concerns itself with men's physiques, with their societies, with the communications and products—the languages and cultures of these societies. It wants to know about particular languages and particular cultures in order to appraise the range and variety of human speech and civilization. Still more does it want to understand speech and civilization in general, in the abstract: the nature and process of language and culture." (Kroeber, 1953: xiii-xiv)

"Men have always been interested in studying themselves. The individual man spends his life understanding himself; a people provides itself with myths; nations write their histories. Therefore, it is futile to speak of a beginning of the study of man. We usually go back to the classical Greeks, but the study is worldwide—a philosopher can appear in any tribe—and it goes back anywhere that records carry us back." (Sol Tax,VOA: 1)

"Anthropology is a young science, as the scholarly disciplines go, but the comprehension of man and his works which it has yielded has been of far reaching significance. Its materials have underscored and documented the need to grasp the similarities that underlie the many different ways of life of human groups that must be understood if, in an age of expanding communications, adjustment between nations is to be achieved. This adjustment can only be reached, however, if mankind is considered in the broadest view, with a respect for differences and with a minimum of that militant centring on self and group, called ethnocentrism, that has been so great a bar to the creating of a functioning world society. And only anthropology, among the sciences, takes this broad view." (Herskovits, 1956: ix)

The vision of anthropology presented in the model UGC curriculum for Anthropology (2001) support this meaning of anthropology as a knowledge discipline.

"Anthropology as a holistic science of Man aims to study human origins, human variation, human nature and human creations as evolved historically, blending the biological and cultural facts and perspectives. Anthropology thus shares frontiers with the natural sciences, social sciences and humanities, or to be precise, it synthesizes the knowledge in order to understand Man as a species and his dynamic world. It strives to create what is known as anthropological knowledge. In a way, anthropology tries to seek answers to the philosophical questions about mankind. Who am I? From where do I come? What is my relationship with other living beings and with Nature? Where and in what direction do I go? Why and how?" (UGC, 2001:15)

"Anthropology as an academic discipline has a culture of its own. This culture of the discipline has to be transmitted to the students to increase the number of anthropologists who would spread the knowledge of human evolution, human creations, human variability and spirit of tolerance and coexistence to the humanity." (UGC, 2001:5)

Anthropology as an academic discipline, as the holistic study of Man and his works or creations, as a study of Mankind since the past into the present and projecting in the future has no boundaries or limits. However, in practical terms, the way disciplines of knowledge and their applications are organized in the knowledge and governance systems, we share the frontiers with the academic disciplines of all sorts.

Anthropology has also been described as jack of all trades, as Mirror for Man, as most humanist of all sciences and most scientific of all humanities. Dr. K.S. Singh, a history scholar and from the cadre of Indian Administrative Service, erstwhile Director-General, Anthropological Survey of India, observed that "humanism and profound concern for the people were strong points of Anthropology...Anthropology teaches respect for all cultures and autonomous identities'. (UGC, 2001: 8)

Actually these issues have been discussed in the UGC Model Curriculum for Anthropology (2001), in the context of training modules designed for university system. We also discuss these issues on the forums of INCAA and Anthropological Society, supported by Anthropological Survey of India.

As we know, classical anthropologists who studied island societies by living with the people compulsorily for one year, since the ship visited the island only once a year, saw and observed the life of the people, until they picked up the local dialect for communication. Non-verbal communication became in the beginning effective, by going 'native'. With verbal communication, they tried to understand the meaning of behaviour and arrived at generalisations of 'function', 'structure' and 'culture'. The Trobriand islanders kept contact with the small islands around, going in small boats, for barter trade, using the principle of 'value-in-use' (kula ring). Such barter trade continues on all international borders, sometimes, even with the people from 'enemy' country.

Classical Anthropology thus started with the documentation of 'queer customs' as an ethnography of other cultures. There has been more focus on finding the equilibrium and stability than change and modification. The public policy would be expressed as culture system interpreted by the elders with experience of dealing with the vagaries of nature and pestilence etc. There were no external forces which could force change in these isolated communities, protected by geographical terrain. Now, these island societies have become Nation-States, and paraded at the Commonwealth Games, Delhi, 2010.

Anthropology is defined as a science of man in totality. In practice, however, primarily, anthropologists are involved in dealing with the tribal issues and are invited as experts about tribal identity. In the classical writings, there has been discussion about the term primitive society in the context of cultural evolution. Anthropological concepts have developed out of prolonged, first hand studies of isolated and island communities and the theories developed are considered useful in analyzing the complex national level cultures and civilizations.

As Kluckhohn says, "The preoccupation with insignificant non-literate peoples that is an outstanding feature of anthropological work is the key to its significance today. Anthropology grew out of experience with primitives and the tools of the trade are unusual because they were forged in this peculiar workshop.... The primitive society is the closest to laboratory conditions the student of man can ever hope to get." (1959: 16-18)

As a result of anthropological studies, primitives as cultural ancestors of humanity got stereotyped. We use the concept of primitive society as an Ancient Society to defend the fieldwork training of students in as remote a tribal area as possible—also to provide them with culture shock—to follow the biological, zoological model of training from simple (tribal) to complex (peasant village and urban habitats). Tribal societies are simple societies according to our parameters about economic, social, religious, aesthetic aspects of culture. We imagine the distant past of humanity while we confront the so-called primitive communities. We have a compelling desire to reconstruct the path of cultural evolution of humanity and of different cultures of human societies.

Robert Redfield has explained the conceptualization about the study of Primitive Society as an abstract used extensively in Anthropology. "In social anthropology it is, I think, quite plain what has been the recurrent reality which the science has tended to conceive abstractly. It is the primitive band or tribe, the small and self-contained human settlement. My science rests upon the kinds of experiences of a single anthropologist living with some few remote people whose common life is for the most part bounded by the valley, hunting range, or island of their ancient habitation. To go to some distant place, to find there a community of people all much alike and living quite according to tradition, to be responsible, alone, for finding out all about the life of people, to need to look no farther than that life of the community, for what is relevant to finding it out—this has been the typical expectation of the young anthropologist; and in most cases he has more or less realized it....In consequence of such a characteristic experience with isolated and self-contained little communities, the social anthropologist developed his methods and came to conceive of his universe of comparisons. From the fact of his sole responsibility to report a remote and unfamiliar way of life the anthropologist became the jack of all social science trades, learning something of the economy, family life, government, and religion of the people he studied....Conceived as a culture, the primitive community was seen as customs and institutions in a unique design of life. Conceived as a society, the social relations described were all, with small exception, to be found right there in that little body of people. Thus arose the concepts of "a culture", "the social structure", "basic pattern", and anthropological holism generally....The primitive isolate, the community that is a whole all by itself, now something of an abstraction derived from many experiences approximate to the abstraction, became the model of research and the typical entity for comparisons and generalizations. Social anthropology came to be a natural history of equivalent and distinct social organisms." (Redfield, 2018: 6-8).

The methodology of 'going native' and the tools and techniques of observation, key informant interviews, genealogies, life history and case study continue to be of significance. Kinship and religion are the two most widely studied aspects of culture in Anthropology and are used as hard aspects while adjudicating between the genuine and pseudo tribal identities. The three universal relationships, of man to man, man to environment, and man to supernatural, along with such concepts as psychic unity of mankind are considered basic in anthropological thought. We have been discussing cultural and social evolution, such as the paleolithic and neolithic on one hand and food gathering, hunting, pastoral and agricultural economies, either following each other in time scale or co-existing as plural economies.

David Mandelbaum has reiterated the wide scope of anthropology, its methodology of studying the alien cultures, its holistic format and need to be able to communicate with non-professionals to sustain the relevance of Anthropology in the contemporary world. This approach is advocated to be a part of training in anthropology.

"It is the practice of field research, of collecting data and testing concepts in the context of real behaviour, that makes the holistic ideal a heuristic guide. The field anthropologist who sets out to study a group's economic activities need not feel constrained from studying mythology or child rearing if he finds that the economy is crucially involved with such other aspects of culture....The student, must move in an alien culture from time to time, even if it is only the unfamiliar environment of a new job or neighbourhood. His movement will be facilitated and his understanding deepened if he can learn to use the approach of the field anthropologist, looking closely, clearly, and dispassionately at what people actually are doing, as well as listening to what they say they are doing and learning, what others say about them; gathering his information at first hand, rather than relying exclusively on documents and statistics; taking his leads from what is important to them, the observed, rather than what may be important to the observer; testing his ideas about them within a frame of ideas which has been developed out of a broad spectrum of knowledge about mankind, rather than one which pertains to a few cultural settings or a single civilization....Professionals in any discipline can communicate with each other in their special technical dialect, they can usually find personal reward in playing out the scientific and scholarly procedures appropriate to their field. Without such internal, professional interchange there can be no real discipline. But without effective communication of the results of that interchange to the non-professional society, the profession can become quite irrelevant to its own culture and eventually inert in itself....The ideas which are repeatedly emphasized in these papers have to do with the whole of human behaviour, as viewed in the context of reality, and as studied in the manner of science. The holistic theme lays down that anthropological studies relate to as many phases of life as does the particular reality which is being studied. This is in contrast with other ways of studying man, in which disciplinary boundaries are more narrowly defined and problems outside the defined limits are not seriously examined. Anthropology takes into consideration both present behaviour and past, familiar cultures and remote, the commonplace in life and the extraordinary, the lowly in society and the elite, the rational in behaviour and the irrational, the cultural and the biological founts of action." (Mandelbaum, David, 1963: 4-5)

One of the pioneer classical anthropologist, Kroebar, has also visualized that anthropology will not remain focused on the study of primitive societies only, and would not claim tribal studies as their exclusive domain of research.

"One thing is certain: primitives and their cultures may remain the special concern, the wards as it were, of anthropologists, since no one else seems ready to take responsibility for them. But the anthropology of the future will not be concerned above all else with primitives, nor will it see in them the primary claim to its own intellectual autonomy," (Kroebar, 1948: 847)

We could experience anthropology gradually shifting from the study of primitive society to village community, however using the conceptual model of tribal ethnography. Village communities in countries like India and China, have been part societies of the great civilizations. Archaeology as a sub-discipline of classical Anthropology was studying the civilization such as Harappan, based on excavations. Particularly during Second World War, association of anthropologists with war office required the understanding of civilizations such as Japanese, Chinese and later Indian.

Both Mandelbaum and Redfield have thought of civilization studies as the natural study subject of anthropology. Study of simple societies follows the method of life sciences to gradually study complex organisms, starting with simple organisms.

"The study of civilization and civilized societies was part of the birthright of anthropology and has never been relinquished. For reasons both internal and external to the discipline, anthropologists concentrated on non-literate cultures and tribal peoples. In recent years, the impetus of anthropological research in such areas as Japan and India, and on problems of civilization and complex societies, has brought a freshet of new data and concepts into teaching." (Mandelbaum, David, 1963:9)

Robert Redfield has written widely about peasantry, about the conceptual difference between peasant and farmer and about India's mythology like *Ramayan*, as the great tradition, in great details. We are aware that *Ramayan* and *Mahabharat* are widely referred and quoted by all sections of the people in India, in the gram panchayats, as also in the Parliament, during discussions.

It is not only the disputes in the kin groups as are discussed in *Mahabharat*, but going in the mythical past about the race to grab a pitcher (*kumbh*) of nectar (*amrit*) among the gods and the demons, which emerged from the ocean, with drops falling at four places in India, that millions of people throng together for a holy dip in the sacred rivers, at these places, as what is described as the largest religious congregation in the world, commonly known as *Kumbh Mela.* In anthropological literature, there are significant analysis about sacred geography, sacred complex, sacred rivers and lakes, and hills at the national-civilizational level as also at the local and regional levels. There are a very large number of *Sadhus*, *Sanyasis* and God-men whom people from all sections revere and consult. Statistically measurable, pilgrimage tourism must be the major objective of tourism in India.

"Anthropologists have also come to study peasants in China, in the Middle East, and, especially in very recent years, in India. In each case the investigator sees a small society that is not an isolate, that is not complete in itself, that bears not only a side-by-side relation but also an up-and-down relation to more primitive tribal peoples, on the one hand, and to towns and cities, on the other....Peasant society and culture has something generic about it. It is a kind of arrangement of humanity with some similarities all over the world." (Redfield, 2018: 17)

The conceptual difference given by Redfield between a Peasant and a Farmer is very convincing. The emotional attachment of peasant to land in China has been nicely portrayed by Pearl S. Buck's Nobel-winning novel, 'Good Earth' (1931). A peasant in a Gwalior village told me in 1958, while I was residing in the village for fieldwork, defining *Kaliyug* as that period in human civilization when *Joru and Zameen* (woman-wife and land) are presented in the market. We have seen village land being supported (to save from mortgage) from urban earnings by migrant labour. Even non-farming occupational groups in the villages, such as a carpenter or an iron-smith would yearn to possess a piece of land (*zameen-ka-tukda*). A classic Hindi movie, *Do Bigha Zameen* has been widely acclaimed for presentation about the emotional attachment to land.

"I shall call peasants who have, at least, this in common: their agriculture is a livelihood and a way of life, not a business for profit. We might say that those agriculturalists who carry on agriculture for reinvestment and business, looking on the land as capital and commodity, are not peasants but farmers....Our cluster of real little societies is now sufficiently well determined. We are looking at rural people in old civilizations, those rural people who control and cultivate their land for subsistence and as a part of a traditional way of life and who look to and are influenced by gentry or towns-people, whose way of life is like theirs, but in a more civilized form." (Redfield, 2018:17-18, 20)

"The culture of a peasant community, on the other hand, is not autonomous. It is an aspect or dimension of the civilization of which it is a part. As the peasant society is a half-society, so the peasant culture is a half-culture. When we study such a culture we find two things to be true that are not true when we study in isolated primitive band or tribe. First, we discover that to maintain itself peasant culture requires continual communication to the local community of thought originating outside of it. The intellectual and often the religious and moral life of the peasant village is perpetually incomplete; the student needs also to know something of what goes on in the minds of remote teachers, priests, or philosophers whose thinking affects and perhaps is affected by the peasantry. Seen as a 'synchronic' system, the peasant culture cannot be fully understood from what goes on in the minds of the villagers alone. Second, the peasant village invites us to attend to the long course of interaction between that community and centres of civilization. The peasant culture has an evident history; we are called upon to study that history; and the history is not local it is a history of the civilization of which the village culture is one local expression." (Redfield, 2018: 40)

"When the anthropologist studies an isolated primitive community, the context is that community and its local and immediate culture. When he comes to study a peasant community and its culture, the context is widened to include the elements of the great tradition that are or have been in interaction with what is local and immediate. If he is interested in the transformations that take place through this interaction (diachronic studies), he will investigate the communication of little and great traditions with each other and the changes that may have resulted or come to result in one or both because of the communication. If he regards the peasant village as a persisting system, as synchronic studies (perhaps limiting his view of the lapse of time to the three generations that are sometimes said to constitute the period within which the recurrent changes that sustain the system take place), he will include in the analysis the persisting and expectable communications from the great tradition to the village as these are necessary to maintain the culture of the peasant." (Redfield, 2018: 52-53)

Redfield has referred to V. Raghavan (1944:57-65) while discussing the Great Traditions in India, including the *Puranas* and the epics.

"Great epics have arisen out of elements of traditional tale-telling by many people, and epics have returned again to the peasantry for modification and incorporation into local cultures....Great and little tradition can be thought of as two currents of thought and action, distinguishable, yet ever flowing into and out of each other....Hindu culture was carried to Cambodia and other lands by endowments made by rulers for the recital, in temples they built, of Hindu epics. With regard to south India, Raghavan traces an unbroken tradition of deliberate provision, by ruler and teacher, for recitation in the vernacular languages of the ancient Hindu epics, especially the Ramayana....The stories were not only recited, they were also expressed in devotional hymns sung by travelling singer-saints. So this Sanskritist, pursuing the great tradition downward, comes into the villages of present-day India. He is thinking of peasant India when he writes that "hardly a day passes without some sweet-voiced, gifted expounder sitting in a temple, *mutt,* public hall or house-front and expounding to hundreds and thousands the story of the *Dharma* that Rama upheld and the *Adharma* by which Ravana fell....The *Ramayana* is the ancient source widely influential in village India today. Derived from oral tales, it was fashioned into a Sanskrit epic by some poet, it is said, one Valmiki-and so became part of India's great tradition.

From the ninth century to the sixteenth century it was translated into many of the Indian vernaculars and in these forms was taught and sung by those processionals of the cultural structure about whom Professor Raghavan has told us. In the sixteenth century, Tulsidas made a Hindi version which became the script for many a village celebration. This writer, an exponent of high culture, made a kind of basic text. We are told that this version is perhaps better known among the common people of India than is the Bible among rural English people. But then, as time went on, the Hindi of the Tulsidas version became hard for the peasants to understand. They added to it accretions from their local popular usage. And now, in village India, this basic text requires interpretation to be intelligible to the villagers. This is how it is done in connection with the festival of *Ram-Lila.* There are two kinds of participants in the dramatic representation of the stories of Ram and Sita and the struggle with Ravan." (Redfield, 2018: 42-48, 52)

Ram-Lila, the drama enacted about *Ramayan* in big villages in the Hindi belt is very common. At Delhi, there is Ramlila ground, where the President and Prime Minister of India are present on the day (*Vijayadashmi-Dusserah*-tenth day of *Navratra*), when the effigies of demon king, Ravana, his son Meghnad and brother Kumbhkarna are ceremoniously set ablaze by using firework arrow, sometimes shot by the Prime Minister of India. This ritual symbolizes triumph of good over evil. Dusserah day is also celebrated as mother goddess Durga, killing the demon *Mahishasur* on this day earning her another name, *Mahishasur-mardini.* The third reference in Hindu mythology refers to Pandavas taking down their concealed armoury which they had kept on a tree, during an year of incognito living in the palace of King Virat, serving him and his family, as subordinates, performing various duties as cook, dance teacher, maid of the Queen etc. The tree and arms were ritually worshipped by the Pandavas, which are continued to be worshipped by Hindus across the country, including offering flowers and sacred *haldi-kumkum* to working tools, vehicles, computers and books. People greet each other by offering leaves of particular sacred trees, symbolizing offering gold.

Robert Redfield's emphasis of studies of peasant cultures in Anthropology, his conceptual difference between peasant and farmer and the concepts of little tradition and great tradition heralded a new era of knowledge about understanding culture and civilization, as the agenda of anthropology. The concept of great-little tradition helps us to analyse the reinterpretations of *Gita* and Bible through hundreds of years, in response to the changing times. The interpretation of *Gita* given by

Lokmanya Bal Gangadhar Tilak, a freedom-fighter, ('Father of Indian unrest') astronomer, journalist given in his book, *'Gita-Rahasya'*(1915) euloging *'Karma-Yoga'* (action), written in the British jail for six years, at Mandalay (Burma-Mynmar) has been widely acclaimed. The Marathi interpretation of *Gita* by Saint Dnyaneshwar, called as *'Dnyaneshwari'* appeal to common men so much that Dnyaneshwar is referred as *'Mauli'* (mother) in Maharashtra, turning the expressions, Dnyaneshwar and *'Mauli'* as synonyms. Vinoba Bhave and Mahatma Gandhi have tried their own interpretations of *Gita*. Vinoba Bhave's *'Gitai'* has been engraved on rocks at Wardha, where he lived at *Paunar Ashram*. Messages from Bible are discussed for half-an-hour before starting a scientific meeting on leprosy in Christian organizations, relating it to the required commitment for addressing the leprosy problem through science and compassion.

Haimendorf while discussing 'Culture History and Cultural Development' in the book 'Current Anthropology' has given examples from the studies by Irawati Karve and M.N. Srinivas as related to epic times and tendencies observable throughout India.

"A study of kinship organization in India by Irawati Karve (1953) extends over an infinitely greater period. Utilizing material contained in Vedic and epic Sanskrit literature, Karve describes the development of Indian kinship behaviour throughout a period of more than two thousand years, i.e. from epic times to the present day....M.N. Srinivas' book *Religion and Society among the Coorgs of South India* (1952) is basically an anthropological study of the dominant caste-group in the small state of Coorg, but the customs and ritual practices current today are set against the background of traditional Hinduism of both the All-India and the provincial type. The clarification of concepts which results is remarkable, and Srinivas is able to explain general tendencies observable throughout India, which hitherto have not been analysed by anthropological methods....From their analysis, supported by extensive illustrative materials, emerges a culture history of Bali in which elements of indigenous pre-Hindu culture (e.g. megalithic sanctuaries, animal sacrifices, ritual cock-fighting etc.) can be distinguished clearly from the Hindu culture introduced, not from nearby Java, but direct from India in the eighth century A.D. ...There was no Indian "colonization" in the narrow sense of the term." (Thomas, William L., 1956: 160-161) In Bali islands, we see huge Shiva temples. The *Ramayan* and *Mahabharat* belle dances are remarkable tourist attraction.

Robert Redfield while discussing the 'Cultural Role of Cities' has observed that "In India the epics and *puranas* have been translated into the major regional languages and have been assimilated to the local cultures. This interaction of a Great Tradition and the Little Tradition of local and regional cultures needs further study, especially in terms of the professional and semi-professional 'mediators' of the process....The role of leading personalities who because they themselves embody or know some aspects of a Great Tradition succeed through their personal position as leaders in mediating a Great Tradition to the masses of people. There is a vivid account of this process in Jawaharlal Nehru's '*Discovery of India*', in which he describes first how he 'discovered' the Great Tradition of India in the ruins of *Mohenjo-Darro* and other archaeological monuments, her sacred rivers and holy cities, her literature, philosophy, and history. And then he describes how he discovered the Little Traditions of the people and the villages, and how through his speeches he conveyed to them a vision of *Bharat Mata* (Mother-India) that transcended the little patches of village land, people, and customs." [Redfield, Margaret (ed): 1962: 343].

"The Great Tradition is one of the emergent characteristics of human society. A full understanding of China or India...requires that we take account of the two traditions....Each civilization is present in peasant village and in the more urbane scholar of the native Great Tradition-Mandarin, Brahmin, or Mayan astronomer-priest. We need to learn how the one is related to the other. Does the Great Tradition continue to affect the Little Tradition: in what ways and by what means?" [Redfield, Margaret (ed.), 1962: 302]

We are also using the concept of great-little tradition to establish the correlation between folk or ethno-medicine in India and the classical texts of Charak, Susruta and Vagbhat, which also requires re-interpretations as about *Gita* or Bible. Charak has said, 'Learn from the shepherd', that is, from the little tradition or what is commonly propagated as the local health traditions. This interpretation has been favourably accepted by those interested in AYUSH in Public Health.

"Anthropology barely hesitated before it redefined itself as a study of all kinds of people in all kinds of social and cultural situations. In 1923 Radcliffe-Brown, in a presidential address, defined social anthropology and ethnology as studies of the non-civilized peoples..... In 1944 he said that social anthropology "has for its field all human societies....American anthropologists have moved very rapidly to accept a part of the responsibility for studying civilized people, national states, and such world.-wide events as industrialization and urbanization....Today anthropology, especially American anthropology, studies just about everything human....The anthropologist no longer studies a primitive isolate, no longer sees only communities that form natural self-contained systems, and no longer works alone. His habits of work are undergoing profound change because of the sudden and wide expansion of his universe of subject matter....The anthropologist moves into his widened world still guided by his primary conception, the abstract primitive isolate." (Redfield, 2018: 9-10)

Margaret Mead's book, '*Cultural Patterns and Technical Change*' written for UNESCO (1955) has taken examples from all-over the world, from primitive and peasant communities to discuss wide ranging subjects, such as cross-cultural studies about aspects of technical change in Agriculture, Nutrition, Maternal and Child Care, Public Health, Industrialization, and Fundamental Education with focus on Mental Health.

"Margaret Mead had led in the study of modern national states by way of the group personality or character of such peoples. She studies national character even from a distance, as in the case of Russia. It is a very different way of work from that once followed in the Trobriands and in the Andaman Islands. Nevertheless, in enumerating the contributions made by anthropology to the study of contemporary cultures, she puts forward the provision which the anthropological approach makes "for the disciplined use of the primitive small society as a conceptual model. The isolated, self-contained community remains the abstract image around which social anthropology has formed itself." (Redfield, 2018:11)

Adam Kuper has endorsed such a shift in Anthropology from the primacy of studies about primitive society with oral history and oral tradition to the civilizations with classical texts and written history by way of epics, *puranas* and other scriptures.

Clyde Kluckhohn has also questioned the idea that anthropology was good enough only to analyse the culture and society of simple people.

"Historians, economists, and political scientists frequently say, "Anthropological methods work well enough when applied to simple peoples. But they are useless for dealing with a diverse, stratified, segmented society..... This reasoning rests upon misapprehension, though there are significant differences between tribal, peasant, and fully industrialized populations." (Kluckhohn, Clyde, 1959: 202)

Anthropology provides us the perspective of understanding issues through various spectacles, unlike the proverbial several blind men understanding an elephant. Many specialized disciplines are like those blind men groping in the dark, to analyse the part reality of culture and civilization, misconstrued as the total reality.

"The economist has attended especially to markets and has developed subtle conceptions of mentally constructed markets and of behaviour in such markets; the usefulness of these abstractions depends upon the fact that they leave out very much of what goes on the human life." (Redfield, 2018: 5)

Anthropology primarily as a study of tribal people in popular image had no variations at global level since the 'primitive', isolated communities had more basic cultural similarities than diversities. Without written history, it was easier to study them in their present period, living with them for an year; which is the unit of life. But in countries like India with people from diverse religious groups, with documented history, mythologies, philosophical doctrines and scriptures, it has not been easy to study the people and their culture. However, there are cultural identities sustained through sacred geography, pilgrimage centres, food and diet, attire, similar rituals and ceremonies and festivals, with no major geographic or ethnic group variations.

The Western perspective falls short of addressing the dynamics of decolonized nations like India which are guided by carefully designed Constitution. No doubt there are similarities in human behaviour at the global level in the patriarchal societies. What Earl of Spencer, Princess Diana's brother spoke as *'Mama'* (mothers' brother) during the funeral rites in the presence of British Royalty, affirming his resolve to protect his sister's sons, the Princes, is what all *Mamas* do, whether in Radcliffe Browns' South Africa, Firth's Tikopia, or Shakuni in *Mahabharat* or what is prevalent in current India, visible on ritual occasions and ceremonies, such as, marriage or sacred thread ceremony.

The civilizational studies required the inputs from all sub-disciplines of Anthropology. Studies of 'primitive' communities in the absence of historical documents, required inputs from linguistics, by way of interpretation of myths and legends, and biological measurements, to identify 'racial' or ethnic identities. Civilisational studies about India could be labelled as Indology or ancient history, but that is Anthropological knowledge.

Although, the term Anthropology may be of recent usage in comparison to other natural sciences, the quest for understanding Man in relation to Environment and Supernatural, goes back to several thousands of years. In ancient civilization like Indian Civilization, the *Vedas,*

Upnishadas, mythologies have thought about the nature of man, his behaviour, kinship group, moral and religious beliefs etc. A system of medicine like Ayurved is a sub-branch of *Atharv-ved.* The concept of universe as made up with *Panchmahabhoota* is also accepted in Ayurved and Naturopathy.

Anthropological thought, and anthropology as an academic discipline, as is taught in the universities, could be different perceptions. Anthropological knowledge, anthropological approach and insights, and anthropology curriculum could be at variance and followed differently in various Universities. At what levels, identity of anthropology as a holistic, knowledge system could be translated as a university based academic discipline, which would be in demand to address the issues or vision of Constitution of India?

It is not uncommon for disciplines or knowledge systems to have variable perceptions and agenda, at the international level, originating in the West with the hegemonic attitude of international leadership as compared to the grassroots realities or struggles of these disciplines or institutions at their respective national or regional levels. As an example, the establishment of International Association for the Study of Traditional Asian Medicine (IASTAM) at the International Congress on Traditional Asian Medicine (ICTAM) held at Australian National University, Canberra under the leadership of an eminent Indologist Prof. A.L. Basham had the scholars from various disciplines in the West who were studying Indian, Chinese and other Asian systems through texts. Prof. Charles Leslie, a medical anthropologist who was named General Secretary of IASTAM had spent an year in India interviewing the Ayurved experts and leaders. While the Indian Chapter of IASTAM was formed subsequently under the leadership of Pandit Shiv Sharma who revitalized Ayurved after Independence, the bulk of members were clinicians with academic affiliations. They were interested in empowering Indian Systems of Medicine *vis-à-vis* allopathy, which became the main system recognized in the public sector, including health care under community development programme. There is great variance between the scholarly agenda of few Western scholars associated with IASTAM and the agenda of Indian chapter with a large membership of clinicians, for its promotion as therapeutics.

Traditionally, Anthropology has been field studying the present with the objective of understanding the past and the process of change up to present, with the use of theoretical formulation such as evolution, diffusion and innovation. The emphasis through the theory of cultural relativism has been to respect the plurality, in terms of functional interpretation for a given structure. The predictive value of anthropology could only be tried with the beginning of applied anthropology.

The moment we discuss future of humankind, we need to analyze two issues from anthropological perspectives:

1. What is our vision of the future from anthropological understanding of present, marching towards future?
2. What is the predictive value of the discipline of anthropology and how could it be further sharpened in terms of theory and methodology?

We also have to introspect as to what is the popular image and understanding about anthropology at the level of lay people and the decision makers at the national level.

As we know the world has changed drastically after Second World War with decolonization. Impact of global economy, United Nations Organizations provides platform to meet and discuss, to agree, to disagree; with communication technology, health care technology and plural system of medicine, Anthropological agenda goes beyond national boundaries. Production and markets at the global level have to take cognizance of large populations of India and China. These processes are also active within nation-states, within provinces/states, districts, talukas, blocks, villages and ethnic communities. Dialogue and active participation go hand-in-hand.

How does Anthropology as a holistic Science of Man studying the historical processes of culture and transformation, the rise, fall and sustenance of civilizations, analyse the march of past into present projecting the future horizons with optimism?

Does anthropology have any active role to play in partnership with other disciplines, be those classified as science, technology, social sciences or humanities. We see anthropology in literature, in *'Yugant'* of Irawati Karve, in poetry of tribal poets, in films providing visual ethnography, life histories, biopics of not only heroes acclaimed globally but also Hindi movies, like *'Manzi—The Mountain Man'* or films by NFDC such as *'Current'*, *'Dharavi'* or about the decadent academic politics in *'Ek Doctor ki Maut'*. There are any number of documentaries showing success case studies.

Anthropological theories based on emic studies of isolated communities are found useful in understanding the static and dynamic aspects of culture. Concepts of soft and hard aspects of culture tell us about the dynamics of change in various aspects of culture. Structural-Functional theories help us to understand as to why some innovations are accepted in preference to others, as to what is the difference between awareness and acceptance. Some of our friends in the universities continue to study all phenomena as if they are isolated phenomena. Projects for studying ethnography of leprosy colonies as leprosy villages are still put up for research funding, using the conceptual model of primitive society, instead of studying the interaction of medical science, health care administration and perpetuation of stigma resulting in incidence of infection and disability, which needs the anthropological concept of holistic study of an issue for meaningful analysis and control strategies.

Anthropology need to broaden its concept of 'Holism' by understanding the micro–macro interactions. The isolated communities represented by our tribal students in Anthropology class-rooms are not interested in the ethnography of their culture, but look forward to theoretical and methodological techniques to plan and implement change, as per their aspirations. The 'whole' has to encompass the global issues, national and regional planning and implementation processes, at the micro and macro levels. There are different actors and stakeholders. The role of modern science and technology cannot be undermined in bringing about change in material soft aspects of culture.

INCAA has shown the sensitivity of organizing a number of Round Table discussions at the annual Anthropology Congress about the theme of 'Identity'. The publications are, such as:

1. Contested Identities in the Globalized World, February 2013.
2. Anthropology and the Future of Humankind, February 2014.
3. Identities, Ethnic Boundaries, and the State, February 2017.

There have been discussions about the various issues related to the term and scope of 'identity'. Philosophically, Man and the groups and communities in which he lives, struggles to survive and meet the aspirations as per his peer groups. The constant pauses in life refer to, who am I, who are we, what is the purpose of life? What are our responsibilities and duties to whom, and how to meet them with dignity, without losing self-esteem? Democracy as a value expressed in the anthropological concept of Cultural Relativism respecting the plurality and diversity also advocates equality among all people. The process of achieving equality and constant desire to improve the quality of life of all people gets translated into the governance at Macro and Micro level, addressing to the Etic and Emic perspectives, with a slogan 'Think Globally, Act Locally.' The constant and frequent meetings on different platforms and forums of the leaders of Nation-States are meant to iron out differences of perspectives and actions towards world peace and economic betterment of all people in the world.

It appears that no academic discipline can survive only as a body of knowledge for its own sake, unless its utility is visible at various levels. One way of understanding this phenomenon is to see as to where and by whom anthropologists are invited for consultation to give their expert opinion. We keep on discussing the future of anthropology and bemoan the dwindling number of students in anthropology departments. Wishes are expressed to multiply anthropology at the junior and senior college level and at the post-graduate level. Rarely do we discuss the role of anthropology in the current issues about human kind and the projections for the future. We are aware that no funding of any sort could be made available unless the utility of the discipline becomes visible. Anthropology as a liberal discipline, that it is, may not find favour in the current scenario of proliferating professional academic institutions. Among the marginalized people where rural to urban migration and mobility for making a living, first generation education is meant for jobs which provide salary every month. Knowledge, skills for making a living, even skills through education or vocational and technical education for making a living do not go well with the academic discipline of anthropology as currently found in the university system. How to change this for anthropology to use its knowledge, enhance it and use it, to show visible result by way of expertise?

There has been widespread discussion about anthropologists limiting their interests to the study of primitive society and shying away from the civilizations having textual history of great traditions.

Anthropology as a knowledge system has also been credited in these words:

> "To see and appraise humanity and its works, and men and their deeds, and beyond that man's relation to nature—to see these free from the distortions of ethnocentricity, with full acceptance of all attainable objectivity whether painful or pleasant; to contribute to such an attitude is perhaps the largest contribution of anthropology." (Kroebar, 1948: 849)

Adam Kuper has commented about the American influence on social sciences in preference to British influence.

"American influence came to predominate in all the sciences and social sciences after the war, and anthropology was no exception. The disarray of European social anthropology in the 1970s and 1980s made Americanization more palatable, even attractive....All the innovations in anthropology from the late 1960s crossed the Atlantic from West to East: the study of gender, the body, medical anthropology, the revamped field of material culture studies, the anthropology of film." (Kuper, Adam, 2010: 152)

Prof. Ajit Danda, Chairman of INCAA and former Director, Anthropological Survey of India has discussed the issues about impact of North Atlantic Anthropological thought, with implications for Anthropology in India, in his paper on "Maladies of Anthropology in India" (2014:49, 227-236). He has discussed the issues of colonial and post-colonial anthropology.

"Emergence and Development of Anthropology as an academic discipline under the British patronage had a fairly close association with the management of the empire. When the need for anthropological knowledge based on local as well as regional specificities is more than ever before, particularly for facilitating administration of pluri-cultural nation-states like India, Anthropology, due perhaps to lack of colonial patronage, seems to have fallen in grace, if not lost its importance to a major extent. It is rather pathetic to observe, how anthropologists of erstwhile colonized nations still appear eager in articulating their respective socio-cultural realities with the frame of research reference once prescribed by their colonial masters. What results, therefore, is a sort of acute identity crisis in Anthropology. This needs to be immediately addressed for the benefit of the people at large as well as for the discipline of Anthropology as such." (2014:49- 227)

I had communicated my spontaneous response to his paper as under:

> "The paper is very scholarly, not just a lead paper but full with appropriate references. The difference between knowledge and discipline discussed in the historical perspective is very meaningful. Similarly the Euro-American background from the North Atlantic region dominating World Anthropology including Indian Anthropology has been boldly brought out. Apart from the Indological references given in the paper, including Ayurvedic texts and Vatsayan, the programme Anthropological

> Society at its Golden Jubillee had organised on alternative voices in Anthropology in which I had an honour to participate with a presentation about Mahatma Gandhi has been a practical manifestation of the knowledge of anthropology. Gandhi's life style including his apparel to win over the Daridranarayan is an exercise in 'participant observation' to understand people's perspectives through their eyes. His Tolstoy farm has been classical action anthropology....In the discussion in UGC curriculum of Anthropology, (2001) I as a Nodal Person, did not discuss knowledge perspective but I was concerned about anthropology as a classical, holistic discipline and the deviations, as we found the way it was taught in our universities. I did advocate Indian Anthropology instead of Anthropology in India....This attitude of Western hegemony continues in all spheres of knowledge. While Ayurvedic time-tested drugs are questioned for efficacy and safety, several modern drugs having gone through animal trials and clinical trials are subsequently withdrawn as unsafe, or with bad side effects. Applied Science appears to be linked to market and is used for money and power....I happened to be face-to-face with a Medical Director of a multi-national pharma company. I asked him an innocent question as to how they prescribed the same medicine and dosage to all the people in the world, while the people were living in different climatic zones, with varying dietary habits, mating patterns linked to kin and non-kin, may be, affecting their genetic characters. The response I got from the Medical Director was, "We are a commercial Company." I could have digested such a response from a Sales Manager of a Company, but not from a medical director...On the platform of INCAA, these issues of knowledge and academic discipline are to be discussed frequently. Otherwise, anthropology becomes what anthropologists do, or teach in the classrooms. Your paper need to be widely disseminated." (Personal communication)

The subject matter of Anthropology, the Man, is an inseparable part of Nature as the Asiatic Society has put it, as its focus of study. Indian culture, particularly Ayurved and Naturopathy spell it out specifically that man is made of the same elements as everything else in the universe (concept of *Panchmahabhoota*). It is the nurturing of man that appears to make a difference. Anthropology is finding new peers among those who are advocates of bio-diversity, environment sustainability and protection, in consonance with the concepts of cultural relativism, plurality, universal values and psychic unity of mind.

To conclude, we agree with Michael Cernea, an anthropologist at the World Bank that, "Applied and development anthropologists need two categories of knowledge: "knowledge for understanding" and "knowledge for action" (Scott and Shore, 1979), to explain and to prescribe. My experience confirms that knowledge for action is indeed a distinct body of knowledge, but one that taken alone can be utterly pedestrian and deceptive. Knowledge for action is valid only if it is incremental to, and relies on, knowledge for understanding, because otherwise, precious as it may be, it is rarely self-standing in the long haul." [2002, 372, In Weaver, Thomas (ed.) "The Dynamics of Applied Anthropology in the Twentieth Century: The Malinowski Award Papers"]

2
Anthropology in India

Initiation in Anthropology

I shifted to Arts stream with Economics, Political Science and Geography after intermediate (12th standard) in Physics, Chemistry and Mathematics due to no engineering college at Gwalior, my native place. I was expected to follow engineering career. After graduation from Victoria College (now Maharani Laxmibai College), Gwalior in 1957, my teacher in Economics, Prof. A.K. Majumdar recommended me to go to Delhi School of Economics despite post-graduate in Economics available at Gwalior. I met Dr. Leela Dube at Delhi at the residence of my aunt, Dr. Sumati Mutatkar who was Director, Music, All India Radio. Dr. Mrs. Dube invited me to Sagar University to join Anthropology while Prof. S.C. Dube had joined Sagar University as Professor and Head of Anthropology Department. Prof. B.N. Ganguly, Director, Delhi School of Economics endorsed the recommendation commending Prof. S.C. Dube.

At Sagar, we witnessed Prof. Dube writing his book on Community Development, 'India's Changing Villages'. Master's level dissertation was assigned to study 'Caste Dimensions in a Gwalior village', now restudied by Anthropological Survey of India under its village restudies programme. As students, we were taken to attend Sociological Conferences at Agra, Calcutta (Kolkata) and Lucknow. I met Prof. Irawati Karve at Kolkata and the Vice-Chancellor of Poona University, Prof. D.G. Karve at Lucknow. This facilitated my selection as a teacher at Poona University.

I and my batch-mate Yogesh Atal were taken up as Research Assistants in a project on 'Communication, Leadership and Decision Making' immediately after the M.A. examination. Both of us were the first recipients of UGC-JRF introduced in 1958-59 interviewed by Sir C.P. Ramaswamy Aiyer chairing the selection committee at Delhi. With two faculty positions falling vacant, both of us were appointed as lecturers in

July 1959 in temporary position, while declining JRF. I got appointment as lecturer in Cultural/Social Anthropology in July 1960 at the Department of Sociology and Anthropology, Poona University, located at the Deccan College Post-graduate Research Institute, to work with Prof. Irawati Karve and Dr. Y.B. Damle. Teaching of distinct Master's programme in Anthropology at Poona University was initiated in 1963, replacing the combined Master's curricula in Sociology and Anthropology with a Master's degree in Sociology. Anthropology was constituted as a separate department bifurcating from the combined Department of Sociology and Anthropology in 1977, seven years after the sad demise of Prof. Irawati Karve, with me as the first Head of the Department.

As a student at Masters level, I was greatly impressed by the writings of Clyde Kluckhohn, Melville Herskovits, and Robert Redfield who has written about Indian great traditions and little traditions. M.N. Srinivas was an Indian Social Anthropologist whose writings on caste and the book on *Coorgs* were greatly appreciated. Prof. Irawati Karve's book on *Kinship Organisation* has been a classic. I had a chance to teach 'We, the Tikopia' by Raymond Firth and 'Religion and Society among the Coorgs' by Srinivas in the very first year of my teaching career at Pune. Prof. Dube was a wonderful teacher in the class and during personal interactions. He personally wrote the research protocol for Masters' village field dissertation and the chapter scheme of the monograph. Dr. Leela Dube was a perfectionist while correcting the writings of essays or project reports. I had a chance to meet the old guard, Margaret Mead while she came to Bombay (Mumbai). She inquired about tribal field trip among the Madia from where I had directly gone to Mumbai. ICSSR had organised seminar-meetings in her honour and S.N.D.T. Women's University awarded Honourary D.Litt. to her by holding a special convocation. While she was being introduced praising her as a remarkable woman, she boomed her first sentence in reply: "I am not a woman, I am an anthropologist."

Introduction

As an academic discipline, Anthropology is visible at the University Departments and Colleges, Anthropological Survey of India and the Museums under the Ministry of Culture, Tribal Research Institutes under Ministry of Tribal Development, Research Institutes of the ICMR and ICSSR and in the NGO sector working on health and development issues. Anthropology continues to be an optional subject with the UPSC and State Service Commissions for civil services examinations.

India as a Culture Region

India is labelled as an ancient civilization. Prof. A.L. Basham, the great Indologist has complimented ancient India in the following statement:

> "Our overall impression is that in no other part of the ancient world were the relations of man and man, and of man and the state, so fair and humane. In no other early civilization were slaves so few in number, and in no other ancient law book are their rights so well protected as in the *Arthasastra*. No other ancient lawgiver proclaimed such noble ideals of fair play in battle as did Manu. In all her history of warfare Hindu India has few tales to tell of cities put to the sword or of the massacre of non-combatants. To us the most striking feature of ancient Indian civilization is its humanity." (Basham, A.L., 1954: 8-9)

The term *Adiwasi* was coined probably by Thakkar Bappa and accepted by Mahatma Gandhi, to denote the indigenous people of India who in earlier Western anthropological connotation were termed as 'primitive' or as tribals. The Constitution of India has enacted an administrative category as Scheduled Tribe (S.T.) to speed up their development and bring them on par with their peer citizens in caste-peasant villages, usually referred as 'Mainstream'. As an agricultural country, India has about 6 lakh villages, although urbanization is a fast process, due to rural-urban migration to seek urban employment, as a result of underemployment in rural sector.

The whole of North East India with seven autonomous states constitute the tribal belt which was also exposed to Christianity during British Rule, due to the policy of exclusion. Several tribal states, districts and taluks were carved out after decolonisation to facilitate self-governance and democratic decentralisation. Affirmative action for participatory governance for tribal people living in geographical isolation and for ex-untouchables (Scheduled Castes) who were spurned, although part of village geography and history, was implemented by way of reservation in elective constituencies at every level, from village to national level statutory bodies. There have been monographs written about tribal communities, as also village monographs following the conceptual model of primitive society, by both foreign and Indian anthropologists. There have been ethnographic surveys of Tribes and Castes of various regions of India during British Rule, redone by Anthropological Survey of India as 'People of India' project.

Ancient Indian Civilization has been understood by the philosophy, mythology, scriptures, astronomy, mathematics, architecture, social and religious organisation, art and music and by sacred geography including trees, hills, rivers, places of spiritual importance and systems of medicine. There is plurality and diversity, philosophy of tolerance and absorption of foreign rulers who settled here. Besides Hindu faith which is inherited by the majority of people, certain faiths like Jainism, Buddhism, Sikhism originated in India. Christianity and Islam came from outside but people following those faiths, largely follow the framework of Indian social organization.

Anthropology in India as the knowledge system by way of the holistic study of Man in all times, gets fragmented with special academic and focused knowledge systems as Indology, Ancient Indian history, Indian philosophy, Archaeology, Linguistics, Folklore etc. If we have to study the past, whether ancient, medieval or recent, we have to correlate various knowledge disciplines. Anthropology is also history. For the pre-literate 'primitive' or tribal communities, oral history and oral traditions, myths and legends tell us about their culture.

In the University system, knowledge disciplines are largely divided into Natural Sciences, Social Sciences, Humanities and Technologies. Anthropology in India is placed under Science or Social Science faculties, depending upon where it originated, and are usually awarded both science and social science degrees. Recently, the terms, ethno-science, ethno-botany, ethno-physiology, ethno-pharmacology, ethno-medicine etc. are being used more frequently to denote focusing knowledge as applicable to people. There has been confusion about Ethnology and Anthropology being used as synonyms. However, the international body of anthropologists is termed as 'International Union of Anthropological and Ethnological Sciences' (IUAES) which holds international congress every five years. India had hosted International Congress at Delhi in December 1978, under the Presidentship of Prof. Lalit Vidyarthi. The post-congress symposium on Medical Anthropology was hosted by the Department of Anthropology, University of Poona, during 19-21 December, 1978.

There has been significant anthropological writing about the culture of India and sub-cultures of various regions in India in vernacular languages before anthropology was introduced as an academic discipline at Calcutta University in 1920. Significant vernacular writings about Indian culture and society have been labelled as literature, and research is carried out under humanities in the university system. In the vernacular literary writings, people's concerns focusing on social reforms for social transformation have been discussed. Voluntary associations were also formed to translate these ideas in action, during British Rule. There have been good monographs about village life, and recently the biographies and autobiographies of some literary figures, what we call life history, have been portrayed as ethnography of marginalised communities, such as the culture of ex-criminal or de-notified groups. Hardly any attempts have been made to analyse or translate such vernacular writing in English. Irawati Karve's anthropological interpretation of the pastoral culture and society of *Mahabharat*, *'Yugant'* received the highest literary award in India, and has been translated in several languages including English.

When we differentiate anthropology as a knowledge system and as an academic discipline in the university system in India, we realise anthropological thought and approach about civilization has been a part of Indian knowledge for long. Even the tribal communities in India had links in the epics of *Ramayan* and *Mahabharat* by way of legends about Eklavya and Shabari, unlike the island communities studied by Western pioneer anthropologists.

The Anthropological Society at the golden jubilee celebration deliberated and published '*Alternative Voices of Anthropology*' (2012) discussing Vivekananad, Gandhi, Tagore, Bankimchandra Chatterjee, Ambedkar and Jyotiba Phule as examples. I had an honour to present Gandhi following the anthropological approach. We are now using Gandhi's spectacles to monitor sanitation programme which he promoted, getting personally involved in popularising latrines, and simultaneously advocating alleviation of the status of 'scavengers' through *'Bhangi-mukti'* movement.

We have another example of cultural idiom being used by Bal Gangadhar Tilak during Ganesh festival which he popularised as public ceremony by using art, music and drama performances to bring people together without hurting the British rulers, who had announced as Queen's Proclamation, not to interfere with people's customs, religion and culture. He used the cultural symbols of Ganesh festival to communicate with lay people, as an example, through a play *Kichakvadh,* whereby Lord Curzon was portrayed as Kichak in Mahabharat, Draupadi as *Bharat Mata*, Yudhisthir as liberal group of Gopal Krishna Gokhale in Congress, and Bheem as militant group of Tilak. The play was subsequently banned by the British, as also the book written by R.K. Khadilkar was confiscated.

While this cultural idiom has been successfully used in Indian literature, visualised in films, it has not been an agenda in Indian Anthropology. The novels and stories by Sharatchandra Chatterji,

Bankimchandra Chattopadyay, Rabindranath Tagore in Bengali and such writings in Marathi or other Indian regional languages have been portrayed as films. Film directors like Bimal Roy, Satyajit Ray, V. Shantaram, Shyam Benegal, to name the few have immortalised the novels by portraying them as films. Mahabharat personalities continue to be portrayed in films. Visual ethnography, showing the struggles of common people, their family life, their houses, their concerns and the way they find solutions within the cultural framework is very effective and have become successful commercially. Special films have been made focusing the lives of Indian diaspora. Life histories of hero-warriors, freedom fighters and now the biopics of living legends are also being portrayed as films. Although anthropology does not have good ethnographic monographs of socially marginalised communities like the so-called denotified or *vimukta jatis*, the autobiographies from these communities provide the ethnographic material as life histories. The British authors compiled crime ethnography by interviewing the elderly persons from the communities branded by them as 'criminal tribes'.

Another area lacking in Indian ethnography is about anthropology of food. Besides the commercial portrayal of cuisine and food recipes in books and TV channels, the preparation of foods, food ethnography is also shown by way of regional variations, using the food products available in the neighbourhood environment. The relation of these recipes cooked in traditional methods with nutrition has not been analysed. Due to mid-day meal programmes and issues about malnutrition discussed at the level of higher judiciary, these policy issues could be addressed by food ethnography. Foods are closely linked with rituals, ceremonies and festivals. International summits and hospitality to visiting dignitaries is linked to what is commonly expressed as 'dinner diplomacy'.

Mahatma Gandhi went 'native' with loin cloth identifying with the *Daridranarayan* (the poor) as anthropologists are expected to go 'native' in their ethnographic fieldwork. These examples tell us the importance of anthropological theory and method in using the cultural framework for change.

While advocating Indianisation of Anthropology, Vidyarthi has said, "Among such numerous social thinkers mention may be made, for example, of Mahatma Gandhi whose teachings and ideals, if looked at, in terms of social sciences seem to Jaiprakash Narayan as the submerged part of an 'ice-berg' which ought to be explored." He has further said, "Along with the series of thinkers, ancient scriptures like the *Vedas*, the *Upanishads* the *Smriti,* the *Puranas* and the epics etc. are full of social facts and they need to be studied carefully to develop 'Indianness' in the social anthropology of India, which should be specially used in the study of cultural process and civilisational history of India." (1978: xviii)

Anthropology in India: An Academic Discipline

The Directory of Professional Anthropologists, brought out on the eve of International Anthropological Congress at Delhi, December 1978, has summarised about the rise and position of Anthropology in India. L.P. Vidyarthi's Foreword to the Directory is summarised as under:

> "Though Anthropology as a discipline in the Indian Universities has a late beginning the anthropological investigation in India was initiated by the British administrators as early as in 1774 under the auspices of the Asiatic Society of Bengal. Since then the British administrators, missionaries, travellers and a few other anthropologically-oriented individuals collected data on tribal and rural groups, and published about their life and culture in the journals of Asiatic Society of Bengal (1784). Indian Antiquary (1872), and later in the Journal of Bihar and Orissa Research Society (1915) and Man in India (1921). Owing to their early efforts we come across basic materials about tribes and the castes of the different parts of India published in a series of hand-books, gazetteers, census reports and a number of tribal monographs....Anthropology in India definitely witnessed a phenomenal growth when it was recognised in the University curriculum of Calcutta University in 1920. It provided initial stimulation to organise anthropological researches on a more scientific level by conducting field expeditions, writing books and articles and by training researchers for undertaking anthropological researches of various types....The Indian Anthropology which was born and brought up under the predominant influence of the British Anthropology continued to mature during the constructive phase (1921-1948) on the pattern and stimulation of British Anthropology. After the global war and specially after India's Independence, Indian anthropology could breathe free air and expand its scope of research. There was a positive increase in contacts of Indian anthropologists with specially the American anthropologists. Some American anthropologists like Morris Opler of Cornell University, Oscar Lewis of the University of Illinois, David Mandelbaum of the University of California, came to India

for fieldwork and stayed with their research teams and in general, they created an atmosphere (1) for the systematic study of Indian villages with a view to test certain hypotheses, (2) for refining some of the methodological frames developed elsewhere, and (3) to assist the economic development programme in Indian villages. With these developments Indian anthropology entered the analytical period of manifold developments in the various branches of social and cultural anthropology....Another field of social anthropology which reflects the British and American influence, and which needs to be mentioned separately is religion. ...Many of the village monographs referred to earlier include materials on religion and its importance in village life is evident from all these studies....The researches of Robert Redfield, Milton Singer, McKim Marriott of Chicago University in India, led to the beginning of an anthropological approach to the study of civilization by studying great and little communities of various dimensions." (1978)

"The tribal and rural community development programme of the Government of India gave further fillip to the Indian Social Scientists to study and evaluate the process of change in tribal and rural India. In such developmental programmes, the concept of Action Anthropology formulated by Sol Tax for the first time, partially replaced the principles of 'Applied Anthropology' developed during the British colonial administration. In some of the later writings of Majumdar, Dube, Elwin, Vidyarthi, and Jay on tribal policy and programmes, as well as the influence of action anthropology in India, have come to be established as an important discipline from theoretical substantive and action point of view....Socio-psychological research got a fillip under the same American influence. G.M. Carstairs, a British psychiatrist conducted field researches about culture and personality in a Hindu village in Gujarat and among the different communities of Rajasthan respectively.... The journey of Indian anthropology still continues. It has gone much ahead under the influence of and in collaboration with the British and then, of the American anthropologists. We have to think where does it go from here to address the contemporary issues in India, taking its rightful place in development planning for the good of the people." (Vidyarthi, 1978: iii-xix)

Anthropology in India: Zonal Updates

The Indian Journal of Anthropology started by INCAA in its very first issue (June 2013) has given zonal updates about Anthropology in India, in northern, north-eastern, western, eastern and southern India.

Abhik Ghosh while summarising about the Departments of Anthropology in Northern India has said, "However, the development of anthropology itself shows that anthropology has been slowly and steadily indigenizing itself (Sinha, 2005) to suit its social and political contours. This is apparent in the way that syllabi and faculty in Anthropology at Delhi University battle to create equality between social and physical anthropology. This battle, though it still continues across Departments all over India, becomes a little muted in the area of Punjab, where the practical nature of its use is most widely accepted while other areas like tribal studies, theories and other issues are ignored. Thus, based on public pressure, political ideologies or even individual whims, certain aspects of anthropology become focuses of attention or key symbols around which Departments of (mostly biological) anthropology coalesce and come into being in different universities across Punjab. These aspects become shattered and fragmented into a variety of departmentalised uses of Anthropology."

"Eventually, however, the holism of anthropology and thus the holistic nature of its analytical frameworks are lost. Their inter-linkages with social relations become inchoate and are eventually left out of any analysis of the region, since social anthropologists and their understanding of the region are underfunded, under-employed and few in number." (Ghosh, Abhik: 2013: *The Indian Journal of Anthropology:* 1: 1: 153-166).

Sarthak Sen Gupta has taken a review of anthropological studies on the people of North-Eastern India (2013). Greater Assam, bifurcated into 'seven sister states' has a tribal population of about 27 per cent as per 2001 Census, Meghalaya with 86 per cent, Mizoram 95 per cent, and Nagaland 90 per cent. After greater Assam was annexed to the British Empire in 1826, several tribal monographs were prepared by British administrators and later by anthropologists like Haimendorf and writings by Verrier Elwin. Due to ethnic diversity, there has been 'insurgent politics' and crisis of identity in the North East. Anthropology as a university based discipline started in 1948 with the Department at Gauhati University, followed by one at Dibrugarh in 1966. Later departments were established at NEHU in 1983, at Manipur in 1984 and recently at Itanagar in Arunachal followed by Diphu Campus of Assam University and in Nagaland. It appears, social anthropology predominates more at these places. Apart from universities, there are cultural, folk-culture or tribal studies centres. There is also a regional office of Anthropological Survey of India at Shillong since 1953.

Sen Gupta while summarising has given his concerns which need to be considered,

> "Research having social relevance is also conspicuous by their absence. It is expected that anthropologists working in the region would apply their work to the solution of contemporary social problems and for the eradication of the social evils. It is often criticized that the anthropological research findings are time and again not practical in approach and, therefore, cannot be utilized by policy makers."

> "There is also an urgent need for greater integration of cultural and biological anthropology. There is a demand for joint efforts to study socially relevant problems. The prospect of anthropology will depend upon a thoughtful understanding of its potency and certainly it lies in the specialized knowledge it can generate. Due weightage should be given to all the branches of anthropology while drafting a syllabus." (Sengupta, Sarthak, 2013: 1: 1: 167-184).

Anthropology in western India was dominated by classical anthropology which was followed by Prof. Irawati Karve at the Deccan College Post-graduate Research Institute with assistance from Dr. S.M. Katre and Prof. H.D. Sankaliya who respectively led linguistics and pre-historic archaeology in India. Irawati Karve with her B.A. in Philosophy, M.A. in Sociology under Prof. G.S. Ghurye at Bombay (Mumbai) and Ph.D. in Physical Anthropology from Germany did not write tribal or village monograph but analysed kinship and caste at national level and interpreted the pastoral society of *Mahabharat* by unfolding the personalities in the context of prevalent cultural values.

However, distinct Masters programme in Anthropology giving equal weightage to physical and social anthropology was initiated only in 1963. After her death in 1970, the department was shifted to university campus, continuing to be in the Social Science Faculty, however, following the model of fieldwork tradition, laboratory work and developing a tribal museum. Medical Anthropology at Pune initiated the establishment of the Inter-disciplinary School of Health Sciences in the Science Faculty. Department also provided leadership in formalising UGC Model curriculum in Anthropology (2001).

Who would cater to the tribal studies in tribal regions, with few anthropology departments such as in Maharashtra, only at Pune? There are universities and colleges being established in all tribal regions. Majority of the college and school teachers, and students, would be tribals in such institutions. They are not interested in the ethnography of kinship and religion. They want to join the mainstream by way of doing professional courses, by becoming doctors, engineers, architects and the like. How does anthropology address these realities of rising aspirations of tribal youth?

In fact, I was invited for consultations in 1985 by the State Government Committee constituted to bifurcate Poona University to form a new North Maharashtra University, encompassing four districts, which together was constituting 40 per cent of tribal population in those districts. I was asked, in what way, as an anthropologist, I would recommend the University to consider the participation of large tribal population, with opportunities of higher education, to address their development issues. I recommended that they could establish Tribal Research and Training Centre, with multidisciplinary faculty to analyse holistically the tribal issues and make recommendations. A conventional Anthropology department with all sub-disciplines of Anthropology, following the UGC guidelines about Anthropology teaching and peer reviews by other Anthropology departments would not necessarily focus on tribal development issues. We are now bemoaning that the conventional expertise of Anthropology about tribal issues is slipping out of our hands. The North Maharashtra University did establish an *Eklavya* Centre which has been upgraded as Tribal Academy in the tribal district town of Nandurbar. Recently, Gondwana University has been established in the Naxal affected tribal district of Gadhchiroli, whose campus has yet to be established for teaching and research, not limiting only to conducting examinations for the award of degrees. There also exists a Central Tribal University at Amarkantak on the border of Madhya Pradesh and Chhattisgarh from where the sacred river, Narmada, originates.

In Gujarat, social anthropology and Tribal Research Institute of the State Government functioned together at the University. Subsequently a regional office of Anthropological Survey of India was established at Udaipur.

Sagar University in Central India became a prominent centre of Anthropology under Prof. S.C. Dube since 1957. It attracted students from Chhattisgarh region and from Andhra Pradesh. Faculty for Physical Anthropology was imported from Delhi University. Research methodology, applied anthropology and village studies were given prominence. The students were not exposed to tribal fieldwork.

With the establishment of Ravishankar University at Raipur and subsequently at Bastar and Bilaspur, anthropology got introduced at under-graduate level in several colleges. Baster district which was geographical bigger than the state of Kerala was subsequently turned into a Revenue Division composed of different districts. However, the Naxal activity has put limitations on tribal studies.

Nagpur has been one of the older regional centres in Central India of the Anthropological Survey of India. However, there does not seem to be viable networking between the Survey regional offices and the Universities or Tribal Research Centres in the neighbourhood. Sometimes, the faculty of the Universities and research scientists from the Survey meet at the Seminars and Conferences. (Mutatkar, 2013. *The Indian Journal of Anthropology*, 1:1:185-190)

If we look around in Central India, as anthropologists or as citizens for understanding the geographical domain, in the context of history, called upon as experts to assist the people and the government, in various tasks confronting them, we have to understand both the basic and applied issues. Central India is a conglomeration of several sub-cultural zones and dialects. Commonly they could be referred as Vidarbha, Marathwada, Khandesh, as sub-cultural regions of Maharashtra, having some universal symbols and traditions such as deities, pilgrimages, saints, warriors, social reformers, and some material cultural aspects like dress, food etc. There are also tribal communities, not co-terminus with the political or governance boundaries. Cultural Zones are also described as Bundelkhand, Baghelkhand, Malwa, Gondwana, Bhil country etc. Each culture region has its own political history, social and economic organization and distinct dialects. Earlier the gazetteers documented these issues, an anthropological document being, '*Maharashtra—Land and its People*' by Irawati Karve.

We have a responsibility of documenting cultural unity and sub-cultural diversity manifested in local history, folk literature, pilgrimage centres and dialects, which is shared by common people in a geographical area. People identify themselves sharing the sub-cultural traditions and local history, providing them self-esteem.

Pradipta Das while reviewing 'Anthropology in Eastern India' in '*The Indian Journal of Anthropology*' (1:1:191-202) has also discussed Anthropology as a body of knowledge in these words:

"Although anthropology as an academic discipline began in India as a hand-maiden of colonial British administration during the early part of the twentieth century, it would be rather improper to make a statement that India was totally void in terms of the production of the very knowledge of anthropology. The earliest account of rise of anthropology as the body of knowledge in India dates back to pre-Christian era.....Another valuable compendium that contributed to our understanding of social organization and economic arrangements of ancient Indian society was Kautilya's '*Arthasatra*' which was dated to approximately 320 B.C.....From all accounts, Kautilaya's '*Arthasatra*' qualifies to be no less anthropological in nature......What is known today as physical anthropology or medical anthropology in conventional anthropological term, its origin as a body of knowledge in India can be traced to the emergence of Ayurvedic system of medicine......When one traces the history of development of anthropology as an academic discipline in India, it is the modern West Bengal, with Calcutta as its capital has been the cradle land of anthropology in India from where ideas and talents diffused to other parts of India (Vidyarthi, 1978). Although anthropology as an academic discipline became established much later as a teaching department in 1920 in Calcutta University, the germination of seed of anthropological studies in fact sprouted with the founding of the Asiatic Society of Bengal in 1774 under the initiative of Sir William Jones. In his inaugural address which was published in Vol. I of Asiatic Research in 1788, he made an explicit presentation of the scope of the society as the study of the entire field of man and nature....Danda (1995) remarked that during the first one hundred years (1778-1883) of publication of the journal, more than 100 papers having anthropological significance were published....Besides colonial administrators, a few missionaries and travellers evinced strong interest in anthropological study, generated data on tribal and rural communities of India, and brought out ethnographic accounts of the natives in different journals, district gazetteers, hand-books, and monographs....British administration issued directives to all the provinces and Princely States to appoint Superintendents of Ethnography for the collection of data for ethnographic studies, Census, Gazetteers etc., and this scholarly endeavour of Risley inspired Indian anthropologists such as Ananthakrishna Iyer, Sarat

> Chandra Roy, and Ramaprasad Chanda to undertake ethnographic studies on castes and tribes of India....Danda (1995) made a dichotomy between anthropology as a body of knowledge and as an academic discipline. He stated that, 'the roots of the academic discipline and the body of knowledge of Anthropology in Indian context are non-identical, in spite of the fact that the former by implication should ordinarily constitute a part of the later.' He further states "that knowledge of Anthropology, however, whether delineated in terms of boundary of the academic discipline or otherwise as already implied, did not altogether lack some traditional moorings." (Das, Pradipta K., 2013:1:1: 191-202)

As known, Calcutta University was the first in India to start teaching of Anthropology in India in 1920. There are now several Universities and colleges in Eastern India such as Vidyasagar University, Vishva-Bharati University, North Bengal University; Utkal and Sambalpur Universities in Odisha, where anthropology is taught at the post-graduate and undergraduate levels. In Odisha, it is taught at some places at the higher secondary or +2 level. There are well established laboratories and museums in almost all places and specialisations are offered in biological, socio-cultural and pre-historical archaeology at several places. Besides there are certificate and diploma courses in 'Forensic anthropology', in 'Visual communication and Culture'. At Utkal, specialisation in 'South-East Asia Culture Area Study' was initiated in 1978, as also Development Anthropology. The Department at Utkal University provided leadership in establishing inter-disciplinary institutions such as 'Centre for Regional Studies' and 'Population Research Centre'.

Francis Kulirani has reviewed Anthropology in Southern India (2013, 1:1:203-228). As we know the coast line of western India, in Kerala and Goa, was visited first by the Portuguese and French voyagers-traders, who settled there and proselytised local caste people. As in other parts of India, castes and tribes of India volumes were documented for south India also, including the Nizam state. Tribal monographs were also written as on the Toda. The physical anthropological studies based on somatoscopy, somatometric and blood grouping were also undertaken. Study of Coorgs by M.N. Srinivas, under the influence of his mentor, Radcliffe-Brown led to new era in village studies, around 1955. The concepts of Sanskritisation-Westernisation, Universalisation-Parochialisation,

Dominant Caste etc. were Indian contribution to anthropological analysis of caste and village. There have also been sacred complex studies in the south. Southern Regional Centre of Anthropological Survey of India at Mysuru (Mysore) established in 1960 contributed to several national and regional surveys undertaken by the Survey. Kulirani has taken an extensive review of anthropological research undertaken in the south. Apart from the studies undertaken in the respective TRTIs, there have been research and training institutes, such as NIRD, CSD, CESS at Hyderabad; CMDR at Dharwad; and MIDS at Chennai; French Institute at Pondicherry (Puducherry), and several other NGO outfits at Bangaluru (Banglore), Tiruvanthpuram (Trivandrum) etc. which have contributed to anthropological studies.

University Departments of Anthropology in the south, besides at Chennai (1945), are located at Waltair (1962), Tirupati, Puducherry, Hyderabad, Dharwad, Mysore, Kannur, Hampi, Kottayam. These departments are functioning in similar fashion as elsewhere, with regional variations. However, in regard to vacant faculty positions in the regional universities and student intake in anthropology departments, the picture is very dismal.

Anthropological Survey of India has established an International School of Anthropology, at its regional office at Mysore, to provide in-service training to the researchers of the Survey.

Kulirani has concluded the survey of south India with the remarks which deserve careful consideration.

"South India has its unique human heritage and has retained varied identities in terms of ethnic, linguistic, religious, geographical and cultural variations within the larger Indian civilizational and geographic whole. The human development index of the region in comparison with many other regions in the country is much higher but people still suffer from many social and economic inequalities. Fieldwork situation in South India demand a new ethnographic approach. Gone are the days when anthropologists could conduct the business of 'participatory observation' on their own choice and terms in any rural or tribal village....The scenario demands a shift from the methodology of participant observation approach to participatory research and its variant in community development programmes—participatory action research (PAR), so that the participating community gains from the research outcome....The job market for the post-graduates and Ph.Ds in anthropology has also changed significantly. Many of them find employment in non-academic set up. Hence, the training in anthropology needs to address the expectation of the students of anthropology to avail these new opportunities in the field of applied anthropology, especially related to development and social change. This is a new methodology for the study of social change and participatory action research (PAR) needs to be given a close scrutiny....Anthropologists and social engineers working in diverse community based projects in education, health, ecology, development studies etc. will find PAR immensely useful and anthropology may be able to make itself relevant to the development demands of the society as such." (Kulirani, B. Francis, 2013:1:1:203-228)

If we summarise the formal positioning of Anthropology as an academic discipline in India, before 1960, about nine anthropology departments were found in India. At the time, UGC model curriculum for anthropology was published in 2001, there were 35 university departments of anthropology in India. Most of the anthropology departments have a museum exhibiting artifacts from tribal areas and a laboratory for training in biological/physical anthropology. The curriculum includes basic courses in all major sub-disciplines such as cultural-social anthropology, physical-biological anthropology, prehistoric archaeology or archaeological anthropology and linguistic anthropology. At the final year, there is provision for specialisation in one of the sub-disciplines. Usually fieldwork training is undertaken in tribal area for the students. In various universities, anthropology is included in science faculty with natural sciences like physics, chemistry, botany, zoology etc. or in the social science faculty with sociology, philosophy, economics, political science, history etc. Both degrees such as M.A., M.Sc. are awarded for the common course depending upon the entry from science or social science stream.

In 1921, the first University Department of Anthropology was set up in Calcutta University, while teaching as a distinct Master's course was introduced in 1920. Other universities, however, were slow to follow. The Anthropological Survey of India, as a national organization for research in the different fields of anthropology was established in 1945 with Dr. B.S. Guha as its first Director. Several States have set up their own Tribal Research Institutes devoted mostly to anthropological research in tribal areas. Tribal Research and Training Institute of Maharashtra (TRTI) was established in 1962 at Pune, with academic links with the University Department of Anthropology.

ICSSR Review

ICSSR established in 1969 was reviewed by Malcolm Adisheshiah

Committee in 1973, with S.C. Dube as its member. The Anthropology Standing Committee had recommended studies on poverty, with focus on tribal communities, as a priority research area, besides studies of small towns and social biology. We seem to have abandoned poverty identifying it as an exclusive economic research issue, as health for a long time was considered as a medical issue. We have to keep on reiterating that Public Health speaks about Public, not focusing on patient, and Health neither refers to disease nor to absence of disease. All advocacy about inter-sectoral coordination in 'Health for All' documents of 1978 (*Alma Ata* declaration), is in-built in anthropological concept of integration of culture.

As we know, social science research projects were initiated under the Programme Evaluation Organisation, a unit under the Planning Commission, before Indian Council of Social Science Research was established in 1969. ICSSR is functioning through regional centres and several Research Institutes in various states in India. Prof. D.R. Gadgil, the Founder-Director of the Gokhale Institute of Politics and Economics, Pune as the first Chairman of ICSSR, in the very first meeting advocated to carry out a quick survey of research in various social science disciplines undertaken so far, to facilitate formulating priority research areas and programmes, for promoting social science research in India. Sociology and Social Anthropology were grouped together for undertaking such survey.

ICSSR's Review Committee to report on the 'Social Sciences in India: Retrospective and Prospective' in 1973, made recommendations about research priorities in Anthropology.

"In last two decades, Indian anthropology has registered impressive growth. It has been able to break out of the monographic shell in which it was encased in the early part of its growth. The first anthropological studies in the country were either carried out by administrators, or with the financial support of the administration, with a view to gathering data on the diversity of manners and custom in the country. For a long time the tradition continued of writing monographs on individual tribes and occasionally on castes."

"Applied anthropology was at first confined only to the narrow area of tribal administration and development. It received considerable encouragement when the community development programme was launched. It has also been utilized under the family planning programme."

"Priorities: Research priorities to meet national needs and the needs of disciplinary growth are listed below. The topics indicated are not necessarily comparable in scope or size or importance:

(a) Cultural dynamics: change, adjustment and emergence of new forces;
(b) Tribal studies: rigorous ethnography of 20 to 30 tribal communities, filling gaps in India's ethnographic atlas; economic and land problems of the Scheduled Tribes; tribes in the regional setting; and tribal rehabilitation;
(c) General and problem-oriented studies of border areas;
(d) Multidimensional studies of the culture of poverty;
(e) Studies in changing stratification and agrarian class structure;
(f) Studies in cultural orientation to medicine and community health;
(g) Cultural dimensions of nation-building;
(h) Anthropological studies of small towns;
(i) Studies in a changing material culture; and
(k) Conceptualizing Indian civilization through a series of micro- and macro-studies." (Vol. I: 1973: 33-37)

It has been recommended that applied anthropology should focus on problems of poorer sections of the community—the study of poverty, its socio-cultural determinants, levels of poverty—particularly in the context of tribal culture should be given top priority. Anthropologists were expected to undertake studies which would provide information base to the government to formulate and implement policies.

Simultaneously, 'A Survey of Research in Sociology and Social Anthropology' in volumes II and III has been presented.

Volume II has given the survey chapters about Sociology of Community Development and Panchayati Raj as Parts I and II, Sociology of Education, Medicine, Law as separate chapters out of the 10 chapters (1974), Volume III provides chapters with anthropological titles such as Cultural Anthropology, Tribal Ethnography in India, Material Culture, Folklore, Applied Anthropology and Research Methodology (1972).

The survey of research in 'Cultural Anthropology' pertains basically to cultural processes, culture area and culture and personality studies, taking the examples of studies undertaken among the tribal communities of India. It has been recommended that culture and personality studies and teaching could be taken up jointly by Departments of Psychology and Anthropology. An exhaustive survey of tribal ethnography starting with the establishment of Asiatic Society of Bengal in 1774 has been attempted by L.P. Vidyarthi classifying them into Constructive Period starting with the establishment of Anthropology Department at Calcutta

University and Analytical Period since 1950. The survey has presented studies according to different geographical regions and States.

The Chotanagpur region has been the most extensively studied area with basic ethnography. "The Chotanagpur Plateau covering six districts of Bihar and the adjoining areas of Madhya Pradesh and Orissa provides a rich laboratory for researches in anthropology. The uniqueness of this area impressed Robert Redfield who advised this author to portray the living sequences from primitivism to civilisation as reflected in the surviving 'style of life' of the food-gathers, hunters, shifting cultivators, settled peasants, craftsmen and emerging industrial urban workers coexisting in close proximity. This conservation of the various cross-sections of societies and cultures of human history as well as the existence of situations characterised by 'vanishing economy', 'vanishing religion', 'vanishing art-form and oral traditions' make Chotanagpur a centre of attraction for cultural historians and anthropologists. The students of cultural processes and applied anthropology whose emphasis is on the study of emerging societies find Chotanagpur an equally rich area for their study because both the traditional and modern processes of change are in full action in this area." (ICSSR-Volume III: 1972: 65)

It would be appropriate to present the gaps and priorities as identified by Vidyarthi in tribal ethnography in his words:

> "The study of tribal dynamics also deserves special consideration. Tribal culture is being rapidly transformed and it is high time that researches are directed to study this process of transformation from primitivism to civilization, from folk economy to industrial economy, from kin-oriented leadership to democratic experiments, from the preliterate society to the emergence of tribal elites and from isolated, stagnant and closed societies to dynamic and open societies. Concepts like tribalisation, detribalisation, tribe-caste continuum, sanskritization, revitalization movement, also need to be studied in terms of long, middle and short range history....The role of women in tribal society, though very significant, has not attracted the attention of any anthropologist except Leela Dube (unpublished thesis)....The study of tribal labour also provides a new dimension for research. The main problem of the tribals is to improve the underdeveloped condition of their economy. Of late, there have been some efforts on the part of the tribals of Bihar, Bengal and Assam to migrate to tea-gardens, just as those of Kerala and Tamil Nadu are migrating to rubber, coffee and

> tea-gardens. The tribal belts of middle India are in the process of large-scale industrialization. All these changes mean diversification in the tribal economy, which eventually leads to basic changes in tribal culture.....Tribal aesthetics, arts and crafts is another dimension to be studied in the wake of change. In general, tribal culture is distinguished from non-tribal culture in terms of folklore and folk dance. The tribal communities, again, are traditionally characterised by their peculiar techniques of producing cloth, iron, cane-goods and several similar items. The faithful recording of tribal technology through the preservation of museum specimens, filming, photographs and description seem to be the need of the hour." (ICSSR, 1972.102-103)

The trend report on Applied Anthropology in India has been compiled by T.B. Naik, Invariably, it quotes Nehru's five principles for tribal development. Prof. S.C. Dube has been referred (1968) for the recommendation that the anthropologists could identify the problems which tribals experience and suggest changes which would not lead to major disruption of their cultural traditions. Commission and Committee reports which were anthropologically oriented have been referred. The main theme has been about land and forest issues of tribals. Community Development studies follow Dube's 'India's Changing Villages' book on Community Development (1958). Education and Medicine have been discussed in the context of tribal communities with few references to village studies. Applied Anthropology in Industry, Law and Crime, and Arts and Crafts have also been surveyed basically with tribal references. T.B. Naik has raised the issues about the scope of Applied Anthropology.

"Looking closely at the total work done in applied anthropology in India which has been surveyed in the preceding pages, the following important points emerge:

1. Nowhere do we find a clear statement of what applied anthropology is and should be. Nor is there any discussion on the method and techniques of this branch of anthropology. It is now time that we at least discuss this and agree on the definition and scope of applied anthropology.
2. Of the researches in the seven fields discussed here, it is found that very little applied anthropological work has been done in (i) Industry, (ii) law, crime and similar other fields, including the problems of border areas, and (iii) arts and crafts. More emphasis should, therefore, be given to these areas.

3. Even in those fields where considerable work has been done, some areas seem to have been conspicuously left out. Applied anthropological studies of poverty, landlessness and indebtedness are very necessary and have to be taken up if we want to understand Indian society and its dynamics at the grassroots.
4. Most of the studies are mere survey work and of a repetitive nature. We must now endeavour to undertake qualitatively more significant studies." (Naik, 1972: 62)

T.B. Naik was associated with the Tribal Research Institute of Madhya Pradesh at Chhindwara for the major part of his professional career. It is not surprising that the survey remains limited to tribal issues. The survey of Social Anthropology Research presented in Vol. III brings home the image of Anthropology as that dealing with Tribal Issues. Community Development although studied initially by Anthropologists, Indians and Americans, has been surveyed with a title of Sociology of Community Development as if caste Hindu peasant village studies are what Srinivas calls Rural Sociology without any distinction with social anthropology. All village ethnographic monographs in India have been written by Indian and Western anthropologists by following the methodology of primitive society as a conceptual model.

The trend report on Sociology of Community Development and Panchayati Rai in two parts by R.N. Haldipur in Volume II of 'A Survey of Research in Sociology and Social Anthropology' by ICSSR (1974) is very comprehensive. It has analysed the multi-disciplinary studies as also the reports of several government committees and commissions. Before the formal start of Community Development Projects in October 1952, several experiments and pioneering efforts were made following the 'holistic and cultural approach' of Rabindranath Tagore and Mahatma Gandhi. The author has linked community development with the 'Sociology of Development'.

"Human well-being, in terms of improved standards of living is the objective of development in practically all under-developed countries. The various components that merit discussion in this regard are class structure, social institutions and value system. It is generally recognised that economic growth is desirable, that the masses of people are teachable and capable of growth and that it is a part of the process of development to help them as individuals or groups to grow." (ICSSR, 1974, 33)

Several anthropological studies have been cited to discuss the structural functional aspects of unity of Indian village or lack of it. My study of 'Caste Dynamics in a Gwalior Village' undertaken in 1958-59 indicate the factional conflicts hampering village development. The village has recently been restudied by the Anthropological Survey of India.

"In his book *Nilokheri*, Dey (1962) also takes a similar view. Since there are communities rather than a community in a village, each with its own customary norms and values,—the intertwining of these groups within a single organisation, with an accepted code which would bring them together, is not an easy task." (ICSSR, Vol. II, 1974:37)

To ensure peoples' participation, democratic decentralisation was considered necessary.

"Panchayati Raj in its present form came into being in 1959 when the Balwantrai Mehta Study Team (1957) submitted its report. It suggested the establishment of a three-tier system for infusing vigour into the working of the Community Development Programme. The recommendations of the Mehta Team were accepted by the National Development Council, thus paving the way for the establishment of Panchayati Raj at different levels of administration. The first states to introduce the system were Rajasthan and Andhra Pradesh, followed by Punjab, Maharashtra, Gujarat and U.P." (p. 64)

One of the significant research gap identified is "Interlinkages between the three tiers of Panchayati Raj and their impact on the overall performance of community development programme and on state and central leadership." (p. 84)

"Some studies on these lines could be useful in identifying areas of cooperation as well as of conflict, between the institution of Panchayati Raj and other village level institutions such as cooperatives, village school, youth clubs, Mahila Mandals, as all of them ultimately have the single objective of contributing to social development." (p. 86)

The trend report on Sociology of Medicine presented by Aneeta Ahluwalia (Monga) deals with the traditional systems of medicine as also with the modern system. Medical scientists as also health administrators are interested in the social science aspects of Health and Medicine or in Disease Control for helping them in their practice of medicine as also in formulation, implementation and evaluation of health programmes. Traditional systems of Medicine have been presented from the tribal and village studies by anthropologists in what is usually referred as ethno-medicine. There is usually description about Shamans, about causation of disease relating to religion, morality and magic.

"For example, there are gods associated with children's diseases, cough, colds, sore throats, boils, blindness, rheumatism, madness, diseases of pregnant women, and disease of animals. Most of these diseases can be cured by supplicating and propitiating these gods directly or through the shamans." (p. 408)

Modern system of medicine has been discussed in the context of several committee reports

> "Examples of such reports are those of the Bhore Committee (J. Bhore, 1946), Chopra Committee (R.N. Chopra, 1948), Udupa Committee (K.N. Udupa, 1959), and Mudaliar Committee (A.L. Mudaliar, 1962)." (p. 411)

The review has suggested studies of nursing profession, paramedical and auxiliary staff and the voluntary organisations of the medical profession. Attention has also been drawn to the underworld of medicine including the quacks, semi-medicine men such as vaccinators, compounders and mid-wives, and the illegal practices such as termination of pregnancies.

"An almost totally neglected area is research into the people's attitudes and action patterns regarding diseases and injuries of domestic animals, especially cattle. This also calls for studies of veterinary specialists and their role performance, as well as of their interaction with the persons concerned." (p. 420)

Academic Organisations

Review of anthropology in India would be incomplete without mentioning the contributions of Asiatic Society, Kolkata, Anthropological Society and INCAA since 2004. IGRMS, Bhopal has been playing a very important complementary role in the march of Anthropology in India. Earlier, the journals, 'Eastern Anthropologist' and 'Man in India' were the major academic journals in Anthropology. Briefly, the academic capital of anthropology in India has been Kolkata and rightly so, since anthropology as a university based academic discipline was first introduced in Calcutta University in 1920.

INCAA has emerged as an apex federating body holding Congress every year since its establishment in 2004 in different regions of the country. There are also impressive publications every year, mostly emerging from the Round Table discussions about a designated theme and the two memorial orations in honour of B.M. Das and S.C. Dube every year.

INCAA is the nodal body of anthropologists who practise the holistic and comprehensive discipline of Anthropology, which has the strength of fieldwork tradition, of qualitative methods useful for analyzing the processes of transformation, through historical times to contemporary issues, of the micro-macro, emic-etic interaction. We can see the change when the island communities studied in classical anthropology present themselves as Nation States at the Commonwealth Games at Delhi with their national flags. The anthropologists functioning in various government departments, institutes, universities and in NGO sector have joined INCAA.I had the honour of serving INCAA as its Chairman for one term of three years. I also had the privilege of organising INCAA Congress in 2007 and 2019 at Pune University.

The agenda of INCAA as a Confederation of Associations and individual scholars, and as an Academy appears two fold. As an academy, we have made a beginning with a Journal. We could take up multi-centric research projects in various basic and applied areas, such as in the areas of Development Anthropology, Medical Anthropology, evaluations of development programmes etc. We should hold research methodology workshops or other workshops in collaboration with the School of Anthropology, Anthropological Survey of India and University departments. As Confederation, we may have to play a proactive role in framing a draft National Tribal Policy, model curricula for Anthropology in the absence of such initiatives from the UGC and at the UPSC, and try out the networking of anthropology and various institutions mentioned earlier.

We do not envisage trade union spirit or activities. But in a political democratic set up, voices matter and voice of solidarity has power. On one hand, we think of humankind. But we also owe to our fellow citizens, particularly the marginalized, to offer the knowledge power of our academic discipline for their human development.

We have to discuss these issues on the INCAA forum objectively but with sincerity and commitment, to use the professional skills and strengths of Anthropology to continue to promote our empirical holistic domain.

The presentations of the anthropologists at the Round Table at INCAA Congress at University of Hyderabad in February 2009, published as an INCAA occasional paper No. 13 (Anthropology In India: Current Epistemology and Future Challenges) in February 2010 is worthy of serious consideration and introspection. The papers by Prof. K.K. Misra, about "Academic Colonialism, Indigenization and Production of Knowledge in Indian Anthropology", by Prof. T.B. Subba on "Anthropological Ambivalences: Are there Ways Forward?, by R.K. Mutatkar on "Emerging Paradigms: Anthropology and Social Realities", by Amitabha Basu on "Anthropology at the Crossroads", by Amitabha Basu and Suhas K. Biswas on "Is Indian Anthropology Dead/Dying?", concluded by Ajit K. Danda on "Anthropology in India: Current Epistemology and Future Challenges" have been found useful in the context of optimistic projection about future of Anthropology in India.

There have been other Round Table discussions at the INCAA organised Anthropology Congresses and subsequent publications about such issues edited by Danda and others in 2013, 2014 and 2017.

Ajit K. Danda has summarised about Anthropology in India and the role of INCAA. "On the whole, thus, Anthropology in India has two very distinct trends having divergent tendencies. As an academic discipline, Anthropology in India is heavily inclined towards the Western tradition. As a body of knowledge, nevertheless, Indian Anthropology is very distinct having scarcely receiving any influence from elsewhere. It is rather unfortunate that even after about seven decades of India's Independence, there has been hardly any cross-fertilization between these two distinct personalities of Anthropology in India. For a healthy growth of the discipline it is extremely important and urgent that the academic discipline receives its sustenance from the body of knowledge that emerged out of indigenous experiences and experiments....The Indian National Confederation and Academy of Anthropologists (INCAA), a national consortium of anthropological associations, since its very inception in 2004, has initiated moves to appropriately meet the inadequacies as are there in Indian Anthropology." (Danda, Ajit K., 2017: 52- 1 & 2, 15)

There are some academic and quasi-academic regional organisations which are open to members not necessarily formally trained in anthropology but engaged in subjects which are discussed frequently in anthropology, such as tribal issues including tribal literature, health and disease issues. Maharashtra Association of Anthropological Sciences (MAAS), Pune and Society for Indian Medical Anthropology (SIMA), Mysuru are two such organisations affiliated to INCAA. MAAS has been publishing a quarterly in Marathi, '*Hakara*' (clarion call) exclusively devoted to tribal issues since 1980. These associations organise seminars and conferences occasionally and undertake research projects funded by the Government (TRTI), ICMR or AYUSH Ministry and such other bodies. MAAS is a recognised Research Centre under Savitribai Phule Pune University (SPPU) and has close relationship with the Department of Anthropology and Interdisciplinary School of Health Sciences at the University.

MAAS has operationally defined the term anthropological sciences. "The term Anthropological Sciences encompasses all the disciplines, which deal with Man and His Works in holistic and historical perspective in relation to environmental, biological, behavioural, economic, social, political and cultural aspects. Anthropological Sciences thus include all social sciences and humanities and all the ethno-sciences such as ethno-botany, ethno-biology, etc. and biomedical sciences." The vision of MAAS has been spelt out as, "To develop, promote, coordinate and apply knowledge of Anthropological Sciences towards comprehensive, sustainable and holistic development of humanity with plural cultures."

Anthropological Survey of India

Anthropological Survey of India established in 1945, bifurcating the Zoological Survey of India is designed to survey the human surface of India. It has surveyed 4635 communities in India under its 'People of India' project. It also does commendable work in biological and palaeo-anthropological work. Some of the ignored communities like 'ex-criminal or denotified' communities have received the attention of the Survey. AnSI functions through its regional centres across the country. However, the co-ordination of the Survey with the Universities and Research Institutes where anthropologists are employed is much to be desired. All anthropologists in India look to Anthropological Survey as the nodal agency of Anthropology as a knowledge system.

Anthropological Survey designed a tool of Social Impact Assessment to assess/certify the impact of development projects which usually dehabilitate people from their ancestral abodes, such as due to dam construction, defence projects or construction of new airports, mining etc. Environment Impact Assessment to provide clearance for such projects was falling short of assessing the impact on the lives of people.

Anthropological Survey of India has also taken up the village restudies programme of the villages which were studied about 50 years ago. Such an exercise is expected to analyse the process of change in the studied villages as a result of programmes and schemes of rural transformation over the period expected due to democratic decentralisation. There are several issues like IVF and organ transplants as also nutrition and growth which require close scrutiny from the Survey.

While the government functions through line departments, knowledge institutions such as dealing with anthropology as the study of man in a holistic way cannot be an agenda of a single line department such as Ministry of Culture. It gives primacy to certain aspects of study to the neglect of other aspects. Such institutions as Anthropological Survey of India need to have status of an autonomous university which could provide freedom to proactively interact with such organisations like ICMR, ICSSR, ICAR, CSIR and other general and specialised universities such as dealing with health sciences and technologies. It could directly have a dialogue with the Tribal Affairs and Social Justice Ministries and with TRTIs in different states.

In the early phases of the study of man, ethnography and anthropology were almost synonymous; the products of this phase were well rounded, comprehensive with descriptive accounts of tribal and other groups. As a University discipline, however, it gradually acquired a greater theoretical orientation. First, the evolutionist and diffusionist approaches made themselves felt; but the first powerful impact was that of the British functional school. The cultural historical approach of the Americans has also influenced the growth of Indian anthropology. The structural approach was later adopted by many anthropologists in this country. Having made some recognizable contribution to the subject, Indian anthropologists have remained in touch with intellectual developments in their discipline the world over, and the subject as taught and studied in India has been sensitive to these developments.

Adam Kuper discussing 'Social Anthropology' in the book '*The History of Social Sciences since 1945*' has commented that rise of structuralism gave fresh impetus to studies about kinship and religion. Fieldwork tradition of Malinowski was continued. About the British anthropologists, he said, "They distanced themselves from issues of public interest. And increasingly they tended to redefine their project as the study of cultural variation. They chose to study isolated, traditional, if perhaps no longer 'primitive' societies, and even anthropologists working in societies undergoing revolutionary changes in India, China, Indonesia, or Latin America typically concerned themselves exclusively with rituals or with kinship terminologies and rules of marriage." To repeat again, he further said, "American influence came to predominate in all the sciences and social sciences after the war, and anthropology was no exception. The disarray of European social anthropology in the 1970s and 1980s made Americanization more palatable, even attractive....All the innovations in anthropology from the late 1960s crossed the Atlantic from west to east: the study of gender, the body, medical anthropology, the revamped field of material culture studies, and anthropology of film." (Kuper, Adam, 2010: 149-152). Anthropology in India was no exception to this influence. While Kroebar and Herskovits were essential in the classroom, Redfield with his writings about India's great traditions and peasant society instantly attracted the Indian anthropologists. Chicago school influenced the studies of sacred complexes and sacred geography. Medical Anthropology has been the direct influence of American anthropologists, such as Charles Leslie and George Foster. However, the fieldwork tradition of Malinowski continues in the Indian university curriculum of anthropology, and continues to be identified as the strength of anthropology, with capability to be with the people, understanding the realities and their concerns from their emic perspectives.

As we know, Anthropology was a compulsory subject at the Indian Civil Services examination. The British civil servants, during their service compiled the ethnography of castes and tribes of India with a view to understand the customs and religious practices of the people to facilitate governance without hurting the emotional identities that could flare up in the popular rebellions as in 1857. These ethnographies, known as Anthropology, branded the discipline as 'colonial anthropology', since anthropologists did not address themselves to the concerns of the people or efforts of the government for development, after Independence, taking a stance of value-neutrality. There have been attempts to study the ethnography of community development but it was not sustained. In the West, Anthropologists were employed in 'Bureau of Indian Affairs' dealing with indigenous American people (American Indians). During Second World War, anthropologists were consulted about dealing with the Japanese in the context of their culture and the status and role of the Emperor. Anthropology in India continued the tradition of tribal monographs following into village monographs by Indian and Western scholars, after Independence, focusing on caste, religion, and kinship.

Development Policy: Early Initiatives

The Independence struggle was also co-terminus with social reform movements against caste, untouchability, issues about widow remarriage etc. There was also thinking about vision of India after Independence, such as formation of linguistic states, about education and health. Mahatma Gandhi's Constructive Programmes about *Adivasi*, *Harijan*, Women, Alcoholism, Health education and Sanitation, *Khadi* etc. were to become the programmes and departments of the Government after Independence.

Community Development Programme started on 2nd October, 1952, soon after the first general election, was the first massive Rural Reconstruction Movement, followed by Family Planning. Several Indian Anthropologists like S.C. Dube, D.N. Majumdar and American Anthropologists like Morris Oplar, David Mandelbaum, George Foster were involved as consultants, to advise on the Extension Approach. This was probably the first attempt by anthropologists to document the process of change. However, the economists and statisticians soon took over the planning process, since the governance by bureaucracy requires numbers, and measurable targets for budgetary allocations. Thus Etic overpowered the Emic. While bureaucracy can function or plan at the macro level, pursuing some foreign models of development, such as trickledown theory of economic development, disciplines like anthropology which study people, function at the micro level. People live their daily lives with the consanguineous and affinal kin-group and with their peers among the kin, neighbourhood and at the work place. Their aspirations have to be met in their world of living. For the women, the world is the radius of marriage distance, which in the tribal and rural sectors did not go beyond 20 kms.

Constitution of India was designed as an instrument to unfold the vision of India and to lay down basic principles of national reconstruction. The principle of equity, fundamental rights, and adult franchise became the guiding principles of functioning democracy, through the arms of legislature, judiciary and executive, monitoring and complementing each other. Anthropology as a discipline claiming holistic study of people has to interpret the Constitution of India, which 'We the People of India' have given to themselves. Public policies in India have to be in line with the spirit of the Constitution. Anthropological paradigms have to be pro-people, since this is the only discipline which studies all aspects of people's lives, instead of fragmenting life into vertical disciplines. The bureaucracy functions through line or sector departments, often lacking co-ordination or networking. The hierarchy in the civil services among the line departments, and hierarchical positions of the revenue collector and newly created development bureaucrat at the district level in the wake of community development and democratic decentralisation is no better than the traditional caste hierarchy. Revenue mind-set appears to rule the bureaucracy although urban land has gained tremendous importance over rural lands and land revenue is no more the prime tax income of the government. The anthropological study of farmers' suicides across the country would provide rich dividends for knowledge analysis useful for policy planning and implementation.

The traditional micro-study area of anthropologists was handled nicely to unravel the emic perspectives through qualitative research tools and techniques. We have an answer to the question, as to why people behave the way they do. Since, culture of an ethnic group has been more homogenous, explainable by Culture and Personality theory, we can predict behavioural patterns and responses. However, when policies and programmes are administered at the national or state level, people have to respond to it within the framework of rules and regulations which are framed to facilitate governance by the bureaucracy. There are common rules for plural, historically derived real life situations, which nullifies the policy at the implementation level, addressed to diverse cultural, social and geographical situations.

What is the visibility of anthropology at the policy planning level which was seen in the early days of community development? Anthropologists are consulted on adjudication issues about pseudo-tribal claims to S.T. status but not on tribal development. In response to governance issues leading to safe refuge of violent groups in tribal belts, Raj Bhavans have been asked to establish tribal cells with an anthropologist as one of the members, to advise about the use of constitutional powers by the Governors.

Human development is an anthropological holistic approach. Anthropological Survey of India as the largest body of anthropologists under one roof, with tribal museums and biology labs, under the Ministry of Culture, has now taken up contemporary issues such as Social Impact Assessment of economic development projects, and capturing the dynamics of change through village studies as also the impact of biological technology on health and disease.

The current debate at the international and national level is about development with various perceptions, such as development as economic growth, inclusive growth addressing equity, or human development. The millennium development goals which India is likely to miss, focuses the plight of the indigenous people to what we refer to as tribal communities. The government has responded to the constitutional provisions about the tribal communities by way of making special provisions such as the tribal sub-plan, and providing mechanism for more powers for self-governance and autonomy by way of 73rd Amendment. At the same time, 78 districts have been officially labelled as Naxal affected. However, anthropologists are rarely consulted on tribal development issues, in spite of the popular image of anthropology as a study of tribal communities. Anthropologists are associated with the committees to adjudicate about the claims of pseudo tribals to be listed as Scheduled Tribe. At the national level as yet, there is no national tribal policy approved by the Parliament. The tribal issues are divided in two ministries, namely, the Ministry of Culture, under which the Anthropological Survey of India functions, and the Ministry of Tribal Affairs. The Tribal Research Institutes as part of Tribal Development Department in the States have been reduced as the appellate authority for Scheduled Tribe certificate verification. The research and training functions of TRTI have been progressively dwindling.

In the specific areas of biological anthropology; molecular biology, biotechnology, stem-cell therapy and organ transplants have provided different dimensions, and challenges to holistic anthropology. Another current issue is about the gender. The concepts of masculinity continue to exploit women as an object of pleasure. Female foeticide has replaced female infanticide with increasing number of sonography machines. In the tribal communities, these practices are totally absent. The concepts of male and female body image and gender equality need focused studies by anthropologists in the context of violence against women and HIV issues. Role and functioning of traditional youth dormitories could be analyzed with the use of anthropological qualitative methods.

Focusing on India, the traditional cultural, social and religious identities such as caste and tribe are being provided legal and administrative identities such as S.T., S.C., O.B.C., D.T., N.T., Others, etc. In the name of equity and development, other identities such as BPL, APL and *Antyodaya* have been created. The approach to development continues to be economic growth with trickle down impact for alleviation of poverty. Liberalization and economic globalization has led to increasing SEZs which target the natural resource rich tribal belts, creating problems of displacements and impoverishment. However, the movements for bio-diversity and environmental protection are in place. Environment Impact Assessment and proposed Social Impact Assessment are expected to play the role as conscience keepers against the onslaught of crony capitalism.

Proliferation of commercial visual mass media including the spiritual channels make their impact pulling in different directions. Democratic decentralization, that is, PRI do not effectively function in the tribal belts, despite 73rd Amendment. Explosion of information about the world does not blunt the social group identities which get strengthened and exploited in the political process of elections. The side benefits of these push and pull forces result in continuation of plural cultures including plural medical systems.

The adoption of soft culture, that is, material aspects of culture including consumption technology like mobile phones and curative therapy or modern diagnostic tools and techniques, seem to sound alarming bells about assimilation in the Western socio-economic system. However, the impact of soft aspects of culture do not necessarily affect the hard core of culture enshrined in the value systems based on religious principles manifested in rituals, ceremonies, pilgrimages, religious congregations and festivals.

Anthropology with its strength of field based qualitative investigations has a capacity to capture the dynamics of processes of change and its impact on the soft and hard aspects of culture. Anthropologists are trained to comprehend the holistic perspective and analyze the issues through the eyes of the people, what could also be called as micro level or emic perspective. The fieldwork tradition in anthropology has been kept alive by training of anthropology students in the tribal belt.

The narrow ethnic identities such as sub-castes may merge into federating caste clusters. The co-terminality of culture and life style may get eroded to develop a new occupational cultural life style promoting endogamy in these groups. More and more studies are required of an interdisciplinary nature under the leadership of anthropology with its strength of holism and field research. Anthropology has proved its academic capacity to analyse the historical processes which led to biological, cultural and social evolution of Humankind. It also has the capacity to predict the future path, considering the psychic unity of Humankind.

Anthropology as Knowledge System, as Academic Discipline and as Professional Discipline

It is worth repeating to say that no academic discipline can survive only as a body of knowledge for its own sake, unless its utility is visible at various levels. One way of understanding this phenomenon is to see as to where and by whom anthropologists are invited for consultation to give their expert opinion. We keep on discussing the future of anthropology and bemoan the dwindling number of students in anthropology departments. Wishes are expressed to multiply anthropology at the junior and senior college level and at the post graduate level to create more teaching assignments. Rarely do we discuss the role of anthropology in the current issues about human kind and the projections for the future. We are aware that no funding of any sort could be made available unless the utility of the discipline becomes visible. Anthropology as a liberal discipline, that it is, may not find favour in the current scenario of proliferating professional academic institutions. Education in the public mind is linked to jobs, skills, employability; not as a medium of liberal thought or knowledge.

Anthropology has been equated with ethnography due to classical monographs which have been highlighting functional stability and equilibrium. By the very elementary theory of culture change, it has to be the study of moving equilibrium in the present context, while planned, directed change for 'development' is the norm of good governance, to address the aspirations of the people.

Tribal Development in the government sector is a conscious attempt to forge Indian (mainstream) identity among all the tribal people of India, recognizing the universal value of equity, enshrined in Constitution of India and using the rights approach to enforce it. Nehru's five cardinal principles about tribal development approaches are in line with anthropological approaches to plan change along the line of culture. "People should develop along the lines of their own genius." The recent Supreme Court direction about 'Vedant project' in Odisha clearly spells out the autonomous authority and wisdom of *Gram Sabha* to take decisions about the development in their region.

Anthropology as a distinct discipline is taught in more than thirty five universities in India. However, Anthropological Survey of India continues to be a nodal institution which uses this trained manpower, to undertake national level study projects, which should provide data for the key issues of public policy. Anthropology with its strength of qualitative methodology and basic theories about the dynamics of culture is most suited to address the issues of public policy with the holistic perspective. Personally, I have also been analysing the public policies about health and disease control which are in the domain of Socio-behavioural Division of ICMR, and newer initiatives in public health in AYUSH. Unlike the yet to be approved National Tribal Policy, there have been two national health policies, now merged into one in 2017, debated as ambiguous about promoting AYUSH.

While we discuss anthropology in terms of knowledge, translated into academic discipline in the university system, the reality of life around us seems to function more by skills or services called as occupation and profession and not by knowledge alone. This affects the knowledge discipline like Anthropology which needs to be reorganized as a professional discipline. The so called globalized approach which in reality is manifested in the market economy, moves in the direction of centralized directions at the global, national and provincial levels. The centralized unitary governance, facilitated by science and technology, more specifically in transport and communication, and now by digitalisation, opens up avenues of inquiry and investigation about planned direction, while market driven forces of change affect the Man and his culture, social groupings, mobility, migration, urbanization and proliferation of slum dwellings. Stem cell biology and organ transplants on one hand and unethical use of sonography to facilitate female foeticide, and violence against women, are challenges for anthropological research about gender related issues in non-tribal communities. The institutional mechanism of anthropology such as the teaching and research departments of anthropology, Anthropological Survey of India (AnSI) and Tribal Research Institutes, are expected to take leads in these areas.

Anthropology, which happens to be a natural academic discipline dealing with tribes and tribal issues, has no say in the affairs of 9 per cent of the Scheduled Tribe population in India. Actually, the Constitutional provision in Article 342 do not talk about the tribe *per se*, but keeps the option open to bestow the status of 'deemed to be Scheduled Tribe, for the provision of the Constitution'. This has given rise to a major politically supported hunger of pseudo tribals, grabbing the S.T. status, thus depriving the real tribals. It is a paradox that it is judiciary which becomes the ultimate authority to decide the tribal or caste identity and not your birth. In spite of the tribal development departments with large budgetary outlays, representatives of tribal communities in the Panchayat system, in the State Legislatures and in the Parliament; Tribal States, Districts and Blocks continue to be at the lowest ladder of any development index. Tribal child malnutrition is pronounced as 'National Shame' by national leaders. What are we doing as anthropologists to analyze this phenomenon in the holistic perspective, and make recommendations in the spirit of human rights and universal values?

The papers presented at the INCAA Anthropology Congresses, broadly cover the bio-cultural perspectives about plurality, variation and diversity. The buzz word in the country is 'development', which may be understood with different connotations and paradigms. Internationally there are human development indices, millennium development goals, PQLI, coming down to district human development reports. There is a confusion between human development and human resource development. All these issues are in the domain of anthropological theory. This also provides us with an opportunity to undertake empirical studies relating to development providing us a challenge to develop theorization about the dynamics and change. We must admit that we are weak in the area of change, since all our ethnography emphasizes the ground level situation of the traditional society. We still continue to use primitive society as a conceptual methodological model. But we are sadly withdrawing from the tribal studies which have been our natural domain of study. AnSI has undertaken village restudy programme in Twelfth Plan which should bring out the rural change during the last 50-60 years. However, the studies of tribal villages have taken a beating since there have not been classical studies of tribal villages except the monographs by Census administration under Dr. Roy Burman's initiatives. But there have been monographs on tribal communities which could be restudied. ICSSR had undertaken restudy of tribes in the mid-seventies under initiative by J.P. Naik and S.C. Dube. We continue to think of poverty as an economic phenomena while linkage of poverty with social categories is a socio-cultural, historical phenomena, which needs anthropological analysis, more so, since tribal communities are the poorest of the lot, which represent the concept of *'Daridranarayan'* of Gandhiji.

Techno-centric, drug-therapeutic, treatment oriented management of symptomatic care which appear to be remote controlled by the multinational pharmaceuticals or insurance companies in some countries, and promoted by treatment oriented medical education in all systems of medicine, does not address the health and disease control concerns of the people. Till recently, two national policies on health approved by Parliament, the second based on AYUSH, have functioned as parallel systems with no convergence even under NRHM. The unified national health policy of 2017 seems to pay lip service to Indian Systems of Medicine. Despite several studies on ethnomedicine in anthropology, indigenous medicine and the practitioners have no place in public health. Anthropology possesses the expertise of understanding people's perspectives by going native, understanding the processes with the use of our qualitative methods. However, we remain content in pursuing ethnography as an end point, titling it as 'ethnomedicine' in areas of health issues, rather than turning focused ethnography as a method to delve into policy research, about health care.

We are invited by research bodies like ICMR to advise them about bio-socio-cultural issues about disease causation and control and to involve community in the government programmes. ICMR has established Socio-Behavioural Research Division. ICSSR-ICMR constituted the Joint Panel on Health, at least thrice which largely remained non-functional, since ICSSR had never taken health as their priority agenda. It continues to be trapped in addressing the caste inequalities, focusing on ex-untouchables. Largely the government wants us to help them in the interventions, in the context of development, or occasionally want us to take up the intervention projects ourselves. The public sector and do-gooder, foreign funded NGOs seek our help to get their schematic agenda accepted by the 'illiterate and superstitious, possibly irrational' communities, in the name of rationality and modern science and technology by our involvement in such programmes as health education, I.E.C. or B.C.C.

The Social-Behavioural Research Division of the ICMR at its first meeting of the Scientific Advisory Committee, was asked to look into gender violence and domestic violence as research priority areas. We know the ICMR institutes are titled after the diseases such as Cancer, TB, AIDS, Malaria etc. and the ICAR institutes after the crops such as wheat, rice, sugarcane, potato etc. But ultimately all are impacting the man who is the host in epidemiological triangle and our subject matter. The acreage under the cash crop of sugarcane eats away the production of pulses and oilseeds which is so important to a pregnant woman, impacting the malnutrition and infant mortality. ICAR may be dealing with agricultural science and technology but what about the farmer who uses that science and technology? Farmer as a man and his culture and society are our research agenda. I remarked to the Director of Vector Research Centre that they seemed to know more about the life-style of mosquito than that of Man which he accepted in a lighter vein. Now, the millets which have been the traditional food of the rural poor is being propagated, with an added argument that it requires less water for production.

The academic NGO, 'The Maharashtra Association of Anthropological Sciences (MAAS)', Pune, which is affiliated to INCAA, has experimented with the intervention projects which are funded by the governments and could be turned into intervention research projects. We had a three-hour discussion with five secretaries heading five line departments of the Government of Maharashtra, as a convergence exercise for them, to discuss a mega project offered to us about sustainable tribal development, focusing on reducing malnutrition, and utilization of Government Schemes by the people. The issue is about the domain of anthropology. Our strength of holistic perspectives, qualitative analysis and expertise in collecting authentic primary data do provide insights for policy formulation and implementation.

As a student, I had read a book on 'Anthropology in Administration by Bartlett. About 60 years ago, we were studying administration in terms of indirect rule as practised by the British to rule their colonies. Anthropologists were also involved in the community development programme in India at its initiation sixty two years ago. What do we do now as anthropologists? Our interaction with the government requires us to understand the government system as it functions at all levels, at the level of the cabinet decision-making process, bureaucratic hierarchies, at all levels of revenue and development administration, lack of convergence amongst various departments, although advocating inter-sectoral co-ordination as given in primary health care approach of WHO, or millennium development goals. In the context of all these, we have to widen our definition of 'holism' which cannot be limited only to the community or geographical boundary, but would also include the political ideologies, globalized impacts, bureaucratic structures, technology and vested interest of the industry and market economy, what all is commonly referred to as stakeholders. The corporate market has reached interior tribal villages through small packages of biscuits and tea-leaves, and kitchen bath corners with 'fair and lovely' cosmetics.

In this complex whole, anthropology has a big space to contribute, because we have the capacity to understand the processes of interaction, integration, hard and soft aspects of culture, which accelerate or hinder change. In this whole scenario, we have to think of the role of Anthropological Survey of India, University Departments of Anthropology, INCAA and such academic anthropology associations to play their role as a knowledge discipline and using the strength of that knowledge for the good of the people.

The civil services administration, following the mindset of British Raj revenue pattern of governance, do not take development initiatives due to ignorance and busy schedule, or fail to effectively implement political initiatives through the process of democratic decentralisation. I had the privilege to attend a meeting of all Secretaries of the State government under the chairmanship of the Chief Secretary to discuss tribal child malnutrition. Never once the term *panchayati raj* was uttered. Discussion centred around what the district level to village level government employees could do and the mechanism of their monitoring.

Initially, we have to be proactive about our expertise, presence and availability. We may not be invited to join, out of the image of anthropology as a study of the past, not going beyond ethnography. Gate crashing is necessary in the initial period as we did for Medical Anthropology, which is not required any more.

The Government administration due to its linkage to budgets, personnel and financial year time line, functioning under a given system, are oriented to statistical numbers. We now know how to turn our qualitative data into numbers. Our strength is to unravel the process which promotes or hurdles positive impact. We have to present it in a case study format, numbers coming from secondary data. Considerable data is available in government records even at Block and district level which can be accessed. Economists who have no know-how about collecting primary data take away the planning positions, since they project statistical numbers once they are available from Decennial Census, NSS, NFHS etc. We study at the micro level and we have good comprehensive knowledge about the issues at people's level. We have yet to develop Economic Anthropology effectively, which is the crying need today, in India.

The questions like, why poverty is a group level phenomena and not an individual phenomena, why are tribal districts like Nandurbar in Maharashtra and tribe dominant blocks at the lowest rung of human development index, according to government reports continue to be there, even after decades of tribal development expenditure? What are the development schemes in TDD *vis-à-vis* survival schemes? How FRA and PESA functioning on the ground—where are the success stories and why, or why not? What are the constraints that poor cannot come out of poverty, that they continue to be poor, despite huge budgetary outlays, programmes and schemes? Is this an economic agenda only?

We are aware about Symington report of 1938, about the tribal areas in Dhule district in Khandesh region of North Maharashtra. He studied indebtedness and made some recommendations, basically not to apply all India programmes to a specific region. Precisely, the taluks and Mahals (under tribal chieftains) studied by Symington were formed into a separate tribal district of Nandurbar after 60 years in 1998. Nandurbar with 62 per cent overall tribal population in a district and 75 per cent rural tribal population continues to be 35th in HDI, as per State Government report of 2002 and 2012 (now 36th due to division of Thane district forming a separate Palghar district).

What is our presence, our knowledge, our study about these phenomena? The study undertaken about health and education issues in Nandurbar have been presented in chapter about Rural and Tribal Development in this book.

There was a National Seminar at the Arunachal University, Itanagar in March 2017 for attempting the first ever discourse on Anthropology and Policy Planning focusing on Development issues. All these years, there have been discussions pertaining to applications of anthropology, but not addressing to policy planning and implementation. With colonisation, exploitation of resources and acquisition of goods for pleasure of the rulers became a norm. There are British documented police records about the conflicts of British with the people in the North-East, for capturing such resources.

There have been several conflicts of the British with the tribal communities in other regions of India. We do not know, how many of these are recorded in anthropological literature, although documented in vernacular literature. Forest as a source of revenue put limitations on the traditional use of forest by the tribal communities, which is now sought to be softened by the Forest Rights Act. Health, education and development of the people were not the concerns of the foreign rulers. Exploitation of resources necessitated infrastructure of transport and communication and governance through indirect and direct rule, required *'Babus'* of various sorts, with education, to maintain accounts and file-records with revenue mindset, not development mindset. Educational institutions in the public and voluntary sector were promoted to get such *Babus* to be a part of state administration.

However, with the withering away of formal political empires and all countries becoming free from colonial bondage, the last being South Africa, and even our island societies studied by pioneer anthropologists becoming independent nations, there is an upsurge for economic development with a lofty aim of all people sharing the benefits of Science and Technology.

Of late, Development Anthropology is emerging as a sub-discipline. Some international books published as recently as 2013 and 2015 on 'Anthropology and Development' are available for discussion. But, the paradigms of development in the West and with us are different. In the West, development is aid to developing countries. Who sets the agenda of aid, of Bill Gates Foundation for example? Or in the World Bank or IMF, or earlier Rockefeller and Ford Foundation?

The definition of what is development is subjected to great debate, as much as, poverty is not being defined properly while schemes are galore. Nehru had set the goal of community development as emergence of a new Man with a vision or perspective. Now the emphasis by Amartya Sen and Maqbul Haq in the book, "*Readings in Human Development*" (2005, second edition) has been on human development (which is misunderstood as human resource development). A quote from the book on 'Anthropology and Development': "Most importantly, we suggest that anthropologists are in a strong position to help redefine what development should be by taking a broader view of the struggles people make to improve their lives, and drawing attention to the growing problems of inequality and the need for social justice." (Katy Gardner and David Lewis, 2015)

S. Leonard Syme, a Social Epidemiologist, writing Foreword to the book "*Epidemiology and Culture*" written by his student, James Trostle has candidly accepted the failure of intervention programmes designed by them based on quantitative studies about identifying disease risk factors and expecting people to take desired or recommended action in the interest of their good health. "We in Public Health have important messages to give to people, but people have lives to lead. There often is a major gap between these two priorities." (In Trostle, J., 2005: xi-xii)

Recently we have been trying to inculcate epidemiological or public health approach in AYUSH. Health and disease control research from anthropological perspectives provides creative opportunities for biological and cultural anthropologists to work together. Only that we have to be proactive since the technology conscious institutions and scientists who parrot the Western clinical and market driven approach do not invite us for what they perceive as clinical work, expecting public to comply to their technological solutions. Anthropologists have been documenting ethnomedicine and the knowledge and practices of herbalists and *Dais*. In the health care system, these traditional professionals with indigenous knowledge are not co-opted nor are their skills updated. We have to show through field research as to how the little traditions in health care are linked to great classical tradition given in the texts of Charak, Sushrut, Vaghbhat. To prove the point we undertook a small study of lady doctors of all systems of medicine about their personal maternity practices when they became mothers themselves. They did the same, followed the same practices as are followed by women across the country. The lady gynaecologists and paediatricians belonging to the families of allopathic doctors owning modern hospitals were no exception. Multi-centric studies of this sort even among Indian diaspora have to be undertaken.

We have been propagating for research on traditional fish medicine since the fisher-folk communities and fish eating people know and follow the do's and don'ts of eating different types of fish and their organs, for prevention, promotion and cure of ailments. We do not document these practices which are side-stepped as common tradition and traditional knowledge, not made use of in national programmes. If this is presented by expert anthropologists to AYUSH Ministry, as public health initiative, it could be favourably considered.

Our greatest strength is the holistic approach and expertise to unravel the processes of action rather than dubious quantitative outcomes. Recently NSSO introduced some questions to elicit information about the use of AYUSH by the people to decide the budgetary outlay for

AYSUH Ministry. They concluded that Indian people were largely in favour of allopathy instead of AYUSH systems. If you ask a question whether a person or a family followed Ayurved or Unani etc. they may so 'No'. If you ask what do you do when you have some specific problems, the answer is likely to be some home remedy by way of use of turmeric, dried ginger etc. which is Ayurved, Unani and documented in the classical texts. We are used to given terms such as Ayurved, Allopathy, Unani, Naturopathy etc. or S.C., S.T., O.B.C. and the like, which people do not use in their day-to-day communication. What people say, and express in their instinctive communication is 'what is', what we call 'Emic'. What we talk to the people to understand their perspectives through our spectacles is 'Etic'. Data generated through etic methods like schedules and questionnaires could not be considered scientifically objective as we are prone to receive idealised answers. It is a common practice in Anthropology to give quotes of the people, without interpreting them. Of course the translation in English language would be a sensitive issue, since language and cultural expressions are significant, not the dictionary meaning of words.

Ethno-medicine would not be considered as system of medicine by the health and finance bureaucracy. Naturopathy although advocated by Gandhi has problems with health bureaucracy, being drugless therapy. There is confusion between the terms, drug and medicine. Food could be medicine. Could ginger or garlic be called as drugs? However, Yoga has been accepted as promotive, preventive and as therapy at the international level. Gandhiji always used the term, nature-cure and not naturopathy. Have we documented the details of forest-dwelling people in their relationship with the nature around them for food, for medicine, for their dwellings and for nursing and nurturing of their cattle? We know, they use natural resources for their immediate needs and not for greed, for possession or for marketable surpluses.

Anthropologists in Europe and North America were hired by respective governments to help them to know the culture and psychology of natives, and of the enemy during Second World War. In India, the ethnography of castes and tribes was compiled by the civil servants who had a research bent of mind without any special funding for the purpose. The volumes were used by the successive civil British administrators to facilitate Indirect and Direct Rule without stepping on the hard aspects of traditions, customs and religious values, in the context of 1857 rebellions and subsequent Proclamation by the Queen. However, several pseudo-groups who claim backward status to get constitutional benefits of affirmative action cite these writings in their memoranda. When we work on the adjudication committees and visit the field ourselves as anthropologists, we realise several factual mistakes in these compilations, which obviously are not research documents.

There is documentation of police records about professional thefts and decoities during British rule. The crime ethnography of thefts, burglaries and decoities by criminal teams have been documented with the help of information provided by elderly key informants specially invited to Bombay Police Headquarters. Several of the ethnic groups were branded as criminal tribes under British Rule who had rebelled against the British and their allies, the feudal, rich peasants, and traders and money lenders. They were later de-notified or called *Vimukta Jati* after Independence, releasing them from barbed wire settlements. Anthropologists were not designated to undertake this work since we hardly had anthropology as an academic discipline in Indian universities. Some studies on these communities were undertaken later and are continuing with the Anthropological Survey of India.

The initiatives taken by S.C. Roy and others to start the journal '*Man in India*' must have been prompted by such compilations about the castes and tribes of India. Later, Anthropological Survey of India under the leadership of the scholar-administrator, Director-General, Dr. K.S. Singh, compiled the volumes 'People of India'.

Anthropologists were designated to help the community development exercise in India, after Independence, whereby American anthropologists and Indian anthropologists studied the change process in rural India. This gave fillip to village studies in India by anthropologists and the production of village monographs during Census 1961 under the leadership of Dr. B.K. Roy Burman.

Democratic decentralisation giving fillip to CBOs like *mahila mandal,* youth groups and self help groups have been important landmarks in rural development. On the other hand, fast urbanisation led to rise of towns and cities. The villages, 50-100 kms around mega and metro cities are closely linked economically and socially to the urban centres, which have given rise to rural-urban relationships, commented briefly by Robert Redfield. This calls for anthropological qualitative research to analyse the available statistical data. Migration and mobility have become major activities in tribal and rural areas, which are not adequately studied by anthropologists. These activities also promote risk behaviour threatening HIV infection.

Health Sector with its linkage with community development through primary health centres reached people to reduce infant mortality and administer disease control programmes. Rise in higher and technical education with employment opportunities led to competing claims for getting the benefits of reservation as SC, ST, OBC, DT/NT etc. Focused ethnography could analyse the dynamics of the process of change in tribal and caste-peasant villages.

The civil administration which continues to have revenue mind-set of British Civil Services in India, with the position of Collector as district king is not equipped to understand the dynamics of societal and cultural change. The district development administration and democratic decentralisation up to village level with 50 per cent reservation to women in such statutory bodies have not been effectively studied, although the beginning was made by way of the book, '*India's Changing Villages*' by S.C. Dube.

Anthropology continues to be the only field discipline which can claim to understand people's perspectives. However, due to ethnographic, qualitative methods of data, although rich in human content, does not satisfy statistics-savvy bureaucrats who like to link all issues to schemes and programmes with budgetary outlays of income and expenditure. It is worth finding out as to whether the content of hundreds of schemes is different or they are presented with different nomenclature, as same wine in a new bottle.

Anthropologists are called upon to function as experts to help adjudication about pseudo- tribal and other pseudo claims for reservation. They are also welcome to help in the public health programmes dealing with chronic and stigmatised communicable diseases like TB, Leprosy, HIV or certain non-communicable, life-style disorders like Diabetes, Cancer, Cardio-Vascular ailments etc. Recently a separate AYUSH Ministry has been formed which need to be utilised for undertaking public health research by anthropologists interested in ethno-medicine. Although human genetics appears to have branched off from Biological Anthropology, Molecular Biology has advanced, providing research opportunities to biological anthropologists. There is considerable international interest in birth defects and disability which requires networking among the geneticists and social workers.

Tribal Development is a special area of development with a distinct Tribal Sub-Plan and tribal administration. However, without anthropological inputs, despite large budgetary outlays, tribal malnutrition continues to be a major problem, no doubt created as a result of regulatory forest department policies which prevented the traditional use of forest for food security by the tribal communities.

The ball of failure of all planned development efforts is put in the court of the people branding them as superstitious and with irrational behavioural practices. A new term like 'Behavioural Change Communication' (BCC) replacing 'Information, Education, Communication' (IEC), which had replaced Health Education, is coined. Social Scientists who are considered experts in understanding community culture and behaviour are expected to help Behavioural Change Communication, which in essence is meant to ensure compliance (now the soft term in medicine used is adherence) on the part of people to follow techno-centric advice given by the health bureaucracy. We have declined to be the 'social marketing agents' of bureaucracy in this regard.

Anthropologists also have to understand some issues while undertaking intervention research. All decisions are taken in a top-down fashion. We cannot be content only with descriptive ethnography of kinship and religion or ethno-medicine. For focused, problem specific ethnography, we have to expand our 'whole', to include the bureaucratic and political stakeholders and to understand their priorities and perspectives. In addition to our qualitative methods, we need to produce quantitative data. Even qualitative data need to be quantified to make an impact on policy and implementation.

There are other issues such as displacement, which have direct linkages with development projects such as construction of dams, inter-city roads and corridors, airports, industry, metro-rail and bullet train, mining etc. Direct cash transfers to millions of bank accounts, due to digital technology, by way of rehabilitation compensation, particularly to tribal people, whose traditional economy was cashless, proves baneful. Tribal students in designated tribal hostels in cities getting such cash, instead of cooked food supplied earlier in the hostel canteen, use the cash for alcoholism or tobacco products. Convenience of administration, probably with good intention to ensure transparency, creates problems of health and malnutrition.

Dharani Sinha, an anthropologist, who was the Director of the premier Administrative Staff College of India, Hyderabad, an apex institution created for the training of senior administrators, in his Sectional Presidential Address at the 78th Science Congress on Anthropology & Archaeology has talked about "Anthropology in the 21st Century: Issues and Challenges." He ended his address on an optimistic note about the role of Anthropology in the complex world.

"The scientific status of a discipline depends not on what it studies, but how it studies. Anthropology has changed its client systems, its subject matter, it has, however, continued its methodological rigour. This is, to my mind, the hallmark of anthropology as an academic discipline. Anthropology is an integrative science, a discipline with a purpose, focusing both on understanding, interpretation, as well archaeological, historical, societal data for human development. Anthropology is a relevant science, an applied science, not only generating knowledge, but also demonstrating how it can be used for societal development."

"In the village study, anthropologists found a natural extension of tribal studies; with the village studies, anthropologists were able to develop new methodological tools and techniques for understanding multi-communities, and enhance its capability to relate a social isolate to a wider world; to handle multiple social phenomena necessary to study complex societies. The village studies graduated Indian anthropology from a descriptive to an analytical discipline, from an orientation of a naturalist to that of a scientist. Mere collection of facts and presentation of ethnographic account was not enough; analysis, interpretation, conceptualisation and building of social theory emerged as one of the basic missions of anthropology. Village studies thus helped to formulate and advance concepts of social structure, roles and relationships, inter-group dynamics and inter-caste relationship and above all, these helped to highlight the processes of social change in India."

While talking about poverty and discrimination, he said, "Despite massive governmental assistance, traditionally poor continues to remain in poverty and ignorance. Poverty has cultural concomitants; the economically poor are also sociologically disadvantaged, and they are no longer willing to accept poverty as the dictates of fate, which cannot be changed. Anthropological studies have addressed to these social issues: social discrimination, social injustice, economic disparities, education, values and development. Since problems do not have disciplinary boundaries, studies on social issues just described have become inter-disciplinary in nature."

About the future identity of Anthropology, he has said, "Anthropology in the future will have to search for a fresh frame of reference, new parameters, and an innovative orientation to deal with its universe. Not long ago, anthropology was concerned about the fragmentation and diversification of the discipline. As a study of man in totality, its sub-disciplines, social anthropology, physical anthropology, pre-historic archaeology (Linguistics have lost their way a long time ago) have grown on their own momentum.....Anthropology is a human science. It has interface with all other sciences and being a holistic discipline, its ability to interface, inter-relate with other bodies of knowledge gives it a distinctive advantage. As a human science, if a human society changes its parameters, anthropology has to change. The change, as I said earlier, is its hallmark; so is its holism....Anthropology as a discipline, however, has some constants about it; some continuity about it. This is in its approach and orientation; its methodology and concern for people and problems its studies. Anthropologists are known for their empathy with their client-systems. This has not disappeared during the last century, and it is not likely to disappear in the next. Another continuity is in the holistic perspective which anthropology pursues. It is an integrative science; it integrates man with nature, nature with spirit, spirit with values, values with society. It pools perspectives from different disciplines, in order to understand man and his society.àAnother hallmark of anthropology is in its empiricism, its intensive participative methodology. Intensive fieldwork and participant observation have been its hallmark. In recent years, the participant observation technique has sophisticated itself into participatory research. Here, it is not observation that matters, but involvement of people in researching their own reality has become an important technology for anthropological research (Chambers, 1983)....The emerging world is large, complex, and challenging; and the change that is likely to happen to the profession in the 21st Century will be unparalleled. Anthropology, as a profession, has to rise to the challenge. It has the comprehensive, conceptual framework; methodological rigour, and qualitative orientation which few disciplines can claim. It has the wherewithal to meet the future squarely. I trust it will." (pp. 1-16)

Although we are recognised as experts about tribal culture, we fail to highlight the high ethical and natural values cherished and practised in tribal communities. Why do we not document and project that there is no gender violence, rape or molestation by a tribal man on tribal women? There is no female foeticide among tribal communities. The only way a tribal woman is harassed is when she is identified as a witch; incidentally witch has become a feminine gender, even Shakespeare discussing it about Lady Macbeth. In our world, female foeticide has a direct correlation with the increasing number of sonography machines as we have studied in the sugar baron Kolhapur district of Maharashtra. It is for these reasons that the tribal activists and tribal poets and litterateurs challenge the call to join the 'mainstream' which is very immoral and exploitative.

Anthropology in India is under pressure to show its relevance in understanding the public issues which are linked to the spirit of the

Constitution of India in aiming at equality of opportunity to all citizens of the country, irrespective of religion, caste, community, gender etc. The roles of executive, legislature, judiciary are structured. Mass Media has established its role. Science academics get linked to industry including defence. What about the social sciences and humanities? The holistic discipline of anthropology with sub-disciplines has created knowledge about Indian Culture and Society during British Rule and after Independence. How is this knowledge used to address the public issues in contemporary India?

To summarise, Anthropology in India as represented in the university system follows the classical curriculum, maybe it is linked to UPSC curricula. The research subjects for Masters level and Ph.D. dissertations also appear to be conventional or addressing such issues as highlighted in Western society at family level. Presentations at seminars, symposia and conferences show some flashes of addressing to contemporary issues. Some individual scholars are invited as experts by the governments, specifically about pseudo-tribal claims. However, there is no consistent effort to develop or use anthropological knowledge, approach and methods to address the issues of people in health, education, livelihood, migration, gender issues and the like. Ideally, INCAA as a voluntary organisation and Anthropological Survey of India as a government body together could take initiatives to prepare a vision document and strategic plan, for the use of anthropological knowledge in consonance with the Constitution of India, in planning and implementation about the programmes and schemes to attain human development goals.

To be brief, the frontiers of knowledge for anthropological interventions in India are immense due to our holistic approach and expertise to understand the emic perspectives at micro level. But we have to be proactive. Nobody would invite us unless the judiciary asks for expertise on such issues as pseudo claims to S.T. status which are directly linked with constitutional provisions. Issues of acute tribal malnutrition affecting child mortality and environmental protection also attract judicial attention. Medical Anthropology has developed, out of proactive analysis and interventions, using theory and methodology of anthropology, which is people-centric. Development Anthropology has yet to develop as a distinct sub-discipline of Anthropology which opens up many avenues for basic and applied research, useful for policy planning and implementation. Anthropology in India has a vision to develop its identity as Indian Anthropology, but lacks initiative to translate it in reality as a professional discipline.

3
Practicing Anthropology

In the context of Anthropology as a knowledge discipline, there have been debates about theoretical and applied anthropology. Malinowski used the term Practicing Anthropology and Sol Tax used Action Anthropology for conventional use of the term Applied Anthropology. George Foster said, "That the teachers like Herskovitz, Kroebar, Lowie consciously kept the students away from applications."

Malinowski firmly advocated "practical anthropology" concerned with answering the issues of the day. He rejected the "erroneous opinion…that practical anthropology is fundamentally different from theoretical or academic anthropology. The truth is that science begins with application. What is application in science, and when does 'theory' become practical? When it first allows us a definite grip on empirical reality.".... "Applied anthropology facilitates such a 'grip' on empirical reality. Even more, it is able to help change social reality." (Malinowski, 1961:5. In Carnea, M., 2002:380)

When a student from the Bhil tribe joined my post-graduate anthropology class, I knew he would not be interested in reading ethnographic monograph about the Bhil written by T.B. Naik. He would be interested to understand the processes of change for influencing the desired outcomes. He would be interested in the culture change issues of tribal world by learning anthropological theory and method, and play an active leadership role in accelerating it. He indeed became a leader by joining a political party and occupied honourable positions in the government system. When young trainees from the Church joined our classes, we knew that they wanted to equip themselves to work with the people. And when anthropology was prescribed as a mandatory subject at the Indian Civil Service, it was done to equip the officers for better administration. The British Civil Servants produced ethnographic accounts of the Castes and Tribes of different regions of India, which again helped their colleagues in administration. Issue of governance was then a dominant theme.

I had a chance to go to Australian National University, Canberra in September 1979 to attend first International Congress on Traditional Asian Medicine (ICTAM) invited by Prof. A.L. Basham who had hosted the Congress. Coming back, at Melbourn, I was the guest of Mr. Bill Deane who represented Red Cross during Bangla Desh war and used to meet Shaikh Mujibur Rahman after he assumed power, very frequently. Mr. Deane invited about six ordained clergy for after dinner coffee at his house to meet me to discuss as to how we as anthropologists work with people in the field.

On another occasion, an international leprosy organisation based in Munich arranged a post-dinner meeting in June 1984 with about a dozen Catholic priests at a church in Munich to discuss the issues about social stigma and social aspects of leprosy in the context of health education. We had met Pope John Paul II at Vatican on June 1, 1984 at St. Peter's church in his office, while about twelve scientists from different medical disciplines and I as a social scientist involved in leprosy research had a week-long meeting at the Pontifical Academy of Sciences, Vatican.

Since anthropologists are identified as having professional experience of interacting with the common people as equal partners, advice is sought about working with the people to understand their perspectives through their spectacles, what anthropologists profess as 'going native'. These are post-colonial phenomena, conceptually people having become the rulers to be self-governed as a democratic Sovereign Republic. Such an advice was never sought from the anthropologists in India during British Rule.

It appears, these debates arose since anthropologists were studying 'other' people and those from the countries which were the colonies of the imperial countries of which anthropologists were the citizens. It is obvious that huge ethical questions would arise since taking positions as citizens of an empire country, about marginalised and isolated communities of subject nations, would be a matter of value neutrality and value judgement. These anthropologists were hired by their respective governments during Second World War to help them to understand the behavioural issues about people in the countries at war.

The debate about applications of the science of Anthropology can be highlighted through the quotes as under:

"Applied anthropology, as I understand it, is a science concerned with the transformation of human society through the knowledge of social sciences....The question is, for whose benefit and for what purpose should social anthropology be used ? If it is for the good of the people, for the common security and prosperity of the great majority, and hopefully even for humanity as whole, if it is used for meeting their growing need for an ever-better material and social life, then, and only then, can science be made to play its proper role in human history..... In other words, genuine applied anthropology must be a science serving the interests of the masses. That is what is meant by people's anthropology. ...That the suffering masses and in need of the knowledge of a social science which reflects objective reality and which will help them build a society where there is peace, equality, and prosperity. And it is the duty of the anthropologists, whose objective is to study human society and culture, to meet the imperative needs of the people and to blaze a new path for anthropology in their service. The purpose of this branch of study is to make the broad masses understand full well the society they live in, to organize their collective life in accordance with existing social laws, and to help satisfy their ever-growing needs." (Xiaotong, Fei, 2002: 141, 148)

"Applied anthropology has now moved beyond the phase where the primary task was that of inculcating respect for and understanding of native customs. The problem is now seen as two-side. The content and structure of the culture of the administered group must still be analysed. The practical anthropologist must also have a systematic understanding of the special subcultures of the policy makers, the supervisory administrators, and the field operators." (Kluckhohn, Clyde, 1959: 143)

"Many, if not most, American anthropologists regard applied anthropology with ambivalent feelings. On the one hand there is a growing feeling that the anthropologist must play a more positive part on the contemporary scene, that his obligation to society cannot entirely be fulfilled by traditional research and teaching. On the other hand there is evident reluctance to come to grips with the "applied" challenge for fear that one's scientific integrity will be compromised. This situation stems from the

> historical and cultural conditions which have surrounded the evolution of the anthropological disciplines." (Foster, George, 1952, 11-3:5)

The ambivalent attitude about applied anthropology is evident from some other quotes:

> "It is obvious that anthropologists have special knowledge and special skills for assisting governments in administering primitive tribes and dependent peoples....An understanding of native institutions is a prerequisite for successful colonial government, though, thus far, anthropologists have been used more to implement policies than to formulate them." (Kluckhohn, Clyde, 1959: 130)
>
> "The technical task of anthropology is discovering the factors in a culture or subculture that make for acceptance or non-acceptance, and pointing out the type of mental climate that must be created if living habits are to be changed. From this point of view the anthropologist's study of culture change may be compared to the physician's work in public health. In what sort of total environment does a disease spread? In what sort is it checked? What are the susceptibilities and immunities of various populations? What are the carriers of infection?" (Kluckhohn, Clyde, 1959: 142).
>
> "All in all, the practical anthropologist will do well to conceive his role as that of the social doctor rather than as that of the social engineer....... Just as the medical doctor has a basic doctrine that he should prevent disease and save life, so the applied anthropologist tends to operate on a basic doctrine that he should prevent friction and violence in human relations, preserve the rights and dignity of administered groups, and that he should save lives...aid in establishing peaceful and self-respecting relations between peoples and cultures." (Kluckhohn, Clyde, 1959: 150).
>
> "To combine and convert knowledge and field findings into predictive and prescriptive policy propositions is intrinsically a theorizing operation." Tom Weaver has written a passionate argument in support of anthropology's potential as a policy science, showing how it engages "the very basis of this field, its

> goals, its subject matter, research techniques, theory, methodology, it's very future." (Weaver, 1985: 203: 27)

As the countries became Independent, and the 'primitive' students joined Universities, they like other citizens have been preoccupied with development issues. The issues of health care, gender, economic development and social disparities are the prime issues for policy planning and implementation. Directed planning for socio-economic change in a democratic set up is significant in governance in India. Politicians, bureaurates, technocrates and people interact in a market guided free economy. Policies of affirmative action in favour of socially disadvantaged people and women are practised using the equity principle to establish egalitarian society.

What role does anthropology as a holistic discipline play in understanding and accelerating dynamics of change?

The debate relates to urge for development in the decolonized countries. Michael M. Cernea anthropologist at the World Bank in his 1995 Malinowski Award Lecture titled "Social Organization and Development Anthropology" has said thus:

> "The first premise is that the kind of development I refer to is induced development. This is development purposively pursued, accelerated, and programmed, often guided by policy based on a mix of knowledge and assumptions, and therefore, distinct from spontaneous development. Thus, while spontaneous development is only observed and passively described in anthropology, induced development is one which anthropologists can influence, if included....The main lesson of my entire experience is that the social scientist's key contribution is to be not only a data collector and offer passive "assessments" of the existing situation: he or she must also actively design the content of induced change and chart the collective action path towards accomplishing it....Putting people first in projects is not a goodwill appeal or mere ethical advocacy....It is a theoretically grounded request to policy makers, planners, and technical experts to explicitly recognize the centrality of what is the primary factor in development processes....It calls for changing the approach to planning." (In Weaver, T. (ed.), 2002:366-389)

India after Independence from British Rule on 15 August 1947 set its agenda to complete the task of preparing a vision and regulatory document, Constitution of India, to enlist the issues to be resolved by using the principle of Equity by democratic means ensuring people's participation in the process. The key agenda has been planned development in a given direction encompassing the public debates mostly on the platform of universal Congress party since the inception of Congress, and such constructive programmes as listed by Mahatma Gandhi. Ever since the Constitution was promulgated, the democratic debates have centred around the people-centric implementation of the provisions in the Constitution monitored through the interaction between the legislature, executive and higher judiciary. The media emerged as the forth pillar of democracy but the academia has not yet established its identity in this process. Where necessary, in order to further empower people's participation, Constitution has been suitably amended. The discipline of Anthropology has evolved to establish a sub-discipline Development Anthropology to address the issues focusing on marginalized communities who are deprived and face the phenomena of group poverty.

S. Parasuraman has discussed the issues of Development Anthropology in S.C. Dube Memorial oration delivered at INCAA Congress at Kannur, Kerala in 2013. "Development Anthropology goes beyond an academic collection of information about change in livelihood patterns in distant communities for rational, scientific purposes; to resolving practical problems associated with the development. At its core, it examines the nature of empowerment and human agency for well-being; and the factors that foster this agency. It actively enquires into the experiences and struggles of marginalised peoples, as they experience, interpret and enact the development process."

"This work provides powerful insights on the skewed relationships that exist between powerful external change agents who conceive and implement projects, and the local groups whose lives such processes seek to improve. One such insight is into the pattern by which modern, development discourses and processes extend bureaucratic power and control over marginalized communities and disempowered these societies further."

"This body of work has also argued a powerful case for viewing people who are at the receiving end of development mechanisms as not just passive beneficiaries, but also thinking and acting subjects capable of informed and principled agency. One key contribution arising from this perspective is its enquiry into collective action and social agency, as alternatives to top down methods of development; wherein people are informed, can provide perspectives and participate in their growth in an equal manner for collective well-being."

In terms of focused ethnography research, the strength of qualitative research method such as 'Listening to the People struggling with their daily lives and/or considered as 'beneficiaries' or 'respondents' is advocated.

Jean Dreze has discussed the issues about research and action in an article in "*Economic and Political Weekly*."

"Thus, my point is not just that research can help action, but also that involvement in action can enhance the quality of research. This statement is bound to raise some eyebrows. What about 'objectivity'? Is personal commitment to a cause compatible with an objective reading of the facts? Is it not important to remove oneself from the situation in order to consider it in an objective light? To this I would respond, first of all, that inaction is not neutrality.... "The case for action-based research appears to me to be particularly strong if the aim of research is to facilitate human advancement and social change. In the academic world, and particularly in development studies, there is often a presumption that this is the case. Most project proposals stress the importance of the proposed research for economic or social advancement, and academic papers routinely end with a section on 'policy implications'. In this perspective, however, the government is almost always perceived as the crucial agent of change, so that 'better policies' become the focus of attention. Rarely is there much acknowledgement of the ability of people themselves to bring about change, and of the potential value of research in assisting the process. If the researcher addresses himself or herself to civil society rather than to the government, research grounded in public action (rather than in the world of policy advice) is likely to have special value....My point is that the value of scientific research can, in many circumstances, be enhanced even further if it is combined with real-world involvement and action. I see this approach as an essential complement of, not a substitute for, research of a more 'detached' kind....The flourishing of action-based research could also pave the way for a healthy 'democratisation' of scientific research. In the social sciences particularly, I see no need for research to remain confined to the ivory tower of academia. Indeed, wider public participation could significantly enrich the entire process. In this respect, once again, research and action belong to a common cause." (2002, 37-9, pp. 817-819)

What should be the context in which the term applied anthropology and practicing anthropology used in a country like India which claims to be one of the fastest growing economies in the world? Applied anthropology as a generalised term has given rise to sort of sub-disciplines labelled as Medical Anthropology, Ecological Anthropology, Business Anthropology and Developmental Anthropology and many others.

Practicing Anthropology is not yet commonly used. There used to be a discussion in a lighter vein in regard to anthropology in administration as to what would be the scenario when anthropologist would himself become an administrator?

Currently at the civil services examinations, anthropology is one of the most popular optional subjects. Several students join anthropology courses at the postgraduate level in a university with an intention to equip themselves for the civil services examinations.

Largely anthropologists in India are invited to be members of committees as experts to adjudicate the claims of pseudo-tribal communities claiming S.T. status. They are also invited to lecture at the training sessions for officers dealing with tribal or backward class issues. They are invited to undertake surveys for Tribal Research Institutes, NGOs working in tribal areas and offered research projects by the ICSSR, ICMR and such other research bodies. They may also be invited to undertake evaluation of programmes usually by the NGOs, as independent evaluations are required by the funding agencies. Several NGOs employ young anthropologists to undertake field assignments, knowing their capacity to communicate with the people in villages. But rarely, anthropologists are asked to plan and execute an intervention project.

In the West, as we know, during second world war, anthropologists were asked to assist the governments in Britain and U.S.A. British anthropologists held important posts in the Foreign Office, the Admiralty, the British Information Service, the Wartime Social Survey, and in the field.

When an anthropologist is included as a member of the multi-disciplinary team or in a team of administrators, he has to contribute in the context of issues under review. He also comes to know the perceptions of other team members about an issue. He, therefore, has to widen his understanding of 'holism' and proactively contribute to the understanding of an issue under review, while offering recommendations.

Practicing anthropology could refer to all such experiences when an anthropologist is interacting with the peers who are not formally trained in anthropology, dealing with a public issue, not limiting only to conventional cultural issues of kinship and religion. I have documented such experiences in this chapter. However, the experiences are also documented in other chapters such as dealing with rural and tribal development, leprosy, sexuality issues, Indian systems of medicine (AYUSH) or dealing with the voluntary sector in the respective chapters of the book.

The major experience of planning and executing an intervention programme dealing with tribal child malnutrition, whereby people's perceptions were not only studied but the real life problems were addressed by offering the services to the people which is usually done by the government, as a part of its governance responsibility as per Constitution. We offered services with government grant but not as per their schemes, to try out a model which was documented in the research format to facilitate evaluation, and replicate it on a larger scale if found useful. This could be termed as intervention research.

In medical sciences, dealing with the disease at an individual level, drugs are administered for cure. Drugs are developed after due process of animal and clinical trials. Drug development research is an intervention research, using experimental and control models. When programmes are designed at mass level, it becomes public health research or health systems research. All research requires intervention, properly designed, planned and executed. If an anthropologist undertakes such programmes, he plans it in the framework of holism, meaning thereby that he would assess the inter-relationship of various sectors, although focusing on one. Several government intervention programmes fail since they are focused only on one sector without reference to other sectors in planning and execution.

Some case studies in which I was personally involved in the study or execution have been presented in this chapter and the following chapters.

Case Study 1: Communication, Leadership and Decision Making in a Village: Chandpur

I was appointed as a Research Assistant on 1st May, 1959 in this project, three days after *Viva-Voce* examination for M.A. dissertation. My batch mate Yogesh Atal was also appointed in the project. Prof. S.C. Dube as Principal Investigator had put up a hypothesis to test the functioning of democratic decentralization, which was initiated in the community development programme. His book '*India's Changing Villages*' about community development programme was just published.

Broadly it was to be documented as to how many decisions were taken independently at the village level by gram panchayat without the directive or assistance of Block Development Officer (BDO) who was the executive head of Community Development Block.

I worked as Research Assistant only for three months since I and Yogesh Atal both were inducted as faculty members upon the two vacancies created by the exit of two teachers, one going abroad and another going back to teach at his native place.

There was an event about visit by a Minister to the village, Chandpur, in Raheli tehsil of Sagar district, as a part of his tour of the area. As the BDO informed the village Sarpanch, a Brahmin, Shri Dayaram Dubey about the proposed visit, series of panchayat meetings were held to decide about several issues such as:

1. Where would the public meeting be held in the village?
2. How would the Minister be welcomed and felicitated?
3. What kind of Memorandum about charter of demands be made with what priority?

The BDO came couple of times and met the *Sarpanch* as he must have met the village heads in other villages to be visited by the Minister. In all these decisions, the dynamics of village politics was evident in the panchayat meetings which I was allowed to attend as an observer. There were two factions among the dominant caste of Brahmins. There was a sizeable population of ex-untouchables who worked as farm labour on the lands of Brahmins besides cultivating their own small land holdings. The women from these Scheduled Caste groups were exploited by the Brahmins, brazenly saying that the beautiful girls in those communities were their daughters. There were other occupational castes like potter, carpenter etc in small numbers.

The visit took place in the following manner: Minister was received by the *Panchayat* members headed by *Sarpanch* by garlanding him at the gate of the primary school. The students made an arch by holding the bamboo sticks under which the Minister walked to the school building for a cup of tea and biscuits, which was supplied from a tea stall owned by a Brahmin, located opposite the school building. The meeting was held in the open space in school premises. A welcome speech was made by the Sarpanch which was followed by presenting a memorandum of demands, properly framed like a photograph, to the Minister. Minister made a speech appreciating the welcome and promising to look into the demands. After national anthem, the programme came to an end, while the Minister headed for another village.

The dynamics of *gram panchayat* was about the demands to be put up by the village to the Minister and their priority. The demands reflected the family interest of the respective members. Finally, the following demands were made:

(a) upgradation of primary school to secondary school,
(b) opening a health centre in the village,
(c) construction of *'pakka'* (a tar road) road in the village connecting the Taluka/Block headquarters Raheli about 7 km away passing through a forest (we used to go by bus from Sagar to Raheli. From Raheli we either walked the distance or went on horseback, hired at Raheli. The horse owner would walk the distance with the horse), and
(d) construction of a '*Dharmsala*' (public guesthouse) for visitors.

The BDO did not play any role in putting up these demands.

The power dynamics in the village became visible subsequently, when the *Sarpanch* was attacked with sticks by two persons, one Brahmin and another Jain, while he was sitting at tea shop. I could see the attack from the school verandah where I was standing A piquant situation arose when a police sub-inspector came to inquire about the attack. He wanted to take my evidence. However, the university authorities told the higher, district level police authorities not to involve us in the police case. The two attackers had instantly left the village and were found gossiping with the villages in the neighbouring village at the thrashing ground, putting up an alibi about their absence from the village at the time of alleged attack. Others who had observed the attack did not give evidence to police, fearing the consequences of getting into these quarrels. After some months, the attackers confided to me that they were concerned while they attacked the *Sarpanch* since I was standing in the school verandah. They said, "this *Sarpanch* is a bad, immoral person. He deserved to be killed. But killing a Brahmin is considered a moral sin. Hence we spared his life." (*Brahma-hatya-ka-patak*).

Thus the field assignment immediately after Masters' examination was not in the area of traditional anthropology of doing ethnography for a village monograph. It was meant to be testing hypothesis using the qualitative method of focused ethnography with the tools of observation and informal interview.

We had a problem of a place of residence in the village. I lived in the school building and ate food in a brahmin's family by turns, on invitation. However, after this incident, it was necessary to keep a distance from the factional politics of Brahmins. Fortunately we could hire a one room in a newly constructed house of a potter who was going away for six months. The house was located at the end of Brahmin locality at some distance/ from where the ex-untouchable locality started. Potter being a clean caste, although occupying low position in caste hierarchy, did not pose any purity-pollution issue. We made our food on a clay hearth (*chulha*), with fuel-wood watched by passers-by people.

Case Study 2: Birla Institute of Medical Research (BIMR), Gwalior

Dr. Ms. Leela Phatak the first Professor of obstetrics-gynecology at the Gajraraje Medical College, Gwalior and later as Dean, Lady Harding Medical College and Maulana Azad Medical College, Delhi, became the Commissioner of Family Welfare GOI. After superannuation, she settled at her native place, Gwalior and was requested to establish Birla Institute of Medical Research at Gwalior by the Birla Group of Industries who had a major textile factory at Gwalior.

There was a move to extend health services to rural areas in Gwalior region. A field station by way of two room tenement was established at village Uprai, in Datia district. Since I belonged to Gwalior and had M.A. dissertation monograph on a village Jaurasi on Gwalior-Jhansi road leading to Datia, Dr. Phatak requested Poona University to send me on three month deputation to initiate the functioning of rural health services in 31 villages around Uprai. I lived at Uprai at the field station in 1981.

A field trip of Master's level Anthropology students of Poona university was arranged to undertake rural fieldwork experience in addition to the usual tribal fieldwork. The students wrote their dissertations about the village and a copy of each was shared with BIMR.

A mobile team of doctor, para-medical worker and a social worker from Gwalior visited the villages on fixed days in a week to offer medical services to the patients. My work was to collect socio-economic data from these 31 villages which could help to prepare a plan of action for providing health care to the people.

The data was collected in a participatory way involving the villagers supervised by village leaders. The villagers were looking forward to upcoming health care schemes to be provided by reputed Birla Textile industry located at Gwalior. I travelled with Dr. Phatak to Delhi to meet

Prof. Ramalingswami, Director of ICMR to report to him about the project. Around the same time, ICMR-ICSSR joint team was working on preparing a health document for India, as a sequel to *Alma-Ata* meeting about Health for All by the year 2000.

I used to interact with the Collector of Datia, Shri Najeeb Jung on a regular basis. (Shri Najeeb Jung later became the Lt. Governor of Delhi). The decoity problem in the region in Madhya Pradesh and Uttar Pradesh around Datia-Jhansi was still active. The 'bandit-queen' Phulan Devi as reported living incognito at Jhansi was discussed between the Collector and Superintendant of police in my presence. The Sarvodaya leader Shri Jaiprakash Narayan had appealed to the dacoits to surrender. There was a surrendered dacoit, as a resident of Uprai village. He hosted a dinner to our students at his residence.

The brief stay at Uprai village for about three months put me in contact with the revenue officials of the district, the villagers and the health personnel, which led to sample survey about the health needs of the people. It also provided with an opportunity to visit the village Jaurasi which I had studied in 1958-59 and mainly discussed the issue of female infanticide with the high caste villagers, which resulted in purchasing the brides from other regions due to adverse sex ratio. Indeed, the two women who were purchased from Khandesh region of Maharashtra were shown to me from a distance.

Case Study 3: Latur (Killari) Earthquake: 30 September, 1993

There was an earthquake in Latur-Usmanabad district region of Marathwada in Maharashtra on 30th September, 1993 around 4.0 a.m. whereby around 10,000 people lost their lives in a fraction of a minute. Earlier, in Maharashtra, there was an earthquake on 11 December, 1967 at Koynanagar, near Koyna dam whereby about 200 persons lost their lives.

ICMR sanctioned a project to assess the gravity of mental health issues to Psychiatry Department of B.J. Medical College. Earlier such a project was sanctioned to study the mental health issues in regard to Union Carbide Gas leakage tragedy at Bhopal on the night of 2-3 December, 1984, but the study remained inconclusive. Due to my association with the PSM Department of B.J. Medical College as a guest faculty, I was co-opted as a member of the BJMC research team. I visited the earthquake affected villages and the epicentre village Killari couple of times to assess the ground level situation using the qualitative methods of observation and informal interviews.

1. There were more deaths in the families whose houses were made of circular stone blocks bound in mud. The stone blocks crushed the people sleeping by the side of the walls in the house. These were relatively well-off families as compared to the poor, whose houses had only mud walls without stone blocks. It is estimated that about 61 per cent people died of house collapse. Destiny saved those who precisely at that moment had gone out of the house for urination.

   In Koynanagar earthquake, few people died since the majority of the houses had mud walls. The mud wall falling on body injured but did not kill.
2. Temporary rehabilitation sheds were erected with the use of tin sheets. All affected families got a standard space as house, irrespective of their social or economic standing, obliterating the sense of hierarchy.
3. I attended a meeting of villagers in a hall of *Panchayat* House whereby every person was introduced in terms of number of deaths in his family, including that of the *Sarpanch. Sarpanch* had no time to mourn since he had to attend meetings about resettlement, or new sights for village settlement, avoiding the line of earthquake.
4. No labour was available to harvest the standing crop.
5. A point of discussion also referred to the distance bullocks would have to tread to go to field from proposed new settlement.
6. The families where a young woman had died leaving back small children were offered by the father of the woman to marry the sister of the deceased (sorrorate) woman to mother the children.
7. Several spiritual discourses such as *Bhajan-Kirtan* by outside groups were visible for offering solace to affected people.
8. Normalcy was defined by people in terms of reconstruction of devastated temples, reinstallation of deities, and marriages being performed as per rituals.

The findings of the psychiatrists related to less mental health ill-effects of this disaster as compared to such studies of disasters elsewhere in the world. The cultural or anthropological explanations could be related to spiritual orientation as an aspect of culture, fortified with spiritual discourses, as also the tragedy striking to one and all. Distinction between rich and poor got obliterated by way of equal space available to all in tin-shade temporary rehabilitation sites. Comparative studies of different kinds of disasters using the theoretical hypothesis about culture and personality could be rewarding.

Pune city had experienced such a disaster on 12 July, 1961 whereby an earthen dam (Panshet) nearing completion of construction, breached and burst another British time masonry dam (Khadakvasla) flooding the city settlements by the side of river, killing about 1000 people and dehabilitating thousands of families. They were provided temporary shelter in school buildings, whereby the occupants made neighbourhood formations in school class-rooms, as they were having in their respective house complexes. This tragedy led to expansion of Pune city by way of new settlements coming up.

Anthropology as a behavioural science is close to psychology and psychiatry. Concepts related to culture and personality have developed jointly by anthropologists and psychologists.

The issues of temporary or permanent displacement due to cyclones, floods, construction of dams, airports, new roads or rail line, new cities, defence establishments etc. keep on coming up. Resettlement and rehabilitation of displaced people becomes a major socio-economic, cultural and political issue. The implementing agencies whether public or private, weigh the production benefits of the completed project in terms of marketable income. The compensation offered in money fritters away in the hands of receivers who are not used to handling large sums of money-currency. People are used to make their living by following certain occupations, usually related to land production. They are not compensated by land for land, of the quality they are used to cultivating. There are certain emotional linkages with the places in terms of being the abode of their gods, pilgrim centres etc. which they would not like to give up or may not be resettled. Anthropologists who are used to give primacy to ethno-centrism about culture are criticized as anti-development. The issue is, do we have any implementable plan and schemes to provide benefits of development to the affected people, as an inclusive policy. Usually the affected people become deprived permanently while the benefits are accrued directly or indirectly to the people who may be termed as 'entreprencurs'. The philosophy of development is based on the concept of 'trickling down effect' supposedly benefiting the downtrodden or deprived.

Prof. S. Parasuraman has discussed this issue with examples from Odisha in S.C. Dube Memorial lecture at the Anthropology Congress 2013, at Kannur, Kerala.

A case study about displacement issues in relation to proposed dam in tribal Bastar is given as appendix.

Case Study 4

International Institute of Population Sciences (I.I.P.S.), Mumbai, the premier institute in demography conducts N.F.H.S. as an authentic health survey of India. Health Minister of India has been an *ex-officio* Chairperson of the governing council. It was reported in the meeting that the fertility rate in Goa was the lowest in the country, conveying that there was no problem of population explosion in Goa. However, the statistical information could not provide the reason for the phenomena. Hon. Health Minister's response was very optimistic that Indian's population explosion could be addressed with Goa paradigm.

The Director's discussion with us brought out that Goa statistics was more comparable to their empire country Portugal and other Portuguese colonies like Angola or Mozambique rather than with British India. Goa was a Portuguese colony until 1961 before the Portuguese surrendered it to India. It was decided to launch an in-depth study of four villages besides studying the records of Goa government written in Portuguese language. The study was supervised at the field level by one of our anthropology trained lady student. Broadly the findings were:

1. Age at marriage of girls has been on an average 27 years.
2. Favourable law about woman's share in property of the father and husband was a significant reason.
3. Recruitment to church by way of ordination as Father and Nun and migration has been significant.
4. Registration about birth, marriage was strictly observed.

At a women's meeting held at Pune about issues of women empowerment, the Muslim women from Goa expressed satisfaction about Portuguese law regarding share in property and did not favour either Indian civil law or Shariat law.

We are aware that the female literacy in Kerala is the causative factor for low infant mortality, not the programme. In Goa, fertility is low due to female education and property rules during Portugese rule, resulting in advanced age at marriage of girls. Fertility in Goa was more comparable to Portuguese colonies elsewhere, than the British ruled India.

Anthropological field study combining qualitative analysis with study of law and records provides explanation for the statistics. Anthropological qualitative methods and holistic approach provides the rationale of statistics.

Case Study 5: Female Foeticide: Kolhapur

It has been commonly alleged that in the patriarchal Hindi belt of north India, female infanticide was not uncommon. The sex ratio in the northern Hindi States confirm this allegation. While I revisited Jaurasi village in 1981 which I had studied in 1958 (Mutatkar, 1978), I asked the villagers about female infanticide which they promptly denied. But to a query, from where they got their brides in case of shortage of marriageable girls, they showed me from a window two women in the fields whom they said they purchased for few hundred rupees from Bhusaval in Maharashtra. Around the same time a case was reported in Parliament about a journalist purchasing a 'bride' named 'Kamla' for Rs. 1500 at Dholpur which is mid-way between Gwalior and Agra.

The technique of sonography is recommended widely to be used in pregnancy to confirm the healthy growth of foetus. However, sonography has also been widely misused to ascertain the sex of foetus leading to female foeticide instead of female infanticide. It has been remarked that "female foetus is not safe even in the mother's womb."

Kolhapur district in South Maharashtra is probably the richest rural district in Maharashtra due to sugar cane cultivation. It was observed that female foeticide was on the alarming increase linked with sonography. The District Collector with assistance from I.T. experts attached a device to all sonography machines whereby the sonography results could be stored up to two years. Any termination of pregnancy including M.T.P. particularly of the female foetus could be linked and traced to sonography. This could be a deterrent to prevent female foeticide since the doctor performing termination of female foetus could be punished according to law.

The District Collector was persuading the State Government to use such device all over the State. On request from the government, UNFPA appointed a committee consisting of retried Director of Health Services, Dean of a Medical College, Professor of Instrumentation from a government engineering college and me as a social scientist, to study and recommend about the feasibility of this techno-centric method of controlling female foeticide at the state level. Director of IIPS, Mumbai was also a member of the UNFPA committee. I was authorized to interview the District Collector, Civil Surgeon, and District Judge to understand the details of functioning of this mechanism, and to verify whether such evidence was admissible in the court of law for punishment. We also organized group meetings of women in the villages to know about the prevalence of use of sonography. It appears, the ANM recommended sonography examination to pregnant women, against which they received some kick backs from sonography centres. We also visited such centres in rural and urban centres. Professor of Instrumentation verified whether the seal of an additional equipment attached to sonography machine could be tempered.

We recommended to the government that the issue of female foeticide could not be conclusively addressed with this technology. We could not expect all government regulatory authorities to monitor such programme with the zeal and commitment of the then Collector of Kolhapur district. Gender issue is a social issue which requires multiple gender friendly awareness and motivational programmes to change the mindset due to historically perpetuating exploitative practices. Why is it that there is no female infanticide or foeticide among tribal communities? Let anthropologists study this phenomena in detail.

Save the Baby Girl

In Maharashtra, the sex ratio from 887 girls per 1000 boys in 2001-2003 went down to 884 in 2006-2008. Kolhapur district had the lowest sex ratio of 839. There has been an issue about strengthening the implementation of the Prenatal Diagnostic Techniques (Regulation and Prevention of Misuse) Act, 1994 which prohibits determination and disclosure of the sex of the foetus. (PCPNDT Act).

Save the Baby Girl (STBG) Web Portal was developed whereby all sonography machines were given a unique login id and password for online recording of all sonographies and MTPs in a prescribed format. Among those interviewed about their perception of sex ratio, sonography machines etc., were the elected representatives, medical officers of PHCs and their health workers, anganwadi worker etc. FGDs of women were conducted in four villages in four talukas. It was found that son preference was maximum among the affluent families and declined gradually with lower socio-economic levels.

The report was submitted to the Additional Chief Secretary Government of Maharashtra. There have been several media reports about some doctors getting punished by law for mis-using sonography technique to terminate pregnancy upon identification of female foetuses. The report could not recommend the operational feasibility of technological solution to the social problem of gender discrimination. Female education and employment seem to be the only socio-economic solution.

Case Study 6: Rural Water and Sanitation Programme: Qualitative Evaluation

Prof. P.V. Sukhatme, the pioneer agricultural statistician of India after serving as Director, Statistics, Food and Agricultural Organization (FAO) at Rome, settled down at Pune and was connected with Maharashtra Association of Cultivation of Science who own Agharkar Research Institute, supported wholly by Department of Science and Technology, GoI. He initiated a DST sponsored intervention project in eight villages with four villages for intervention and four as control. Dr. N.S. Deodhar, Director (Retd.). All India Institute of Public Health and Hygience, Kolkata provided public health inputs to the project.

Prof. Sukhatme had put up the hypothesis that nutrition to children was not the single determinant of childhood growth and development. The infections leading to morbidity such as childhood diarrhoea was the result of bad sanitation and un-potable water. The programme was, therefore, launched to construct latrines and provide potable water by disinfecting the village wells, which was the main source of drinking water.

The social worker was co-ordinating to ensure community involvement.

I was asked to undertake quick assessment of the programme which had no benchmark. I made trips to one village and had informal discussions in a village. The following points emerged:

About the construction of latrines: Financial provision was made to have a latrine per family. However, the provision was barely enough to cover the cost of pot, and the platform on which the pot was to be fixed. It was conceived that the roof, walls and door would be fixed by the respective families as per their facility; meaning, it could be made of bricks, tin sheets or branches of thorny bushes or other such material as gunny bag material. Little was the realization that the visual image of a latrine in the minds of the people was what they had seen in the PHC compound or in Tehsil office which had proper brick walls, a ventilating window, mud tiles or tin for roof and proper single or double wooden door. The community rejected the proposal of such a latrine. It was then decided to construct a latrine as recommended in a village meeting, to be shared by three families, which covered all costs.

I asked the key informants, sitting in a newly constructed temple without external aid, by the village community, as to what was the benefit of these latrines. The prompt reply was, "Elderly people have added years to their lives. "On asking to elaborate, they said, "earlier the old man would avoid eating sufficient dinner, lest he may have an urge to go for defecation at night, in darkness, to the field. There could be a chance that he may fall and would have fracture. The daughter-in-law who would have to care for him would blurt out that the old man ate too much. So, he avoided food in the evening. Now, with a latrine at the backyard and an electric bulb with a switch in the house, he had no such fear. So, he ate a normal dinner which was good for his health."

On making inquiry about the construction of the temple, they said, "we collected funds, we selected an architect and builder, we went to Jaipur to purchase marble idols of deities, we did everything without any external aid." When I remarked that I had to jump over an open drainage, just outside the temple, they said, that was to be managed by the government. People had the capacity to manage construction of a temple but that capacity could not be harnessed for constructing a proper drainage. Why not?

The well water was disinfected (chlorinated) occasionally by the social worker early in the morning coming all the way from Pune in a jeep of the Institute. On a rainy day, in darkness, it appears, large quantity of disinfectant was dropped in the well. As a result, small fish in the well died. They were taken out in darkness and were thrown in the drain linked to well. The dead fish got stuck on the mud side-walls of the drain and were visible to the villagers. That day, the tea made in the houses also smelt of disinfectant and as reported, the *'dal'* (pulses) could not be properly cooked. There was an outrage in the village and a meeting was called to punish the social worker and driver of the jeep. However, at the meeting, some elderly people argued that "these persons were working for our good. They had no intention to harm us. And if we look at the picture of diarrhoea in our village, we have less diarrhoea this year than last year. Similarly, in comparison to other villages in our nighbourhood, we have less diarrhoea, for which the credit goes to the disinfection of our well." The social worker was cautioned to be careful in future about disinfection of drinking water in the well.

This case study educates us to look at issues holistically. Latrine is not only a technical solution for better health for the people who are used to open defecation for ages. People have visible image of a proper latrine, which has to be addressed. People understand the logic of science if properly demonstrated.

Case Study 7: India: Rural Infrastructure Project

National Council of Applied Economic Research (NCAER), New Delhi had embarked India Rural Infrastructure Survey Project supported by Sir Ratan Tata Trust during 1999-2002. Alumni of Department of Anthropology, University of Poona, Dr. Jyotsna Bapat was the project coordinator and I was one of the three project consultants. Around the same time, UGC curriculum development committee for Anthropology of which I was the nodal person used to meet frequently at Delhi. Dr. Jyotsna Bapat offered to the respective anthropologists to conduct field studies in couple of States each, about the ground level situation of rural infrastructure in four sectors: telecommunications, power, roads and transport, and water and sanitation, NCAER had selected the two districts in each state with good and bad performance and two talukas in each district in every selected state for collecting primary data, using the mix of qualitative and quantitative tools, such as observation, group meetings, key informant interviews, case studies of innovative projects and questionnaire. The primary data was collected in 10 States from 1100 villages. The final report has been published as a book by SAGE publications. (2007)

We had taken the responsibility of doing field studies in Maharashtra and Madhya Pradesh. In transport sector, even now, media keeps on reporting deaths of marriage parties travelling in tractor-trolleys, tempos and trucks, not meant for human transport. The private jeeps in tribal areas are overcrowded, to the extent that only the driver's face is visible. Nothing of the jeep is visible, except the human bodies.

Tribal village roads are not connected to the main roads or state highways. Mobile phones have increased which could be used for telemedicine in difficult tribal belts, if mobile towers are raised in sufficient numbers Telecommunication and cyber cafes provide prices of agriculture produce at different markets. For electricity, there are different sources of energy. Some private enterprises have produced solar lamps. The issue is how many hours is electricity available and for how many days in a year? There is also an issue of theft of electricity, mostly to run irrigation pumps.

In Maharashtra, Kolhapur, the rich peasantry district and Gadchiroli, the tribal district were notified for study. 92 villages were visited. Electricity was available for 16 hours for 4 days in a week and out of 90 days, it was available for 46 days. As expected, the situation in tribal district was dismal in all respects. Some people have to travel for livelihood every day. It is a common sight in tribal taluka town for the public sector functionaries as school teachers, anganwadi workers, ANM's etc. to travel to their place of work in the morning by whatever transport is available and return back in the evening. Drinking water sources are usually wells, hand pump and river. In Maharashtra, people listed he priorities in the order of water and sanitation, internal and external roads, electricity and telephone.

In Madhya Pradesh, being a large State, four districts and 8 talukas were selected for study. 185 villages were visited by the research team. The priority listed in M.P. related to electricity, roads, drinking water and sanitation and telephones in that order.

These studies are a good example of focused ethnography under the supervision of anthropology trained personnel. It was easier to convene village meetings at a public place to discuss the issues relating to infrastructure. It appears, for the first time, anthropologists were involved in such a large national level study, combining the qualitative and quantitative methods of data collection.

Case Study 8: Tribal Malnutrition: Government-NGO Partnership about Tribal Malnutrition: An Intervention Project

In the context of '*suo motu*' observations by the Mumbai High Court about the alarming infant mortality and malnutrition among tribal children in Maharashtra, the tribal development department offered a health related tribal development project jointly to two voluntary organisations: Comprehensive Rural Health Project, Jamkhed headed by Dr. R.S. Arole (Jamkhed model) and Maharashtra Association of Anthropological Sciences, Pune headed by Professor of Anthropology, R.K. Mutatkar, to work in seven tribal dominant districts, in nine talukas as proposed by the organizations. The then Principal Secretary, Tribal Development Department of the State Government offered to Dr. R.S. Arole and Prof. R.K. Mutatkar, "Let us be partners in tribal development."

We had the privilege of undertaking an experiment in practicing anthropology through our voluntary agency, the Maharashtra Association of Anthropological Sciences (MAAS) established in 1976, to conduct interventions in about 250 tribal villages in seven districts and nine tehsils of Maharashtra, covering a population of about 1,70,000 tribal people. The intervention was wholly funded by the State government and primarily addressed, as per the government order, to bring down under-nutrition of tribal children in response to *suo motu* injunction of Mumbai High Court. This intervention could have been administered by a religious charitable organization by feeding all the children in a given time in the name of God, with compassion, as is usually done. We launched a project entitled- "Comprehensive and Sustainable Human Development of the Tribal People of Maharashtra." Using the anthropological theory of holism and functionalism, our initial inputs were in the area of health. But as per the concept of functional integration of culture, we also provided inputs in education, in community organization, such as empowering the Grampanchayat members and *Mahila Mandals*, involving the Integrated Child Development Services (ICDS) and health department functionaries etc. We also introduced puppetry and trained volunteers to supplement traditional art forms to generate awareness. We aimed at raising the self-confidence and self-esteem of the tribal people. The programme was implemented by about 250 male and 250 female volunteers who were the citizens of their respective hamlets and villages. They were paid Rs. 250 p.m. honourarium for the voluntary work. The traditional health care providers such as Dai and herbalist medicine man were involved. The approach of 'confidence building' by keeping medicine box for common ailments with every volunteer, distribution of seeds for kitchen garden, distribution of clothing to new born to protect against respiratory infections and the supplementary food fortified with Ayurvedic herbs to lactating women, and ready to eat, pre-cooked *'Sattu'* powder to children under three years of age, was followed. The pregnant women were given normal fresh meal one time a day from fourth month to ninth month of pregnancy in the house of the volunteer. There has been a measurable impact on the birth weight of new born, and reduction of under-nutrition as per the Anganwadi scale. Due to 'capacity building' exercise, these 500 volunteers were empowered to undertake programmes of similar nature in their respective villages. They also understood the cause-effect relationship of weight and malnutrition, since the children were weighed every fortnight and charting of weight and other documentation was done by the volunteers. Dai huts were constructed in the villages where a particular *Dai's* services were sought after by the people, as a sanitary place for institutional delivery by the *Dai*. Training in birthing practices was given to female volunteers as also to *Dais* to upscale their skills.

To put it briefly, anthropological approach has been practised to understand processes of human development and to address the needs of the people. It was found necessary to understand the functioning of the government system about tribal development. This programme has also provided a model of Government-NGO partnership by installing the joint monitoring system at the State and Block level. As anthropologists, we have learnt the necessity to widen the definition of holism going beyond the ethnography of culture of a tribal community as if it was an isolate. We have to understand the interaction between the macro decisions and issues of micro level implementation. We have been successful in this project due to emic perspectives implemented at micro level. Vision development of volunteers motivated them to work for their own communities which enhanced their self-esteem and self-confidence, bestowing on some of them formal positions of authority and employment, such as members of *gram panchayats* or as *anganwadi sevika*. The 500 male-female volunteers and some PRI members were presented in person to a tribal cabinet minister and tribal commissioner of Maharashtra, and to the media, at Nasik on 22 November, 2012. Some of them publicly articulated their experiences about the skills and empowerment they received from the programme. The tribal women who had not travelled beyond 20 km distance, the marriage distance, got opportunity to travel, and interact with tribals from other ethnic groups. The issue is how to use these empowered human resources for tribal development.

In pursuance of the G.R. the actual functioning of the project "Comprehensive and Sustainable Human Development of the Tribal People of Maharashtra", titled in Marathi as *"Adivasi Utthan Karyakram"* (AUK), started in January 2005. As advised by the government, gram panchayat was taken as a unit of action covering about 15000 tribal population in each of the nine talukas. All ethnic tribal communities in Maharashtra including the three 'Primitive Tribal Group' (PVTG) communities have been covered in the programme.

Adivasi Utthan Karyakram was operative during 2005-2013 in Jawhar-Mokhada talukas of Thane (Palghar) district, Karjat in Raigad district, Akole in Ahmednagar district. Dhadgaon (Akrani) and Akkalkuwa in Nandurbar, Dharni in Amravati, Zari Zamni in Yavatmal and Etapalli taluka in Gadchiroli district.

Focusing on malnutrition and infant mortality, the programme components included health, education, livelihood and income generation, community development, empowerment, training and orientation of development functionaries, and self-esteem and cultural identity in the descending order of priority, following the anthropological concept of holism based on integrative functional interaction among the aspects of culture.

Government-NGO partnership was made functional by structuring joint monitoring committees at each of the nine field sites, at the level of Tribal Commissionerate and an Apex committee at the Mantralaya. The committees have been chaired by the government functionaries, respectively by Additional Tribal Commissioners, Tribal Commissioner and Secretary, Tribal Development and with the *Adivasi Utthan Karyakram* functionaries as Secretary of the committee. The other members at various levels have been BDOs, MLA, *Panchayat Samiti Sabhapati,* Project Officers of ITDP etc. The periodical meetings discussed the progress of the work and provided guidelines for future work.

AUK programme activities have been carried out by the male and female tribal volunteers totaling about 450 in nine centres selected at the respective village meetings. Through the mechanisms of fortnightly and monthly training and monitoring meetings, the activities were planned. Each village/hamlet based volunteer has been paid an honourarium of Rs. 250 per month. Supervision has been provided at the local level by senior volunteers as peer supervisors or *'Margadarshak'* assisted by educated local tribals selected for the job, under the guidance of programme coordinators selected from the region as full-time employees of the programne. The assistants and coordinators met every quarter for orientation and feedback meetings under the guidance of Programme Directors.

Activities had been planned and administered as confidence building and capacity building activities.

Confidencc Building Activities

1. A medicinal kit box for common ailments with each volunteer, medicines to be dispensed free of cost.
2. Seeds of vegetables distributed free, first to families having malnourished children and then to volunteers for their kitchen gardens.
3. Fish seeds for fish ponds in the villages.
4. Health camps specially for women and children.

Capacity Building Activities

As a human development programme, it was designed to develop the capacities of tribal volunteers, assistant co-ordinators, co-ordinators and general population. Various training programmes have been organized.

1. Fortnightly training of 450 tribal volunteers about programme activities by assistant co-ordinators and taluka co-ordinators involving the locally available resource persons from other block development functionaries and others.
2. Feedback and training of 9 field coordinators and 80 peer supervisors and assistant co-ordinators at Pune, Jamkhed and other field sites to plan and execute the programme activities, every quarter.
3. A batch of 20 tribal trainees from each field centre in puppetry and appropriate technology respectively at Karjat, district Raigad and Phaltan, district Satara.
4. Training in tailoring to about 300 tribal girls from 9 centres.
5. Training in bamboo work to about 200 tribal youth.
6. Panchayati Raj training to about 200 gram panchayat members.
7. Training about processing of medicinal herbs to make medicine to about 350 Vaidus.
8. Training of about 500 Dais and other women about birthing practices by experienced lady trainers from Jamkhed once a year.
9. Exposure visits of tribal volunteers to specific sites about horticulture, medicinal plant nurseries etc.

Programme activities: Focus on malnutrition and child mortality

1. Appropriate three types of weighing machines to volunteers to weigh new born, children up to 3 years of age, pregnant and lactating women. The Anganwadi has these machines, which could not be used unless a baby child is brought to anganwadi. Programme instruments were taken to the respective houses and growth-weight charts filled.
2. Two sets of culturally acceptable undergarments *(jhabala)*, body covering *(dupata)* and a cap *(topada)* to cover the new born baby to protect from respiratory infections. Garments have been stitched by tribal women who underwent training in tailoring.

3. Ready to eat wheat-bengal gram roasted powder *'sattu'* for the age-group 6 months-2 years given at home.
4. This *'sattu'* fortified with Ayurvedic drug tonics and lactogens supplied to lactating women to improve lactation.
5. Pregnant women provided one time full square meal in the house of tribal lady volunteer from the 5th month of pregnancy to increase the birth weight of expectant baby.
   Lady volunteers were given authority to make purchases of food items and vegetables from the village shopkeeper or weekly market and maintain accounts. She was not given any additional wage besides the honourarium of Rs. 250 per month, which every volunteer received from the programme. She was permitted to share the food with pregnant women and her children up to the age of 2-3 years, free of cost. During meals there has been discussion about care during pregnancy, delivery and about baby care based on the booklets prepared by the programme.
6. Experienced trainers and female village workers from Jamkhed went to each of the nine centres once a year to provide training to *dais* and women who were interested in undertaking *dai* work about safe birthing practices and identifying the risk situations in order to refer the cases to safe institutions for delivery.
7. *Dai* huts were constructed in the villages where the *dai* was in great demand for delivery. It is difficult for women to be taken to the primary health centre at a distance in a difficult tribal terrain with lack of easily manageable transport facility. Clean places for delivery in and around the village are preferred where other siblings could also be around the mother.
8. In certain areas like Karjat, district Raigad and Zari Zamani, district Yavatmal, the tribal people lived in exclusive hamlets in the neighbourhood of caste peasant villages. Since the anganwadi are located in the villages, tribal children from the hamlets could not utilize anganwadi services. The programme started *'khelwadi'* in these hamlets which were taken over by the government as mini-anganwadi.
9. The activities in ashram school and other academic activities included computer education, reading room, special coaching to Class X students, bio-gas, bathroom repairs and solar lights in girls ashram schools, plant nursery in ashram school having land and irrigation facility etc. Bijudhavdi Ashram school in Dharni, District Amravati was developed as an ideal ashram school.

10. Current activity is to make at least two anganwadis in each of the 9 centres as ideal, meaning thereby 100 per cent compliance of Anganwadi guide book of the government.
11. Where applicable, small bunds were constructed by the community for irrigation and increased agricultural production.

Besides these focused activities, some of the centre specific activities included soak pits, drinking water on festive occasions where thousands of tribals gathered for celebration of *Holi* festival, repairing *'ghotul'* in Madia villages and *'chawdi'* of Kolam, facilitating getting Antyodaya cards, providing traditional musical instruments etc.

Outcome

1. The measurable outcome is the reduction of malnutrition grades of children as a result of intervention of providing supplementary ready to eat food supplement *'sattu'* for the age group 6 months–2 years.
2. The *'sattu'* fortified by ayurvedic tonic drugs given to lactating women has also shown weight gain for the babies up to 6 months while the infants were only breast fed.
3. Providing one square meal a day to tribal pregnant women from the fifth month of pregnancy has resulted in increased birth weight of babies born to these women.
   These outcomes analysed by a demographer faculty member have also been confirmed independently by the spontaneous quotes of tribal women about the impact of these interventions. The sustainable impact is reflected in the understanding of people about the relationship of malnutrition measurable by weight and not only by expressions like looking pale, not playing, inactive, neck not straight but declining towards a shoulder etc. So, large number of weighing machines for weighing children would be used, instead of one provided at the anganwadi.
4. Capacity of tribal volunteers to take weights, fill in growth charts and mobilise people for action has increased. Their capacity to access government schemes has increased.
5. Capacities of *dais*, gram panchayat members, *vaidu* and about puppetry, bamboo artifacts, tailoring etc. increased substantially in their respective vocations and domains.

Many volunteers got elected to gram panchayat, as ASHA, as anganwadi *sevika* etc. due to the skills and the popularity they gained due to their community work.

The interventions were planned and carried out with an eye on replicability in the government sector, including the financial viability of the programmes. Some of the programmes like kitchen garden, supplementary ready to eat food, clothing for the new born etc. have now been introduced in some ITDP centres.

This also indicates that Government-NGO collaboration or partnership is possible and would show substantial results if fund flow is done regularly as estimated. Breaks in the programme due to uncertain funding leads to loss of confidence of the people in the programme and people's involvement becomes shaky. The government functionaries at all officer cadre levels keep on changing due to transfers. There is no mechanism for the new incumbents to be oriented to the special issues of tribal development, for which a special tribal sub-plan has been devised.

In short, the outcome of *Adivasi Utthan Karyakram* to develop capacities of tribal volunteers and peer supervisors to function as agents of change has been achieved to a great extent. However, for empowering the tribal people to demand and access the tribal development schemes and to do micro-planning, continued training, monitoring and sympathetic supervision may be required for few more years.

The total intervention project was not pre-conceived except the integrative approach of graded interventions in different sectors. The details of interventions evolved in consultation with local people and by experiencing in the field, the felt needs of the people which would win their confidence, to equip them for capacity building. (Mutatkar, 2018)

This project has provided confidence that anthropologist could undertake intervention programme for model building using anthropological concepts and methods with due consideration of ethical objectivity. This is a good example of action anthropology.

Case Study 9-10: Participation in Government Statutory Bodies as Nominated Expert Member

As mentioned earlier, Government of India directed to constitute Tribal Cells in Rajbhavans to help the Hon. Governor in discharging constitutional responsibilities about Scheduled Tribes by directing the state governments to take steps accordingly. I had the honour to be consulted about the nature of tribal cell to be constituted. Subsequently,

I have been nominated on two statutory bodies, viz. Statutory Development Board of Maharashtra and the Tribes Advisory Council, a body of selected tribal MLAs and MPs, chaired by the Chief Minister. I also had the honour to prepare a draft Memorandum of Association for the TRTI to be made autonomous body, as per law about Charitable Associations and Trusts. As governing board member of TRTI, there are opportunities to advise about the research studies to be undertaken by the TRTI.

There are Statutory Development Boards in Maharashtra, separately for the geographical regions of Vidarbha, Marathwada and Rest of Maharashtra, directly under the authority of the Governor functioning logistically through Planning Department, to address the issues of regional imbalances since the formation of the linguistic State of Maharashtra on 1 May, 1960. Governor has directed the Boards to undertake research in respective geographical jurisdictions under the Boards. As an anthropologist member of the Board nominated by Hon. Governor, we can be partners in these efforts, particularly about the issues of tribal development. Apart from the regional imbalances, the tribal pockets in each region suffer from imbalances in development efforts, despite Tribal Sub-Plan. The recently constituted Kelkar Committee in regard to regional imbalances, has conceptually treated all tribal areas and communities as a distinct region, recommending 50 per cent of TSP money to be given to PESA village gram sabhas to administer the development schemes as per their choice. What is the role of anthropology in all these development efforts?

Tribes Advisory Council

As mentioned earlier, TAC is a statutory body of selected tribal MLAs and MPs which is chaired by the Chief Minister. The Tribal Development Department puts up the agenda for discussion and decision, which may be added by the members. The prominent issues which are discussed relate to pseudo-tribal claims for S.T. status, which are actually political issues. Education is another issue, as also the forest rights and tribal lands.

I as a nominated member raised the issue about the role of colleges and universities set up in the tribal areas for the benefit of tribal students. Anthropology's natural and historically evolved expertise about tribal culture has to be put to use through such institutions. The major effort has to be in the area of upscaling the indigenous knowledge towards skill development. Biological anthropology can contribute to such issues as sickle cell and goiter. There is good scope not only to document ethno-medicine but to upscale it by linking with public health.

As members of such committees, we learn different perspectives and priorities which we have to link with our theoretical concepts, or develop new theories to analyse the dynamics and process of change, and the role played by different stakeholders such as legislators, bureaucrats, markets and voluntary or people's sectors.

Summing up

In Anthropology, different terms have been used to connote the process of knowledge used for analysing or recommending solutions to certain public issues. Anthropological concepts and methods of analysis are used for such purpose. From general term such as 'applied anthropology', Malinowski used the term 'practicing anthropology' while Sol Tax has called it 'action anthropology'. However, the examples found in Western anthropological literature refer to 'other' cultures. In India, the urban born anthropologist would consider tribal issues as of other people. But, when we are addressing the national or regional issues as trained citizen anthropologists, we are not dealing with other people. Tribal students, students from rural areas, people's elected representatives from village, block, district, state up to national levels are not dealing with other people. At some point of time, we have to play the advocacy role for voiceless people identified by the Constitution and endorsed by the judiciary by way of entertaining PILs and *suo motu* injunctions.

"Malinowski held that ethnographers who have studied culture contact and assessed its potential and dangers have the right and duty to formulate their conclusions in a way in which they can be seriously considered by those who frame policy and carry it out. They also have the duty to speak as the natives' advocate." (Firth 1981:195).

As an example, a tribal girl from an ethnic group of Thakar was molested by a non-tribal shop keeper. A tribal leader who happened to be a Thakar decided to organise a protest *'morcha'* and prepared a hand bill for distribution accordingly. Since, I was staying with his family for my research work, I was shown the handbill. I advised him to refer the victim not as Thakar but by a more general term *adiwasi* and calling upon *adiwasi* to join the protest march. As a result people belonging to all tribal ethnic groups in large numbers joined together in protest, with good results. I get this insight not from my political education but from field insights about ethnic groups and the solidarity which a general popular term like *adiwasi* could convey. This, I think is action anthropology.

The voluntary organisations or small NGOs, also referred to as tribal activists working in tribal villages mostly on issues of tribal land in relation to forest lands and rules about ownership, constantly kept contact with us. They used to organise meetings about land-forest issues coming together with other activists from other regions of the country and invite us to address them.

Most of these 'activists' were educated up to post-graduate levels and had no formal links with any political party. Some of the activists, who were tribals themselves had reservations about non-tribal activists, which they voiced publicly. This is comparable to the issues such as Mahatma Gandhi championing the cause and concerns of untouchables calling them Harijans, while Dr. Ambedkar himself belonging to the ex-untouchable community suffered the discrimination as a victim, despite his high education and urban and defence background of parentage. However, the tribals do not suffer from the discrimination and deprivation of the kind suffered by ex-untouchables. The tribal activists who live in deprivation and poverty feel that the non-tribal do-gooders and intellectuals who have had no experience of their deprivation could not be effective advocates about their plight.

Our university background, however, provided us with immunity of objectivity in this regard, since we were not linked to any geographical tribal region. When I proposed to the 'activists' whether they would appreciate my joining their cadres, they declined saying that they appreciated joining university seminars or workshops where they 'charged their motivational batteries', since sometimes they felt lost in the day-to-day mundane activities, functioning in their small geographical boundaries, forgetting their aim in starting their respective voluntary organisations.

Our interaction with the public sector or voluntary sector provided us knowledge of issues at the policy level, as also at the micro level about the logistics of implementation. Since, tribal people do not possess legal or written documents about the ownership of land or house, they being traditionally pre-literate people, controversies arise in the government system. Even amongst caste-peasantry, due to illiteracy, the revenue clerk called as *Patvari* or *Talathi* used to commit frauds about inheritance of land property.

Practicing anthropology would require an anthropologist being a part of a muti-disciplinary team where his expertise about community culture and traditions would be valued, his recommendations about such issues as pseudo-tribal claims to S.T. status are honoured by the government and confirmed by the judiciary.

Besides brief case studies given in this chapter, other issues of applicability or practice are given in respective chapters. The case study dealing with designing and administering an intervention programme about tribal malnutrition all over tribal belts in Maharashtra is real action anthropology. The model developed on the basis of holistic and integrative concept of culture, applicable for sustainable change, is based on implementation of programme by the community, rooted in people-centric anthropological paradigm. Anthropology in action with constant dialogue with the people, provide insights to correlate theories about stability, equilibrium and change with the existing ground realities, and understand the aspirations or need of the people to change the reality of living in deprivation into a life of dignity. Is it enough to document and discuss the etic perception of poverty, and the top-down national schemes, or find ways to come out of it, to reach out to help in framing the policies and considering logistic micro-details about implementing them to meet the emic goals of good life?

Appendix

Cultural Dynamics of Resettlement: A Case Study

The following case study about proposed hydro-electric dam construction in Bastar affecting the tribal people and the Sal forest is presented here on the basis of anthropological field four. The project was abandoned not so much since it would affect the tribal people but it would have destroyed the Sal forest.

Introduction

Bodhghat Hydro Electrical Project in Bastar was submitted to the Government of India for clearance under the Forest Conservation Act, 1980. The Ministry of Welfare, Government of India constituted an in-depth study group on possible displacement of tribals due to Bodhghat Project in Bastar and their rehabilitation, in August 1987, the report of which was to be submitted to the Prime Minister. Other committees, such as one from the Ministry of Environment and Forests, Forest research institute, Jabalpur and Forest Research Institute, Dehradun were also appointed to assess the Bodhghat dam project. All these committees had given a negative report. Simultaneously, the Government of Madhya Pradesh constituted a committee of four university level academicians and four administrators from Madhya Pradesh to assess the likely impact of Indira Sarovar (Bodhghat) Hydro Electrical Project on socio-economic, cultural, and religious life of the tribals, to be displaced by the project. This committee briefly called, the State Committee, collected empirical data in the project submergence area using quantitative and qualitative social research methods. The report was submitted to the Government of India in December 1987.

The State Committee administered household schedules to 133 families from 13 different villages on a purposive sample to represent villages on both the banks of the river Indravati and to represent various tribal, Schedule Caste and caste Hindu groups. This was supplemented by discussion with the villagers to assess their views and opinions. Resettlement sites were also visited.

The report is presented in three parts. Part I deals with the present status and situation of the people living in submergence area. Part II covers the perception and awareness of the population to be displaced as well as the host population around the new settlement location. Part III reviews the resettlement and rehabilitation plan as proposed by the project authorities and Government of Madhya Pradesh.

The final committee which was appointed constituted the retired forest officials from Madhya Pradesh and Maharashtra. Several forest officials from Maharashtra earlier were located at Nagpur since Nagpur was the capital of Central Provinces before Madhya Pradesh State was formed. The retired Director General of Forests, GoI, who was a Maharashtrian was the Chairman of the committee. I was inducted as an anthropologist to study the effect on tribal people in the tribal villages under threat of submergence. I was known to forest officials from Maharashtra, since in the Marathi Journal '*Hakara*' (Clarion Call), published by our academic NGO, MAAS, which was exclusively devoted to tribal issues, carried several articles about forests and tribe relationships. Several forest officials also contributed articles to this journal. With this experience, I was invited to assess the impact of Bodhghat on people's lives in the submergence areas, study the state committee report in detail, and make recommendations about resettlement. I invited my faculty colleague Dr. B.V. Bhanu to join me to form our team. We formed part of a larger investigating team consisting of experts in forestry and engineering, from Madhya Pradesh and Maharashtra.

We had an access to the MPEB project report of 1987 at Pune. The reports by other committees, and the State Committee report were carefully studied and the findings were assessed fresh in the field.

Incidentally, all teachers and students of the Department of Anthropology, University of Poona (now called SPPU) had visited Bastar and stayed for two weeks in a village Munchnar, 3 km from Barsoor, in November-December 1977 to give tribal field training to the students.

Methodology

While embarking on the two-week field tour of Bodhghat project area in Bastar on 21 November, 1990, we had decided to adopt qualitative research strategy for collection of primary data from the people. It was obvious that 10-11 days stay in the submergence area was not enough to collect quantitative data without winning the confidence of the people. Moreover, a team of junior investigators would have to be recruited from local colleges, given training and provide supervision. It was also felt that the affected people may not open up their hearts and minds to answer questions on a topic which was to affect their lives in future. It was, therefore, decided to use the anthropological technique of observation and informal interviews for assessing the views of people on displacement and resettlement.

The most important step in qualitative social research to ensure scientific reliability and validity about the data collected, is to minimize the communication gap between the researcher and the respondents. This is possible by playing the role, which is neutral from people's point of view, the role not associated with the problem with which the people are exercised. We told the people that we were teachers. Thus, we could speak to the teachers first by asking them about their education and occupational problems. Since, the teachers were like students to us, the role they accepted easily, they used to be very free with us. We told people that we were on way to join our students in Orissa tribal area and in 1977 we had brought our students to Barsoor area for studying tribal culture. We told them, we wanted to assess changes in their lives during the last 13 years since our last visit. We also told them that we had heard about Bodhghat Project and that we had studied similar projects. We are accompanying our friends from forestry division from Maharashtra whom they saw surveying the forest with the help of local forest guards and some other local help. We told them, we stayed at the camping huts of the MPEB, with our friends.

We used to stop and talk to the people wherever we found them. We accepted their hospitality readily, sat with them on the ground, entered their houses, made curious inquires about their artifacts and their problems.

We discussed their marriage customs, rituals, observed house making, cock fights, agricultural operations and rope making. We made no distinction in choosing people to talk, from *Patel, Kotwar* to landless labour. The informality in our approach made them free with us. We never started discussion about the dam, but we made inquiries about their culture and discussion about the impact of dam on their culture followed in the natural course of communication. No interview lasted less than an hour.

We never used paper and pencil in the presence of the people realizing that historically, they had often been exploited by the literate people in administration and by money lenders or traders with the use of paper and ink. As a result, we could establish our role as senior teachers, as their friends, willing to listen to them patiently. Some people actually asked our opinion about the dam and asked us if we had inside information about the decision about dam construction.

People saw us travelling in MPEB jeep for short distances but they saw that the forest personnel went to the forest with their instruments and with the forest guards. They also saw that the bearings and *khaki* dress patterns of our forest colleagues was different from us. We always mixed with people, ate with them, sat with them and visited their *Devgudis*. We offered no advice, no solution but listened patiently to their individual and communal problems. The teacher who was staying at Harrakodar for 16 years probed about the real purpose of our visit, while we rested in his house on his bed. We shared with him that we were genuinely concerned about the problems of displacement and resettlement and that we wanted to understand the minds of the people so that we could convey them to the decision makers in the government. We could convince him that we had not taken any sides and we had no views of our own but that we wanted to collect the unbiased views of the people.

The people could see that we did not seek any help from the local government functionaries as our forester colleagues took the help of forest guard. We did not engage any interpreters although in group discussion, help was offered by some members of the group. We had experienced at other places that the local interpreters also acted as respondents and interpreted not only the language expressions but took liberty of interpreting the views, according to their own biases.

We tried a combination of Hindi and Marathi since many people knew Halbi which has many Marathi words. With gestures and communication of the eyes, we could express ourselves and could also understand people. The exercise of understanding each other's expressions itself narrowed the communication gap between the researchers and the respondents.

Out of 33 villages to be submerged, 12 villages had a population of less than 100. We decided to personally visit about 10 villages, depending upon the transport available. After reaching Bodhghat, we realized that we could not go in the jeep beyond Harrakodar on the right bank and beyond Neurnar on the left bank of Indravati River. We visited the villages up to Bhatpal on bicycle one day. On another day, we walked to Binta from Neurnar, a distance of 18-20 kms and had a night halt in the village.

Observations

Following is the sequential account of our visits to places and people during November 23–December 3, 1990. On November 23, at Jagdalpur we met Principal Jha, a retired Principal of a local college whose brother was also Principal and whom we had met in 1977. He appreciated that power generation was of regional and national interest but voiced concern about disturbing the eco-system and the problems of resettlement. Earlier he was associated with the Bastar *Prakriti Bachao Samiti*. We met Dr. R.K. Saha, Regional Officer of the Anthropological Survey of India, Government of India, who was also a member of the state committee. He regretted the human problems created by development projects like Bodhghat dam, and wondered if it was avoidable by harnessing nuclear energy.

After returning from Bodhghat fieldwork, we had a planned meeting lasting two hours with the senior citizens of Jagdalpur on December 3, 1990, who were associated with the Bastar Prakriti Bachao Samiti. We met Advocate Ravishankar Bajpai, Mr. Sharad Verma and Mr. Aswathi. They were concerned about the destruction of precious forest wealth and species, due to Bodhghat project. They appreciated the need of power generation to the State but voiced the concern that Bodhghat power would not bring development to Bastar. They opined that the tribals were ignorant and innocent people and they would suffer on account of displacement. They also felt that there was always a wide gap between promises and practice and that MPEB, or its agents were not capable of providing solace to the affected people. They expressed doubts about compensatory afforestation, as to whether it could compensate the loss of Sal forest and eco-system.

On 3rd December at Jagdalpur, we had an hour long meeting with Mr. K.B. Prasad, the research officer in the office of the Deputy Commissioner, Tribal Development, who met us on behalf of Deputy Commissioner, who had to go out at the time. The research officer could not convince us as to why the Tribal Development Department was not involved in any studies regarding Bodhaghat project. He, however, suggested that if any responsibility was laid on the Tribal Development Department, they would share it. It became apparent that there was no dialogue between MPEB and the Tribal Development Department of the State Government.

On November 24th we were taken round the dam site by Mr. Gupta, Chief Engineer, MPEB at Barsoor. He informed us of the compensation scheme which was also given in the project report. He, however, expressed doubt as to how many people would like to shift to resettlement sites in view of the prospect of employment at the dam construction site. It was reported that power generation would not be of direct local relevance since it would get into the State Electricity Grid System.

On the same day, Asst. Engineer Mr. Dwiwedi took us to a model village, Pharasmadhur about 60 km from Barsoor. We saw a hut with an attached bath made for Rs. 32,000. Having seen many specious tribal huts which exemplified their ethnic character, we were unimpressed with the hut. We also saw the buildings of school and community hall and were told about land development. The young engineer expressed that the displaced people be given compensation and they could find their own ways of resettlement. Little did they realize that the cash compensation may not reach the pockets of tribal who could not count large sums of currency notes. The money may vanish into the pockets of money lenders and traders or may be frittered away in flashy consumer items. If the tribals had capacity to organize themselves for future, they would not have remained underdeveloped and branded as backward.

During our three trips to MPEB Office at Barsoor and during our interaction with MPEB officials, we clearly felt the prevailing atmosphere of despondency. The indecision in regard to construction of the dam and the visits of various teams to assess the feasibility and impact of dam on forest, wild life and people would definitely dampen the morale of MPEB staff. The engineers were without engineering work for too long. The officials, it was apparent, had to follow the ritual of taking round the members of various committees to dam site, model village sites, and to provide hospitality to them. Pending the decision about construction of Bodhghat dam, all matters about resettlement appeared hypothetical and without any immediate relevance.

We had a long dialogue with a revenue inspector at the MPEB office and with a senior Naib-Tehsildar, Mr. Premlal, on deputation to MPEB. The Naib Tehshildar whose services were to be reverted to the revenue department in the absence of any concrete rehabilitation work at Bodhghat, apprised us of the problems of displacement, compensation and resettlement.

He reported non-cooperation from people in respect of measurement of land, trees and huts in regard to assessment of compensation to be paid to them. He also reported that the land for resettlement available in revenue records was, in places, actually encroached and cultivated by people in the host villages. It was a difficult task to vacate the encroachments since the host villagers were not willing to accept the displaced persons from Bodhghat. On being asked about the rules and practices of inheritance of land after the death of a person, he reported that generally the tribals did not seek any legal partition of their ancestral land between surviving sons/brothers, although in actuality, they divided the land. The tribals did not have precise information of the land ownership of the land under their cultivation.

An encroached land was considered property to be inherited by the sons, in the absence of clarity of records, matching with the land under cultivation. The Naib-Tehsildar felt that the land to be allotted to ousters in the host villages was partially developed by encroachers. He also felt that the land could be developed and houses could be built by the ousters, of their own efforts, as per their tradition, instead of giving them a readymade house, which was culturally incompatible.

Village Field Visits

While planning village visits, it was contemplated that villages on both the banks of Indravati would be visited. It was felt that villages of varying sizes would be studied. But this was not possible since the transport problems were not anticipated. It was not known that the villages could not be reached by jeep in November. Moreovcr the concept of village in Bastar (Bodhghat) where there was no central settlement, except in Binta village, was based on having a common *Devgudi* and a common *Thanagudi*. Otherwise, every house was a separate entity, surrounded by a spacious *Badi* (Kitchen garden) having a compound of bamboo mats. Every village was divided into *Pasas* (Hamlets), i.e. settlements for each tribal or caste group. In some villages like Harrakodar and Binta, the houses of non-tribals were nucleated in a row.

Following 11 villages were visited on both the banks of Indravati.

Sl. No.	*Name of Village*
Left Bank	
1	Koyam
2	Neurnar
3	Begtlur
4	Bhatpal
5	Udenar
6	Raigundi
7	Binta
8	Bheja
Right Bank	
9	Airpund
10	Harrakodar
11	Picchikodar

The villagers from both the banks of the river cross over the river and visit the villages in the *Donga*, i.e. a dugout canoe.

The submergence area consisting of 33 villages is like a bowl surrounded on three sides by the hill and proposed to be closed by a dam on the fourth side. The area is in contact with Barsoor weekly market (almost 20km) up to Bhatpal village. From Udenar to Binta, the villagers climb the hill at Mardum and keep in touch with Lohandiguda, a place of weekly market and the primary health centre.

The first village on the right bank is Airpund which we visited on 29th November, i.e. on 6th day as our field stay. On earlier two occasions, we had gone to Harrakodar passing by Airpund. The leader of the area, Mr. Ishwarsingh Ran who stays in this village is a rich Halba peasant and a money lender. His rate of interest is reported to be 50 per cent per annum. When we visited him he was busy with several workers in thrashing operation. He offered us tea without milk. While we were talking to him, the two teachers from his village were also present. We were accompanied by the teacher from Harrakodar who was being harassed by the local MLA and about whom Ishwarsingh used abusive language. He also used rough language about Prarasmadhur which he had visited. He said, their beautiful lands required another god Hanuman who could lift the land and take it for resettlement. In case of resettlement, he wanted equal area of land of good quality. He was in touch with local MLAs and MPs and was in contact with the social activists at Jagdalpur.

He knew about Narmada dam dispute. He said, they had given a memorandum to the Prime Minister V.P. Singh when he visited Jagdalpur. He did not mention about forest submergence or displacement of deities. He had met the members of all previous committees and was appreciative of those who kept MPEB officials at a distance.

While we asked the reasons for desertion of villages in earlier times, Ishwarsingh said the desertions in many other villages, took place on account of menace of man-eater tigers. These deserted villages like Hitameta in the Reserved Forest could again be resettled. Actually many villagers in the villages on left bank told us that they would settle down at Hitameta in Reserved forest outside submergence area in case of displacement, instead of going too far off places.

We went to the village school with teachers where we found children of *Anganwadi* age group. On inquiry we were told that they came to school in place of their elder sibs who had gone for work to help their parents. This was the first time in our experience of 30 years in tribal areas, we came across children who came to school in place of somebody else. These children remained in the school till 2.30 p.m. when they were given porridge to eat. The villagers told us that they sent the kids to school lest the teacher would lose his job.

We went to Harrakodar three times. A non-tribal teacher from Durg region had been residing in the village for the last 16 years. Due to his long stay, he was one with the villagers, particularly the non-tribals. The village got a middle school and a big building was constructed in 1986-87 at the instance of the Collector of Bastar who was reported to have remarked the development activities in the submergence area could not be stopped due to prospect of dam coming up after 10 years. We spent more than an hour with Muria Sarpanch's brother at his house. He gave us curd made from cream of the milk, from which he made ghee. They required ghee for performing religious rituals. They milch buffalos but not cows. He had been to Pharasmadhur but did not like the hut which he said would cost Rs. 300 if they made it. He was set to go for cockfight next day. He was unaware about the amount of compensation to be paid in case of displacement. We went in his kitchen and saw the dark store room where grain was stocked.

At the next village Pichikodar we met the *Patel*, a Muria. He was busy constructing another room in front of his house in his compound, about 4 m × 2.5 m in size. He said it would be ready in 10 to 12 days. He had three married sons. He produced enough rice to last for the year. His house had two big rooms and a store room to keep grain. His wife and daughter-in-law were preparing *'Landa'* the rice beer which we saw being prepared in other two houses in the neighbourhood also. There was a colourful photo-print of *Shankar-Parvati* and *Ganesh* on the outside wall which was purchased at Barsoor market for Rs. 3. He identified *Shankar-Parvati* as *Sitaram*, and *Ganesh* as some kind of demon. He did not know how much compensation would be paid to him in case of displacement. He did not show much concern about the dam but in view of the forest dependency, would prefer to shift to the nearby forest region. He was at a loss to know what kind of hospitality he could provide to us. He was willing to come with us even to Bombay in case we reached him back in about two weeks time. Patel showed us the certificate whereby his loan from bank had been waived *(Rinmukti).*

On way back, we met a Maria and his son who had worked at the bridge construction at Bodhghat and received Rs. 12 per day as wages from a contractor. They had visited Pharasmadhur resettlement site but did not feel attracted. They did not know about the amount of compensation but said, they would accept money if paid.

We visited more villages on the left bank since we travelled on bicycle and on foot on two occasions, first to go to Bhatpal and then to go to Binta, the last village under submergence area. We could not visit other villages on bicycle as the bicycle track was also non-existent. Bicycles would have to be carried in hand.

Koyam is closest to dam site. People had been paid compensation. The eldest of the four brothers was a MPEB employee who could not count his salary of Rs. 1450 on the salary day. He showed us a bank pass book on which the photograph of the four brothers were pasted. He nor his brothers could tell us about the details of compensation paid to them. Some amount was credited to the savings bank account while some other was put under fixed deposit scheme which could not be withdrawn without the permission of the Collector. All the land was in the name of the eldest brother although he shared it and the bank account with his three brothers. There was no family problem about sharing land or money.

Neurnar is on the bank of the Indravati river and Bengloor is close to Neurnar. We met a *Harijan* family at Neurnar who enjoyed *Sulphi* and chicken in celebration of winning the cock fight previous day whereby they got the defeated cock from sarpanch's brother from Harrakodar, as a trophy (We had met the looser at Harrokodar, two days earlier). He said, baiting at cock fights was of the tune of Rs. 200-300 per day at the *Murgabazar* (Day and place of cock fight). They were landless. They had worked at bridge construction at Bodhghat and were paid Rs. 10 per day by the contractor.

They were paid two *'payali'* of grain per day as agricultural labour in the village. The young Harijan had gone to Pharasmadhur to see the house and the village but was unimpressed. They had *Tulsi* plant and *Mahadeo* in their backyard. He was advocating encroachment of land since the experience was that after paying the fine or a jail term, the land was transferred to the encroachee. The young Harijan took me aside in the unoccupied school building to plead to start Bodhghat Project so that they could get work at the dam site. He again reminded when we met at Barsoor market after few days.

While at Neurnar, we saw many people going towards Barsoor. It was reported that the Collector was camping there and would issue fresh *'Patta'* for land. People had been called for hearing at Barsoor. It was reported that the *Pattas* were issued for regularizing encroachments as per government decision.

The Kotwar of Neurnar conveyed that the threat of displacement was a matter of constant grief to the people. He said, forest dependency of people was maximum during monsoon. There was a group of Harijans in Kotwar's compound when we discussed for more than an hour. They were not confident that the compensation money would be paid to them. They said the villagers on whose lands the mud from the tunnel had been poured had yet to receive the compensation. The Kotwar had been to Pharasmadhur and said nobody liked the place. The social contact of the tribals and non-tribals did not extend beyond 30 kms as their marriage ties were limited to that area. Cross-cousin marriage was preferred. They said, there was only one community *Devgudi* in each village but a family could have private *Devgudi*. On being asked about the school, they said the teachers were very irregular but people tolerated, since they did all writing (applications etc.) for the illiterate people. He said, people had planned to migrate to nearby forests in case of displacement. He said, once a meeting was organized by MPEB at Harrakodar where schemes of displacement/resettlement were informed to the people. No medical facilities were available to the people in the submergence area. He said, when the need arose for community decisions, *panchayat* members from 4-5 villages came together to take decisions. Kotwar lamented that the ancestral lands, trees and deities could not be discarded.

At the next village Bhatpal, we had a firsthand observation of the cock fight. Cock fighting was a major source of recreation for people below 35-40 years of age. Children also went to observe the fight. None of the persons present except outsiders like us were without a cock. Even children bring small birds in their arm-pits. At one time, only three or four fights may take place although there may be more than 50 cocks on the ground. Weights of cocks (weighing it by lifting) and willingness to fight were judged before fights are engaged. Baiting took place ranging from 25 paise to Re. 1 and Rice beer *landa* was sold by women, in leaf-cups.

At Bhatpal, we crossed river to go to school in a canoe. There were two teachers, one Halba and another Muria (both non-graduates) in the school. There were 7-8 students in two rooms. The teachers hailed from North Bastar. They stayed at Barsoor and came to school on bicycles everyday. The teachers who were well dressed were in favour of a change. They said from their own experience that education was important input for change in tribal way of life. They said, people were annoyed about dam construction and did not like to discuss it.

Another Muria young man educated up to 4th standard had a wrist watch worth Rs. 500 purchased from Gidan. He asked the purpose of our visit. His kinship circle in the village consisted of 80 persons. How could they divide themselves in case of displacement ? Their agriculture activities were on a communal basis, that is, members of the kin group helped each other in agricultural work. He demanded similar quality of land. Family was the disciple of Kanthimaharaj, a local God man in Bastar at whose instance they gave up alcoholism, non-vegetarianism and started worshipping Hindu deities like Mahadeo and had *Tulsi* plants. The house of this family was big with exquisitely carved doors. There was a good crop of papaya fruits in the kitchen garden.

At Udenar we met a tribal person who claimed to be a disciple of Kanthibaba. On being asked whether he gave up alcohol, he said with a smile "Oh ? I do have it, I take Ram's name and take the drink." Udenar is a spread out village and it took us about 50 minutes walking to cross the village boundaries.

At Raigundi, we had lunch which we had carried with us, in the house of a non-tribal Dhakad. The house was very clean. They had their own *Devgudi* with *Tulsi,* Mahadeo and Terrocota figurines of cows. The lady who gave us water to drink did not speak about dam. The house was small, having a kitchen and lot of open space which was covered with a roof.

Binta was a big village having many mango trees. The village was known due to a settlement of Oriya Brahmins who were prosperous. They claimed, they were invited by the King of Bastar who had Oriya kinship connection. They had *Rathyatra* as in Jagannathpuri. But they also had common *Devgudi* for the village although they had private *Devgudis* in their spacious houses. We saw Oriya working or rather supervising the work performed by tribals on their farms. They had all varieties of cattle, including sheep. The Oriya had linear settlement, the houses in a row as in caste Hindu villages. They travelled widely going for pilgrimages all over the country. They had claimed compensation for their lands according to market price of land around Jagdalpur since they would have to purchase land from the compensation money. They were willing to shift if proper compensation was given for the house, lands and trees. Some of them had acquired properties in Lohandiguda. Every time, people in Binta travelled out of the bowl-shaped valley, they had to climb a difficult and steep Mardum hill.

A young man Badri (Oriya Brahmin), having an ascetic appearance felt concerned about the people. He said, he had a magnetic attraction to the village where he was born and would not leave Binta even after submergence. The Oriyans told us that they had heard about Bodhghat since their childhood. There was no point in becoming panicky since nobody knew whether the dam would ever be constructed ?

We had an occasion to see Barsoor weekly market. Having seen the market in 1977, we realized that the weekly market had grown in size, may be due to MPEB settlement. The transactions unlike in 1977, were in cash. Most of the traders selling cloth, utensils, cosmetics, ornaments, tobacco and Mahua fruits were from Gidam. Tribal women sold vegetables and fruits, mostly papaya and banana. Many women sold *'Landa'* while men sold *'Sulphi'*. Men were selling live fish and smoked and dried fish. Pictures of Hindu Gods were on sale for Rs. 3 each. Cock fights were a side attraction at the market.

General Observations

According to the State Committee Report, a total of 8775 people residing in 33 villages in the submergence area would have to be resettled. The population could be considered to have grown by 2 per cent to 3 per cent annually. Of these 71 per cent were Scheduled Tribes, 8 per cent were Scheduled Castes and 21 per cent belonged to caste Hindu groups. Among the tribals, Maria were 42 per cent of total population of 8775, while Maria were 8 per cent, Gonds 9 per cent and 6 per cent were Halbas who are good cultivators and are closest to caste Hindu culture. Although there were about 30 per cent non-tribals, the ethos of Bastar is tribal. The marriage distance of non-tribals was also short as of the tribals. Every village had one common *Devgudi* which is tribal in character. Even Oriya

Brahmins respect it as a village *Devgudi*. The chief mode of transporting goods in the submergence area is *'Kawad'*, weights properly balanced by a stick kept on the shoulder. There were hardly any road, unless made and repaired by forest department. We found the whole area criss-crossed with footpaths. If we had no local assistance, we too would have easily lost our way, not knowing which footpaths led to which village or *pasa*. We did not notice any bullock cart.

Although non-tribals looked down upon the tribals, the tribals observed untouchability. They did not eat in the houses of Harijans. The forest dependency for food, house construction and agricultural implements and saleable minor forest produce was maximum for Muria tribals and kept on decreasing for Halba, Scheduled Caste and caste Hindus in that order.

One of the deficiencies in submergence area was the total lack of health care facilities. There is one primary health centre at Barsoor and another at Lohandiguda. The sub-centre at Binta was functioning while the multipurpose health worker at Harrakodar was always absent. There were borewell pumps in some villages towards Bodhghat side. The tribals, however, preferred to use them in monsoon only. Rest of the year they preferred to use the river water for drinking. The non-tribals or the people who lived in the vicinity of the borewell used it.

The weekly markets as mentioned earlier were located at Barsoor and at Lohandiguda on the Mardum side. The transactions progressively developed in cash and not in barter as seen by us in 1977.

The tribals were independent in all respects. They went to forest whenever they had no agricultural work. During day time, the able bodied men were difficult to find in the villages as they went to forests. They constructed the houses on their own and as observed, did land levelling or bund raising on their own. Since kinship bonds were strong, kin helped each other in such activities without payment. Food was offered for such help, not considered as wages.

Discussion

We have been in general agreement with the State Committee Report about perception of the people and about the Resettlement and Rehabilitation packages as offered by MPEB. However, there was so much difference between what was offered and what was implemented as per general experience of people, that people had lack of confidence in what was promised by the government.

For various reasons, there was total lack of communication between the people and MPEB. People were ignorant about what exactly was in store for them. The host villages were also ignorant about the plans of resettlement. MPEB felt despondent due to lack of decision-making on the part of Government. At the same time, to expect revenue officials to plan and implement resettlement of people whose worldview had not extended beyond 20 to 30 km was unacceptable. People had been managing their own affairs for so long, that it was wrong to feel that they lacked the capacity of community organization. If people were told that construction of dam was not negotiable and everything else could be negotiated, they would come forward with various alternative suggestions which could be supplemented further by the experts. This is a common experience of all grassroots level workers that people came forward with suggestions during discussions.

It must be understood that unlike an irrigation project, a lobby of beneficiaries did not get created in a hydro-electric project. No visible benefit was seen by local people in a hydro-electric project. However, a power project had more profit and industrial production potential which could be shared by people who had to be displaced. Special efforts were, therefore, needed to provide benefits to the affected people and to the people of the geographical region in general.

The human aspects of development projects have generated international discussion on the concept of development.

The situation under review relates largely to the tribals living in forest region. The tribal world does not extend beyond 20 to 30 kms of their habitations. Their life as compared to that of caste Hindu peasantry is frozen in the time capsule. Their symbiosis with the environment is harmonious, appearing almost ideal to the urbanites. It is unbelievable that the tribals in the forest regions can live by themselves without reference to the outside world. Commercial exploitation of forests is believed to have led to extinction of wild life and has endangered the autonomy of the tribals. The increasing population and its pressure on forest has also led to deforestation.

There has been a great debate on the balance to be struck between development and protection of environment. The debate has particular relevance to the situation of tribals caught in the development projects since the capacity of tribals to adjust with the new environment is rated low. The projects are not necessarily designed for the development of tribal areas or people. The projects designed for exploiting the national resources of water or minerals, located in the tribal area displace them and threaten their impoverishment.

The tribals are not in a position to exploit the opportunities of development offered by development projects since they are pre-literate and are unaware of future implication of development process. The development projects located in tribal areas are usually meant for development of areas and people outside the tribal belt. The tribals are, however, brought abruptly in contact with cash, market economy which endangers their identities and self respect. This situation may apply to non-tribals also but the capacity of non-tribals to adjust to new situations is considered relatively better than that of the tribals. The pertinent question that is asked about projects in tribal areas is "Why should tribals be sacrificed for the development of others? What do they get in return?"

For the sake of argument, a different scenario can be thought of. If no development projects are initiated in tribal areas where would the tribals be as a part of national culture? Will they develop according to their own genius, as propagated by thinker-politician Jawaharlal Nehru? What efforts have been initiated for their development with what effect? Having been brought in the regional and national political stream through elections, what is happening to the tribals?

If no dam is constructed and if the tribals are left to themselves, what would happen? Will the tribals develop skills and resources according to their own genius ?

Are not the tribals being exploited today by the local non-tribals? or are not the primitive tribals in Bastar being exploited by the good cultivator tribals? Are not these exploiters opposed to development since that will cut the very roots of dependence of them? will the Muria and Maria children go to schools unless attempts are made by devoted, committed NGOs or unless Ashram Schools are opened ?

It is nice to see nature in its wild beauty. The more sophisticated, the more imdustrialised, the more synthetic, the more complex, the greater is an urge to go back to nature temporarily, to meet people in harmony with environment. Tribals in the submergence area are living in a human zoo, along with wild life in the forest. It is true that these people are incapable of quick adjustments if they are exposed to complex market forces too suddenly. Fortunately, in Bastar, they can be resettled in similar ecological atmosphere. If proper care in resettlement is taken, the agonies of displacement can be turned into a challenge and an opportunity to develop a model which can be replicated in similar situation elsewhere, by preparing village-wise micro plans.

Recommendations

The human problems of Bodhghat in quantitative terms are small since about 10,000 people would be displaced. Bastar being a tribal district under forest cover, the resettlement sites with proximity of forests are not difficult to find.

The most important aspect is to establish direct ground level communication with the people to win their confidence. People must get the proof that those who want dam have a genuine concern for their problems.

The host villages should also be taken in confidence. The *Thanagudi* and *Devgudi* in the host villages could be renovated, beautified and strengthened with musical instruments or such other temple artifacts which the people would cherish.

The packages offered by the project are attractive, if they are implemented faithfully.

1. For long term changes, education is an important input. Looking into the experiences and solutions in Maharashtra, the schools in the submergence area be closed down and be replaced by Ashram Schools. The ashram schools should be provided for all tribal and casts groups in the submergence area. Tribal people send their children to schools if they are fed in the school. Tribal students can study only under residential schools. The present school buildings which will get submerged after 5 to 6 years could be used for the purpose till then.

   If possible the ashram school, the vocational training school at Barsoor, and the I.T.I. at Jagdalpur currently financed by MPEB be handed over to a reputed NGO like Ramkrishna Mission.

   This arrangement will properly equip the tribal youth to take up the jobs which MPEB has promised to offer after the completion of the Dam. This will be a step in the direction of fulfilling one of the items of training local youth as per the Panchsheel of tribal development propagated by Nehru.

   If NGO is not available or unwilling, the educational programme be managed by the Tribal Development Department under the supervision of village panchayat.
2. People should be educated about harnessing second crops of potato or tubers immediately. Technical advice or involvement

of NGO like Bhartiya Agro Industries Foundation be sought in the matter. Unless marketing mechanism are developed production alone will not help the people. Second crops of wheat, pulses, vegetables, fodder or buffalo rearing are other avenues of new adoptions.

One of the steps to win the confidence of the people is to present them with articles of day-to-day use such as utensils, blankets, clothes and ornaments for women, as is done under relief measures in times of crisis like fire or earthquake.

People's love for cock fighting should be understood. Inter-village cock fighting could be encouraged with rewards to develop poultry.

Buffalo dairy development is possible since people know the technology of producing curd and *ghee*. They will have to be educated about the nutritive value of milk to children since they already know its value for calves.

3. The landless non-tribals be resettled immediately. They could be provided with wages at the resettlement sites, slightly more than what the contractor would pay them at dam construction site. Wages could be paid for house construction, land development and afforestation.

   No contract labour be employed for construction of houses or land development. Material be provided for house construction, in addition to already promised transport for present house material to new sites. People will feel emotionally involved in the house and land, developed by their own efforts. They can be provided with technical guidance.

4. The forest villages outside submergence area which were deserted in the past mainly on account of menace of man eating tigers could be reactivated. It is reported that encroachment in these areas has already begun. A pragmatic approach to resettle some primitive tribal families on these lands be made.

   People opting for resettlement at nearby places could be offered lesser amount of compensation while those going away could be offered more. This could be discussed with the people and their suggestions be invited.

5. Schemes of development such as bee keeping, pisciculture, *amber charkha*, bio-gas could be taken up with the help from KVIC.
6. Processing units for minor forest produce be started and training provided accordingly. This will also lead to area development.

The compensatory afforestation can provide such opportunities.

7. All host villages accepting resettlement should get the extra benefits of absorbing more population. All such villages be electrified now. They may be offered more packages in terms of Ashram schools, Health care delivery, in consultation with them. All these suggestions are illustrative in nature. A detailed Master Plan, based on data about each family, pasa and village as also the data about host villages, will have to be commissioned. A master plan of resettlement has to be made possible by a committee as under:

   1. A tribal IAS officer from M.P., Rajasthan or Maharashtra, Andhra Pradesh.
   2. An action anthropologist.
   3. A management consultant with an experience of behavioural organization.
   4. An activist with constructive approach.
   5. MLA/MP.
   6. Representatives of Forest, Revenue, Tribal Development, Commercial Departments and MPEB.
   7. One or two Muria Sarpanch or Manjhi.
   8. Representative of BAIF, or similar organizations who have done concrete work in tribal development.
   9. Volunteers with experience in rural technology.

The data required for preparing a master plan should be the responsibility of Tribal Research Institute, Government of M.P. who can seek help from MPEB and relevant departments for collecting data. The implementation has to be done at the family level. Tribals should not be made to run from pillar to post to meet their needs of resettlement. As per Nehru's guidelines, a single administrative agency and not multiplicity of agencies be created to meet the needs of affected families.

Persons trained in Social Work or having experience in resettlement be recruited through all India advertisements. Some devoted persons from NGOs may be recruited on deputation for implementation of Master Plan.

Conclusion

Forced displacement is always a painful experience. However, the people in Bodhghat submergence area are psychologically prepared to shift. All they have been asking are the good quality lands. None of them said about shifting of deities or the problems therein. Whenever they were invited to see the alternate site, they went and saw but were disappointed. There has been no discussion. Their suggestions have not been sought. They have no proof that those in authority have a concern for them. People do not feel comfortable with packages on paper, what they can understand is action and warmth.

Utmost effort has to be made to implement Nehru's Panchsheel of Tribal Development.

Resettlement of displaced persons could be accepted as a challenge and as an opportunity to implement Nehru's Tribal Panchsheel in resettlement pockets. This also affords an opportunity in developing an administrative set up suitable for development of backward regions. Development of human resources is also a national responsibility, more important than development of natural resources.

The two important prerequisites before dam construction activity starts are:

1. A Master Plan for resettlement highlighting as to how—
   (a) Each family will get due consideration irrespective of whether tribal or non-tribal.
   (b) Mechanism of dialogue with the people, sometimes in *gram sabha* in the submergence and host villages.
   (c) Benefits to the affected people and to the region in general by way of industrial growth in stages which the region could absorb.
2. Implementing authority and mechanism be evolved and be known to people and be accessible to the innocent and ignorant persons easily.
3. Subsequently, the dam construction project was withdrawn mainly due to risk of submergence of precious Sal forest.

4

Ethnic Identity

Backwardness and Affirmative Action

Contemporary Indian social-political system is based on democratic principles, visualized and guaranteed by the Constitution. Equality of opportunity for development of the groups and individuals has to be the sheet anchor of democracy to develop the emotional bonds of nationhood. On account of historical, sociological and geographical factors, all social groups in India, be them castes, classes or tribes, are not at a position whereby they are socially, educationally or economically equipped to take the advantages of equal opportunity. The Constitution of India has, therefore, provided for certain special provisions to bring the principle of equity into operation for a designated period, by bestowing special protective and developmental facilities, more particularly, for the Scheduled Castes and Scheduled Tribes.

The whole exercise of development gets reduced to identities such as ST, SC, OBC, DT, NT or such as BPL. Our Tribal Development Department at the Centre and in the States with Tribal Research Institutes are constantly engaged in adjudication about the contested identities. Judiciary puts the final stamp of caste-tribe identity which actually is ascribed by birth. The birth identity and the court identity could be justified as same or different depending upon the transparency of the judiciary and competence of Government advocates pleading the cases. Similar is the case with BPL identities. Of course, the majority of tribal population continues under BPL at the mercy of Public Distribution System for food security. Tribal Development Schemes continue to be survival schemes despite huge funding of Tribal Sub Plan and despite the Rights approach validated by the Higher Judiciary. But we have as yet not approved National Tribal Policy.

Tribal communities continue to be the study basket of Anthropology at the Anthropological Survey of India, at the Universities and Tribal

Institutes due to continued apathy of other disciplines not engaging themselves in tribal studies.

Tribe *(Adivasi)* and Caste

The caste groups designated as scheduled castes are those who suffered from the stigma of untouchability in the Indian caste based social structure. The Scheduled Tribes in the original lists are those who were commonly identified in the Indian society as *Adivasi.* Several synonyms are used for the term *Adivasi,* such as *Adim Jati, Vanvasi* and *Girijan* which were discussed during the debates in the Constituent Assembly. Neither the term Tribe has been defined in the Constitution, nor has there been an agreed definition among the academia. According to Article 342 in the Constitution of India, the Scheduled Tribes are the tribes or the tribal communities or parts of or groups within tribes or tribal communities which the President may specify by public notification. It is the special developmental schemes as also the reserved seats in political representative bodies which prompt groups in Indian society to claim inclusion in the list of Scheduled Tribes by virtue of their claims as being tribals *(adivasi).* Special administrative structure, including separate Ministries in certain States of India, have been carved out for the development of Scheduled Tribes.

The term *Adivasi* has been objected to on the ground that it connotes that they are the original inhabitants of the Indian subcontinent, on the same lines as are the tribals in North America and Australia. There are references to tribal communities in *Ramayana* and *Mahabharat*, and in history, whereby they helped the rulers from the plains. They were also exploited on certain occasions by the ruling class as in case of Eklavya in *Mahabarat.* However, instead of going into the literal meaning of the word *adivasi*, it would be expedient to understand the concept which the word conveys. If a group or an individual is respected as an original inhabitant of the land, they deserve the care of protection and nurture from the majority. Anyway, the theories of social and cultural evolution recognize primitive or tribal culture as the earliest forms of organized human life which have evolved into the pluralistic cultures in the contemporary world. It is believed that the tribal communities due to isolation and other factors such as invasions, remained in a relative time freeze which hindered their evolution with the river valley civilizations of the settled agricultural communities. Tribal communities live in symbiotic relationship with nature and are free from greed of accumulating possessions.

There is great difference between the concepts of tribe and caste. Caste system is based on the principle of inherited inequality, caste groups being hierarchically graded on the principle of ritual purity and pollution. As a consequence, they maintain social distance from each other. Each caste has a traditional, hereditary occupation and these occupations are hierarchically graded. There is division of labour and specialization of occupations and trade. An Indian caste village is linked with the outside world through markets, administration, pilgrimages, marriage distance, educational facilities, sacred geography of rivers and mountains. Caste system has been criticized on account of its segmentary and divisive role. A sizable group of caste population was relegated to the status of untouchables, as *Avarna* in the *Varna* hierarchy. It is to remedy this situation whereby the citizens of one nation were divided in hereditary unequal groups resulting in their social, educational and economic backwardness, that the Constitution of India through Article 16(4) came out with appropriate measures. The categories of Special Backward Classes, Other Backward Classes, *Vimukta Jatis* and Nomadic Tribes (includes castes) in Maharashtra are the result of action in conformity with Section 16(4).

Status of woman in caste society degraded gradually in historical times, although women discovered agriculture. Settled agriculture gave rise to surplus production which necessitated the protection of crops. This gave rise to a class of professional protectors as institution of kings came up with militia. This also sprang up markets, distribution system and exchange through currency. These systems became male dominated and the woman was subjected to become a sex consumer product. Consideration by way of dowry was negotiated for a woman to obtain a position in a family of higher status.

A caste group living in a tribal area may also have subsistence economy, may not be the owners or custodians of the natural resources as the tribals claim themselves to be, but they still would have the psyche to look outwards and organize themselves to enjoy the fruits of development, whenever such an opportunity is presented. In Rayagada district of Orissa, as a result of special efforts by the Government for development, the Dongri Kondh tribals have taken to horticulture and turmeric production. However, all marketing of tribal produce to the plains is done by local Scheduled Castes, who are 30 per cent of the local population and share territory with the tribals. As a result, the Scheduled Castes in this region are more forward in their outlook and have made progress.

It is not uncommon for tribals to get marginalized if large scale development projects suddenly get located in tribal areas, since the tribals have no mental skills or equipment to exploit the opportunities to their advantage. The tribals, therefore, need to be protected from the exploitative forces and have to be drawn in the development process with great sensitivity. It is precisely for these reasons that the tribals are provided with constitutional safeguards by designating them as Scheduled Tribes.

When a non-tribal group or a caste group with similar nomenclature or with tribal suffix or prefix to their name claim tribal status, they are not only harming the interest of a tribal group with whom they are trying to identify by putting up a tribal claim, but they are also harming the interests of all tribals in the state and the country, since the benefits of Scheduled Tribe are bestowed according to the generic category of Scheduled Tribe and not according to a specific tribal group. The pseudo-tribal group, therefore, nullifies the constitutional guarantees of all the Scheduled Tribes in a State and the country.

The claimant caste or non-tribal groups who profess cultural similarities with a tribal group in historical times, do not in reality, show any social interaction or commonality or participation in each other's rituals or religious festivals. They do not even worship each other's gods or deities, or do not have the same deities and gods and shrines, let alone intermarrying (affinity) each other.

Culture and Personality of a group or a community are holistic and integrated configurations. Similarities in parts of culture without the holistic context do not make two groups same. The Presidential notification about designating certain tribal groups or parts of them as Scheduled Tribe is based on the distinctness of culture and personality of the tribal group and is not limited to a name of a tribe which may also be the name of a caste group in the Hindu caste system in some parts of India. Constitutional provisions are meant for Scheduled Tribes and Scheduled Castes only and not meant for the caste groups whose name happens to be common or similar to that of a Scheduled Tribe or a Scheduled Caste. Thakar or Thakur is a tribe and a Scheduled Tribe in Maharashtra, while the names of several Kshatriya groups in caste society of North India are designated or addressed as Thakurs including the great Hindu gods, Rama and Krishna, who are commonly addressed as Thakurji, in the villages.

Saint Mirabai in her devotional songs has consistently referred to Lord Krishna as Thakurji. The village temples in Hindi belt are called

Thakurji temples. The notifications are meant only for Scheduled Caste and Scheduled Tribe, but caste groups in open category taking advantage of similarity in names seem to stake claims for notified Scheduled Caste or Scheduled Tribe status.

I had the privilege of chairing an expert Backward Class Committee of the Government of Maharashtra in 1992 when Shri Sharad Pawar was the Chief Minister of Maharashtra. My name was recommended by Shri Shankarrao Kharat, an intellectual, litterateur/author who was earlier Vice-Chancellor of Dr. Babasaheb Ambedkar Marathwada University at Aurangabad. He knew me as an anthropologist at the university and also having established an academic NGO, MAAS which provided an objective apolitical platform to discuss land-forest issues of tribals. We were given 147 files from communities demanding SC, VJ, NT, OBC status. No file about ST status was marked to us by Social Welfare Department since ST was exclusively the preserve of Tribal Welfare Department.

Recommendations were made on the basis of field studies visiting the areas where the applicant castes were preponderant in number. Hearings were given to delegations of applicants in different cities in Maharashtra. Our report with recommendations, based on field studies and hearings of deputations coincided with the Supreme Court judgment about Mandal Commission whereby a permanent OBC Commission under the Chairmanship of a retired High Court judge was to be established in each State. Our report was referred to this Commission in Maharashtra of which I was also a member. The report was totally endorsed by the Commission along with recommendations. I abstained myself from discussion on my report during meetings but was available as an adviser.

The Mutatkar Committee observed that a large number of claims were put forward for NT status and none for SC status, unless the group having SC status in their native state were claiming the same in Maharashtra. SC status carries the stigma of untouchability, thus preventing the pseudo claims. Demand for VJ status is also not claimed, since the certification requires some evidence of punishment or proof of living in settlement by the forefathers of the claimant. Since there is no fixed criteria or parameter about nomadism, and it also does not denote social stigma, many communities claim nomadic status. It is pertinent to note that of the 147 applications received, 57 applications were from metro cities of Mumbai, Pune and Nagpur. The organised effort to take the benefit of reservation emanating from big cities is as expected, due to awareness on the part of caste organisations located in cities.

As a backward caste committee we received delegations of caste groups seeking reservation. They said, "Put us in some reserved category." When asked—first tell us, who you are, before seeking some given category, they would narrate their backwardness by saying, "Sir, we have a lone girl in our group who has educated upto graduation. We have a problem of finding an eligible match for her in our community."

In a representative democracy and electoral politics, certification of a community as backward also tends to become a political issue. In the recent past, Vanjari claiming Banjara VJ status, Halba-Koshti claiming Halba ST status, fisherfolk Koli claiming Mahadeo-Koli ST status, Dhangar claiming ST status, Lohar claiming Gadia Lohar (from Rajasthan) NT status, Govari claiming Gond-Govari ST status, Maratha claiming Kunbi OBC status, now claiming distinct status as backward, and many such claims have been backed by political leaders. The Government of Maharashtra created a category of special backward class (SBC). However, to a query from Khatri Commission, it was accepted by the government that there were no objective parameters to certify a particular group as SBC.

But we have now caste based agitations for getting backward reservations. There are also positive visible results of reservation. My barber's son is doing Ph.D. in Mathematics in Germany and daughter is also doing post-graduation. The two daughters of a vegetable seller, who is from a SC (Mahar) community, selling vegetables in a vegetable market, are electronic engineers.

Poverty and development issues have got linked to equity which is addressed in India through positive discrimination, what is commonly understood as affirmative action about reservation. There is a competition to be officially labelled as backward. As Chairman of Backward Class Committee of the Government of Maharashtra and later as member of statuary Backward Class Commission, we have been requested by delegations to place them in some backward category to provide opportunities for technical education and government jobs. Social Justice and Tribal Departments and Research Institutes of the government are continuously preoccupied with the validity issues of so called caste certificates. Judicial Courts are occupied with litigation appeals on these issues. Anthropologists are best suited to adjudicate these issues due to understanding of culture pattern, language, custom, genealogically establishable kinship connections, religious rituals, deities worshipped etc. Due to political influence and money power, many pseudo groups have achieved positions of authority, thus depriving the needy for whom the constitutional provision were made. We have had memorable interactions with the political leaders who while in power or out of power could not influence the anthropological investigations. Backward are those who cannot utilise the development infrastructure offered to them or who cannot verbalise their needs and requirements. The groups who can organize themselves into urban violence such as bus burning, *rail roko*, *rasta roko* for (blocking rail and road traffic) agitating for backward status cannot be backward.

Methodology of Study

The caste or non-tribal groups claiming tribal status on the basis of similarity in names or sharing common territory or certain aspects of soft or material culture have a tendency to give citations from the British time gazetteers or from the writings of British administrator-scholars. The citations are part sentences or paragraphs quoted out of context to justify their claims. It need to be reiterated that in many cases, the gazetteers were authored by the same scholars who wrote ethnographic volumes on castes and tribes on India. These volumes were written to serve as guidelines to newly recruited young British administrators, and attempts were made to group together the descriptions of various communities. These writings were not the result of any research exercise according to the authors themselves and the information was collected under severe limitations of finance and personnel. As a result, there are several contradictions in these writings which may not wholly serve the purpose to determine the tribal or backward characteristics of a claimant group. The writings from early twentieth century deserve praise as it provided basic documentation upon which the Anthropological Survey of India, Government of India, tried to improve in the current decade, under 'People of India' publications.

However, the surest and scientifically most valid and reliable method to study the culture, society and basic personality of a community or a group is to undertake ethnographic field studies by the professionally trained personnel, who have an objective and unbiased view. It must, however, be clear that ethnographic studies are meant to study the culture of a group and not to authenticate the geographical spread of a group which may be possible only through Census or through surveys specially designed for the purpose. However, Census statistics cannot be taken as a last word since census enumerators are expected to record the information provided by the respondents. In census of recent decades, some non-tribal groups and individuals from Halba Koshti community declared themselves to census enumerators, as Halba *adivasi* taking advantage of similarity of nomenclature with the Halba scheduled tribe.

In the discipline of Anthropology, a standard method which is designated as fieldwork, to collect ethnographic data by interacting with the common people in the geographical area has been time tested and found scientifically reliable and objective. The crucial question is what do the common people in the area consider each other's community to be, as a tribe or as a caste in the Hindu social structure, since they are interacting with each other in social, economic and ritual activities and have reached a degree of symbiotic relationship over the years. There is a tendency to tutor the people about the questions that may be asked by the expert committee members. Women are the custodians and transmitters of culture and they, therefore, are more reliable in giving correct information about the customs, as we found while talking to Banjara women.

It is true that certain tribal groups or parts thereof who have been living in close proximity with the majority Hindu caste peasantry or who as a result of political and developmental processes may have acculturated, on way to adopt and assimilate the culture of caste peasants. However, field anthropologists know the difference between soft aspects of material culture which may be used without affecting the hard core of culture manifested in faith, life cycle rituals, religious ceremonies and festivals and pilgrimage or sacred geography. Adoption of soft material aspects does not result in the rejection of hard aspects of culture or complete assimilation with the other group.

These processes are recognized by the makers of Constitution who made provisions for Constitutional safeguards for a certain period until they reached the level for competing for equality of opportunity from a position of near equality. Till such time, the Governments have created various categories within backward communities commensurate with their level of development, such as under OBC, or designating some Scheduled Tribes as primitive groups. A category of "creamy layer" has been instituted among OBC. Likewise, in a graded time period, it may be necessary to make a judgement as to which Scheduled Tribe groups or parts thereof have attained a degree of development or assimilation so as to warrant its descheduling or put it in a higher position in a ranked order of scheduled communities. Probably, Scheduled Tribe groups may have to be graded using development parameters. Governments have identified primitive groups among the Scheduled Tribes and have made special provisions for their development.

There is clearly the very high decadal growth rate among the Scheduled Tribes as compared to the total population. In case of STs the decadal growth does not reflect the natural biological growth. Several caste groups or other social groups who have similar names or live in close proximity of the tribal community claim to share some cultural similarity with the tribal people have already been listed as Scheduled Tribes. Such claims are continuously made in order to get the constitutional benefits accruing to ST population. The claims of pseudo-tribals, if granted, give them the status of ST and bloat the ST population which eats into the affirmative action and positive discrimination made in favour of genuine tribal communities. In effect, within the ST population, there are various tribal communities who occupy the development ladder at various steps; some of them may not be labelled as tribal people by anthropologists. As yet there is no mechanism whereby some developed Scheduled Tribes could be taken out of the constitutional category and be treated on par with other caste peasantry population. According to classical anthropological parameters, all ST may not be tribals; the ST are those who are labelled as tribal community by the government. In the original list of tribal communities notified as Scheduled Tribe in 1950 with the promulgation of the Constitution, the genuine tribal communities were listed as ST. In subsequent years, new groups have been accorded ST status. This phenomenon as mentioned earlier captures the benefits of genuine tribals or indigenous *'Adivasi'*. Very few tribal communities who are believed to be in the pre-agricultural or collection stage have been designated as primitive tribal groups (PVTG) and get some special benefits such as cheaper food under PDS than other STs.

The claimants to tribal status with a view to claim ST status invariably show similarity in nomenclature with a notified ST group, pleading to ignore the suffixes or prefixes. They do not seem to know that the President is empowered to notify 'parts of or groups within tribes' as a ST. Similarly, the President notifies a tribe and not a caste as ST, although, there may be similarity in nomenclature of a tribal and a caste group as in the case of Thakur tribals in Maharashtra and the Thakur as a high caste in other parts of India. It needs to be surmised that the Executive has an authority and mechanism to scrutinize as to whether a group or an individual is a tribe or a caste, since the ST status can be given only to a tribe by notification and not to a caste. Anthropologists have not been able to define the tern Tribe for the sake of constitutional notification.

Among the SC in Maharashtra, the Mahars who were generalists in the village economy took benefit of taking to education and migrating to urban areas following the advice of Dr. Ambedkar who was himself a Mahar. SC persons from Maharashtra occupying high positions at national level, as Vice Chancellors, members of Planning Commission, at the UGC, ICSSR etc. are Mahars. Others with skills as occupation could not give up their occupation of living, like the Mahars who migrated to urban areas and took to education. This is a significant research issue.

The *Charmakars,* leather workers who considered themselves as the Brahmins among untouchables, above the Mahars in traditional caste hierarchy, did not accept Ambedkar's leadership but went with Gandhi's Harijan brand. They have been provided with Charmakar Development Corporation to give funding for their occupational development.. Such ethnic disparities also occur within ST.

The expression backward class in Art. 16(4) takes in Other Backward Classes (OBC), SCs, STs and may be some other backward classes as well. The accent in Art. 16(4) is upon social backwardness. Social backwardness leads to educational backwardness and economic backwardness. They are mutually contributory to each other and are intertwined with low occupations in the Indian society. Economic criterion cannot be the sole basis for determining the backward class of citizens contemplated by Art. 16(4). The weaker sections referred to in Art. 16 do include SEBCs referred to in Art. 340 and covered by Art. 16(4).

During debates in the Constituent Assembly, there is a discussion about what could be the parameters of backwardness and who would determine them. It was clearly stated that the State could determine these parameters. Similarly, during hearing of the Mandal Commission report at the Supreme Court, the Court has accepted that the Governments were within their rights to make different categories among the backward class in view of Article 16(4) of Constitution to enable all sections of the people to share the governance of the country. The Scheduled Caste and Scheduled Tribe have not been mentioned in these debates.

On the point of Backward Classes, Chairman of the Drafting Committee of the Constitution, Dr. B.R. Ambedkar Clarified as under:

> "....there are three points or view which it is necessary for us to reconcile if we are to produce a workable proposition which will be accepted by all. The first is that there shall be equality of opportunity for all citizens. ....if this principle is to be operative.....there ought to be no reservation of any sort for any class or reservations of any sort for any class or community at all, that all citizens, if they are qualified, should be placed on

> the same footing of equality so far as the public services are concerned. ...although theoretically it is good to have the principle that there shall be equality of opportunity, there must at the same time be a provision made for the entry of certain communities which have so far been outside the administration.....the administration which has now for historical reasons, been controlled by one community or a few communities, that situation should disappear and that the others also must have an opportunity of getting into the public service....If honourable Members understand this position that we have to safeguard two things, namely the principle of equality of opportunity and at the same time satisfy the demand of communities which have not had so far representation in the State, then, I am sure they will agree that unless you use some such qualifying phrase as 'backward' the exception made in favour of reservation will ultimately eat up the rule altogether. Nothing of the rule will remain. That I think if I may say so, is the justification why the Drafting Committee undertook on its own shoulders the responsibility of introducing the word 'backward' which, I admit, did not originally find a place in the fundamental right in the way in which it was passed by this Assembly....Somebody asked me: "What is a backward community"? well, I think anyone who reads the language of the draft itself will find that we have left it to be determined by each local government. A backward community is a community which is backward in the opinion of the government." (quoted in 1992: 59-61)
>
> "In short, the objective behind Article 16(4) is empowerment of the deprived backward communities—to give them a share in the administrative apparatus and in the governance of the community." (1992:61)

To quote him from the debates in the Constituent Assembly,

> "..... although theoretically it is good to have the principle that there shall be equality of opportunity, there must at the same time be a provision made for the entry of certain communities which have so far been outside the administration.... If honourable members understand this position, ... then I am sure

> they will agree that unless you use some such qualifying phrase as "backward" the exception made in favour of reservation will ultimately eat up the rule altogether. Nothing of the rule will remain....The Drafting Committee undertook on its own shoulders the responsibility of introducing the word "backward" which I admit did not originally find a place in the fundamental right in the way in which it was passed by this Assembly."

This is what the Article 16(4) in the Constitution is meant for besides the Article enabling the State to make special provision for SC and ST.

Ambedkar was asked as to what is a backward community? "A backward community is a community which is backward in the opinion of the Government." That is how we had Mandal Commission interpreted by the Supreme Court and reported in A.I.R. 1993 Supreme Court 477. Indra Sawhany *vs.* Union of India dealing with OBC reservation under Art.16 of the Constitution.

We are aware that Ambedkar has extensively studied caste and has written about it. And he said, "There would be outcastes as long as there is Caste." We are also aware about M.N. Srinivas writing about strengthening of caste in politics. Irawati Karve had exception about reservation since she thought it would be difficult to withdraw such provision. Kalelkar Commission had refuted reservations on caste basis as it would perpetuate caste phenomena. But it could not suggest any viable or practical indicators of backwardness. Why are there backward groups and backward regions? Why is poverty a group phenomena? What do we mean by the term 'backward'?

However, following the spirit of Supreme Court Judgement, it is not inappropriate to devise more categories within the ST to place the different tribal groups or subgroups on a hierarchical ladder according to the socioeconomic and development parameters. In fact, the grouping of certain ST groups such as, the Katkari, Kolam and Madia Gond in more primitive category in Maharashtra as PVTG groups, is a step in that direction.

A caste can be and quite often is a social class in India. If it is backward socially, it would be a backward class for the purposes of Art. 16(4). Among non-Hindus, there are several occupational groups, sects and denominations, which for historical reasons, are socially backward. They too represent backward social collectives for the purposes of Art. 16(4).

On caste-class relationship the Supreme Court holds:

> "The Court now held that a caste is a class of citizens and that if a caste as a whole is socially and educationally backward, reservation can be made in favour of such a caste on the ground that it is a socially and educationally backward class of citizens within the meaning of Article 15(4)." (Mutatkar Committee Report:1992: 74-75)

Backwardness is not defined with precise parameters on the basis of which a community is certified as backward. In the Indian context, the backward community could be a social class as defined by certain occupations such as rickshaw pullers, but it is usually a caste group, which is identified as backward. While discussing the Mandal Commission, the Supreme Court in its judgement has observed that the context of Article 16(4) as enacted was the accent on social backwardness which led to educational backwardness and both together led to economic backwardness, which is a vicious cycle perpetuating social and educational backwardness.

As noted earlier, caste groups and their associated hierarchies are also a feature of non-Hindu religious groups in India such as Muslims, Christians and Sikhs. It is believed that conversion to Islam and Christianity in the past may have largely occurred among low-caste Hindus due to atrocities against them. However, as per government notifications, only the former untouchable caste groups among Hindus, Buddhists and Sikhs are eligible for being included in the Scheduled Caste category. There is no such restriction with respect to religion for being eligible for the Scheduled Tribe or other backward classes category. The Mutatkar Committee did recommend number of Muslim groups following the same or similar vocations as the Hindus, for OBC status, since religion is no bar for OBC status, if the criteria of social and educational backwardness is viable.

In recent years, the issue of deprivation among the Muslim community in India has come into the limelight with the report of the Prime Minister's high level committee (Sachar Committee) which enquired into the social, educational and economic status of the Muslim community of India (Government of India, 2006). The report indicates the low socio-economic level of the Muslim community in India according to various indicators. The committee has made a number of wide-ranging recommendations to address the deprivation and concerns of'the Muslim community. Among its more general recommendations include the setting up of an equal opportunity commission, which would look into the grievances of deprived groups. The report has also observed that Muslims in India in terms of their social structure consist of three groups that broadly correspond to high-castes, OBCs and SCs respectively in the Hindu community. These are '*ashraf*', '*ajlaf*' and '*arzal*'. The report has recommended that the *ajlafs* need affirmative action policies, which could be similar to that of Hindu OBCs, while the *arzals*, who have similar traditional occupation as that of the SCs, may be designated as 'most backward classes' and a number of multipronged measures be adopted to address their cumulative deprivation. (Mutatkar, Rohit. 2012, pp. 25-27)

Mandal Commission Parameters

A. Social

1. Castes/Classes considered as socially backward by others.
2. castes/Classes which mainly depends on manual labour for their livelihood.
3. Castes/Classes where at least 25 per cent females and 10 per cent males above the State average get married at an age below 17 years in rural areas and at least 10 per cent females and 5 per cent males do so in urban areas.
4. Castes/Classes where participation of females in work is at least 25 per cent above the State average.

B. Educational

1. Castes/Classes where the number of children in the age group of 5-15 years who never attended school is at least 25 per cent above the State average.
2. Castes/Classes where the rate of student drop-out in the age group of 5-15 years is at least 25 per cent above the State average.
3. Castes/Classes amongst whom the proportion of matriculates is at least 25 per cent below the State average.

C. Economic

1. Castes/Classes where the average value of family assets is at least 25 per cent below the State average.

2. Castes/Classes where the number of families living in *kuccha* houses is at least 25 per cent above the State average.
3. Castes/classes where the source of drinking water is beyond half a kilometre for more than 50 per cent of the households.
4. Castes/Classes where the number of households having taken consumption loan is at least 25 per cent above the State average.

Caste as a hierarchical and divisive system has been exercising the minds of social and religious reformers for centuries. Several religious and social movements tried to counteract caste system but ended up becoming a part of it. Caste has been abolished in India by the Statutes but functions as a social reality and a political force. Caste hinders equality, yet it is used to usher in equality by providing reservations to so called backward classes which in effect are caste groups from the lower rungs of caste hierarchy.

What is the unit of social action in India—a caste, class, kin group, extended family or a nuclear family? Caste has an identity, a name, not the other groups, except a family. Caste is identified by endogamy, traditional occupation, hierarchical ranking, social and ritual distance expressed in rules of commensality and an autonomous juridical system.

Leaders of modern India like Mahatma Gandhi and B.R. Ambedkar, launched their struggle against the caste system. Relevant provisions in the Constitution of India bear testimony to the success of their struggles. At the same time, forces of modernization, industrialization and urbanization have introduced class in caste, thus breaking the co-terminous character of class and caste. Creamy layers have appeared among the backward classes threatening the interests of the needy, among the backward classes.

Chinnappa Reddy presented the data on membership and presidentship of *Zilla Parishads* according to caste as also the caste membership of legislatures and parliament from Karnataka state. The castes of the members of the Judiciary has also been scrutinized. The caste members who declared surplus land under land ceiling and the analysis of land holding according to caste is revealing. While discussing educational backwardness, caste-wise data of students, appeared and passed at the SSLC examination, those admitted in the professional colleges and at post-graduate courses as also employment in various categories of services in public institutions has been presented with a view to identify backward classes. Chinnappa Reddy has recommended the Caste/Community/Tribe/Religious/Occupational groups of people as socially and educationally backward classes as under:

> "I have divided the Socially and Educationally Backward Classes identified by me into three categories. Category-III consists of the occupational groups. Categories I and II consist of the Caste/ Community/Religious/Tribal groups identified by me as Socially and Educationally Backward. The Division into Categories I and II is made on the basis of the comparative backwardness of the community as well as the size of the community, bearing in mind that some of the castes etc. groups are either so extremely backward Socially and Educationally or are so small in number that they cannot possibly hope to compete with the larger groups or those who, though socially and educationally, backward are more advanced than themselves. The reservation in favour of Category-I shall be 5 per cent, the reservation in favour of category-II shall be 28 per cent and the reservation in favour of Category-III shall be 5 per cent. (1990:170)

> "For a long time, caste has been identified as the villain on Indian social scene. Only in the last fifty years has the caste system shown real signs of breaking down, thanks to the many inventions of the West.....the spread of Western education, growing national sentiment, and the intensive propaganda of enlightened leaders....it will take many years before all trace of caste feeling is eradicated; but when Mahatma Gandhi persuaded his followers to sweep their own floors and clean their own latrines, he sounded the death knell of the old Hindu social order, which for all its faults, has preserved the identity of Indian Society over centuries of foreign domination" (Basham, 1954:151)

The report of Kalelkar (1955) and Mandal (1980) Commissions and the Supreme Court Judgement (1992) thereupon have discussed the issues of caste and class endlessly. While the Constituent Assembly discussed reservations for backward classes with a view to open the gates to the disprivileged, to share State power, what has emerged after is that the few have entered and become privileged, denying entry to more disprivileged, all in order to abolish caste, but using caste as a tool to strengthen their respective positions in economy and polity. Majority of the claimants examined by the committee are drawn from metropolitan urban areas.

Another issue is, to what extent reservation *per se* helps to remove backwardness. Female literacy is low even amongst some of the affluent groups because of a different perception about female roles. There are schools in villages and tribal areas where no map of Maharashtra is available. Can they compete with others, with better facilities, in spite of reservations? If new groups are added without any exclusion, and with poor economic growth; for a given number of jobs, more persons from backward classes would compete with each other. If the category of Scheduled Caste was devised to compensate the historical stigma which weighs on the mind, what about people who want to be labelled as Scheduled Caste, for reservation benefits, although they do not suffer from the stigma of untouchability?

Tribal people and their groups historically labeled as primitive people have been the subject matter of Anthropology in terms of understanding of cultural and social evolution of human institutions, as a sequel to biological evolution of man. Karl Marx and Engels have developed their theories designating primitive economy as primitive communism. Theories in anthropology about culture, change, acculturation and personality have been formulated on the basis of empirical evidence from tribal studies all over the world.

In India, references to tribal people are found in *Ramayana* and *Mahabharat*. It is with the help of forest dwelling tribal people that Ram could wage a successful war against Ravan. Eklavya was exploited to protect and promote the supremacy of rulers. The genocide in North America, Australia and the white rule in South Africa which was personally experienced by Mahatma Gandhi are well known. The British rulers in India took cognizance of the abject poverty and exploitation of the tribal people. Symington Report about the present Nandurbar District in Maharashtra is one such example. (1938)

In consideration, Mahatma Gandhi included *Adivasi* as one of his 18 Constructive Programmes. The Constitution of India has provided a comprehensive framework for the socio-economic development of tribal people and for preventing their exploitation by other people, pledging loyalty to the principle of equity and social justice. However, the term tribe has not been defined or explained in the Constitution although the Constituent Assembly debates clarify the spirit of affirmative policy.

Article 342 of the Constitution about Schedule Tribes reads as under:

1. The President may with respect to any State or Union territory, and where it is a State, after consultation with the Governor thereof, by public notification, shall specify the tribes or tribal communities or parts of or groups within tribes or tribal

communities which shall for the purposes of this Constitution be deemed to be Scheduled Tribes in relation to that State or Union territory, as the case may be.

2. Parliament may by law include in or exclude from the list of Scheduled Tribes specified in a notification issued under clause (1) any tribe or tribal community or part of or group within any tribe or tribal community, but save as aforesaid a notification issued under the said clause shall not be varied by any subsequent notification.

It has to be borne in mind that the President/Parliament shall notify a tribe, not a caste as Scheduled Tribe. Who decides whether a particular social group is a tribe or a caste particularly when they bear similar nomenclature? This needs clarification.

Characteristics of Tribe

For the purpose of Article 342, for a group to be included as a Scheduled Tribe, Government of India has recommended the following broad parameters:

1. Primitive traits
2. Distinct culture
3. Geographical isolation
4. Distinct dialect
5. Animism
6. Clan system
7. Shyness of nature
8. Backwardness

These parameters conform to the characteristic features of an ideal tribal society as put forward by Anthropologists, out of their sustained studies of tribal societies all over the world.

Tribal communities usually inhabit the isolated forests, hills and valleys which are not easily accessible. As a result, they have remained cut off from the outside world and have to lead their lives in isolation. They are very close to nature and meet their sustainable needs from the local environment, which includes food, shelter and medicine. Most of the tribals have been the collectors of forest and river produce for consumption and not the producers of surplus food. Although, they have been cultivating land, they had no emotional attachment to land comparable to that of caste peasantry till recently. They have a production-consumption economy, which is not linked with market and currency economy. Their production and collection tools are simple and handmade which do not give them enough surplus to need a bullock cart for transport since production can be transported on head load. As a result, tribals do not have craze for private property and much of the resources are shared commonly. Cultural evolutionists label their behaviour as primitive communism, in view of their handling resources according to the principle of "each according to his needs". There is no division of labour in tribal society except based on sex. Everybody does everything unlike the caste society. Work is shared and not accomplished by payment of wages. This community spirit has recently been acknowledged by the 73rd Constitutional Amendment whereby more powers of self-governance and control over natural resource have been given to Gram Sabha in tribal villages in comparison to those in caste Hindu villages.

The tribal groups have their own dialect which cannot be written for want of a script. The tribals are called as preliterate and not as illiterate, since illiteracy connotes existence of literacy in an area, group or community. The transmission of culture is, therefore, through oral tradition, through songs and folk tales.

They live in symbiosis with local environment which they protect. A body of folk mythology has developed which is linked with the ritual relationship with the flora and fauna. For a long time, they have been facing the forces of nature unitedly, following their indigenous wisdom and knowledge. They are used to self-government under the authority of a leader. Magic is used for protection, promotion, cure and occasionally for destruction of evil forces. They have their own mythology about the creation of universe and the origin of their group. The tribals are animistic and their deities are made from natural products, the deities in most of the cases have no relationship with the mainstream Hindu icons. Their social, economic and ritual life does not extend beyond a distance of 20-25 km. which they can traverse on foot. Although some of the tribal groups may be large in number, they are divided into sub-tribes, and clan is a functioning exogamous group.

Status of woman is relatively better than that in caste society. Bride price has to be paid as a consideration in marriage. A girl has a choice of selecting a mate and divorce is easy. Man-woman relationship is patterned according to custom and protected by the tribal elders. The government judicial machinery is relatively non-functional as also the police administration, except in case of serious offences.

As a result of self-governance for a long time, and as a result of experience of the outsiders, who only went to exploit them, the tribals are non-communicative and occasionally hostile to the aliens. However, due to the experience of destructive power of the outsiders, they are timid and shy and shun any external contact. In case of any external threat, they usually flee from the village into nearby forest and reappear only after ascertaining the nature and purpose of visitors if sizable in number. If the tribals and caste groups share a common territory, caste people are prone to develop external contacts, while the tribals withdraw in their tortoise shells of forests or hills. In consequence, they remain backward and in a time freeze which have made them ideal subjects for study by those who wanted to understand the process of cultural evolution. Their backwardness makes them incapable of exploiting the opportunities of development such as education and health care facilities, fair price shops and other development schemes such as modern agricultural or horticulture technology, offered by the Welfare State. Backwardness has to be understood in terms of lack of motivation and vision, to seize the existing opportunities of development, let alone demand them or lobby for them in the democratic political set up.

Acculturation and Change

These ideal tribal characteristics were found in India in majority of tribal communities until Independence in 1947. Due to contact with the outside world and as a result of development efforts and drawing them in the democratic political process, acculturation has been taking place among the tribal communities. However, acculturation does not destroy the hard core of culture which is manifested in their rituals, beliefs, ceremonies and festivals, in the dialect, and in music and dance. Everywhere, women are the preservators of culture, which gets transmitted to the next generation in the process of child rearing. Usually, the birth, marriage and death rituals do not change beyond recognition, which may obliterate the ethnic identity. In case of economic betterment, the traditional rituals are solemnized with more gaiety, with better food and enjoyment, more gifts to kin and more invitees, as a visible show of prosperity. If all aspects of culture undergo change, that is, if a subgroup or a kin-group totally gets assimilated in another cultural group, such an assimilated group cannot claim the social or cultural membership of the original group. That is possibly the reason why the President is empowered to notify even a part, or a subgroup of a tribe, as Scheduled Tribe, since a part or a subgroup can also achieve assimilation with the majority community in the neighbourhood.

If caste groups and tribal groups are put together by history to share common territory, transculturation, that is mutual borrowing of each other's culture traits, follows. However, the process does not seem to have led to assimilation of either of the groups. Their identities are still distinct. Actually, it is these different identities which groups claiming tribal status are trying to obliterate to their advantage, by showing similarities in nomenclature or some letters in their names, common territory, some soft customs in material culture and wishing away the major cultural or linguistic differences by the argument that they got acculturated and hence gave up the cultural characteristics of the original tribal group.

The crucial question as to the identity of a group in a given geographical area, is the identity bestowed by the local communities about each other. Whether a particular subgroup is *adivasi* or not is best identified and labelled by the local communities. It is very natural for a group to put its claim for *adivasi* status, since such status opens the gate for labelling as a Scheduled Tribe under Article 342 of the Constitution of India. However, it would be expedient to verify whether the local communities address or refer such claimant groups as *adivasi.*

PVTG: Katkari

The 'primitive tribal groups' or 'particularly vulnerable tribal groups' represent some of the most deprived sections of Indian society. From a policy perspective it is important to understand the constraints faced by people from these ethnic groups, which prevent them from coming out of chronic poverty. This note describes a profile of deprivation among one such ethnic group, viz. the Katkari primitive tribal group based on a field study in a Katkari populated hamlet in the tribal region of Jawhar tehsil in Palghar district, Western Maharashtra (Mutatkar, 2007). The profile of deprivation includes their living conditions, livelihood pattern, food consumption pattern and health status, educational status, position in social hierarchy and socio-economic relations with other groups, their perceptions of government schemes and institutions and their perceptions of development. The profile of deprivation is summarized below by way of the broad pattern regarding these aspects, as indicated by the case study in the Katkari hamlet.

(A) Living Conditions

- *Kuccha* houses or *pucca* houses constructed through a government scheme.
- No sanitation facility.
- Dependence on well, public tap for drinking water.
- Use of wood as cooking fuel.
- No electricity connection.
- No consumer durables (such as television etc.).

(B) Livelihood Pattern

- Landless.
- Dependence on wage labour for livelihood.
- Work for other landed scheduled tribe ethnic groups in the agricultural season—male members work as attached labourers, female members as daily wage labourers and children work in activities such as cattle grazing.
- Seasonal migration between cultivation and harvesting period and in post agricultural season. Migration pattern that of seasonal migration with children.
- Work on employment guarantee scheme in post-agricultural season, in stone breaking activity.
- Borrowing for consumption purposes (food/cash) by way of credit-labour market interlinkages through attached labour.

(C) Food Consumption Pattern and Health Status

- Food purchases in piecemeal quantities before every meal.
- Depend on public distribution system for food grain requirements.
- Coping mechanisms for food shortages—seasonal migration, liquefying and grinding food, consumption of wildly grown food, borrowing of food.
- Anthropometric indicators indicate severe under-nourishment among children (0-6 age group).
- Morbidity highest in monsoon during agricultural season, when absence from work due to any illness results in loss of wages in case of daily wage labour.

- Work related injuries due to wage labour activity, including that in stone-breaking.

(D) Educational Status

- Majority of children in school going age group not attending school.
- Maximum educational level in most households below middle school level.
- Perception regarding education—unable to relate education to survival concerns; ascribed status of wage labour leading to perception of no utility of education; lack of success story regarding completion of education and education as an instrument of upward mobility, in familiar cultural setting of Katkari.
- School going children enrolled in village government primary schools, but not in government residential Ashram schools for tribal children. Socio-cultural constraints in enrolling children in Ashram schools due to social discrimination from children belonging to other Scheduled Tribe ethnic groups.
- Other constraints to education-opportunity cost of wage labour of children; school dropout or low school attendance due to seasonal migration; peer group effect of other dropout children and neighbourhood effect; structural problems related to government primary school.

(E) Social Hierarchy and Socio-economic Relations

- Regarded as lowest in social hierarchy among scheduled tribe ethnic groups in the region-women from other ethnic groups refuse to accept water and food from Katkari.
- Exclusive Katkari hamlet in terms of demographic composition; social interaction with other groups limited.
- Social atmosphere within hamlet-addiction to drinking and gambling, which may be interpreted to be an outcome of psychology of defeat and escapism due to magnitude of deprivation.
- Landed farmers of other scheduled tribe ethnic groups from surrounding hamlets exclusively dependent on Katkari for labour requirements. Education and upward economic mobility of

Katkari against the interest of such farmers as they perceive it may lead to shortage of labour.

- Narrow geographical spread of kinship networks; no permanent migration from anyone in the hamlet and no exposure to mass media.

(F) Government Schemes and Institutions

- Perceived by the Katkari people that government schemes are biased in favour of the landed households; e.g. of employment guarantee scheme in which only landed households are eligible for horticulture schemes.
- Perceptions regarding employment guarantee scheme—access to only stone breaking work due to being landless; perceive that number of work days available under employment guarantee scheme too little to address livelihood concerns; delays in receiving wage payments perceived as drawback of work in employment guarantee scheme.
- Perceive that public distribution system has weakened over time, since pulses, sugar and edible oil no longer available.
- Categorized as Antyodaya under government's poverty classification. Food ration card of public distribution system and tribe verification certificate perceived by people to be the most important documents required for accessing government welfare schemes.
- Mid-day meal in government primary school perceived to be of very low quality.
- No Anganwadi in Katkari hamlet and located in nearby hamlet of another Scheduled Tribe ethnic group, in spite of that hamlet having lesser population. Constraints in attending Anganwadi-low attendance of children in agricultural season, since parents are engaged in wage labour and there is no one to accompany especially the smaller children to the Anganwadi; low attendance after agricultural season, due to seasonal migration with children.
- Lack of health care facility in the region, especially specialized care for women and children.
- Katkari people disempowered in the local power structure and not represented in the local Gram Panchayat. Perceive that government schemes intended for them are diverted elsewhere and taken advantage of by people from other Scheduled Tribe ethnic groups.

(G) Perceptions Regarding Development as Expressed by Key Informants and Local Leaders

- *Inter-generational change*—'Our forefathers were engaged in the occupation of catechu (*kath*) making, then we started making charcoal from the forests working for private contractors, now we break stones for a living. We have always led a life of dependency on others.'
- *Reason for backwardness*—'People from other ethnic groups call us backward. But without land and without education, how can we come forward?'
- *Demand for redistribution of land*—'Some people from other ethnic groups have lot of uncultivated land. Even if our families were to be given one acre each, we would have something to live by.'
- *Importance of education*—'Education is the only way for the landless to come out of poverty.' 'There should be a separate Ashram school for tribal children.'

The above profile of deprivation based on a case study indicates the range of social and economic processes because of which people from a primitive tribal group such as the Katkari have remained trapped in chronic poverty. It is evident from the above description that integrating groups such as the Katkari into the development mainstream will constitute a major challenge in the present policy objectives of promoting inclusion in the economy and society. In this regard, it would be important for government interventions to focus on sustainable livelihood interventions, in addition to improving the nature of and functioning of relief interventions. Education would be a common entry point for intervention, but is more so in case of landless groups such as Katkari. Primitive tribal groups or particularly vulnerable tribal groups would require more targeted interventions in addition to those already existing for the scheduled tribe category.

Denotified/*Vimukta* and Nomadic Groups

In the rural social organization in Indian caste peasant villages, some communities who had traditionally useful functions got marginalized due to their nomadic occupations and some others who were branded as 'criminal groups' by the British rulers. After Independence, although denotified from the identity as a 'criminal' community, they continue to be stigmatized. For no logical reason, the two communities, that is nomadic and denotified or *'vimukta jati'* are put together as V.J.-D.T./N.T. in the common category for getting statutory affirmative benefits. The possible argument could be that no criminal groups are likely to have permanent settlements, which is also not tenable, since the womenfolk and children do live at fixed places for a longer duration. All nomads are not engaged in 'criminal' activities.

A village with a predominant occupation of agriculture pursued by caste—peasantry and supported by artisan castes such as carpenters, iron-smiths, potters etc. also needed other specialists who would meet other requirements. These requirements were provided by nomadic groups, who could not settle in one village due to infrequent and seasonal requirements of settled communities. Such groups organised in small bands consisting of few families have been historically mobile moving from one village to another performing socially useful functions. These nomadic groups were engaged in activities such as the following:

1. Performers like musicians, dancers, acrobats, story tellers, puppeteers and entertainers with performing animals like monkeys, bears, snakes etc.
2. Pastoral groups grazing, hunting, gathering herbal medicine in the forests adjacent to villages, and protecting crops of peasants with specially trained dogs.
3. Artisans using iron, bronze, bamboo, bell metal etc. to make various implements and selling to the villagers or in small towns.
4. Individuals wandering and regularly visiting villages with spiritual messages, fortune telling etc.

These nomadic groups are now labelled as nomadic tribes (NT), though the term tribe is usually associated with an isolated geographical territory. Some of these groups (about two-hundred in number) were notified as criminal tribes by the British through the Criminal Tribes Act of 1871. This took place in the context of the 1857 war of independence, which had made the British extremely sensitive to potential threats to their security or social conflicts creating law and order issues. Thus, some groups like Ramoshi (Berad in Karnataka) with martial characteristics and who had offered resistance to the British were also put into the category of criminal tribe. The criminal tribes were isolated in settlements by the British. The Criminal Tribes Act of 1871 was repealed after

Independence and these communities were denotified to be later called *Vimukta Jati* (VJ) in Maharashtra.

The Criminal Tribes Act was however, replaced by the Habitual Offenders Act, 1952. This Act is often misused by the police to harass these groups when a crime is committed in the neighbourhood areas of their localities. The denotified and nomadic tribes by virtue of their mobility remained houseless since they used to live in tents in the periphery of rural or urban areas. Over a period of time they have lost their traditional occupations due to mechanization and urbanization in the modern market economy, emergence of modern forms of entertainment, and legislations preventing street performances and use of animals, wildlife protection etc. Thus, these communities have no proper source of shelter or of livelihood. They are excluded from citizenship rights like ration card and voting rights, and basic facilities such as schooling for children, anganwadi etc. Due to difficulties in census enumeration, there are no authentic population figures of these communities available.

Due to a nomadic way of life and suspicion in case of crime, women from these communities suffer the most. There is domestic violence due to suspicion of adultery and there are also instances of molestation by regulatory personnel. Under abject poverty, some women have to earn livelihood for their children by commercial sex work. Autobiographical literature has emerged in Marathi highlighting the plight of these communities in their day-to-day lives, which has informed mainstream society of their deprivation.

Currently, the denotified and nomadic tribe communities are spread across (included in) the Scheduled Caste, Scheduled Tribe and other backward classes category in the categorization in various states. In Maharashtra, separate reservation benefits are available for the VJ and NT categories in education and employment. In the Hindi belt, they are included under the OBC category.

A National Commission for Denotified, Nomadic and Semi-Nomadic Tribes was constituted by the Government of India, under the chairmanship of Shri Balkrishna Renke, which submitted its report in 2008. The Commission has made a number of recommendations for the welfare and development of these communities. These recommendations include a "tent to tent" survey of these communities, special housing schemes, education of their children through Ashram schools, upscaling their traditional skills through training, and measures to check atrocities and harassment.

It is necessary to constitute an advisory council for these communities on the lines of the Tribal Advisory Council in the state. Similarly, there may be need for special budgetary provisions on the lines of the tribal sub-plan. The denotified and nomadic tribes are more backward than communities in the other backward classes category. In particular, the denotified tribes or *Vimukta Jati* also suffer from the stigma of criminal history, real or imposed, proof of which has to be produced by them for certification. Thus, the constructed identity under the British continues to stigmatise the present generation. An option of abolishing the *Vimukta Jati* category and merging them into the Special Backward Class (SBC) category in Maharashtra, may be considered. *Vimukta Jati* and nomadic tribe categories need not be clubbed together in policy discussions, since the *Vimukta Jati* have a stigma of criminality, unlike the nomadic tribes.

There have been other prominent cases about claiming Scheduled Tribe status by non-tribal groups in Maharashtra. There are Govari, Gond and Gond Govari in Vidarbha region of Maharashtra. There was a Gondwana kingdom with capital at Chanda (now Chandrapur). It is believed that some groups migrated from outside, tending the cattle of feudal Gonds, as herdsmen. Living in close proximity of Gonds in separate hamlets, a hybrid group developed out of the alliances of Gonds and their herdsmen, labelled as Gond Gowaries, like the Anglo-Indians. Govaries are claiming S.T. status with the pretext that there is no difference between them and Gond Govaries. Matter came to prominence since about 125 Govari women and children died in stampede at Nagpur while they were brought from rural areas for a demonstration at the Vidhan Sabha in session.

The other big group is that of Koli, a fisher folk community from the Konkan coast, including Mumbai region as north Konkan, who claim that the Scheduled Tribe, Mahadeo Koli who are actually living in the forest and hills, are the sub-tribe of Koli. "If the sub-tribe is Scheduled Tribe, why not the main tribe"? The '*Kul-Devta*' (clan/lineage deity) of Koli is '*Ekvira Devi*' with the piligrimage centre near Lonawala, a hill-resort, on Pune-Mumbai highway, which is also the lineage deity of CKP caste group, including that of the 'Shivsena' supremo Thakare, who belongs to CKP caste.

The shepherds (Dhangar in Maharashtra) are claiming ST status with an argument that the 'Dhangad' believed to be some Oriya migrant families in Gadchiroli are the same as Dhangar. However, there are no Dhangads in Maharashtra. Dhangar shepherds are already listed as nomadic groups. Sometimes the Lohars (ironsmiths) were claiming the nomadic status while claiming affinity to Gadiya Lohar community from Rajasthan, Chitorgarh, when they vowed not to return to their native place after their leader Raṇa Pratap lost the war with Mughal King Akbar. Since Lohars were the '*balutedars*' in Maharashtra getting payment in grain for the services rendered to peasants, which is not given to nomads, how could they be nomads? (*Jajmani* system in the Hindi belt has been often referred in anthropological village monographs, titled as *Balutedari* in Maharashtra)

The prominent or dominant caste in Maharashtra, the *Kshatriya* Maratha have been claiming the Kunbi status who are listed as OBC. The Kunbi are marginal farmers who call themselves Maratha. Incidentally the first king (*subhedar*) of Gwalior, Ranoji Shinde, who as warrior-attendant of Bajirao Peshwa who annexed Gwalior to Maratha empire, was a Kunbi. The high caste Maratha in Maharashtra consider the king of Gwalior as Kunbi and would have no affined relations with them.

Now the Maratha on their own, not claiming as Kunbi, are claiming backward status for getting reservation benefits. They have successfully organized huge silent, non-violent *'morcha'* (processions-marches) all over Maharashtra, as to show of solidarity.

The media reports huge silent marches organized by Marathas in Maharashtra in different cities seeking reservations, as socially, economically and educationally backward, which are the criteria identified by Mandal Commission and endorsed by the Supreme Court. The sugar barons and educational barons as proprietors of sugar factories and private educational institutions such as deemed universities are also Maratha. Government of Maharashtra has filed an affidavit in the Supreme Court with data about the backwardness of Maratha as reported in the State Assembly.. The immediate cause of these marches was also the rape and murder of a Maratha minor girl in a village Kopardi in Ahmednagar district allegedly by Scheduled Caste youth. About an year ago, at a village Khairlanji, SC women were gang raped by high caste people. There is an atrocities Act which is meant to protect the dignity of SC and ST by taking immediate punitive action. It is alleged that this Act is misused by SC particularly by falsely implicating the high caste persons. So the demand of the Maratha marches, as memoranda finally submitted by the young ladies to respective district collectors to modify the atrocities Act and offer reservations as are applicable to OBCs. These kinds of organized demands through huge gatherings combined with agitations, like *Rail Roko*, *Rasta Roko* are also witnessed in Rajasthan, Gujarat and Haryana, by caste groups which have been identified traditionally as middle level peasantry, probably incited by rich peasantry with political clout.

During the last couple of months, there have also been silent counter-morchas by non-Maratha Communities in Maharashtra demanding no modifications in Atrocity Act and implementation of the principle of Equity as per the spirit of the Constitution.

There have been *morchas* to celebrate Constitution Day, (*Samvidhan Din*) at Pune and at Kolhapur, the seat of Maratha rulers. There was participation by Muslims, SC, VJ, NT also. Predominantly there were blue flags of Republican Party of India with the photo of B.R. Ambedkar on the flag and yellow flags of another SC group—The Matang or Mang Community.

Why should Dr. Ambedkar be projected by S.C. only? We know he had an argument with Mahatma Gandhi about the term Harijan which led to a pact between Gandhi and Ambedkar in 1931, commonly known as Poona Pact whereby Gandhiji agreed about reservation to the ex-untouchables.

Why do we create dichotomies dividing the people of the country in two sections such as backward and forward, thus directing the reservations not going beyond 50 per cent, or such category as BPL and APL? How do we address these issues based on our field experience, looking at issues from peoples' perspectives? What is peoples' definition of poverty or backwardness? How does it go with or contradict universal values of human rights? What is development and human development, not human resource development?

These issues are discussed and adjudged at the Macro level in an etic approach. How do we anthropologists study these issues at Micro level from emic perspective, since that is our methodological and theoretical strength?

Coming back to caste and Ambedkar, he embraced Buddhism of Indian origin, to be out of caste hierarchy and ritual status of pollution and purity. There have been any number of reform movements against caste and untouchability in historical times, all ending up as becoming endogamous caste groups themselves. There have been saint-poets from all caste groups in Maharashtra including from untouchable group, propagating humanity and equity. Kabir continues to be a pan-Indian phenomena and now Sai Baba of Shirdi has attained that status.

It may not be easy for people to organize themselves for implementing socialist economy as per the Directive Principles of Constitution, but it is easier to organize themselves on the platform of caste. Maximum social science and Indological writing has been on caste from such scholars as Hutton, Risley, Ghurye, Irawati Karve, Srinivas and also village studies with focus on inter-caste relationships projecting the structural-functional holistic entity of a village.

Surprisingly, caste as a distinct research area has not been discussed in the ICSSR. Research Review Reports of 1973-74 for Sociology and Social Anthropology. Kinship, village and community development have been discussed without much about caste as a group or as an institution.

There have been discussions about all India macro concept of *varna*, endogamous castes and sub-castes at the regional levels. Irawati Karve has defined caste as an endogamous group of actual or potential kin. For her, caste is the basic extended kinship group after family and lineage. Several endogamous groups with same name is termed as caste–cluster, such as several endogamous groups among potters or Mahars, Maratha, Brahmin etc. Although, the essential caste-traditional occupation relationship may have dissipated, though not totally, endogamy continues to be the anchor, since caste is also a cultural group, facilitating the day-to-day living of an affinal family with patrilocal residence in a joint or extended family format or culture complex. Since we understand the hard and soft cores of culture, and the difference between material and non-material aspects, we understand what is changeable easily and what is not. As anthropologists, we have been studying kinship and religion which refer to hard values in culture.

The fission of caste and fusion as caste-cluster by intermarriage among the sub-caste or caste endogamous group, in Irawati Karve's definition, and the fission among political parties, and fusion or alliances at election time are of great academic interest.

As we know, caste is a big force during elections particularly in rural areas. When we talk of vote bank, it is the kinship-caste which is significant. Even for defeating a candidate, another candidate from the same caste is prompted to contest, thus dividing the votes due to kinship. I once asked a Sarpanch of a group gram panchayat as to what was the secret of his getting elected every time, he said, he had two wives and both affinal kin were in the geographical area of his *panchayat* electoral constituency. He was not a rich peasant and with a clean image, he said he did accept consideration for the vote bank he commanded at state level or national level elections, since he had no other source of good income to get his daughters married with a dowry. We have to get such case studies. Questionnaires are not of great use for the kind of data we need in anthropology.

If we asked villagers as to what was the population of the village, they would tell the details of electorate, caste-wise, not the population.

This much political awareness is visible due to constant elections at different levels.

Interestingly, the processes of Sanskritisation about which Srinivas has written is still in vogue in terms of those in power becoming the role models for those who aspire to gain in social standing. As a strategy, to grab constitutional affirmative provision, there are agitations using the vote bank politics to acquire backward status, as per parameters of Mandal Commission. The legal backwardness does not contradict with social backwardness at the ethnic identity or endogamy level, since the efforts are a group level activity. The capitation fee at the private medical institution for MBBS is very high while for MD it is astronomical. It is far easier to grab a fake backward class certificate by purchasing it at market price at the individual level and continue to support the cause of ethnic, endogamous kin group, i.e. caste, for joining the agitation as a group level activity.

Who suffers in the game? People think of their respective caste or tribal group since they have to live their daily lives within these groups. Once they are included in a backward category, the genuine suffer, since they cannot stand the competition from the 'haves' within the statutory category.

When a non-tribal group or a caste group with similar nomenclature or with tribal suffix or prefix to their name claim tribal status, they are not harming the interest of a tribal group with whom they are trying to identity by putting up a tribal claim, but they are harming the interests of all tribals in the State and the country, since the benefits of ST are bestowed according to the generic category of ST and not according to a specific tribal group. The pseudo-tribal group therefore nullifies the constitutional guarantees of all the scheduled tribes in a State and the country.

The claimant caste or non-tribal groups who profess cultural similarities with a tribal group in historical times, do not in reality show any social interaction of commensality or do not have the same deities and gods and shrines, let alone intermarrying (affinity) each other.

We had a case of Banjara or Lambada-Lambadi who are internationally known as Gypsy with a distinct dialect and rituals and ceremonies. They are DT/VJ in Maharashtra, ST in Andhra and SC in Karnataka. We had two Chief Ministers, uncle–nephew, from this caste based in Vidarbha, since they did not pose any threat to Maratha leadership in Western Maharashtra. The Vanjari in Marathwada who are cultivators like Kunbi in Western Maharashtra claimed to be synonym of Banjara with an argument that there was only an accent difference between Vanjari and Banjara (V and B) as is found in eastern India. Vanjari is pronounced as Banjara—Vovels become bhovels, Van becomes Ban in Bengali accent. As members of the expert committee, we went to the field and classified the details of distinctive cultures, to pronounce the obvious, that these communities had distinct identities and there was nothing common amongst them. The Vanjari leader became a Union Cabinet Minister and after his accidental death, one daughter is an MP and another a Cabinet Minister in Maharashtra.

As one of the members of our expert committee remarked that "even a village child sitting by the roadside for defecation, knows the difference between Banjara and Vanjari. And we have an expert committee." (Appendix A)

So the issue boils down to demand to get backward status to get the benefits of affirmative reservation benefits in public sector jobs and entry into the backward quota in colleges of technical education.

The matter for us as anthropologists is what is our role as subject experts. What research issues are relevant for us? What should be the content of our curriculum? How do we upscale our expertise so that we are not questioned at any forum particularly by the judiciary?

How do we capture the forces of change and their impact on the welfare and development of the people as per Human Rights guaranteed in the Constitution?

Our holistic approach, emic perspectives with knowledge and understanding of etic forces at work, our qualitative methods combining with quantitative data, understanding of interaction of micro and macro is what would make our academic and applied role unflinching for the good of the people and State. Let us be good anthropologists—the only social category as anthropologists—as humanist on the side of the people, marginalized people.

Although 'we the humanity' may be a distant ideal, 'we the people of India' has to be the reality to which we can contribute with the use of our academic discipline.

The following recommendations emerged from the discussions at the Mutatkar Committee whose member-secretary was retired Director of Social Welfare, Government of Maharashtra.

Recommendations (Examples from Maharashtra)

The problems could be identified at various levels:

(a) The notified list in Bombay State prior to formation of Maharashtra State on 1 May, 1960 and after its formation do not seem to be property coordinated. The Bi-Lingual Bombay had a different geographical spread and Maharashtra was formed by merging and deleting the regions which earlier were part of other States.

(b) Certain names of the tribes have been taken from the descriptions by British authors, such as, Bison Horn Marias which is a description of bison horn adornment on the head, but is not the name of any group.

(c) The transliteration or spellings of names of communities between Marathi and English have created certain problems prompting certain groups to claim Scheduled Tribe status by showing similarity in nomenclature.

It is, therefore, necessary to scrutinize the lists very carefully to avoid the contradictions. A committee of experts need to be urgently constituted to overcome these problems.

It has been observed that most of the petitions and especially in their verbal depositions, the delegations complained about rejection of their claim for ST certificate by the scrutiny committee. It is on these points that most of the petitions are subjected to judicial adjudication. It is also found that many claimants to the ST status originally belong to the States which are adjoining Maharashtra. It is, therefore, necessary to take following steps in this regard:

1. There should be an inter-State committee to sort out issues regarding the immigrants from one State to another. The issue is much wider than what is dealt in domicile rules.
2. The departments and the officers therein, need to be oriented and formally trained about the parameters to identify the genuine tribals who need and deserve constitutional safeguards and developmental facilities. A special departmental examination could be devised for the purpose. In fact, the Tribal Research and Training Institute at Pune has been given the status of a recognized research Institute by the Pune University. It is, therefore, possible to reorganize training courses at TRTI for the officers under the guidance of Pune University. The course designed by Anthropology Department, Pune University with the involvement of Director, TRTI, Commissioner, Tribal

Development and some of the elected representatives could be run at the TRTI.

3. There could be a state level expert committee or a commission which could act as an appellate authority over the scrutiny committees. If the commission is given statutory status, it may reduce the burden on judicial adjudication in the courts of law.

It is felt that the individuals who mislead the authorities by wilfully putting up false claims to ST status need to be punished according to the existing law and if such law does not exist or is inadequate, such law need to be enacted that provides for the cancellation of all benefits including academic degree and promotions obtained on a fraudulent declaration.

Last but not the least, the TRTI as an Institute need to be strengthened in its academic aspects to take up the responsibilities of research and training of the University standard. The recruitment of the research staff, their training, continuous education, exposure, and evaluation need to be streamlined.

Question 1: How to bring about a casteless society?

Process of fission of caste based on the development of class and creamy layer is a continuing process, to form new caste in a larger caste complex, bearing a common name, differentiated by a suffix or prefix which ensures enjoyment of caste benefits.

Recommendation: The unit of enumeration for backwardness in case of OBC should be family and not caste. Enumeration can be based on indicators where caste and class would be prominent indicators among the many others, much as female literacy, bide price, infant mortality particularly among the female infants etc. These could be different for different geographical areas and can be standardized after pretesting in pilot studies.

Question 2: How to remove social backwardness which does not automatically disappear with economic betterment?

In order to develop culture of Self-Esteem and Self-Confidence, women have to be literate and educated.

Incentive to female education is possible only with female employment which would bring about democratic relationships within the family, and start demolition of caste endogamy. Kalelkar Commission had recommended all women to be treated as backward for the purpose of reservation.

Recommendation: At least 30 per cent of employment and entry into portals of higher education be reserved for women in the reserved quota meant for backward classes.

Question 3: How to create Data base on the people of Maharashtra and document the changes brought about by progressive policies? Caste groups claim similarity as synonyms, having common names and occupations. They claim to be nomads or VJ/SC/ST. How to find ground reality?

Recommendation: To commission field study on the people of Maharashtra under the supervision of professional social scientists.

Question 4: What is the role of Social Welfare Department and how to perform that role more objectively?

Recommendation: Research cells and Institute under Social Welfare Department be strengthened to raise the level to the standards of academic training and research. At least half the senior staff should be recruited directly from the social science disciplines.

Continuing education in social sciences be designed for the staff of Social Welfare Department.

Inputs in human resource development go a long way to improve the quality of life. Caste either explicitly or implicitly cannot help the process of human resource development. The dynamics of Indian Society will soon revolve around family groups and not around traditional caste. If we do not equip ourselves with reforms, the caste will continue to dominate the scene by changing its colour like a chameleon.

To conclude, in what way anthropologists could contribute to understand the group level phenomena of backwardness and poverty? To what extent the administrative categories of group identity match with the socio-cultural identities to justify the affirmative actions? What about creamy layer in all categories and ethnic inequalities in each category? How do we assess a group in terms of female literacy and empowerment or employment, neonatal and infant mortality, migration for survival or better prospects? Is anthropology as an academic discipline equipped to address these issues through their research ?

Appendix

Introduction

Halba/Halbi community resides in Vidarbha region of Maharashtra as also in some parts of erstwhile Madhya Pradesh including Bastar. They are notified as ST as per Art. 342 of the Constitution. Halba Koshti, a weaving community also resides in Vidarbha. They are usually identified as a sub-caste of Koshti, the weavers. Halba Koshti claimed that they are the tribal Halba with weaving as their occupation. So, they claimed Halba Koshti to be notified as Halba ST. The opposition from all tribal MLAs in Maharashtra assembly, across all political parties to which the tribal MLAs belonged, made the State government appoint an expert committee in June 1984 under the Chairmanship of Prof. J.V. Ferreira, Professor of Anthropology, University of Bombay. I was a member of this committee and conducted field tours in Vidarbha. The terms of reference required the committee to examine as to whether the Halba and Halba Koshti were the same community. Whether Halba Kosti were real Halba or real Koshti and if not with what difference?

Apart from the secondary data and data about Court cases, it was decided to conduct anthropological field visits to Halba and Halba Koshti villages and places associated with them such as temples, pilgrimage centres and places of work, such as handlooms and power looms of the Halba Koshti weavers, mostly located in their houses.

The report was submitted to the State government in June 1985. Work of the committee was coordinated by TRTI, Pune. The State government in a court case about Halba-Halba Koshti in the Supreme Court presented the expert committee report with the admission, on demand from the Court, that the State government accepted the findings of the committee.

This case study about the field study has been presented very briefly as an example of practicing anthropology.

Case Study 1: Claim of Halba Koshti as Halba: Halba Report 1985

Trained investigators visited three predominantly Halba/Halbi Villages and two Koshti villages. They administered their schedules on 20 per cent of the families in each village. The expert Committee also visited eight villages in Bhandara and Gadchiroli districts over a period of five days in their field tour, independently of the investigators. The data so collected clearly indicate that the Halba/Halbi tribals and the Koshtis do not interact at all at economic, social or religious level.

The Koshtis continue their weaving of fine cloth for which they do not get reasonable economic returns. Their Hindu deities, as among other Hindu Castes, are well installed in temples and are looked after by specified families. All caste Hindu festivals and ceremonies are performed according to well-established Hindu norms in the region. The Halba/Halbi religious practices clearly brings out its tribal character.

The worship of Durga Mata and her sisters at the pilgrimage centre of Palandur, near the Madhya Pradesh border, in the Bhandara district, seems to indicate a matrilineal connection with South India or even a Bengali connection. Ravan worship on Dassera also indicates a Dravidian connection. As a result of acculturation, many Hindu festivals are followed by the Halbas/Halbis, as for example, that of Durga Mata. But the members of the Expert Committee saw for themselves that the temple, deity and sacred platform bore all the testimony of a typical tribal culture as against Hindu pilgrimage centres and their well-kept temples. Often, tribal deities have been bestowed the names of caste Hindu gods and goddesses in the process of acculturation.

The tribal deities Jangaldeo, Jhikati, Narayandeo, and Mothadeo were located on the fringes of the village or in the fields, badly kept and not worshipped everyday. Some of these deities, who are connected with the harvest and hunting, cannot be worshipped or even visited by women, thus exemplifying the tribal tradition of the ritual impurity of women, which is in contrast with the caste Hindus among whom women have an important role to play in the rituals.

On many occasions, the members of the Expert Committee happened to enter the Koshti houses or temples and were confronted by women. The women invariably identified themselves as Hindu Koshtis, but the temporarily absent menfolk, who hastily returned on learning about the presence of visitors, claimed to be Halbas. It is instructive to note that the Halba/Halbi tribals in Maharashtra usually call themselves Halbas/Halbis while the Halba Koshtis call themselves Halbas. In Madhya Pradesh, these tribals are called Halbas/Halbis and the Koshtis are called Koshtas/Koshtis. It is reasonable to assume that the Koshtis, who are called Halba Koshtis in Maharashtra, migrated from the Halba region of Madya Pradesh. The Halba Koshtis are very few in number today in Madhya Pradesh. This leads to the conclusion that the Halba Koshtis once occupies more or less the same territory as that of the Halbas, but were not themselves Halbas. This has been further substantiated by the fact that the Halba Koshtis are an artisan caste with no tribal origin or tribal characteristics.

It has been observed that during the process of acculturation, culture undergoes changes particularly in the soft areas, such as in various aspects of material culture. However, as far as the hard core of culture, such as religion is concerned, the culture does not exhibit substantial changes easily. If one culture gets completely assimilated in another culture, there is no reason whatsoever for the assimilated group to claim the benefits bestowed on a disprivieged people in order to help them to come out of their isolation and backwardness and to join the mainstream.

It is, therefore, untenable that the Halba Koshtis who claim to be originally Halbas should have no interaction at all with the Halba/Halbi tribals living in the same region. The Halba Koshtis claim that they have been completely assimilated in the mainstream of Indian economic life and caste Hindu religious organization, and hence do not show any traces of tribal characteristics. However, if such an assimilated group claims the constitutional benefits meant for tribals, it would defeat the very spirit of granting constitutional safeguards. These claims would not only harm the interests of the Halba /Halbi tribals alone but would also jeopardize the interests of all the Scheduled Tribes in the state of Maharashtra.

The Koshti is not the only caste having various subcastes which are endogamous. Other artisan groups such as potters, who are also found at an all-India level, are divided into sub-castes. Iravati Karve has discussed the problem of caste and sub-caste in her book *Hindu Society—An Interpretation* (1961). In discussing the caste of the potters she says, "The Kumbhar caste cluster is chosen as representing an artisan caste cluster. From east to west in Maharashtra there are a dozen castes making pottery. Each is endogamous; each goes by a specific name and each has slightly different ways of making pots or has some other peculiarities exclusive to itself" (page 26). The case of the Koshti caste and sub-castes such as the Halba Koshtis is similar.

The Marathi-speaking Brahmins in Gwalior, Banaras or Allahabad are called *Dakkhani Pandits* (Deccan *Pandits*). In similar fashion, the Koshtis who have migrated from the Halba/Halbi area or are living in the Halba neighbourhood are called Halba Koshtis by other Koshtis. The potters and the washermen, who have migrated from outside Maharashtra, are called *Pardeshi Kumbhar* and *Pardeshi Dhobi* in Maharashtra state. These *Pardeshi Dhobi* and *Pardeshi Kumbhar* clearly exhibit their ethnic and cultural traits in the observance of rituals and worship of deities. Similarly the Halba Koshtis exhibit a Koshti cultural identity and not a tribal Halba-cultural one. A cook in Vidarbha may be called '*Pandit*' or in Delhi '*Maharaj*', but they cannot claim to be Brahmins. Nomenclature alone cannot be taken as a criterion to establish one's cultural identity. It has been seen that similar names of the deities among the Halbas/Halbis and the Halba Koshtis do not make for similarity in the observance of rituals or even in the upkeep of the temples and the deities. The Halbas/Halbis and the Halba

Koshtis are as a part from each other as are the Indians from the American Indians.

The martial connection of the Halbas/Halbis is clearly indicated by sword worship in the Halbi temples as also on ritual occasions. In a peasant society, possessing the land is the highest aim of every citizen. The Halbis have been rewarded by kings through the grant of *zamindari* rights in land in accordance with the practice of the kings to grant land to warriors. People with a martial tradition are not known to have turned themselves to acquiring the skills of the artisans anywhere in the world. In the process of detribalization, the tribals have become a part of the peasantry. In some cases they have become industrial workers as in Jamshedpur or in Belladilla in Bastar. But, nowhere in the process of detribalization, have the tribals become specialized artisans such as weavers.

Whenever a peasant loses land, he becomes a landless labourer working on the land. This reflects the general problem of land alienation among the tribals all over the country whereby the tribals are losing their lands to non-tribals and they themselves are being reduced to the category of landless labourers. The Halbis/Halbas are either agriculturists or work as agricultural labourers but by no stretch of the imagination is there any proof of their turning to the art of weaving.

One of the important features of a caste is its association with a traditional occupation. While agriculture and military service have been mostly open occupations in caste organization, other occupations particularly those associated with the skills are traditional occupations. The artisan groups enjoy relatively lower status in the caste hierarchy. Weaving is an all-India occupation and is a basic one. The castes of weavers have different names in different parts of the country and the names vary in different religious groups. However, all these caste groups are endogamous groups.

It is well-known that division of labour is the hallmark of the caste system and absence of specialization of occupations is the most important characteristic of tribal society all over the world. There are no artisans among the tribals, since their simple, barter economy does not envisage surplus production or complex tools. They work with primary tools such as an axe, a hammer, a sickle etc. The tribals living close to nature in the forests, the valleys or the hill tops are known for their half-nakeness except in regions such as Nagaland, Mizoram or Arunachal Pradesh, where the human bodies have to be covered by cloth to protect them from inclement weather. At places, where the tribals weave their own cloth, the production is meant for consumption and a surplus for the market is never produced.

In fact, one of the characteristics of the tribal economy is that it has not been drawn into the market and cash economy of the so-called civilized world to any significant extent. Even in agriculture, it has been seen that there is a lack of surplus production. As a result, a bullock-cart (load carrier) is a luxury article in the tribal area.

The Halba Koshtis/Koshtis, on the other hand, are not only specialized and skilled weavers but they are known for ages as highly skilled in weaving silk and super-fine cotton of export variety. They have been a part of the market economy since long. The poverty of the weavers in Vidarbha is not due to their tribal origin, as claimed by some of them, but due to their exploitation by the middlemen. Their problems have been similar to the problems of the weavers all over the country, which prompted Mahatma Gandhi to champion the cause of the weavers.

Religion represents the hard core of culture. Inspite of acculturation, the religious practices do not undergo great change. The deities of the Halbis/Halbas on the out-skirts of the villages, their worship by the *bhagats* and sacrifices offered, are all typically tribal. The deities of the Halba Koshtis are those of the caste Hindus and form a part of the Great Hindu tradition. While Dhapewada is the most important spiritual pilgrimage centre of the Halba Koshtis, the Halbis/ Halbas have not even heard of it. The Halba Koshtis living in the Halbi villages do not visit the Halbi shrines nor do they interact with them is socio-religious life. In spite of the celebration of some of the Hindu rituals and festivals by the Halbis, they have not given up their original deities, shrines or religious. Moreover, the Hindu festivals are celebrated by the tribals according to tribal norms and not according to caste Hindu norms.

The pilgrimage centre of Durga at Palandur has been typically tribal, and the deities of the seven sisters are kept in pitchers there. This indicates a matrilineal phratry system and the Dravidian origin of the Halbas/Halbis, a point which has also been made by earlier scholars. The practice of Ravanpuja also supports the above argument.

The widespread custom of burial among the Halbas/Halbis is also strongly tribal. However, acculturation is exemplified by the practice of cremating the head of the family pursued by or few well-to-do Halbis.

It is pertinent to note that the Halba Koshtis have always been recognized as a sub-caste of the Koshti caste by the Koshtis. The Halba Koshtis have, however, never been recognized as an offshoot of the Halbas/Halbis by the Halbas/Halbis themselves. It appears that realizing the benefits that would accrue by successfully claiming as Halba, Koshtis also started claiming the Halba tribal status following in the footsteps of the Halba Koshtis.

All the evidence, derived from the field tour conducted by the members of the expert committee and from the field investigations conducted by the investigators, clearly demonstrates the tribal identity of the Halba/Halbi Scheduled Tribe and the caste identity of the Halba Koshti, as a sub-caste of the Koshti caste, in the Vidarbha region of Maharashtra State.

Case Study 2: Claim of Vanjari as Banjara

Introduction

Some of the Vanjari from Marathwada region had procured caste/tribe certificate claiming to be ST and/or *Vimukta Jati* which was not admitted by the appeallate authorities. Such litigations were pending in the High Courts. Thereupon the Administrative Tribunal directed the State Government of Maharashtra to appoint an expert committee to decide as to whether Banjara and Vanjari communities were the same as claimed by the Vanjari leaders in their memoranda. An expert committee under the Chairmanship of Prof. D.C. Wadhwa, Director of Gokhale Institute of Politics and Economics was constituted in 1992 with me as a member besides some retired social welfare officers of the State Government. I was incharge of visiting the Banjara-Vanjari villages and hamlets in Marathwada for field study.

The political angle referred to the Chief Minister being a Banjara and leader of the opposition being a Vanjari. The Committee besides meeting the delegations of Banjara and Vanjari associations visited the Banjara pilgrimage centre and the villages in Vidarbha, besides the villages in Marathwada.

The report was submitted in 1993 which was accepted by the State Government. The case study has been presented on the basis of field study bringing out the differences in various aspects of Banjara and Vanjari culture.

On the basis of the field study including group interviews with the Banjara and the Vanjari in villages, the distinctive aspects of culture of both the groups and the differences in their cultural traits are summarized as under:

Banjara	Vanjari
Location	
Reside in *Tandas* (hamlet) away from the main villages.	Live in the main settlement of the villages.
Economic Organization and Material Culture	
Occupation: Are traditionally pastoral, having changed over recently to agricultural labour and in some cases are in possession of land. In some cases, dairy is a supplementary occupation (as they are eligible for loans from VJNT Corporations).	*Agriculture:* Most of them, if not all, possess land between 5 and 10 acres. Dairy cooperatives formed in few villages.
Housing: Semi-*pucca* houses and thatched huts. The entrance of all the houses faces the east.	*Pucca* and semi-*pucca* houses of stone and lime. Entrance of houses displays figure of Ganpati/Radhakrishna.
Dresses and Ornaments: Men wear shirts and *dhotis* with turban as headwear. *Dhoti* worn to knee length.	Shirt and *dhoti* as among other Hindu caste men.
Traditional dress of women is *ghagra,* and backless blouse with *odhni*, made of multi-coloured cloth. Dress is beautifully embroidered. The women sew their own dresses. Some *cholis* (blouses) are embedded with mirrors.	*Sari* and blouse is common among women as in other caste Hindu women.
Married women do not use *mangalsutra* but use *topli* and *ghugri* which have the sanctity and symbol of marriage with living husband.	Married women use *Mangalsutra* as a symbol of marriage with living husband. Use jewellery as other caste Hindus.
The unmarried women use *garathani,* an ornament like necklace which is removed at the time of marriage. Women use huge earrings, headband made of silver and horn bangles and ornaments made of brass.	Unmarried and married women apply *kumkum* (red powder) on the forehead. Widows do not apply *kumkum*.
Food Habits	
Non-vegetarians mainly; goat sacrifice common. Women eat mutton and cook non-vegetarian food. 'Saloee', mutton boiled with blood,	Vegetarians mainly; Vanjari women are strictly vegetarians. Mutton is a taboo for them. If the men desire to eat, they cook the same themselves

(*Contd.*)

considered to be a delicacy, a marriage cuisine.	and clean their own utensils.
Liquor drinking is common in both the sexes particularly on all social functions, namely, marriages, birth, death etc.	Liquor drinking is not common.
Social Structure	
Gor-Banjaras comprise Ade, Chavan, Pawar, Rathod, and Wadatiya/Jadhav, sub-groups.	The main sub-groups are Bhusarjin. Ladjin and Raojin Vanjaris. The surnames are generally Adhav, Dhatrak, Ghate, Ghuge, Karad, Mundhe, Patil, Phad, Pimple, Sanap, Sankhe and Wade.
Individual Life Cycle	
Birth: First delivery takes place in the husband's house. After the birth of the child the woman stays in an isolated hut near the *tanda*. If a son is born, his birth is announced by beating *nagara* (big drum). They celebrate the naming ceremony on the 3rd day of the birth.	Normal custom of the wife having her first delivery at her mother's place. Naming ceremony is celebrated generally on the 12th day as among caste Hindus.
Marriage: Proposals made by the family of the bridegroom. Bride price is common among the Banjaras.	Marriage proposals made both ways; dowry system common. The social reform movement is underway to decrease the amount of dowry.
The custom of '*vetadu*' (the bride-groom staying with the family of the bride for a month, these days for a day or two, before marriage and not seeing the face of mother-in-law is observed.	Horoscopes maintained by parents and verified by the Brahmin priests. The couple seeks the blessings of Devi Ambe after the marriage.
Haveli custom is followed, the main feature of which is to make the bride stand on bullock so as to oversee village in all directions and bid goodbye before she is sent to her place. With the change of times, the bride now is made to stand on a wooden platform.	All customs like other caste Hindu peasantry.
In case of Banjara widows, the younger brother of the husband has the first claim for marriage with her	No levirate but in some cases widow re-marriage among Vanjari is permissible.

(*Contd.*)

(Junior Levirate), only in case he declines to marry her, she is married outside the family of her husband.	
Brahmin priest officiates during marriage ceremonies and in case he is not available, the Waditya/Jadhav can solemnize the marriages.	Only Brahmin priests officiate at the marriage ceremonies.
Death: The unmarried deceased are buried, only the married deceased are cremated.	Unmarried and married deceased are cremated.
Period of pollution not observed. '*Pitru Paksh*' (fortnight of ancestor worship) not observed.	Pollution observed for 12 days, '*Pitru Paksha*' observed.
Religious Organizations	
Festivals and Ceremonies: Main festivals are *Holi*, *Deepavali* and *Ramnavami*. *Holi* is observed early in the morning on the second day after full moon at 4.0 a.m. *Teeja* is observed by unmarried girls. Goat sacrifice undertaken on *Holi*. *Ramnavami* is celebrated at *Pohra* with goat sacrifice on second day.	Main festivals are *Dassera, Deepavali* and *Pola, Padva, Gokulashtmi* and *Holi.* Women generally observe *Purnima Vatsavitri, Nagpanchmi, Tulsi Puja* and *Sankrant* as is common among caste Hindus. Vanjaris observe *Holi* on the first day in the evening. At *Harinam Saptah,* that is, week during which mythology is recited by the community, Rs. 2,000 to Rs. 20,000 are collected from the community in various villages.
Deities: Pohra Devi in Akola district. Seva Bhaya, a saint, pioneer reformer, is also worshipped. Hingla Devi in Rajasthan.	They worship Ram, Maruti, Mahadeo, Ganpati, Krishna, Shankar, Vitthal, the Gods and Goddesses of the caste Hindus.
Pilgrimage: Main place of pilgrimage is Pohra Devi in Akola district. Visited by about 2,00,000 Banjara on Ramnavmi when about 10,000 goats are sacrificed by the devotees. Annual pilgrimage undertaken by some Banjaras to Hingla Devi in Rajasthan.	Main centres of pilgrimage are Alandi, Pandharpur, Trimbakeshwar, Nasik, Tuljapur and other holy places of Hindu worship. As members of Warkari cult, many people go on annual pilgrimage to Pandharpur.
Language	
Gormati is the common spoken dialect. They speak corrupt Marathi also.	Marathi is their mother tongue.

(*Contd.*)

Education	
Educationally backward, due to concessions they are getting educated.	Progressive in their outlook, relatively educated.
Status of Women	
Women are social and participate on an equal footing with men in all discussions. System of ritual weeping among women termed as *'thanko'* and *'dhavlo'* is a special feature on the occasion of marriage and death.	Vanjari women do not participate in discussions. System of ritual weeping does not prevail.
Aesthetics	
They have different folk songs and dances for different occasions, festivals, birth, marriage etc.	Folk songs like other caste Hindus.
Special Characteristics	
Headman of the *tanda* is the Naik who commands respect from the residents of *tanda.*	Vanjari follow the traditional system of village *panchayat.*
Social Reforms/Acculturation	
Banjara are traditional in their outlook. The women still wear traditional dress and ornaments. Some Banjara who are educated and are gradually changing their dress pattern. Pohra Devi, traditionally represented by a flag, has been replaced by a marble idol of Goddess about 30 years back.	No distinctive acculturation apart from what is seen in a caste village. Reforms about reducing dowry is underway.
Interaction between Banjaras and Vanjaris	
No interdining, particularly among Banjara and Vanjari women. No intermarriage. Banjara not invited to functions organized by Vanjari.	Vanjari do not mix with Banjara. They consider themselves as higher in the local caste hierarchy.

We visited Pohra Devi pilgrimage centre in Akole District in Vidarbha. The deity is traditionally symbolized by a flag, called '*Nishan*' in the sacred room in the building. It is understood that the two Chief Ministers of Maharashtra, uncle-nephew Shri V.P. Naik and Shri Sudhakar Naik who had a long stint in office, being Banjara, installed a marble idol of mother goddess which is visible in several Hindu temples of mother goddess (Devi). The marble idols were in the vicinity of '*Nishan*'. It was remarkably visible that the marble idol did not show any sign of having been worshipped with flowers, *kumkum* or such other sacred material as was visible at the '*Nishan*'. The Banjara community continued to follow the traditional way of rituals to a traditional symbol of mother goddess.

On the second day after Ramnavmi, about 10,000 goats are sacrificed including the one from Chief Minister's family. It was reported that on several occasions, Chief Minister visited the temple on this particular day. There is no Vanjari connection whatsoever with this temple and pilgrimage centre. Besides worshipping the caste Hindu deities, the Vanjari have their own pilgrimage centres.

It will be seen that the Vanjari, as they are found in Maharashtra today, satisfy all the features and characteristics of a caste and are inseparable part of the village economy and village culture. The Banjara, on the other hand, as they live in *tandas* today show largely tribal characteristics in terms of their self-sufficient and all inclusive social structure. They have occupational groups among themselves. They have apathy in contact with the mainstream village life. They have distinctive culture and language, and religion and rituals dominated by animal sacrifice. They also have equal status for women.

The study of the Tribal Research and Training Institute and the ethnographic studies made by this Committee do not find any similarity in any aspect of culture or language of the Banjara and the Vanjari as they live today in the villages. Any acculturation, even bordering on total assimilation, would show the relics or survivals of the original culture and language. In the case of the Vanjari, there is no similarity or survivals of the Banjara culture and language in the Vanjari culture. The Vanjari culture as seen today is indistinguishable from the culture of the Maratha Kunbi and other caste Hindu peasants. The total assimilation of one group in another group is very difficult unless it is forced by military power because during the process of acculturation, cultural borrowing is always selective. The educated Banjara, who are in the process of acculturation, due to contact with other settled Hindu caste groups and due to education, as also due to urbanization, have adopted the dress patterns and other material culture of the caste groups but do exhibit the earlier signs of their culture and language in their rituals, pilgrimages and distinctive food habits, etc. Even if they do not follow certain cultural customs, they are aware of those customs as having been practised at the time of their grandparents or parents. Such is not the case with the Vanjari. It was observed during the field study that the Vanjari did not know the Banjara culture and language except the distinctive costumes of the Banjara women which are visible.

5

Rural and Tribal Development

Dr. Rajendra Prasad, President of India:

> "The terms 'Community Development' and 'Community Project' are new, but the concept is very old. Basically, the concept is of many-sided development as distinguished from development relating to particular aspects.... All aspects of rural life are inter-related, and that no lasting results can be achieved if individual aspects of it are dealt with in isolation." (1955: 3)

Pandit Jawaharlal Nehru, Prime Minister of India:

> "People talk of money, and money is, no doubt, useful. But it is the human being that counts in the end and it is human being who have made history and who have advanced the cause of humanity, not money. If we train and prepare the right type of human being in India, then the rest is easy." (1955: 8)

Introduction

In India, ideal democracy by way of listening to the wishes of the people and acting on it, is paraphrased in traditional role model as Ramrajya. Democratic decentralization as an ideal form of democratic India after Independence, required some steps which were taken on priority basis. Feudal princely states, which were given freedom and autonomy by the British, during the process of their exit from India were merged as units of Indian Union with federal structure. As a compensation, the princes were given, what is called 'privy purse' on an yearly basis, which was abolished in 1971 by constitutional amendment. Some of the princes were given the designation as *Rajpramukh* (status equivalent to Governor) of the newly formed states, merging a number of princely states, such as the Maratha ruled states of Gwalior, Indore, Dhar, Dewas etc. as Madhya Bharat, until the linguistic states were formed in 1956 onwards. Similarly, Jagirdari and Zamindari were also abolished. Several feudal lords took to electoral politics and occupied positions of ruling power, which they continue to do so.

In a massive programme of rural transformation, on 2nd October, 1952, Community Development programme was launched all over the country with separate district and taluk-tehsil level development bureaucracy, complementing the already existing revenue administration. Revenue units of *taluk-tehsil* level were co-terminus with the community development block units in the beginning. In tribal areas also, the tribal development blocks were formed with some variations.

Conceptually community development programme was conceived as a movement for rural transformation, to modernize India through participatory democracy at all levels. What is modernization?

Is modernization a process or an end to be achieved? Does modernization mean change? Is change desirable? What should be the direction and rate of change? Is everything western modern? Is there anything like a capitalist model of modernization and a Marxist model of modernization? What should be the period for study of modernization in developed countries and developing countries? Is modernization unilineal? Who are the agents of modernization? What are the main components of modernization? In the Indian context, do modernization and Westernization mean the same process and product? What are the prerequisites of modernization? Is modernization value free or does it involve value judgement?

The discussion about modernization amongst the social scientists has been focused around these and similar questions.

According to Lerner "Modernization is the process of social change in which development is the economic component." (1968: V.10:387). Aiyar understands modernization as the total transformation of society. He understands it as a movement propelling in a consciously chosen direction.

Dube understands modernization as a process "denoting a movement from a traditional or quasi-traditional order to certain desired types of technology and associated forms of social structure, value-orientations, motivations and norms." The essence of modernization, according to him, "is to be found in the capacity of a society to operate highly complex formal organizations." (1971:67-68) Srinivas has discussed the distinctions between Westernization and modernization. According to him, "The term Westernization unlike modernization is ethically neutral. Its use does not carry the implication that it is good or bad, whereas modernization is normally used in the sense that it is good." (1966:52)

Eisenstadt has discussed the sociological approach to problems of modernization in "Modernization: Protest and Change." (1969). According to him, "The common characteristics of modernization refer both to what may be called socio-demographic aspects of societies and to structural aspects of social organization." Social mobilization (Socio-demographic aspects, refers to 'the process in which major clusters of old, social, economic and psychological commitments are eroded and broken, and people become available for new patterns of socialization and behaviour.' Structural Changes (structural aspects of social organization) refer mainly to 'the separation between the different roles held by an individual, especially among the occupational and political roles, and between them and the family and kinship roles.'

We are interested in studying the process of modernization as it affects the social structure and is affected by it. In India, the social scientists are prone to accept the meaning of modernization as expressed by Dube. According to him, "Modernization is not just another term for economic development and technological change. It has an important bearing on social organization. The social structure has to be adopted to the changing conditions, and ways have to be found to minimize the injuries of change and reduce its social costs. Modernization generates a variety of forces which make a powerful impact on society." (1971:96)

Srinivas has put forward the concepts of Sanskritization and Westernization to explain the features of socio-cultural changes in India. According to Srinivas, Sanskritization has occurred throughout the history of India and it still continues to operate. Westernization refers to changes brought about during British rule. These changes, according to Srinivas are continuing even now under the new title of modernization. "Sanskritization is the process by which a low Hindu caste, or tribal or other group, changes its customs, ritual, ideology, and way of life in the direction of a high, and frequently, twice-born caste. Generally such changes are followed by a claim to a higher position in the caste hierarchy than that traditionally conceded to the claimant caste by the local community." (1966:6) The reference group for imitation may be a dominant caste in the local community. The dominant caste need not be a Brahmin caste. Besides stable economic position, high ritual status and a sizeable population, new factors of dominance have arisen. Western education, jobs in administration and urban sources of income are significant factors of dominance acting at the regional level. After Independence, these dominant castes are playing major role in regional politics. They are many times responsible for fostering the divisive tendencies.

The dominant caste in a village community acted as 'the watchdog of a pluralistic culture and value system'. It also motivated, unwittingly, the low castes to imitate their customs. Wherever the dominant caste changed their ways of life, it affected the entire region. Recently, the dominant castes have Westernized many of their culture patterns in the regions where cash crops have brought in quick affluence. This has resulted in tremendous stresses for the traditional value systems and have broken the joint families at least at consumption levels. Sanskritization has been a modernization process all through the Indian history, whereby the low castes tried to improve their ways of life after the models of the dominant castes.

The contact with the British and Western education created in the Indian elite an urge to change their traditional society. However, the urge to freedom gained ascendancy and forged solidarity of all the caste, religious, linguistic and regional groups. The revivalist movements like the Arya Samaj were started by Western educated intellectuals, and people like Swami Vivekananda and Tilak tried to restore the identity of the nation. It is often said that Gandhi was acceptable to masses because he dressed and lived like a *Sanyasi*, though his views about untouchability and women were modern.

Due to communication and panchayati raj, secularization has reached villages. The village leaders give more attention to their diets, clothes, personal hygiene and at least publicly criticize untouchability. They have to do something for all the castes and for villages other than their own to get the image of universal leadership, and votes. They hire rooms to reside at district or State capitals to keep in contact with the district and state leaders. They are receptive to new ideas. They have started challenging the disparities in standards of urban and rural living. They are also trying to educate their children in higher and technical education, even sending them abroad. They, however, still look upon education as an end and not as means to certain objectives. Education has yet to show its impact as a socialising agency.

Communal organizations act as political parties and sub-regional loyalties exist. But in emergencies, national consciousness is adequately expressed. In the social sphere, the emphasis on achieved status and equality of opportunity are growing. There is definitely a mood of modernization and secularization in India.

India wants to modernize itself so as to meet the basic amenities of life for its citizens and uphold national self-respect. But, why the modern and affluent Western youth is seeking spiritual quest and Yoga from the Indian *Sadhus*? Is it modernization?

We are aware that several American anthropologists such as Morris Opler, David Mandelbaum and George Foster had come to India to help try the extension approach in community development in collaboration with Prof. D.N. Majumdar and Prof. S.C. Dube. Dube in his Presidential address at the Social Anthropology session at Indian Sociological Conference at Agra in 1958, about the study of Indian village communities has discussed the issues: "In the last decade there has been a noticeable shift in the orientation and the focus of interest of social anthropology in India. Anthropologists are no longer concerned primarily or even mainly with the study of tribal cultures; in increasing numbers they are now operating nearer home in village communities where they have discovered challenging possibilities of theoretical and applied social science research. ...It must be conceded immediately that the village communities studied so far and those being studied currently, do not approach anywhere near a statistically acceptable sample for the country as a whole. But, such critics appear to ignore certain essential characteristics of anthropological research. What we lose by not working on an extensive and statistically adequate sample, we more than compensate by acquiring depth and coverage of overt and covert norms in our analyses....Some anthropologists have tended to ignore basic sociological realities by viewing the village as a biotic community, although in essence it is a synthesized community. Because of their theoretical and methodological orientation towards tribal studies some anthropologists indeed have tried to study village communities in a biotic frame of reference regarding it as an isolate; in consequence the unity of the village has been emphasized more than its extensions....The concepts of great and little traditions, *sanskritization,* and universalization and parochialization offer us a good starting point, and from here we should build step by step a series of hypotheses and concepts that would ultimately lead to meaningful generalizations regarding the structure and processes of Indian Society. ...To place the study of change in one particular community in the proper perspective, it will be necessary to relate its changes to the wider national, regional, and local area developments. An historical survey of the major trends would prepare the ground for the characterization of change, and would help in determining its cumulative, concentrated, or sporadic nature....It would be essential to discover and identify the reference groups, and the agents and carriers of change. Who provides the model for change? And who are its promoters?" (Dube S.C., 1958)

Foster as a medical anthropologist has also thought and commented about primary health care as health wing of community development

"By the end of World War II it was becoming apparent that efforts of meet the material and social needs of the countries we now call 'developing' or 'third world' through the traditional technical services or national ministries would require financial and personnel resources far beyond the capacities of the countries concerned. Clearly, innovative low cost approaches socially and culturally appropriate to local communities would have to be developed to satisfy these needs."

"Two generic types of programme, or 'movement', have appeared in response to this challenge. The first to appear was community development (CD), a rural across-the-board developmental approach stressing agriculture, health, education, and communication. The second is primary health care (PHC), designed to cope with the basic health needs of developing countries, and set in the context of integrated socio-economic development." (Foster George M.: 1982: in 'Medical Anthropology', 6: 183-195)

The *Alma-Ata* declaration of 1978 about 'Health For All by the Year 2000' has given primacy to the inter-sectoral coordination which is implicit in the concept of integrative nature of culture in anthropology. At the *Alma-Ata* conference it was stressed that "People are the most important resource of any country, but all too often this resource remains untapped. Primary health care, however, has to make full use of all available resources, and therefore has to mobilize the human potential of the entire community." [WHO 1978a:61 in Foster, 'Medical Anthropology', 6, 186, 1982 (Page: 186)]

"Again quoting Mukerji, "Community development....has to be an integrated and multipurpose programme dealing with all the major problems of the people... (it) has to comprise activities in the fields of agriculture and animal husbandry, irrigation, cooperation, village and small-scale industries, health and sanitation, education and social education, communication and housing, economic and social welfare of women, children, youth and the under-privileged classes." (Mukerji 1961:67 in Foster, 'Medical Anthropology', 6: 186, 1982)

Governance during British rule was limited to revenue collection and law and order, combined in one position of a district collector having both authorities combined in one with limited judicial authority as magistrate. When development, particularly rural development through C.D. blocks became the priority agenda of government after Independence, new bureaucratic structures were created, since the majority of people's representatives at district and down below, had no vision or competence to manage or guide development administration. The bureaucracy, therefore, had an upper hand as executive authority.

P.H. *alias* Raosaheb Patwardhan was a freedom fighter from Ahmednagar and was closely associated with Nehru and Patel who were lodged in Ahmednagar jail. As member of the Congress working committee, he was closely associated with the planning process.

"Today, the emphasis is on the administrative and departmental bureaucracy. A series of new village officers are rapidly being appointed. Jeeps of new officers are visiting the villages oftener, the initiative is obviously with the managerial staff. The people are the missing link. In some of the States they are transforming the present Revenue Department into Development Department." (Patwardhan, P.H., 1955: 445)

Some of the greatest problems encountered in CD programmes stem from the basic nature of bureaucracies. Four bureaucratic characteristics that have handicapped CD programmes follow:

"*The need to show results:* Bureaucracies, to justify their budget requests, are under pressure to show quick results, particularly those that can be quantified. Consequently, even those workers philosophically committed to qualitative changes in people inexorably were drawn to support activities producing visible, quantifiable results. Progress in creating communities with self-reliant citizens able and anxious to make decisions about their futures is much more difficult to measure than material improvements." (Foster, George M., 1982: 191)

"*The intersectoral approach:* PHC statements emphasize this point, including the need to cooperate with and/or strengthen CD programmes. Yet medical people assume they will make the basic decisions, that they will be the team leaders. The potential for inter-ministry friction may be almost as great in PHC programmes as in CD programmes if they attempt to encompass broad-scale development." (Foster, George M,: 1982: 192)

"There are, thus, good reasons to believe that PHC will be more successful than CD, particularly with respect to eliciting community participation. But one major 'positive factor' that I would like to have included, but cannot as yet, is the incorporation of basic social science research in PHC programmes. While much lip service is paid to this need, relatively little research is being carried out, and much of what is done is of poor quality."

"PHC committees that pass on social science research are dominated by medical doctors. With their biomedical backgrounds, most of them cannot conceive of non-quantifiable research methods; they believe survey research is the only way to find out about human behaviour. Until the participant observation, open-ended interview method is also accepted as a valid research methodology, behavioural research done on PHC programmes is likely to have limited operational value. Probably the most effective way to change this picture is for medical anthropologists to work as members of medical health research teams. When medical researchers see the behavioural information that anthropologists provide that bears directly on their interests, they are much more likely to be convinced than if their knowledge of behavioural factors is limited to reading anthropological articles and reports." (Foster, George M., 1982: 193)

Rural Development

Carl Taylor, a pioneer public health and international health expert, a mentor to Indian heath luminaries like Dr. R.S. Arole and Prof. Ramalingaswami, was closely associated with India about public health issues.

"There was one item of observation which I was unable to make to my own satisfaction, viz. whether landless persons were being mobilized to assist in Community Improvement Projects. Where they were involved, I was sure that they were much more than labour battalions working under subtle social pressure without much evidence or promise of improvement of their own lot. I believe I saw some evidence that the lower economic and social classes were often not as completely mobilized and served as the higher and intermediate classes." (Taylor, Carl C.: 1955: 483)

"My opportunity to visit with Collectors was fairly limited. What little I saw and heard led me to believe that neither Collectors, sub-district officers or *Tehsildars* yet have very great understanding of the philosophy of Community development methods or of the details of Community Projects." (Taylor, Carl C., 1955: 485)

In the evolution of anthropological thought, village studies initiated by anthropologists followed the studies of isolated island and primitive tribal communities. However, the conceptual model of isolated primitive society was followed in single village studies. In the evolution—diffusion debates, domestication of animals and plants have been discussed in the context of pastoral and agricultural societies. Irawati Karve has analysed *Mahabharat* characters in '*Yugant*' in the transitional process of pastoral society turning into an agricultural society, with discussion about the relationship of seed and soil in the context of planned insemination, leading to the distinction between biological and sociological fatherhood. It is believed that Lord Ram's stay in forest with the tribal people for 12 years was an attempt to develop symbiotic relationship between the agricultural and forest economy.

Robert Redfield brought out the distinction between Peasant and Farmer. A peasant is one who has a longing for land and would never think of selling it. In an Indian village, the occupational communities, commonly known as *Balutedars* in Marathi like the carpenter, ironsmith, potter, goldsmith who have been given OBC status now, always cherished a desire to own a piece of agricultural land. Pearl S. Buck's Nobel prize winning novel, '*Good Earth*' has brought out the emotional attachment and concern about the land in a Chinese village. A peasant in Jaurasi, a Gwalior village studied by me in 1958 and restudied by Anthropological Survey of India, defined '*Kaliyug*' as an era when land and women would become marketable commodities.

Starting with the first village monograph, 'Indian Village' on Shamirpeth, by my teacher, Prof. S.C. Dube, who was also Superintending Anthropologist at Anthropological Survey of India's Nagpur office for a brief tenure, several anthropological village monographs have been produced across the country. Incidentally, now Shamirpeth has almost merged in Secunderabad city. All these village monographs have stressed the unity of a village rather than its extensions. Srinivas and others like Milton Singer or Mackim Marriott have discussed the vertical and horizontal solidarity of an Indian village in the context of caste. Srinivas has discussed about the myth of village self-sufficiency. All these ethnographic village studies have described the traditional functioning of a village. In discussing the dynamics, there has been more debate on caste than on agrarian issues. The foreign scholars in British India like Hutton and Risley have written more on caste than on village which was being administered in a feudal set up of kings, *zamindars* and *jagirdars* who belonged to the higher castes. The Indologist-Sociologist like Ghurye were on the offensive with knowledge of Sanskrit. It was only after the abolition of Princely states and *Zamindari-Jagirdari*, that the agrarian situation started changing. The feudal lords were co-opted in the political system by joining parliament and legislatures and continue to be so. How much land ceiling Acts made a difference in redistribution of land is a matter of research. Bhoodan movement by Vinoba Bhave was symbolic since, even the donated land was not redistributed except probably in Communist Kerala. Although India had to import food under PL 480 scheme, to feed 35 crore people, with the use of technology, India can now feed 125 crore people, although there are food security issues and under nutrition in tribal areas due to faulty distribution or regulatory forest policies not different than during British Raj. The Supreme Court had directed free distribution of wheat from Punjab which was rotting, for which the government had shown inability to do so.

It is a common criticism about Anthropology that the theory of culture and cultural relativism, structuralism-functionalism are more prone to project stability and equilibrium than change. This is an obvious outcome of studying 'other' societies, mainly the isolated communities to unravel the processes of social-cultural evolution, to understand the origin of our institutions and their meaning by "Going Native." The concept of value neutrality as a scientific dictum was also weighted in favour of stability, what now could be branded as tacit or unintended pro-establishment stance. Anthropology in some quarters is misunderstood or branded as a colonial discipline, due to such arguments downplaying action anthropology for change.

However, with the end of colonial rule, starting with India, in the Third World, issues of self -rule for development became prominent. Until then, the ethnographic monographs about villages focused on inter-caste relationships to present the holistic picture of a village community. Following the model of the study of primitive society, the emphasis has largely been on rituals, festivals and kinship. The traditional economic relations among the occupational castes and farmers have also been documented. The massive community development movement in India has been one of the first national planned programme towards rural reconstruction. However, agriculture and poverty remained and continue to be so, as an agenda of the discipline of Economics. There have been recommendations in the ICSSR Review reports for Anthropology to bring in poverty issues as anthropological research agenda, but with little success. It took quite some time, for ethnography, for focused ethnography, to be used as a method, as a research technique, rather than as an end point. In medical anthropology, focused ethnography has been widely used to analyse health and disease control programmes. Similarly, in adjudication about pseudo-tribal claims for getting ST status, focused ethnography has been effectively used. However, ethno-medicine predominates about health and disease issues, presented as ethnography about knowledge of medicinal herbs and about the herbalists, not providing leads for policy planning in health care and disease control.

The first book on community development came from Prof. S.C. Dube as '*India's Changing Villages*'. While I had to select a village in Gwalior region, for my Master's dissertation study, in 1958, it became easier to move with the Block Development Officer in his four-wheel drive open jeep, which he called and used as a 'mechanised bullock cart', crossing the agricultural fields and rivulets, where villages were not connected by motorable roads. When I revisited the study village, Jaurasi, after 22 years in 1981, villagers accepted that there was change in terms of increased production and increased agricultural income, but bemoaned that in real terms, it did not mean progress, since the prices of all other essential consumables also increased proportionately. They concurred with my visual observation that the houses and the roads remained in the same condition, as before.

Currently, the agrarian situation in India strikes in the eye due to large scale farmers' suicides as a result of indebtedness. The common man has to face the sudden price rise of essential food like onions, which are next only to salt as a traditional food supplement with bread. We can see a poor man eating his bread with salt and onion, as complete food. That is the reason why salt *satyagraha* against the British initiated by Gandhiji was a great success

While I established a Centre for Social Science Research on Leprosy, a WHO sponsored Project at Gandhi Memorial Leprosy Foundation, Wardha in 1985, I received a gift parcel from an International Leprosy Funding Organisation, based in Munich, wishing us success, on the first day of the Centre's functioning. The parcel contained bread and salt to be shared among the Centre's staff, symbolizing it as international basic food of the humans.

While I joined Pune University in 1960 as an anthropology faculty, there were no sugarcane or grapes in Maharashtra. These cash crops created sugar barons, who have also become education barons owning deemed universities and technical educational institutions, Maharashtra pioneered cooperative sugar industry with academic initiatives from Prof. D.R. Gadgil, the founder-Director of Gokhale Institute of Politics and Economics. Currently, all these cooperative sugar factories are privately owned by politicians. We had a small project about health issues of migrant sugar cane cutters as a part of our 'AYUSH in Public Health' programme, funded by AYUSH Ministry. The migrant contract labour live in abominable conditions, at the outskirts of villages, uncared by the sugar factories, and health and educational facilities being inaccessible to them. Are these not the research agenda of anthropology?

There has been an Expert Committee Report on Agricultural Indebtedness under the Chairmanship of economist Prof. R. Radhakrishnan (July 2007). Few excerpts:

"There has been a distinct slow-down in agricultural growth during the past two decades, in spite of substantial acceleration in the growth of the Indian economy. The slow-down is accompanied by a significant reduction in the share of agriculture in national product, but without much reduction in the share of workers depending on it for their livelihood. The two faces of the emerging distress are the manifestation of agrarian crisis that threatens the livelihoods of farmers, particularly those of the small and marginal ones; and the agricultural development crisis of reduction in its overall growth rate accompanied by declining profitability. The support systems to farming have weakened, public investments in agriculture have declined and institutions have become unresponsive. In the absence of any breakthrough in cost reducing technologies, the rising input prices have made cultivation un-remunerative. The result is the manifestation of agrarian crisis, often, in the extreme form of distress that results in suicides by some farmers." (Radhakrishnan, R., 2007)

TISS had submitted a report to the Mumbai High Court on March 15, 2005 about causes of farmers' suicides in Maharashtra. Out of 644 suicides till 2004, 5 per cent, i.e. 36 cases were studied. Following conclusions to be reflected.

"Repeated crop failures, inability to meet the rising cost of cultivation, and indebtedness seem to create a situation that forces farmers to commit suicide. However, not all farmers facing these conditions commit suicide; it is only those who seem to have felt that they have exhausted all avenues of securing support have taken their lives."

"It is not only the landed who have a crisis of indebtedness to deal with. There were a number of landless families who had leased land on a short- or long-term basis by securing loans. It was also noticed that many landless families managed to acquire money through migration to cities and purchased lands in the late eighties and early nineties. Many such families were caught up in cycles of debt and destitution, which ultimately led to the suicide of the head of the family. Thus, the survivors were reduced to landlessness due to debt. Among those committed suicide, included medium and large landowners who were also affected by a high level of un-payable debt."

"In the cotton belt, the crop seems to have failed more than once in the last four years. This crop failure has always not been associated with natural calamities, such as failure of rain or un-seasonal rains leading to destruction of crops. The causes are an increase in pest attacks in the last few years, especially from 1995 onwards. This meant that the farmers needed more money to pay for pesticides, though, in the end, a high level of pesticide use did not prevent crop failure."

"Longitudinal data available with government sources indicate declining productivity of land. This meant increased use of fertilizers to enhance productivity of land. The information available indicates that farmers have been spending more on fertilizers even while crop performance has been showing a declining trend. The group discussions and case studies point to the fact that the quantity of use of fertilizer per acre rose in the mid-nineties and has now reached a saturation point. There appears to be a decrease in the production per acre in the same area."

"Most families indicated that they did not have access to extension machinery of the government in giving sound information on how to deal with pests and declining productivity of land. The farmers are dependent on agents of fertilizer and pesticide companies for advice on seeds and crop care. The information base of the farmers is, thus, limited to the data provided by the agents and their products. A false perception of prosperity is being created in the minds of the cultivators that prompts them to take serious risks in terms of fertiliser-based cropping pattern." (TISS: 2005)

A peasant from Nashik, Shri Shivnath Borse has written a book on farmer's problems in Marathi. He has also mentioned about the agricultural crisis, since the economic reforms in 1990. The paradox of economic progress according to global parameters and decline of agriculture leading to farmer's suicides has been discussed. The contribution of agriculture to national income has declined from 51 per cent in 1973-74 to 22.7 per cent in 2003-04. He has also analysed the ignorance, lack of planning on the part of farmers about crop planning. Over-use of fertilisers has disturbed the soil-health and has made it dry. The example how a polyester shirt becomes dry faster *vis-à-vis* a cotton shirt which holds the water dampness for a longer time has been compared to making the soil dry, losing its capacity to hold water. He has also advocated side business, subsidiary occupation to farmers.

Referring back to my field experience, while standing on an agricultural field, full of pebbles, in a tribal block in Jawhar-Mokhada region of newly created Palghar District (earlier Thane district), in the 1970s, I asked the tribal farmer as to why the pebbles were not removed. He lifted the pebbles to show the damp soil underneath, as evidence of the utility of a pebble which protected the dampness from scorching sun. We neither know, nor appreciate this indigenous coping mechanism, unless we undertake traditional anthropological fieldwork. He was not sure about the ownership of the land he was cultivating, saying he cultivated it this year while in the previous year, some other tribal family cultivated it.

What is the contribution of Anthropology in the analysis of these phenomena? Or do we give it up as an economic exercise based on secondary, quantitative data, linking it up with the financial institutions to find a solution ?

We get the national level analysis from the expert committee report by Radhakrishnan Committee (2007). We get a quick glance from the report by TISS (2005) for Mumbai High Court, undertaken under a time frame for the State of Maharashtra. TISS headed by a trained anthropologist and following social work tradition of TISS, went for FGDs and case histories. We may not call them case studies as we understand case studies as holistic documentation and presentation in anthropology, while case history is a method used in social work and in medicine, for symptomatic treatment or counselling therapy.

We have to think about good qualitative research about the farmer's suicides, which is still pending. A Hindi movie has also been attempted on the issue. National level leaders visited the victim's families, economic packages have been unfolded and discussed among the neighbouring districts as to how to attract or grab those suicide packages. We have documented examples from *vimukta jati* whereby a person would pawn his wife to a private moneylender, since he had nothing else to pawn. He did get back his wife after couple of years, even with a child. *Mahabharat* war happened since Draupadi was pledged in a game of dice. I wonder whether any suicide has happened due to the demand of a moneylender for the pleasure of a woman from the indebted family. We cannot get such details without a qualitative in-depth comprehensive case study.

Bhatinda in Punjab is labelled as the cancer capital of India, thanks to indiscriminate use of insecticides and pesticides, and the train carrying them to a cancer hospital in Bikaner is called Cancer Express. Commercial advertisements of all the products such as detergents, dental creams, insecticides, pesticides, fertilizers and seeds etc. make tall claims in the name of science. In the encyclopaedic volume, '*Anthropology Today*', there is a reference that in America, magic was being sold in the name of science. I had once asked an International Medical Director of a Multinational Pharmaceutical Co., as to how they recommended the same dosage globally while the climatic conditions, nutritional standards, dietary patterns, genetic issues due to endogamy and other mating choices differed, he replied, "They were a commercial company."

What do we do as anthropologists with our strengths of holistic perspectives and qualitative people-centred methodology? We can launch multi-centric studies about agrarian situation or collect case studies of suicides, not case-histories as in social work or medical case paper. We have to study the farmers with various land types, size, crop patterns, use and knowledge of technology of modern methods of agriculture including irrigation. We have to interview the women in the families across generational age groups. The farmless labour and their problems are important. In a cash economy, the landless farmers have a choice of migration, while the landowners have to take care of their cattle also, as family members. Anthropological methods are strong in analysing the process of development or deterioration. We are already aware about the macro situation, as projected by the economists, but do not have data at micro level for good ground level analysis.

The *Wadi* Programme of the large NGO, Bhartiya Agro-Industries Foundation (BAIF) working in the tribal belt, for propagation of horticulture, required the tribals to follow the timeline of irrigation and monitoring of fruit trees. The tribals expressed regrets that sometimes, they had to miss dancing sessions since they were tied to the time-line technology of Wadi. We have to study the ethnic groups individually instead of following the governments' administrative or constitutional categories such as SC, ST, OBC, Others etc. We normally get statistics according to these generalised categories, which are used by government administration for policy planning and budgeting. So far, anthropologists have not gone into marketing issues and the advances given by private moneylenders to farmers and landless as migrant labour. It is reported that such cash crops like turmeric, ground nut etc. are purchased by traders before the crops are harvested. We can catch these processes through qualitative methods such as case studies and FGDs. Even if we desire to launch major quantitative studies in partnership with peers from other disciplines or as partners of government, the qualitative studies would help us to design valid and reliable quantitative instruments.

There is a fundamental paradigm difference between us and the ruling administration. We learn from the people while communicating with them.

Administrators want people to comply with their advice and follow the given schemes, designed for administrative facility of implementation and audit requirements. Our discipline as Science of Man in totality is people friendly. In Medical Anthropology, we have declined to play the role as social marketing agents to sell the bacillus killing technology. The Western people are turning to alternative systems such as Chinese or Indian Medicine including Yoga, not because of the love of it but since they have experienced the bad side effects of modern medicine. That is why we have to get the cross generational experiences of farmer's families. We have to bring agriculture, technology, nutrition, diet, health and disease, public health, AYUSH as anthropological agenda for research, directed towards people friendly policies and implementation logistics.

Tribal Development: Contemporary Issues

The Constitution using the principle of equity, with good intentions, provides some facilities as affirmative action, to the backward communities classifying them in categories, such as ST, SC, OBC, DT/VJ, NT etc. The term 'Tribe' does not have a universally accepted definition. The term, ST is a given term giving deemed status for the purpose of the Constitution. We are aware that the peasant communities, such as Gujjars in Rajasthan, Jats in Haryana, Patels in Gujarat or Maratha in Maharashtra agitating for getting backward status for ensuring reservation in jobs and in technical education. We anthropologists are called upon to adjudicate as experts on such issues. Besides listening to the pleadings of delegations, and looking into the literature and their memoranda, we undertake ethnography as a method to find out the details of culture traits and complexes of the communities and compare them with those, whose status they demand. We are aware that although the tribal lands are inalienable by law and cannot be purchased by non-tribals, the ever growing metropolitan Mumbai has been extending towards north into the tribal area. The builder mafia managed to get tribal lands by getting a certificate from revenue officials that the owners of land were non-tribals. While I was called by the Tribal Research and Training Institute of the State government to adjudicate in the matter, meeting the tribal owners of land, I drew the genealogies of the family members. Their kins were spread out in the neighbouring villages and carried the certificate as being tribals, how is it that the owners in a particular tribal village could be non-tribals? My certification was accepted by the Judiciary, but a lady activist who contested the case on behalf of the tribal owners of land was murdered at her residence. The fact also remains that we do not have a tribal policy approved by the Parliament. Are we, as anthropologists, incapable of drafting such a policy?

The Human Development Report of Maharashtra (2012) has computed district Human Development Indices (HDI). Nandurbar and Gadchiroli, the two tribal majority districts, rank lowest among the 35 districts of Maharashtra [YASHADA, 2012: 257 (unpublished)]. The status of tribal communities is lower than the general population on every indicator relating to health, education, infrastructure, civic amenities and utilization of government services.

The Taluka Development Index (TDI) computed by YASHADA further indicates that among the 356 talukas in Maharashtra, the bottom fifteen are all tribal-majority talukas (Annex **7.3).** This index (TDI) is not strictly comparable with the HDI and has also been separately computed by YASHADA. The difference between the topmost taluka (Pune 0.888) and bottom-most taluka (Akrani 0.059) is dangerously high. This is a clear picture of uneven regional development in the State. It is further highlighted by the fact that in Thane district the talukas of Thane, Kalyan, Vasai, Ulhasnagar and Ambernath belong to the top 15 whereas the adjoining five tribal talukas of Mokhada, Vikramgad, Talasari, Jawhar and Dahanu belong to the bottom 15. This is indicative of the lopsided development in the State and the position of tribal people at the bottom of the pyramid.

The poverty-line survey conducted by the District Rural Development Agencies showed that 63.7 per cent tribal households were below the poverty line in 1980 whereas the benchmark survey in 1996-97 identified 91.1 per cent tribal households below the poverty line in the sub-plan areas [GoM, 2012(a): 467]. Although comparative data is not available, the prevalence of poverty in the State as a whole was 43.4 per cent in 1983 and 36.9 per cent in 1993-94 (Planning Commission, 2011:267). Poverty among the tribal people was nearly double that of the State. No recent statewide data on this were available from the Tribal Development Department, Government of Maharashtra.

There is a government sector and a peoples' sector. We have to understand both the sectors thoroughly for meaningful analysis to help the policy planning and implementation. When I was a student in 1957-59, we had a lone book by Bartlett on Anthropology in Administration. Now, we have to understand tribal administration in its relationship with line/sector departments. In Maharashtra, TDD has a budgetary outlay of Rs. 8000 crore annually co-existing with issues of malnutrition, and tribal taluks and districts at the lowest rung of Human Development Index as per government reports. We are asked by the well meaning bureaucrats and Ministers to provide analysis and give expert opinion. Are we academically prepared? We are being asked to provide a Tribal Development Index to measure the inputs-output in Tribal Development.

I think AnSI undertook several growth studies which could be useful in identifying the degrees of malnutrition if we can simplify the technique at the village level. It is also nccessary to develop anthropological, cultural inputs in nutrition and diet. Otherwise, we continue to provide wheat in rice eating Gadchiroli in the ration shops or purchase *chikki* or biscuits to feed supplementary meals in *anganwadis* and schools.

Exasperated by the poor and apathetic governance of tribal areas and people, by the state governments, turning development issues into law and order problems, the Government of India activated Governor's constitutional authority about scheduled areas by asking to establish tribal cells in Rajbhavan. The tribal cell in Maharashtra Rajbhavan is fairly active and has been issuing some directions about PESA or tribal employment directly from Rajbhavan.

We know that the tribal people have traditionally been the collectors of food and not primarily the producers of food. Due to regulatory practices of Forest Department since British times, increasingly looking to forest as source of national revenue and the forest dwellers only as labour, the tribal people started becoming mal-nourished. The pieces of land in the forest cultivated traditionally by tribals were denied to them. The Forest Rights Act bestowed by Government of India have been used successfully by some tribal village communities which have been documented by tribal activists and journalists.

In Gadchiroli district, in a village Mendha—under the leadership of Devaji Tofa—*gram sabha* has recently earned the forest rights for collection and sale of minor forest produce—Bamboo, despite stiff opposition from Forest Department. The Governor and Chief Minister of Maharashtra and Union Minister of Environment and Forest, went to the village to bestow the statutory rights. This has been the first *Gram Sabha* in India which has successfully used the statutory powers given by 73rd Amendment to Gram Sabha by having a turnover of Rs. 1 crore with a profit of Rs. 50 lakh. Their slogan, "We have a government at Delhi and Mumbai, but in our village we are the government" has become popular. The success story of Mendha Lekha hamlet in Gadchiroli has to be presented as an anthropological monograph. People know about Ralegan Siddhi which was transformed by a retired army sepoy Anna Hazare, who shook the country giving some rights to *gram sabha*.

Another important initiative has been PESA which offers us areas of research about the interaction of people and government administration. There are several NGOs or voluntary organizations working in tribal areas who have field knowledge but no backing of theory to crystallize their thoughts and activities. Since they are starved of funds they undertake fund-driven activities. They crave for intellectual support from us not necessarily as partners in their advocacy work. We could study their functioning, their agenda, their field level expertise. They have always remained in constant contact with us for inputs of anthropological concepts and methods of investigation.

Departing from the classical stance, we anthropologists are now debating the Special Economic Zones (SEZ) resulting in dehabilitation and exploitation of tribal people and rightly so, in consonance with the universal value of justice. The Supreme Court has to apply its mind to malnutrition and food security; to such issues as spiritual, environmental and ancestral relationship of the tribal communities with the land and the forest. Even tribal tourism in Andamans has to be monitored, since the tourists were taken there to show the Jarawas as zoo specimens.

Supreme Court intervenes to uphold right to life with dignity not as dispute management justice, but as universally accepted moral value. The Government has identified about seventy eight districts which are *Naxal* affected. Why are the tribal belts affected? There is a constant debate as to whether these are development issues or issues of law and order. To counter these, we have 73rd Amendment to the Constitution acknowledging the traditional self rule and autonomy of the tribal communities, resulting into what is commonly understood as PESA Act. Going backwards, the Constituent Assembly and the leaders like Mahatma Gandhi and Jawaharlal Nehru could understand that the tribal development issues had to be tackled or handled differently than those of the caste peasantry community development. A respectable term '*Adivasi*' coined probably by Thakkarbappa was adopted by Mahatma Gandhi giving the status and respect of the original dwellers of the land, or as ancestors of the mainstream Indian citizens. However, the terms like *Vanvasi* and *Girijan* with political overtones tried to replace the term *Adivasi*. In consequence, the term 'Tribe' is not defined in the Constitution of India. As affirmative action, for administrative purposes, we have created the administrative categories such as Scheduled Tribe (ST) and Scheduled Caste (SC) and later on added *Vimukta Jati* (VJ) or Denotified Tribe (DT), Nomadic Tribe (NT) and Other Backward Classes (OBC). This has led to the issues of pseudo-tribalism, increasing the ST population, defying all parameters of decadal growth rate. The Scheduled Tribe population in India is about 9 per cent of the total population. The population of certain tribal ethnic groups keeps on increasing with every decennial census. The Census shows us that the decadal growth rate in ST population transgresses all principles of biological growth including that of the mythological Gandhari, as mother of hundred sons, meaning thereby that every tribal woman being a Gandhari could not have multiplied so much growth of the ST population. It is to sort out the pseudo-tribal issues that anthropologists are invited as experts and this expertise is respected by the judiciary. Our report on Halba-Halba Koshti has been upheld by the Supreme Court. Actually, the tribal research institutes all over the country have been reduced to functioning only as appellate authority for certification, to the neglect of research functions. The OBC Commissions have to adjudicate with the ever increasing demands of the communities to be identified as backward. The high profile dominant *Kshatriya Varna,* caste-cluster Maratha in Maharashtra, are claiming to be identified as the OBC. The Gujjars in Rajasthan, who can organize agitations in urban areas are staking their claim to the ST status in competition with the Mina community which already enjoys ST status and have captured the maximum civil services quota for ST. Interestingly there are no pseudo claims to get the SC label due to stigma of untouchability or for DT/VJ due to record of crime to be shown as evidence. Maximum claims are made for getting status as nomadic or scheduled tribe, besides the OBC status. Some states have introduced a new category, special backward class (SBC) due to inability to award ST status to them, without any parameters to list them as SBC.

We are aware that the British labelled some geographical territories inhabited by the tribal communities as 'excluded' and 'partially excluded'. To help the British administration for peaceful governance by understanding and respecting the customs and manners of various ethnic groups, civil servants turned scholars compiled the volumes on the ethnography of castes and tribes of various Presidencies. The Anthropological Survey of India (AnSI) followed this model in the 'People of India' publications, written by anthropologists and not by civil servants, as under British rule.

Interestingly, the tribal issues, may be due to north-east connection, and international borders, were looked after by the Ministry of External Affairs before passing it to Ministry of Home Affairs, perceiving probably as the law and order issue. The tribal communities were put into the lap of Social Welfare Departments at the Centre and in the States which were later re-christened as Social Justice Ministry. It is recently that the Tribal Affairs Ministry has been created, without yet a National Tribal Policy. However, Anthropological Survey of India (AnSI) which is a prime institution studying the tribal communities continues to be with the Ministry of Culture which has under its umbrella several museums, giving a message of primacy to documentation and preservation. We are not aware as to the mechanism of coordination between the Ministry of Culture and the Ministry of Tribal Affairs on tribal issues. It is now that the AnSI has completed the task of preparing a Social Impact Assessment Module addressing the issues of dehabilitation of tribal people due to proliferating SEZ, recognizing that the Environment Impact Assessment falls short of protecting the livelihood and cultural interests of the people. We are aware about the N.C. Saxena Committee and recently delivered Supreme Court judgement about 'Vedant' in Orissa. This is being put forward to emphasize the relevant agenda in Indian Anthropology. Some of our colleagues are advocating for the term, Anthropological Impact Assessment to replace Social Impact Assessment.

The draft National Tribal Policy, for the Scheduled Tribes of India, based on the constitutional provisions about Scheduled Tribes is linked with the *Panchsheel* (five principles) about tribal development enunciated by Jawaharlal Nehru and translated in the Dhebar Commission Report. It has been further spelt out in the 73rd Amendment with ramifications in the Forest Rights Act and PESA Act. The issue as to why the tribal areas get ranked lowest as per the human development parameters need to be analyzed. That means, focusing on infant mortality and under nutrition in the health sector, lower literacy and higher drop out in the educational sector and low productivity, issues of food security and seasonal migration in the livelihood sector, are distinctly low as compared to the other identified categories, such as the SC, OBC and others. Within Scheduled Tribes, there are wide disparities among the ethnic groups and in geographical regions, as between the North-East, Andamans and the rest of the so-called mainland India.

My understanding is primarily based on the first hand anthropological research and intervention research, in all the scheduled areas in Maharashtra and among all the major tribal ethnic groups. I had the privilege of analyzing the lowest ranked 35th district in Maharashtra, Nandurbar, a tribal district with 75 per cent tribal rural population as per Human Development Report of the State Government, on parameters of health, education and livelihood. Interestingly, a British Civil Servant, Symington in his report about poverty and indebtedness in 1938, about tribal pockets in Western Khandesh in north Maharashtra, had mentioned the *tehsils* and areas under tribal chieftains which precisely were carved out as a separate tribal district of Nandurbar in 1998. It took sixty long years to carve out a tribal district from the erstwhile Dhule district. Symington's comments about the tribal areas and people continue to be relevant after 65 years—"It has hitherto been usually assumed that whatever measures were suitable for the country at large were suitable also for the tribal areas. This assumption is now being queried, and I submit that the conspectus of these areas contained in the following report will show that, in point of fact, the common law of the land is in many respects highly unsuitable for the tribal areas and produces serious oppression and exploitation. My position is that, at any rate for the next generation, we must regard the aboriginal as being in the nursery. Like a child he must be protected from outside interference and victimization and like a child he must be taught how to hold his own. In short, the State's attitude must be parental." (Symington: 1938: 2-3)

As a student of Anthropology, I had to understand the governance issues, that is, the structure and functioning of Tribal Sub-Plan administration in relation to revenue and development administration of the line departments. The decentralized democracy of Panchayat Raj Institutions (PRI) cannot function with 25 group gram panchayats for 163 revenue villages and more than 260 official hamlets, spread over more than 1100 settlements, in Dhadgaon hilly tehsil in Nandurbar district. With such a scenario, what would be the relationship of *gram sabha* with hamlets, village and group gram panchayat? To top it, one *gramsevak* is a secretary of more than one group *grampanchayat,* following the revenue model of a *patwari/talathi* who looks after the revenue issues of three or four villages. As students of Anthropology, we cannot be content only with the ethnographic studies of kinship groups or class and caste, social, economic, cultural and religious organizations, but we have to understand the functioning and impact of statutory institutions, on the life in the hamlets and villages, in the forests and the hills.

The government's policies, schemes and the tribal development administration is decided at the macro level. That is a top down planning and implementation procedure with the firm belief that the bureaucracy from the State to the District to the Tribal Sub-Plan and at the block level could bring about the desired development, aimed at meeting the millennium development goals. Our participant observation revealed that, never ever, the existence of *Gram Sabha, Gram Panchayat* and its role discussed in the meetings of high level state level bureaucracy. I have been a witness to observe the discussion where only role of government functionaries from district to village level was mentioned as a panacea to tackle the issues of registration of births, deaths and malnutrition.

Despite the existence of PESA, Forest Rights Act and legislation about alienation of tribal lands, the ground level situation is entirely different. Anthropology as a discipline and anthropologists by training, are best equipped to study and analyze the ground level reality, which is so very essential in the implementation of various Acts and Schemes at the household, hamlet and village level. The micro level situation and understanding of the concerns and experiences of the people through their eyes, through their perceptions, is the strength of anthropology. On the ground, we may find wheat being 'distributed' in the public distribution system (PDS) shops among rice eating people. While the under five or under two child mortality is high, the *anganwadi* appears to be visibly functional at the age group of 3+ level with a directive to under-report and manipulate malnutrition grades. The maternity benefit scheme designed to provide special health benefits to pregnant tribal women in Maharashtra was to provide tonics manufactured by multinational pharmaceuticals instead of food items like pulses and edible oil to meet her requirement of protein and fat. Even the suggestion to do this to the Tribal Development Department was thought to be implemented by the Health Department, not by the grampanchayat at ground level.

The interview schedules and questionnaires can never bring out these ground realities. The traditional anthropological tools and techniques alone can document the processes that accelerate or impede change. Similarly, the use of the category of Scheduled Tribe can never bring out the real problems of infant mortality and under nutrition, since there are wide disparities among ethnic tribal groups within the scheduled tribe category. The ethnic tribal groups who had formal kingdoms or the leading family functioned as Chieftain, have a different vision, exposure, self-esteem and confidence. However, the disciplines which use secondary data for analysis continue to use the administrative categories of SC, ST etc. as research categories. Actually the technical research organizations like the Indian Council of Medical Research (ICMR) and Indian Council of Agricultural Research (ICAR) whose institutes are titled respectively after diseases and crops, when directed to pay attention to tribal situation, for which funding is provided from the Tribal Sub-Plan, continue to use administrative label, ST as research category, which does not present the grassroots realities.

The institutions such as the *anganwadi* and *ashram* schools in the tribal areas which are administered and monitored by the state and national level administration do not analyze the data for understanding the processes of change. Often, the health centres or the ashram schools and *anganwadis* put the blame on the people for non-utilization of these institutions. Never does it occur to them that the answers which they provide for non-utilization, such as superstition, illiteracy, low self-esteem, etc. are the questions or the concerns for which the answers, the solutions have to be found. It is wholly within the theory and methodology of anthropology to study these issues and offer recommendations. The tribal people are branded as backward. Actually the backwardness of tribal communities refer to their lack of capacity to utilize the infrastructure to meet their needs, or expand their development choices. It refers to their weakness in articulating their concerns or desires whereby we brand them as shy and dumb. On the other hand, the pseudo groups who aggressively strive to be labelled as backward for seeking the benefits of affirmative reservation is something which need to be studied and rectified in favour of genuine tribals. This is best done by the use of ethnographic methods such as genealogy, observation of rituals, and life cycle ceremonies and sacred places, including pilgrimage centres, which reveal the hard core of culture. Their concepts of their own origin and the origin of universe, the concepts of life, death, their deities and spirits would unfold their cultural values.

The sole object of development in the government perception is aimed at infrastructure development of the geographical area of the tribal belt, (area development approach) towards aiming the tribal communities to join the mainstream of Indian society. The term human development is of recent origin and wrongly refers to human resource development. The tribal activists' perception of mainstream is the rape of women, domestic violence and dowry deaths. They would, therefore, question joining such a sick mainstream. Field anthropologists know that a tribal woman is never molested or raped by the tribal man, that there is bride price among the tribal communities, which ensures better gender equality. There is no adultery but there is freedom to annul the marriage and get into new relationship, following the socially prescribed or approved norms. We have seen 15000–20000 Bhils-Pawaras dancing whole night on the *Holi* festival on full moon night *(Holi Purnima)*, in the Akrani hills in Nandurbar district, at Kathi, with adornment of girdle of bottle gourds and peacock feathers etc. Not a single police constable is required to maintain law and order. No rape, molestation or thefts from the street shops of small traders ever happen. These strengths of tribal cultures are not properly documented or analyzed, which should contribute to the mainstream value systems in Indian culture. There is no female foeticide in tribal communities. There has been female infanticide, now replaced by female foeticide in relatively affluent and strong patriarchal north India, or now reported widely from sugar cane rich rural district of Kolhapur in Maharashtra, where universal sonography examination has become an instrument of female foeticide, changing the demographic composition of population.

As anthropologists, as students of tribal communities and caste peasantry, and some anthropologists having tried to analyze national cultures, the issue of what is the mainstream, and what are plural cultures is our research agenda. We understand the implications of issues about ethnic identities at birth or ascribed identities, statutory identities, and lastly the identity adjudicated by the judicial court. The issues of certifying the ethnic identities of communities as per constitutional categories are resolved by anthropologists as experts. The concepts of development, i.e. development of infrastructure, economic development measurable in GNP and GDP, and human development are debated widely. Several clitches are used such as development with human face, or development with social justice, inclusive growth etc. to capture the vote bank of the poor and deprived communities. We have the paradoxes of being the fastest growing economy with largest number of undernourished children and infant deaths. The tribal regions in mainland India maximally contribute to undernourishment and child deaths, bringing down India on the human development scale.

Tribal Development: New Role for Anthropology

What is the role of anthropologists in understanding these processes while macro level massive tribal development programme is launched as Tribal Sub-Plan? Who is going to study the ethnography of the functioning of the Tribal Sub-Plan and the impact that it makes on the lives of the people? As students of anthropology functioning at the micro level or grassroots level, trying to understand the emic perspectives, we realize that the administrative management of tribal development is planned without reference to people, for whom it is meant. It continues to be provider-beneficiary relationship, contrary to democratic principles of partnership. PRIs are in place but without any effective powers. Group *gram panchayat* nullifies the cultural functioning of hamlet as a unit of social action. In response, PESA Act has been formulated acknowledging the traditional capacity of tribal communities about self-rule, including management of tribal kingdoms. The principles and functioning of PESA are the subject matter of anthropology. The issues of interrelationships of group *grampanchayat,* revenue village, hamlets, habitations and *gram sabha* jurisdiction can be better analyzed by anthropologists due to understanding of micro and emic perspectives. There are tribal states in India, tribal districts, tribal *tehsils* and tribal *gram Panchayats*. In the democratic set up, there are tribal representatives of the people at all levels including the ministers and chief ministers. The issues of governance and administration like the issue of indirect rule during British regime, should normally be the subject matter of the discipline of political science and public administration. However, we find that in our university system, the other social science disciplines do not study anything tribal, neither the tribal economy nor the tribal law or administrative system about development. Anthropology as a holistic study of 'Man and His Works' has to study the contemporary issues of development. The hierarchy within civil services affect the development process. Tribal areas are to be governed by the Collector, Chief Executive Officer of the *Zila Parishad* and Project Officer (PO) of Integrated Tribal Development Project (ITDP) under Tribal Sub-Plan (TSP), as a team. The Collector, age old revenue officer collecting land revenue since Mughal or pre-Mughal times, is the senior member of the team. The PO of ITDP has no powers to monitor the functioning of the line or sector departments of *zila parishads* or state governments in TSP area, which are actually funded under Tribal Sub-Plan. There is no other academic discipline which bothers to look into these issues of tribal India. It is worth quoting S.C. Dube from his International Anthropology Congress Speech at Delhi in 1978, "The discipline continues to maintain, by and large, a value free posture; is uncertain about the role of the anthropologists in society; and is shaky in determining the criteria of the relevance or research. In consequence, its analytical handling of gut issues, such as poverty, exploitation and population growth is feeble."

I have voiced similar ideas in Panchanan Mitra Memorial Oration at Asiatic Society, Kolkata, in 2010: To quote from the lecture:

> "When we practice anthropology in the area of tribal development, our ambit of study becomes wider, not limiting itself to micro level communities. The impact of parliament or state legislation about land and forest, education and health, construction of dams and SEZ in tribal areas, on the lives of the tribal people, need to be studied in the context of human dignity. To understand and analyze the ethnography of administration is

> a new challenge to anthropology. When we say, we have to redefine the holistic concept in anthropology; we mean, we cannot be satisfied only with the ethnography of microcosm. The macrocosm is impacting the microcosm; the global macrocosm is becoming powerful enough to be termed as neo-imperialist." (Mutatkar:2010:35-36)

We, field anthropologists who have a very close and intimate dialogue with the people are in a position to understand the issues at their level, from their perspective. If we try to understand the issues holistically, we can identify the various stakeholders and their respective roles and functioning, which could offer solutions. We need not become activists, not even play an advocacy role, unless we are called upon to join the government committees, but our research data and analysis can help advocacy efforts by the advocacy groups, including the lagislators. We, researchers, cannot undertake research unless we formulate a research question. While looking at tribal malnutrition, we have to see, among which ethnic group, there is a recurring problem. We also should find a local solution by analysing as to why there is no malnutrition among some ethnic groups and among the majority of families? But, instead, we isolate the affected families and provide them with some fancy food or tonics imported or gifted by foreign agencies, which are not sustainable solutions. Anything connected to market has a tendency to lead to kick-backs.

We tried intervention research in tribal malnutrition from the platform of an academic voluntary organization (NGO), in nine tribe dominant blocks in seven districts of Maharashtra, in 250 villages, with the help of 500 male and female volunteers in equal proportion. After the initial base-line survey conducted with the help of local literate youth, interventions in various components such as health, education, livelihood, community development, tribal identity by way of art and culture etc. were tried in a participatory format. One time full meal was provided to about 2000 pregnant women everyday in the houses of respective tribal volunteers, *sattu* [roasted wheat and *bengal gram* (*chana*), in powder form] fortified with Ayurvedic lactogenes for lactating women, and *sattu* to children up to 2 years was given. Impact was visible in increased birth weight and improvement in grades as per ICDS scale. Seeds of vegetables for kitchen gardens were supplied free. Medicine box with Allopathic and Ayurvedic drugs for common ailments were kept with tribal volunteers for free distribution. Some aspects of the programme about meals to pregnant women have been adopted by the state government as its programme. (Book: Tribal Health and Malnutrition)

In Maharashtra, the convention is that percentage of the total budget of the state government should go to tribal development, commensurate with the tribal population. That means, if ST population is 9 per cent, then 9 per cent of the budget should go to the tribal development, which would make it the richest department in the State. Of course, they never get 9 per cent, they get 6 per cent or 5 per cent or 4 per cent, even then, it remains unutilized, and then as the minister and the secretary say that the department only functioned as post office. We are only distributing the budget to various sector departments. The tribal development department has no authority to monitor the utilization of funds allotted to sector department.

Health and Malnutrition

As far as health is concerned, we have got so many schemes. We have had a Matrutva Anudan Yojana; that means tribal pregnant women are provided with Rs. 400 cash and Rs. 400 by way of some medicine. On examination of the Government Resolution about this Matrutva Anudan Yojana, it was found that, the Rs. 400 medicine were all tonics of the multi-nationals. Dr. R.S. Arole suggested to give them edible oil as fat and pulses as protein. This was to be supplied by the health department from the budget of tribal development department. Why cannot the *Gram Panchayat Samiti* do that by purchasing these things locally. This is the kind of centralized approach. The point is, such schemes are bound to fail, since there is no dialogue with the people. In our tribal project, we were feeding 2000 tribal pregnant women once a day, with food which includes *chapati*, rice, *dal* and vegetables. This has resulted in increased birth weight of babies.

Education and Ashram Schools

As far as the education is concerned, and actually if we look at the institutional set up, *ashram* schools and *anganwadis* are the two best institutions in tribal area. How do they function is a different matter. But concept-wise these institutions are good.

We have seen in hilly Dhadgaon area of Nandurbar district of Maharashtra in the 1970s, a child going to a grocer, asking for sugar for 25 paisa. He has no bag or any container and cannot take it on his palm. So the grocer took out a piece of old newspaper which was under the gunny bag and gave sugar to the child on it. That is probably the only printed word that the child had seen in his life. That is the reality we knew. That child could study only in *ashram* schools.

Which tribal ethnic group among the tribal belt are the school teachers taking the benefit of reservation? In Maharashtra, they could be predominantly—Mahadeo Koli, Kokna or Raj Gond ST, not the Warli, Thakar, Dhor Koli or PVTG Katkari, Kolam or Muria.

In the area of education, particularly tribal education, there is much to contribute. A good institution like *Ashram School* in tribal belts is coming under red line since it is not managed properly by TDD. Since it is called a school, Education Department wants to take it under its umbrella, as primary health centres are under the Health Department. According to Education Department, *ashram* school is an expensive institution, since it is compared with conventional schools. What is the basic concept of *ashram* school as per recommendation of Wandrekar Committee? It was expected to be a centre for personality development and a nodal agency for tribal development. *Ashram* schools were supposed to have land around it for giving the students training in agriculture. If it has not happened, it is not the fault of the concept of *ashram* schools, but issues of implementation of policy.

Unfortunately, we do not have a national tribal policy approved by the parliament as yet, and that should be one of our agenda to make a draft policy. We anthropologists are also responsible for it. It happens that anthropology continues to be the only discipline dealing with tribal issues. Strength of anthropology lies in qualitative process analysis at the micro level, which makes it viable and relevant for bottom-up policy planning and implementation.

Constitution of India using the principle of Equity has bestowed special provisions for the upliftment of the tribal communities and geographical territories of their habitation, by using the terms Scheduled Tribes and Scheduled Areas respectively. The Governors of the States have been given special powers to protect and promote the interests of the Scheduled Tribes, overriding the legislative and executive powers of the State Governments, when necessary. 73rd Amendment to the Constitution has further enhanced the autonomous authority and functions of tribal hamlets and villages. Forest rights of the tribal communities have also been accorded statutory regulation.

To provide support to the Governments by way of studies to collect, collate and analyze data sets, to train the administrative personnel and those in the voluntary and people's sectors and to evaluate the schemes and programmes of development, as also to preserve the cultural identity of tribal culture by way of museums, Tribal Research and Training Institute was established in Maharashtra at Pune on 1 May, 1962.

To facilitate the objective functioning of TRTI, it has been decided to give it an autonomous status as an Association/Society under the Societies Registration Act and Bombay Public Trust Act.

To take a brief resume of tribal development in India:

- In bi-lingual Bombay State during British Regime, there were two important reports dealing with tribal issues: (1) Starte Committee (1930), and (2) Symington Committee (1938).
- Leaders, like Godavari Parulekar, organized Warli against the *Zamindars* (landlords). Sarvoday leaders, like B.G. Kher, Acharya Bhise, tried to organize the constructive work by forming forest labourer co-operative societies and starting the schools for the tribal children.
- Wandrekar Committee made recommendations about *Ashram Schools*.
- Tribal Development Department became a distinct department around 1975 with the creation of a joint post of Secretary-*cum*-Commissioner.
- The Constituent Assembly debates clearly bring out the resolve to apply the principle of equity to bridge the time gap between the so-called tribal communities and caste peasantry mainstream. Obviously, the affirmative action by way of reservation policy, scheduled area, special powers to the Governors, and later calling out separate Sub-Plans for Tribal Development, have been instituted and administered.
- The TRTI had to play the role as knowledge partner of the tribal development administration and assist the planning process. However, Article 342 of the Constitution which has mentioned a tribal group or a part thereof to be given the status as deemed to be Scheduled Tribe has created problems of pseudo tribalism. Several non-tribals taking the advantage of similarity in nomenclature claimed and continue to claim the ST status.
- Gradually, the TRTI's function got diverted as in appellate authority to adjudicate these claims which were widely used to get the benefits of professional education in medical and engineering and to get the benefit of reservations in the jobs in the public sector.

- Due to absence of clearly defined meaning of the term 'tribe' in anthropological literature, some operational criteria were devised by a Government Committee. Many pseudo tribal claims are challenged in the court of law which is disputed by the lawyers with little knowledge of the culture of the people including that of the judiciary in this regard.
- The pseudo tribals claiming the benefit of genuine tribals are estimated to range about 50-60 per cent, many of them outside the scheduled area, after the withdrawal of area restriction. The population of some ST groups has grown more than 100 per cent according to decennial census.
- The tribal people who have been basically the collectors of food from the forest got deprived and exploited due to regulatory forest legislation and administration during British Regime. It is recently that the Forest Rights Act in favour of tribals about the minor forest produce is being recognized. Mendha Lekha village is probably the first tribal village in the country getting the community forest rights due to personal intervention from the Minister of Environment and Forest, Government of India.
- For those tribals whose agricultural produce does not last beyond three or four months and for the landless, education is the only panacea of all ills. *Ashram* School, therefore, becomes a very important institution in tribal development. The tribal districts and blocks continue to be at the lowest rungs of the human development index. Proper analysis and planning is required in this direction.

Community-Driven Development in Tribal India: Prospects and Problems

It is presumed that the tribal development efforts in India are not addressing themselves to the concerns and problems of tribal people. While large amounts of budgets are being sanctioned and utilized, whose development are they aiming at, if not of the tribal people? Tribals are designated as backward signifying that they lack the capacity to utilize the schemes and infrastructure of development. The peasantry in India particularly the high caste land owning peasantry can grab the fruits of development and lobby for more benefits.

What are the mechanisms of tribal development and how has it evolved historically? Anthropologists are considered to be the 'natural academic and research guardians to tribal studies', in the absence of other disciplines owning different aspects of tribal studies.

The tribals who got isolated in different and inaccessible geographical terrains remained in relative time freeze. They attracted the scholars who studied them for various applied and theoretical reasons, who later became pioneer anthropologists. Anthropological theories of culture, cultural relativism, integration of culture, based on studies of static and equilibrium oriented tribal communities have been found useful, although not adequate to study dynamics and change. Major contribution of anthropology has been in the area of methodology of 'going native' for the simple folk, trying to minimize the gap between 'we' and 'they,' between the investigator and the subjects of study. The methods now commonly labelled as qualitative methods have tried to understand the people's perspectives through their own eyes. The participatory approaches have directly developed from the techniques of participant observation.

The concepts of democracy, civil society, welfare state enjoined upon the State to take the responsibility to identify and develop the backward classes and bring them on par with the citizens in the mainstream society. In India, the constitutional provisions in regard to Scheduled Tribes and Scheduled Castes are the steps in that direction. During the struggles for political freedom and social reform movements, tribals attracted the special attention of the leaders and bureaucracy. The various committees appointed during British period and in Independent India about the development of tribal people and tribal areas have formed the tribal policies and administration of tribal pockets. The tribal sub-plan and Integrated Tribal Development Projects have been a big, though unsuccessful effort towards tribal development. Mahatma Gandhi had a constructive programme for tribal development which attracted Elvin to write monographs on tribes and be an architect of government's tribal development policy. Nehru had a special feeling for tribals and his '*panchsheel*' of tribal development focusing on tribal development according to their genius is oft quoted.

What has been the effect of budgetary provisions, distinct autonomous administration on the development of tribal people? Majority of them, up to 90-95 per cent continue to be under BPL, malnutrition deaths of children are on the rise, migration for survival is increasing, lands are getting alienated. Against Nehru's advice of single window administration and reducing multiplicity of schemes of development, there are literally more than 300 schemes under tribal development. More than 80 per cent of tribal people do not know anything about these schemes except the school and those who know cannot take the benefit since the help to do paper work for the proposal is not available.

Seventy third Amendment to the Constitution has given more powers to tribal *gram sabha*. But a close look at the concept of revenue village, group gram panchayat and the reality of hamlet as the locality of action nullifies the functioning of *gram sabha*. No financial powers have developed to the Panchayati Raj Institutions except some powers at the district level. Recently, in Maharashtra, 5 per cent of TSP funds are being placed at the disposal of *gram sabha* with the resolution to raise it 10 per cent. It is the business of anthropologists to assess as to what is happening on the ground about the implementation and impact of this provision.

What role do the NGOs play? They really are non-government organizations implementing the government's welfare functions in a given area, with government grants. Due to constraints of funding, they largely follow the agenda of funding agencies. NGOs are also outside agencies, they have visiting relations with community. Personnel in the government change due to transfers; at the NGO, there is frequent turn over due to funding problems who are unable to ensure promotional channels or job security to the workers. The CBOs such as *mahila mandals* or SHGs and youth groups are now being formed performing some voluntary activities.

Abraham Lincoln's definition of democracy as 'by the people, of the people, for the people' is followed by representative political democracy as 'for the people' only in their manifestos. The divide of 'We' and 'They' continue while some of 'They' are co-opted as 'We'. The anthropological field research approach of bridging the gap between 'We' and 'They' translated into participatory approaches provides clues to community-driven development.

Tribal people are used to self-government. Although they were not development oriented but continued with subsistence and coping mechanisms, they have the mechanisms of self-help. Due to lack of property concept and other reasons, there are not too many hierarchies or gender problems. It is possible to orient hamlet level women and men facilitators to take up development skills and roles. The local herbalist has to be co-opted in the health care delivery and use his indigenous knowledge of herbal medicine. More revenue villages as gram panchayats, instead of group gram panchayats, have to be formed in tribal areas. As a general policy, there should be a separate gram panchayat for each revenue village. There need not be any group *gram Panchayat* in the scheduled area. The policy of an administrative or development unit, such as a school, a health centre being located, per unit of population or geographical area in square kilometres is defective. Distance in kilometres is not the proper unit of measurement, the time required to travel the distance on foot in the tribal terrain has to be the criteria for locating institutions.

Instead of bemoaning that the tribals do not take advantage of development infrastructure or institutions, the question need to be asked as to why should they use these institutions? How does it help them according to their perspectives and needs?

Anthropologists are best suited to find answers to these questions.

The issues of displacement have cropped up in a big way due to Special Economic Zones (SEZ). The displacement of people due to construction of dams, defence projects etc. are genuine concerns. They never get properly rehabilitated since the concerns of the people are never understood by the techno-centric administration who believe shelling out money as rehabilitation and the money disappears quicker than water vapour. The bane of political democracy is that every issue is politicised for election, including war, famine, flood and terrorist activities.

Millennium Development Goals cannot be reached without addressing the issues of deprivation which are expressed through social group disparities; regional disparities, gender disparities and rural-urban disparities. We do talk of equity and inclusive growth, or economic growth with social justice, but with our experience of fieldwork in tribal and rural communities, how do we analyse the micro situation, using the strength of anthropology?

It needs to be assessed as to what were the goals of community development for rural and tribal transformation as outlined by Shri S.K. Dey, ICS, as India's first Cabinet Minister for Cooperation and *Panchayati Raj* who spearheaded Community Development:

> "The motto of the Community Projects is 'Destination Man'. The Project will succeed to the extent that it can approach this objective. It will fail to the extent that it leaves 'Man' behind and attempts to push things along to the fore." (1955: 100)

Anthropology as the 'Holistic Science of Man' has theoretical and methodological strengths to contribute to 'Destination Man' as per the spirit of the Constitution of India.

6

Medical Anthropology

Medical Anthropology (Initiation)

We had one course (out of ten) on Applied Anthropology at the Master's curriculum in Anthropology at Sagar University (1957-59) designed by Prof. S.C. Dube. It included applications from biological as well as cultural aspects, the reference book being '*Anthropology Today*' (1953) (ed) by A.L. Kroebar. The oft quoted example of applied anthropology in the text books was about 'Golden Stool' in the country now known as Ghana. Anthropometry was widely used for 'Growth and Development' studies at a later date. Examples about health came from William Caudill's paper 'Applied Anthropology in Medicine' in 'Anthropology Today' (1953), Spicer (ed) 'Human Problems in Technological change' (1952), Benjamin D. Paul (ed) 'Health, Culture and Community' (1955) and Margaret Mead (ed) 'Cultural Patterns and Technical Change' (1955).

At Pune University, a distinct Master's course in Anthropology was started in 1963 with a paper on Applied Anthropology. Irawati Karve, Professor and Head of the University Department of Sociology and Anthropology, located at Deccan College Postgraduate and Research Institute, commonly known by its earlier name, Deccan College, was invited in 1963 to deliver a lecture at the Armed Forces Medical College (AFMC), Pune to the Army Medical Corps (AMC) officers undergoing postgraduate course in Preventive and Social Medicine (Advanced Preventive Medicine). Besides being a well known anthropologist, she had kinship connection with the Defence forces, her brother, Rear-Admiral Karmarkar being the Chief of Western Naval Command at Bombay. She was not happy with the interaction, and directed me to deliver the lectures recommending my name accordingly to AFMC. Since 1963, I continued to deliver lectures for the next thirty years, the arrangement having been formalized by an order from the Defence Ministry.

The civilian B.J. Medical College, Pune had a competitive relationship with newly established AFMC. The Preventive and Social Medicine Department under the leadership of Prof. N.S. Deodhar also started inviting me to speak about social aspects of health and disease to the post-graduates, and formalized the arrangement with a government order from the State Government. Both the medical colleges were then affiliated to University of Poona. The State Government had also directed that the post of District Health Officer (DHO) could only be held by a doctor with a post-graduate Diploma (DPH) or M.D. in Preventive Medicine. As a result several serving Medical Officers of the Government as also junior faculty members in PSM Department joined the course to upscale their qualifications. I had the advantage of close interaction with them till they retired from service, going up the ladder of holding senior positions in the government.

When we designed and introduced the course on Medical Anthropology, we wanted the PSM faculty from BJMC to deliver lectures to the Anthropology students at the University. Realising the difficulty of PSM faculty to travel to University, without reimbursement of the travel cost, anthropology students went to BJMC every week on designated days. On a particular health/disease related topic, after the presentation by PSM faculty, we would immediately discuss the socio-cultural issues. The Ayurved faculty from the Ayurved college came to the University to deliver series of lectures to Medical Anthropology students. The course on Medical Anthropology was standardized through this process.

The International Anthropological Congress (IUAES) was held at Delhi in December 1978. Our request to organize post-Congress symposium on Medical Anthropology was accepted. This symposium attended by 50 anthropologists from Europe and North America and subsequent publication of a special number on this symposium in 'Social Science and Medicine' [Charles Leslie (ed.), 1980] provided credibility to Medical Anthropology at Pune University. The Symposium brought me in continuing personal contact with Prof. Charles Leslie, George Foster and Arthue Kleinman. The interaction with Prof. Pertti Pelto from University of Connecticut and his students led to several collaborations, since Prof. Pelto resided in Baroda (Vadodara) and later at Pune for considerable period.

This opportunity opened gates for further interaction in the areas of leprosy, public health, sexuality and sexual behaviour, and AYUSH. The anthropological inputs in these health and disease related issues have been presented under respective sections of this chapter.

Medical Anthropology

"The anthropologist differs from the doctor in studying the well more than the sick. The difference in outlook between psychologist and anthropologist arises primarily out of the fact that the psychologist has his eye upon the individual, the anthropologist upon the group and upon the individual as a member of a group." (Kluckhohn, Clyde: 1959: 225)

"We trace contemporary medical anthropology to four rather different sources, each of which developed in relative (but not absolute) isolation from the others: (1) the interest of physical anthropologists in topics such as evolution, adaptation, comparative anatomy, racial types, genetics, and serology; (2) the traditional ethnographic interest in primitive medicine, including witchcraft and magic; (3) the "culture and personality" movement of the late 1930s and 1940s, with collaboration between psychiatrists and anthropologist; and (4) the international public health movement after World War II." (Foster, George, & Anderson Barbara: 1978: 4)

Introduction

Medical Anthropology has emerged as the fasted growing sub-discipline of Anthropology joining together the biological, social-cultural and paleolithic, archaeological and linguistic branches of classical Anthropology, in relation to health.

Medical Anthropology was first introduced as a special course at University of Poona in 1974. That paved the way for organizing a largely attended international symposium on Medical Anthropology, following the International Anthropology Congress at New Delhi in December 1978. The proceedings of one session on Medical Pluralism were brought out as a special number of 'Social Science and Medicine' edited by Charles Leslie (Vol. 14 B-4, November, 1980).

'Society for Indian Medical Anthropology' (SIMA) which was established by Prof. H.K. Bhat and Prof. P.C. Joshi, having attended the Poona International Symposium in 1978, had its first Conference at Mysore on Medical Anthropology and Health Sciences in November 2007. Medical Anthropology in India is now actively taking initiatives in the health and disease research and control programmes relating to Mother and Child Health, Leprosy, Tuberculosis, HIV and AIDS, Malaria, Nutrition and Growth etc. Initiatives have been taken by anthropologists in the areas of Human Population Genetics and Human Biology and are now closely collaborating with molecular biologists and biotechnologists.

Significant contributions have been made in the area of Palaeo-pathology. The discipline of Psychiatry is borrowing freely from the anthropological theories about culture and personality.

Medical Anthropology with its holistic and cultural bias has taken policy initiatives in Indian systems of Medicine (AYUSH) and their role in public health. With the theory of cultural relativism at our command anthropologists are holding leadership positions in bio-ethics. The most recent initiative is coming in the area of palliative medicine.

Epidemiology, Psychiatry and Traditional Medicine are the natural allies of Medical Anthropology in Medical Sciences, due to theoretical formulations about Culture, Environment, Tradition, Personality etc. The Millennium Development Goals have brought back the focus on disadvantaged groups, more particularly the tribal communities which continue to be the preserve of anthropologists. Medical Anthropology in India in its comprehensive bio-cultural, bio-social, bio-psychic ramifications has a tremendous research and training potential to influence the policy planning in the areas of Health.

At one of the conferences of the Indian National Congress around 1930, it was decided to accept Ayurveda and other Indian systems of medicine as national health systems after Independence. We are aware that after Independence, modern medicine has operationally become the national health system. Officially plural systems of medicine exist in India by way of medical colleges, research institutes, pharmaceutical industries, and Government departments in all systems. The Indian Systems of Medicine and Homoeopathy are brought under the newly created Ministry of AYUSH. The plural systems of medicine are governed by such bodies as Central Council of Indian Medicine, Indian Council of Medical Research, Medical Council of India, Central Council of Research in Indian Medicine and the like. There are national and regional institutes for all systems of medicine, across the country. There are disease specific national institutes as per modern medicine. However, the budgetary provisions and the infrastructure of public health care delivery system clearly indicates bias in favour of modern medicine. Indian Systems of Medicine do not figure in primary health centres, attached to community development blocks, except in some states where the Ayurvedic Health Centres function as OPD clinics.

In States like Maharashtra, Ayurvedic doctors are appointed in PHCs usually in tribal areas, to perform all duties as their allopathic counterparts. There is a total mismatch between the postings of ayurvedic personnel and supply of ayurvedic drugs. In some States like Chhattisgarh, Madhya

Pradesh, Himachal Pradesh, the allopathic and the ayurvedic public health systems function as parallel systems without any worthwhile communication with each other. However, PHC model has sub-centres with paramedics as ANM while Ayurvedic Health Centres function only as OPD for treatment.

The prime subject of the study of Medical Anthropology, focusing on Ethno-medicine in terms of home and herbal remedies as also traditional healers with indigenous knowledge of herbs and healing, including TBA (*Dai*) are totally out of the public health care system.

The Nobel Laureate in Economics. Dr. Amartya Sen, has identified India's basic problems as deep seated poverty and severe inequalities in social and economic opportunities. Income, according to him, provides opportunities but the opportunities or capabilities also depend upon such factors as health which have to be considered while measuring welfare.

Health is no more considered as absence of illness, which is more of a therapeutic and biomedical concept. Health is now widely understood as a bio-cultural and psycho-social phenomena. Emphasis has now shifted to the understanding of the life styles of men after knowing the 'life styles of bacteria and viruses' which have capacity to mutate, since human life styles threaten to disrupt the harmony of the human body and the mind, particularly in regard to non-communicable diseases.

From Social Science perspectives, health refers to total biological, social and psychological fitness of an individual which ensures performance of socially prescribed roles to optimum efficiency. Health, therefore, encompasses all those socio-economic and political systems as also the scientific and technological systems which contribute or hinder human creativity and productivity.

In Ayuved, physical health is understood in terms of harmony of the three *Doshas* or *Dhatu*, namely the *Kapha,* the *Pitta* and the *Vayu*. In Unani, *Mizaj* refers to psycho-physical equilibrium which is commonly understood as psychic mood. Mental health is understood in terms of harmonies of different types of elements. Man's position and relationship with other living beings in the universe is based on concepts which are philosophical in nature. Health would be determined by the symbiotic relationship of man with environment.

The medical colleges and institutions belonging to various therapeutic systems address themselves to morbidity, to disease and illness. Training is imparted in the diagnosis and treatment of diseases to cure a person of his illness. Researches are carried out in improving the tools and techniques of diagnosis and treatment. Research outputs from modern natural sciences help these researches to develop new products and techniques. Researches in social sciences help to bring out the role of human institutions and culture in health, disease and illness, across the world. Concept of life style is a variant of the concept of culture which is being identified as an important causative 'organism' in the transmission of both non-communicable and communicable diseases. Research outputs from social and behavioural sciences are being used in managing individual and community issues in health care.

The emerging discipline of Health Science, therefore, calls for interdisciplinary and holistic approaches to understand issues concerning human health. Health Sciences to develop as a unified discipline thus need research outputs from various natural and social sciences. Human variation and human types and human evolution need to be studied from biological and socio-cultural angles to understand the implications for health and disease. Researches in all aspects of human genetics are, therefore, needed, more particularly to understand the genetic factors in preventive, promotive and curative factors in health and disease. So little is understood about the immune system of man which continue the bottlenecks in the control of chronic communicable diseases such as leprosy. New disease syndrome such as HIV and AIDS baffle the common man and scientists alike. Claims about understanding and solutions in plural therapeutic systems are researchable issues in health sciences.

Nutrition is another area in which there are varying rational, non-rational and irrational beliefs and practices across geographical areas. How much and what kind of food is required by humans in varying climatic zones for their physical and mental growth that would ensure their optimum productivity, and reduce morbidity and mortality? Bio-statisticians like Prof. P.V. Sukhatme spent their life time in addressing the issues of inter- and intra-individual variability in nutritional requirements of people.

These issues have significant implications for agricultural production, commerce and politics. People's perceptions and practices about nutrition and diet are based on the concepts in traditional medicine, while what is being advocated as prgrammes is based on modern science. This has opened new vistas in regard to validation of traditional health practices and perceptions, from the standpoint of modern science.

Malnutrition, under-nutrition, food security, draughts and famines are the commonly used key words in health, economics, commerce and politics. Poverty and welfare could be measured in terms of adequacy and quality of food available to people. Physical and mental growth or retardation is attributed to intake or denial or non-affordability of certain kinds of foods and nutrients. As Amartya Sen has proved, it is not the production shortfalls that would necessarily lead to famine but the deficiencies and mismanagements of the distribution of food that could result in food shortages leading to famine. Thus, measurement of malnutrition and its impact on human growth continue to be researchable issues in health.

Prof. Sukhatme led a debate as to what impeded growth, recurring bouts of infection or malnutrition and undernutrition? Making it as a researchable area, he tested this hypotheses in eight villages. According to him, it is a problem of providing potable drinking water, personal hygiene and sanitation which were more responsible for bouts of infection, reducing the capacity of body to take food, rather than the opposite, pronounced in some Western studies. The programmes that have to follow such research in controlling morbidity are obvious.

In the process of evolution of production systems leading to surplus production of food, patriarchal systems developed giving prominence to male muscle power for protecting the surplus production. Kingship, markets and armies developed, reducing women to a secondary position. Wars needed males and marching armies always captured land, and molested women. What followed over centuries has led to what is now identified as gender inequality.

It is now common knowledge that the sex ratio in post-Independent India has been progressively getting adverse against women, that female foetuses continue to get destroyed in large numbers. Family planning is not contemplated until the required sex composition of the family, that is, at least one son in the family is ensured. The two most change resistant phenomena in Indian social life relate to stagnant age at marriage of the girls and overriding urge for a male progeny. It, therefore, follows in biases in favour of males while providing nutrition, education and health care. All programmes about limiting the size of the family are directed towards women although men are the decision makers in matters relating to sex and size of the family.

Reproductive health of women has emerged as a priority research area. It is believed that many reproductive morbidities are not perceived as morbidities but are considered part of normal female physiology. As a result, no action is taken by women in regard to several discomforts which, however, affect their health and sex life and lead to problems such as sterility, resulting in desertion by the affinal family. Adolescent girls attaining puberty and becoming teen age mothers are totally ignorant of the reproductive physiology. They are vulnerable for exploitation by the wrongfully informed adolescent boys and deviant perception of masculinity, who get their knowledge from yellow books and blue films.

The Welfare State of India has created a vast public sector infrastructure of health care through primary health centres. There are vertical programmes for control of certain chronic, communicable diseases and programmes like family welfare. This calls for health administration, manpower training and logistics of manufacture of drugs and their unhindered supply. These problems are being addressed in WHO terminology as health services and health systems research. One of the key problems relate to lack of community participation in government programmes. A specialized branch of health education has developed to inform the people about the scientific aspects of health and disease, which in effect expects compliance to modern bio-medical programme of regularity of intake of drugs. Mahatma Gandhi has included health education as one of his 18 constructive programmes, and he talks more about behaviour in relation to health, hygiene and food, rather than about disease. One of the problems identified by social scientists relate to the government programmes addressing themselves to the annihilation of the bacilli, by techno-managerial management, in preference to addressing the programme to the concerns of the people. Health and disease management thus becomes a specialized subject in the hands of professional health managers while the ground realities of human living are taken for granted, not considered necessary for planning and implementation.

World Health Organisation (WHO) at its World Health Assembly represented by all member States of UNO, agreed in 1978 at *Alma Ata*, to ensure health for all people of the world by the year 2000. The Primary Health Care approach was propagated which emphasized inter-sectoral coordination among the various sectors of development to be able to ensure health to the people. This conceptually put more importance on the traditional non-health sectors such as agriculture, education, water and food, sanitation etc. for promoting health and preventing disease, in place of treatment with drugs.

History tells us that improvement of socio-economic conditions played an important role in eradicating communicable diseases from the West before effective medicines were invented. The primary health care approach has, therefore, put primacy on the holistic study of health involving the inputs from natural sciences, social and behavioural sciences, and plural medical sciences.

The so called industrial development which has led to rural to urban migration, has created considerable health problems. The pollution levels have increased by polluting the river waters and air. Noise pollution has emerged as a health issue. Forests have dwindled leading to soil erosion and degradation of river waters. Research in environmental pollution affecting health and issues of bio-diversity have gained international priorities.

Medical Anthropology translated in current popular expression as Health Sciences, thus offer opportunities for research which would have a direct bearing on improvement of health programmes. Interdisciplinary researches are needed for better understanding of the variables and their interplay to understand health from holistic perspectives.

Social-Behavioural Health Research

Social-Behavioural research in Health has been initiated by health scientists in the historical perspective with the concept of welfare state developed after Second World War. Health care of the people was accepted as the responsibility of the state. Earlier the state responsibility was limited at the level of controlling epidemics. The terms, Public Health and Epidemiology gained currency and with *Alma Ata* declaration, made it an inter-disciplinary domain.

At WHO level, social science research got into focus after *Alma Ata* declaration, which emphasized non-health sector impacting health issues. Inter-sectoral co-ordination was emphasized which continues to be utopian strategy in the government sector. The functionalist integrative nature of culture discussed prominently in Anthropology goes well with intersectoral approaches. However, it does not get translated into doable strategies at the micro level.

In India, Family Planning became a major population control programme with mandatory participation by all government line/sector departments, under the umbrella of Community Development in rural India. KAP studies and IEC strategies became dominant themes.

Social Sciences conventionally never considered Health as its research agenda. At the international level, Medical Anthropology and Medical Sociology developed as sub-disciplines only in mid-seventies. In India, Medical Anthropology was introduced at Pune University in 1974. At the Armed Forces Medical College, Pune, social science inputs were introduced in 1963 at the D.Ph. and M.D. level in Preventive Social Medicine followed by B.J. Medical College. Social Science was sought by Gandhi Memorial Leprosy Foundation in 1967 to facilitate health education with an objective of promoting voluntary reporting in leprosy and obtaining patient compliance (now adherence) in therapy.

At the WHO level, Social and Economic Research (SER) position was created in TDR around 1980 with one of the first assignment to write a working paper about 'Social and Economic Aspects of Leprosy' given to me. That was the focal working paper to discuss the issues at an international joint meeting of the social scientists and leprologists and programme managers at Kuala Lumpur in 1981 and in subsequent meetings.

The ICSSR-ICMR joint panel on Health was constituted while Dr. Paintal was DG. ICMR and Prof. T.N. Madan was Member-Secretary of ICSSR. The joint work of ICMR-ICSSR between Prof. Ramalingswami from ICMR and Shri J.P. Naik from ICSSR with significant commitment and inputs from Dr. N.H. Antia from FRCH brought out a document of 'Alternative Strategy about Health for All' suitable to India. This document greatly influenced the National Health Policy of 1983. Almost all the members of this group who discussed the issues were drawn from the public health field.

Public health thus came into focus in preference to disease control programmes. However, it has to be noted that para-medical personnel have been visiting the homes of people and not the doctors of Primary Health Centres, for health care and disease control programmes. The MPW, PMW, NMS, ANM, CHV/ASHA, AWW workers who are women workers continue to do the work in the communities. In tribal areas, the local herbalist and *Dai* continue to be the first line of health care. Neither basic nor operational research has documented the contribution of paramedics in health care or their training.

Sociologists contributed more about the studies of hospital systems. Plethora of slum studies done by sociologists have not highlighted health issues in a comprehensive manner. Anthropologists have given ethnographic accounts regarding health while discussing food, rituals, herbalists or medicine men and child rearing practices. A special branch labelled as Ethnomedicine developed with considerable publications in anthropological journals about the herbs and herbalists including magico-religious practices for cure.

Policy research from the social-behavioural perspective is the need of the hour. The issues of embarking vertical programmes and abandoning them after few years, emphasis on RCH/MCH, geriatric care, anaemia amongst women are some of the important policy issues. Gender research focusing on women is the prime agenda, providing opportunities for anthropological research.

There are certain administrative issues concerning networking within ICMR and with other institutions undertaking allied research on social-behavioural issues. There are social scientists located in other divisions at the ICMR HQ at Delhi and in several national institutes of the ICMR. Recently 'Social Forum' has been initiated at the ICMR to facilitate research networking among the social scientists in ICMR institutes and the universities and other research institutions. AYUSH has become an independent Ministry with their national institutes for each system, such as Ayurved, Unani, Siddha, Yoga, Naturopathy and Homoeopathy. However, there are issues about drug focused therapy and drugless therapy as in nature-cure, propagated by Mahatma Gandhi. There are parallel public health infrastructure of AYUSH and modern medicine in some states along with PHC organization from block to district to state level. Research organizations, like Anthropological Survey of India, undertake both biological and social-behavioural research about the people of India focusing on tribal communities. Tribal Affairs Ministry also provide funds for research among the 9 per cent tribal people of India. ICMR's regional centres at Jabalpur and Bhubaneshwar are engaged in tribal health research.

The establishment of a distinct Social-Behavioural Research Division at the ICMR HQ deserves compliments for the vision of ICMR policy leaders. However, social-behavioural issues are embedded in all health and disease transmission and control issues which need to be addressed consciously by bringing the research personnel, as outlined above on a common platform for cross-disciplinary dialogue. The active functioning of the S-B division will make a qualitative difference in research directly linked to the communities and enhancing the scientific understanding and analysis of the epidemiological triangle.

Medical Anthropology: A Sub-discipline

One of the short-cut method to understand the scope of Anthropology is to reflect upon the first encyclopaedic inventory, prepared under the Chairmanship of A.L. Kroebar, published in 1953 under the title 'Anthropology Today', quickly followed by a supplement 'Current Anthropology' published in 1955. Out of the 50 research articles in 'Anthropology Today', 21 are about the classical, conventional anthropology, 5 about research methods, 14 about theory and 10 under the section of 'Problems of Application'. Under Application, there is one with the title, 'Applied Anthropology in Medicine' by William Caudill. In a lengthy 30 page review article, about 7 pages are given to review of 'Primitive Medicine in Non-literate Societies'. Paper starts with the curiosity about social anthropologists, in recent times, participating in meetings and conferences with physicians, about social medicine, mental health, public health and about teaching in medical schools. While eyebrows are raised about anthropology interacting with the overcrowded medical curriculum, comments are made about, "Medicine today is itself in a state of flux: old definitions of disease and health are being called into question, there are many competing concepts of comprehensive medicine, environmental medicine, social medicine, psychosomatic medicine, preventive medicine etc.; and fields of medicine have become so specialized that it is only with difficulty that they can achieve integration even in a hospital....If anthropologists and physicians are successfully to achieve a much-to-be-desired collaboration, both groups need to be aware of the many hidden pitfalls in interdisciplinary research." (Caudill: 1953: 799). There are separate chapters about 'Applied Anthropometry' and 'Growth and Constitution'. Out of 10 chapters on applications, 4 are given to 'Applied Anthropology in Governments'.

As mentioned repeatedly, anthropological, ethnographic monographs have not discussed using the term 'Health' since tribal people rarely discuss the positive connotation of health as is dicussed in Ayurved or such other medical systems. They follow the cultural patterns of behaviour in respect of life cycle, rituals, festivals and ceremonies. Basically, with symbiotic relationship with environment, following the principle of 'primitive communism—each according to need' and not given to accumulation of surpluses, collected from nature, there is no conscious discussion about health. In case of discomfort or disease, combination of ritualistic and herbal medicine is given, if necessary, by harnessing the services of local herbalist-*cum*-priest and medicine man. In monographs, we find the descriptions about food as offered on ritual occasions, child rearing practices, about herbalist-medicine man or priest-medicine man, *dai* and all these put together by the term, ethnomedicine.

Medical anthropology as a term seems to have emanated in relation to health issues in their relationship with culture, lifestyle, concepts of nutrition and healthy diet, disease etc. in non-tribal communities in the West. In ancient civilizations, such as India and China, there is also textual material on health and disease. The development of human genetics in its relationship with health and disease developed the concepts of bio-cultural paradigm of health. With the development of the concept of welfare state, particularly after Second World War, with UN organizations such as WHO, UNICEF, FAO, and health being recognized as a human right, Medical Anthropology and Medical Sociology developed as sub-disciplines to become the academic sub-specialities.

Right to Health makes it obligatory for the States to design the policies and programmes that would make health care accessible to one and all. We are expected to make people-centric policies and implement them as to reach out to them. So, we measure 'how much' poverty, 'how much' health care delivery and 'how much' population. Today's world is the world of measurement—measurement of happiness, wellness, health and development, consumption of modern technology and the like.

We try to make quantitative assessment of how much we are reaching Millennium Development Goals, where are we according to Human Development Indicators, about infant and maternal mortality, about fertility and about patterns of migration and the impact of all of these on quality of life.

We express happiness about economic growth, despite economic recession and the upward march as fastest growing economy of India. We aim at yearly targets of economic growth, not of reducing infant mortality.

Economists are preoccupied with measurement of poverty and poverty line, and politicians proclaim to reduce it in election manifestos. Health care is measured in terms of infrastructure of health care delivery, expenditure on drugs, and personnel employed for the purpose. Mostly, it is related to disease control measures with drug therapy. Special relief packages are floated to ensure food security to the poor by way of providing subsidized food in Public Distribution System to ensure consumption of required calories. Our studies about the purchasing capacity of poor people as to how much food is lifted from these shops in a week or a month is not a very charitable exercise. How do we assess consumption of food, and what kind of food, including the junk food, by whom, with what effect?

Our intervention project in 7 tribal districts in Maharashtra whereby we provided one square meal to pregnant women, vastly improved early registration with the Auxiliary Nurse Midwife as also the birth weight of babies. On the other hand, childhood obesity among the urban rich has become a public health research issue, due to consumption of junk food and TV/mobile phone addiction.

Even amongst the poor, there are wide disparities among ethnic groups, among the farm holders and farmless labour. There is migration for survival, and mobility and seasonal migration for adding income to meet the aspirations of possessing consumable durables like TV, mobile phones etc. As we know, the chronically poor do not commit suicides, it is the transient poor who are unsuccessful in using technology for dream production, promised by product marketing, who commit suicide, and we have witnessed significant number of farmers' suicides during the last five years or so.

For poor people, illness is an additional factor of already existing disorganized life. It does not warrant special attention to the people who are afflicted by psychology of defeat and frustration. Those whose lives are organized, who have set goals about the development of the family and children are the one who take prompt action if illness threatens disorganization.

Motivation for action in health care or illness care differs widely in different situations. While early signs and symptoms of leprosy among women in strong patriarchal societies may be ignored, an adolescent girl of marriageable age may invite prompt action. An unmarried daughter in the culture of universal marriage would invite shame to the family and if it is on account of leprosy, would stigmatize the family and kin-group.

Interestingly, leprosy programme inadvertantly continues to perpetuate stigma by stamping the life time 'patient' status to the leprosy afflicted who have completed treatment by referring to him as 'cured leprosy patient', or 'ex-leprosy patient' even in leprosy institutions and control programme.

HIV problem is scaring to the parents of young persons in rural areas, who work in metropolitan cities, with cash in their pockets, no proper living space and anonymity. The scientific community and media by writing HIV slash AIDS (HIV/AIDS) give a message that HIV and AIDS are synonyms while the counsellors try to wean the fears of HIV^{+ve}, that with a proper life style and prompt symptomatic treatment, AIDS could be postponed indefinitely. There are no takers for this advice if HIV and AIDS are projected as synonyms.

Actually the concepts of immunity in different systems of medicine have different connotations while for the lay people, it is also linked with moral issues. Disease in a way is a moral, spiritual deviation which attract the evil spirit or bacteria or virus.

Why all the CSW's not HIV^{+ve} although all of them for their sheer survival may require multiple partners?

Our strategy for community participation is to educate the people, in the name of modern science, about the causation and cure of a disease. Our health educational material is meant to scare the people so that they would come to us and comply with what we tell them. Say, in leprosy health education, information of what is not leprosy is more rewarding in suspecting and voluntary reporting, than in telling, that all patches should be suspected unless otherwise ruled out—what we mean is differential diagnosis. The current message to go to health centre and do what you are asked to do, is the surest way for the leprosy suspects to go underground or consult a quake. So our health education programme is a social marketing programme to bring them to the providers.

The methodological issues in micro-macro studies and quantitative-qualitative methods are very significant for scientific validity and reliability of community based research. International Institute of Population Sciences, Mumbai several years ago were advised by President, General Council, who is Minister of Health and Family Welfare, Government of India, to replicate the model of low fertility in Goa, to the rest of India, as a solution to population control. IIPS had reported that the fertility in Goa was the lowest in India. However, they could not give the reasons for lowest fertility in Goa. The then Director had a meeting with us, to launch anthropological studies to find out the reasons for low fertility. We selected some villages in 'old conquest' and 'new conquest' areas of Goa for micro level studies. Goa was a Portuguese Colony, until it was annexed to India in 1961. The civil and property laws of Portugues-ruled Goa, and registration of births, were responsible for advanced age at marriage of girls. There has been considerable recruitment to Church clergy from Goa, and migration for employment elsewhere, which seemed to be making an impact on fertility. Obviously, the Portugese Goa model was not replicable to India, which was earlier ruled under British Presidencies and by the Princes. Kerala has a different picture about sex composition than the Hindi belt, especially Haryana. Sex ratio has become adverse in rural rich district like Kolhapur in Maharashtra.

We find in tribal areas, maternal mortality is low while infant mortality, more so, neonatal mortality is very high. In areas where obstetric services and referral services are absent or are poor, low birth weight babies or small babies could be preferred for easy delivery. Tribal pregnant women would eat less during pregnancy, for a small foetus for easy labour. In communities where bride price has to be paid in marriage, losing a wife would be a calamity, since to procure new bride would cost substantially. In a community where a girl brings dowry in marriage, there could be more domestic violence, female foeticide, and less value for a young daughter-in-law. In India, there is great difference in the status of women in different regions and the age at marriage variation is significant which cannot be accessed through quantitative methods. In tribal areas, with the custom of bride price and total absence of female molestation by tribal men, the sex ratio is commendable as compared to non-tribal sex ratio in India. In South India, where cross-cousin marriages could be preferred, it would have a different scenario as compared to North India where such a marriage would be considered incest.

In Ballabhgarh region as field station under AIIMS Delhi, we interviewed village women about diarrhoea to comprehend that their classification was according to the colour and consistency of fecal material and the perceived causes and home treatment were different in each case.

Recently in our studies about Indian Systems of Medicine in Himachal Pradesh, Madhya Pradesh, Chhattisgarh and Maharashtra, we found all the village women practicing herbal treatment in their homes for common ailments as the first line of defence. An elderly ANM in H.P. pronounced her kitchen as the home dispensary, since kitchen condiments were of medicinal value according to the great traditions in Ayurved or Unani or Siddha system of medicine. We covered all households in selected villages as per anthropological method, whereby, we may select a village as per sampling method, but the universe is covered in the village.

In an assessment of latrine programme in 8 villages, initiated by late Prof. P.V. Sukhatme, former Director of Statistics, FAO, as a project from the Department of Science and Technology, we found the elderly improved the quality of life and as villagers said "added age to their lives" since the presence of latrines in the backyard of the house liberated them to enjoy their dinner, which they avoided for danger of visiting the defecation sites in the field at night. They were afraid of falls and fractures resulting in displeasure expressed loudly by the daughter-in-law.

All these studies could give us the causes about diseases in relation to health, as people perceived them, through our qualitative research methods and tools and techniques of observation, informal interview, group discussion and even genealogical method.

There are issues of theory, methodology and ethics in all studies. The mix of micro-macro, quantitative-qualitative have to be networked for valid results. The best ethical principle would be to give patient listening to people in order to learn about their concerns, and target the programmes to their concerns, by abolishing the terminology of providers—beneficiary and compliance.

In health sector it is necessary to use the services of herbalist medicine-man and *dai* for providing the services to the people in rural and tribal areas. Their knowledge and skills could be updated for better result. These recommendations have evolved from the ethnographic knowledge of tribal culture from fieldwork experience in anthropology.

To quote from my editorial about 'Social Responsibility of Social Scientists' in the journal, '*Social Science and Medicine*':

> "The Alma Ata declaration on Primary Health Care proved a turning point in the interaction between social scientists and health professionals. The emphasis on intersectoral coordination and the development of non-health sectors for their impact on health sector, as also the emphasis on community participation, self-help, traditional medicine and appropriate technology, all provided an independent role for social scientists. However, the initiatives continued to come from the health professionals, with positions for social scientists being created in medical colleges and health institutions. Social scientists continue to collect baseline information, to become involved in training and to undertake evaluation research in developing models of health development programmes." (Mutatkar, 1994: 755-56)

Medical Anthropology thus offers opportunities for research which would have a direct bearing on improvement of health programmes. Interdisciplinary researches are needed for better understanding of the variables and their interplay, to understand health from holistic perspectives.

Anthropological perspectives, therefore, cannot be limited to the cultural eye of the native subjects but has to be extended to their responses, and understand those responses from Malinowskian functionalism of need satisfaction. Health care delivery packages are discussed in Geneva and transmitted to New Delhi to State capitals to District and Taluka headquarters. Who among the delivery system, who are called providers, and the so called beneficiaries understand these packages, with what expectations?

Family planning targeted programme is supposed to bring down the population of the country. National Malaria Eradication Programme was supposed to wipe out malaria. As a result we know more about the life style of mosquito, its biting habits, biting times, flight heights and speed of travel and what not. The malaria workers had to be rehabilitated as multi-purpose workers in the PHC set-up, after the programme was abandoned. Leprosy control programme is supposed to bring down prevalence which hypothetically should result in decrease of incidence. Leprosy programme is also supposed to bring down deformity. *Anganwadi* is expected to bring down child malnutrition. Tuberculosis is supposed to bring down prevalence and incidence of TB. We seem to be struggling with problems of drug resistance and look forward to more potent drugs. HIV is struggling for vaccine and microbicides, but is content with counselling. HIV has provided immense bio-medical and socio-cultural potential for research due to HIV-TB co-infection. With plural systems of medicine in India, India has had two national policies about Health, National Health Policy and National ISMH (AYUSH) Policy, until they were integrated in 2017. A distinct Department of AYUSH has been established at Delhi. In some States, there are parallel systems of Health and AYUSH sector, the two remaining parallel except that AYUSH personnel have to participate in national health care and disease control programmes. In some States, AYUSH doctors are appointed in the Primary Health Centres, without AYUSH medicines, with the declared philosophy of integration, but in reality, when MBBS doctors are not available to work in rural or remote tribal areas.

This scenario of health care delivery or what we would prefer to call health care, is in the study domain of Anthropology. We have to apply our theory and research methods to understand the health-care systems in totality. Holistic approach is the strength of anthropology. We are advised to use health systems approach. Anthropologists were the first to talk about culture system. The only problem with anthropology is, we still have our mind set on studying primitive society in isolation. We have adopted primitive society as a methodological model and ethnography as the output. What is required is, we have to have peasant society as part society, as a model, using the concepts of Great Tradition-Little tradition interaction and focused ethnography as one of the important qualitative method of data collection and presentation, leading to qualitative analysis for policy recommendations. Anthropology is weighted in favour of equilibrium, due to pioneering studies of isolated communities, resulting in our inability to grasp the dynamics of change. We discuss change only in the context of disturbing stability and equilibrium, when new programmes for change are announced or implemented, to which we do not subscribe. However, the modification by way of adoption of soft, material aspects of culture, does not necessarily affect the basic human values, enshrined in the hard aspects of culture, and cannot be taken as an effective indicator of socio-cultural change.

Our young scholars continue to present a research proposal for studying leprosy colony as a leprosy village, while in reality leprosy village is an asylum to put the patients rejected by society at one place, as stray cattle are trapped in an enclosed compound. When Gandhiji was invited to open a leprosy asylum, he said, he would rather come to close it. Asylums in the past represented the failures of curative science and ignorance about infection and lack of compassion, manifesting helplessness due to untreatability of the affliction. When they were discharged from the colony, they developed their own settlements which could sustain in an urban area due to beggary and stigma, which prevented physical action against them by police or municipal personnel for fear of transmission. They are also voters. The study of leprosy settlements would not throw any new light or analysis, or would be of no use to anybody unless the case studies or life histories of inmates could document the process of onset of symptoms and signs of disease to the level of rejection. Now the recruitment to leprosy asylums is going down due to available domiciliary treatment, resulting in several institutional asylums functioning as hospitals for treating all disease conditions, besides leprosy.

What we are driving at is that the anthropological perspectives of health care have to go beyond cultural definitions of health and study of traditional healers, which could continue only as ethnomedicine, not as medical anthropology. The whole as propagated in anthropology has to become a wider circle to include health care delivery system and the interaction of people's perception of health and disease on one hand and the so called delivery systems, put in place by the governments. Now that health is being recognized as a right, it becomes a justiciable issue, which would put more pressure on the government to improve health care delivery system. Panchayati Raj Institutions have been established following the historical, cultural model of self-rule by elders which in the present context is expected to facilitate community participation. *Gram Sabha* is expected to receive more authority and funds for self-rule as per constitutional amendments.

It would be appropriate to understand anthropological perspectives in health care by studying some examples, which have been discussed as in respective sections of this chapter.

We often hear people exclaim, why do people behave the way they do? The policy planners and implementers while blaming the people for failures of programmes, exclaim, why don't people behave the way we advise them, in their own interest ? George Bernard Shaw in his play, 'Pygmalion' turned into a movie 'My Fair Lady' says in a lighter vein, through a character, 'why don't women behave like men'?

Behaviour is discussed more in the context of deviation than normality. An eminent psychiatrist, Dr. R.V. Shirvaikar, often said that psychiatrists were dealing with abnormal behaviour without knowing exactly, what was normal behaviour. He expected anthropologists to throw light on normal behaviour. The first Professor of Medical Anthropology in the world at Harvard University, Prof. Arthur Kleinman, has been a psychiatrist turned anthropologist, as also his pupil, Prof. Mitchell Weiss. Prof. Klienman developed an Explanatory model, now turned into Cultural Epidemiology, by Prof. Weiss.

Human behaviour is considered to be acquired behaviour, through the process of enculturation and socialization, as compared to the instinctive behaviour of other animal species. When we domesticate some animals, we train them for acquiring some communication commands from us and they acquire some directional, behavioural traits from us. However, they then become unfit to live with their peers in the wild or in the nature, if released from domestication. Human sexual behaviour has been one of the areas of inquiry for its variability, cultural branding and tolerance, and its association with some afflictions. Gay behaviour in the past, was not discussed publicly and was reported as deviant behaviour. Now, in some states in the world, gay marriages have been legalised. One of my Indian students in New York reported to me that he was making his living by professional counselling to the same sex partners, in case of their discord.

There are two models dealing with health and disease management, at the individual level or as a public health issue. In respect of communicable diseases, the agent, usually a bacillus, is targeted to be killed with a drug. In chronic, long lasting ailments, such as leprosy or TB drugs have to be consumed for a longer duration. It is argued that in respect of irregular treatment, what is commonly branded as non-compliance, or lack of adherence, the microbes become resistant to drugs. Health bureaucracy pivoting the techno-managerial disease control programmes blame people for irregular treatment. They expect the social scientists to educate the people advocating behavioural change in respect of regular treatment. The bio-medical hypothesis proposes that with decreasing prevalence, the load of infection and bacilli would go down, and thus the incidence would also go down, thus eliminating a disease as a public health problem.

As per the epidemiological triad, the relationship between agent, host (Man), and environment decides the spread and control of diseases as a public health issue. As we see, the programmers focus on the agent with the total neglect of host. When I remarked to the Director of Vector Research Centre, Puducherry, that they knew more about the life style of mosquito, in terms of its flight limits, horizontally or vertically and the biting hours and their implications, in terms of getting different types of infection, as compared to their knowledge about the life style of man, he responded in a lighter vein, that 'the mosquitos knew the life style of man. The mosquito followed the man and they followed the mosquito'.

In respect of non-communicable afflictions, for which the public health programmes had no palliative drugs to offer, they profess people to amend their life style. As a result, wellness industry has developed. Yoga has acquired international accreditation. However, the Western model of targeting an individual employee is followed with a view to enhance his productive efficiency at the work station. In Indian society, a person lives in a family guided and supported by kinship solidarity. Behaviour is not an individual phenomenon, but a close kin-group phenomena. So, any programme about informing the people about the traditional or modern knowledge about health and disease need to be directed to the family and the peer groups.

S. Leonard Syme in his Foreword to a book, '*Epidemiology and Culture*' by his pupil, James A. Trostle, 2005 (Cambridge University Press), has said that when 20 years ago, "Trostle pointed out in the class, that Culture was important in the discussion about Epidemiology, he thought that the paths of his understanding of Social Epidemiology and that of an anthropologist about Culture were different. However, Syme confessed that now he thought that Trostle was right. We have planned several intervention projects. We thought, people would listen to our advice, rush back home and change their behaviour for their benefit. But our intervention programmes after intervention programmes have failed. We now understand that people have lives to lead everyday. We have to understand their concerns and priorities in life."

Among the poor people, whose concerns are food security and a roof cover, whose daily lives are disorganised and crisis driven, health disorganisation is another one to be added to their woes. And when they seek medical intervention, in order to be able to attend the work place for earning their wages, as early as possible, they are misguided and exploited by the greedy medical profession.

How do we explain the medical termination of pregnancies only in respect of female foetuses? We had an occasion to study the correlation of extensive use of sonography, during pregnancy and the decreasing sex ratio in peasant-rich Kolhapur district in Maharashtra, comparable to that in Haryana, on behalf of UNFPA. The District Magistrate and the Civil Surgeon tried some new instrument to be attached to a sonography machine, termed as 'Silent Observer' whereby sonographies could be stored, to view them at a later date, verifying the termination of female foetuses, with the stored ones. Although the intentions were commendable, the technical intervention was not found feasible for replication at the state level, as a solution to the behavioural issues of female foeticide. When sonography technique was non-existent, female neonates were exterminated by throttling them or giving tobacco water from the smoking hubble-bubble, or using such other gory methods. In patriarchal societies, to be born as a female, is a curse, a disability. However, in tribal communities, which are also patriarchal societies, there is no rape of a woman by a tribal man, thus no female foeticide. There is a custom of bride price, instead of dowry as amongst the majority of non-tribal Indian communities. The cultural factors of behaviour evolved historically need to be analysed, before any change is planned, involving the community in the change process.

In India, we have seen the fate of our disease control programmes of Leprosy, TB, Malaria and such programmes like Family Planning, which cannot be certified as successful. We blame the people for not changing their behaviour to accept the programme as organised by us. We do not appreciate that there are plural systems of medicine. The Ayurved system dates back to textual treatise compiled more than 2000 years ago, which are being followed in professional schools even now, and the local interpretations are followed as local health traditions. People are aware about the medicinal qualities of food and observe restrictions when ill, or in such conditions as pregnancy and child birth. Certain foods are avoided during varying climatic seasons. In Unani medicine, behavioural temperament, *Mizaj*, is a medical term, which is a combination of physical and mental balance. In Ayurved, individuals are classified according to combination of physical and mental types, termed as *Prakriti*. Even, behavioural traits are associated with *Prakriti*, as also vulnerability to certain health disorders. Several studies have shown that common people have knowledge about several medicinal herbs which they use as the first defence in manging common ailments. Traditional herbalists and *Dais* have been providing first aid services in treating common ailments and in child birth and child rearing. People's health seeking behaviour, therefore, combines the use of plural systems of medicine, for different health and disease conditions as per the perceptions of the people, accessibility of traditional health care workers and faith about their capacity to cure. We have the recent example of acceptance of faith healing in respect of Mother Teresa, annointed as Saint by the Catholic Church.

The social scientists were approached by health care and disease management programmers to educate the community to accept the drug technology, based on laboratory science, mainly chemistry, for cure. Health education of the people, by way of transmitting knowledge about causation and cure of diseases, based on modern bio-medicine is desirable as an exercise of knowledge empowerment of the people. However, in practice, health education remained limited to informing the people about the capacity of modern health care facilities, and asking them to make use of them. We have seen some top health bureaucrates telling their staff to put fear in the minds of people, so that they would comply with the programme schedule properly. But, we have also experienced that the fear of affliction particularly in respect of stigmatised diseases, such as, leprosy, HIV and AIDS, lead people to hide or conceal the early signs and symptoms, resulting in the progression of the conditions when it becomes too late for cure. The role of social scientist was thus carved out to be the social marketing agent of health bureaucracy. The term, health education was replaced by another term, 'Information, Education and Communication'(IEC) without changing or modifying the process of implementation. In Leprosy programme, based on the 'Survey, Education and Treatment' (SET) model, the evaluation of 'E' undertaken for the ICMR by us in the states of Odisha and Andhra Pradesh, indicated the absence of 'E' in the implementation of the programme. The current term used for ensuring community involvement in health care and disease control programmes is referred as 'Behaviour Change Communication' (BCC). The strategy of community involvement in these programmes thus continue to bring people to accept what has been designed by health bureaucracy, without any dialogue with the people in planning the strategy. Communities have been taking care of their health through centuries with the combination of traditional knowledge, local healers and faith in supernatural benediction. People have been managing their lives within the limitations of resources of food and other basic conditions of life, with dignity. People have the traditional capacity to own their programmes of livelihood. If taken in confidence, they possess the capacity to incorporate the knowledge from plural systems of medicine to put it to judicious use. Asking the people to change their behaviour to facilitate the administrative delivery and management of health care and disease management programmes, amounts to mistrust inflicted on the traditional wisdom of the people. People are amenable to accept and implement new knowledge if they are taken into confidence, and provided with total information about an issue, not the select some, to ensure compliance to the programme.

Practicing Medical Anthropology: Research Agenda

- Plural systems of Medicine
- Body Image, Metabolism, Immunity
- Health Care System in India
- Disease Control Programmes
- Primary Health Care Approach, HFA, 1978
- Universal Health Coverage
- National Health Policy
- Ethnomedicine and AYUSH
- Leprosy: People's Concern and Biomedical Model
- Family Planning, RCH, MCH
- HIV-AIDS, Sexuality
- Health Education, IEC, Behavioural Change
- Culture and Life Style
- Medical Anthropology and Health Sciences

Anthropological Perspectives: Health Research and Policy

Medical research is intervention research; it is aimed at finding solution to the problem. Traditional social science research has nothing to do with the interventions or solutions. We associate interventions with the value judgements. In addition, medical sciences or health sciences are understood as technologies of which the social scientists are ignorant. Only the biological anthropologists can communicate with them using the same terminology, accepting the subordinate role, but such biological anthropologists have no effective communication with social anthropologists and other social scientists. Health has not figured in the earlier classical monographs of the anthropologists as an aspect of culture, although health related data was collected and presented under such headings as nutrition, diet, rituals, shaman etc.

Health scientists or managers had no use of social scientists until after Second World War, when the ideas of welfare state emerged and the independent democracies assumed responsibilities for providing health care to the people. The health problem could be identified by the health bureaucracy at the national and global level. A large army of doctors and paramedics was trained and recruited for running the vertical and horizontal national health programmes. Way back in 1956 or so, senior social anthropologists like N.K. Bose, M.N. Srinivas and S.C. Dube admitted in a meeting that in their academic disciplines, they had never given thought to solutions of problems. Economics has been the only discipline which has been discussing issues and problems and offer solutions to such gut issues like poverty. The situation has not materially changed since then in the University based Social Science disciplines.

It is only when the blueprint techno-centred health programmes did not show desired results that social scientist were approached. This also was the result of the extension approach proposed in community development started in India in 1952. The emphasis was on educating the people about the modern agricultural and health technologies. The resistance to acceptance of technology was labelled as superstition and backwardness, due to illiteracy which was sought to be changed through extension education. Community's culture and social fabric was branded as at fault. Social scientists were drafted to educate the community, to understand their behaviour, to redesign the progammes at operational level. So, the agenda was set by health programmers for social scientists. All this would be done in the health institutions like WHO or Health Ministries, discussing issues of communication, education, culture and motivation. In all this planning, indigenous systems of medicine did not figure, even now it does not figure in satisfactorily except paying lip service with a view to use AYUSH manpower for administering blue print models of health care. When we discuss social science and health, we discuss modern medicine and blue print models designed by global health experts, while anthropologists keep on documenting ethno-medicine, mainly from tribal communities.

In this scheme, the role of social scientists were limited to training, baseline surveys, evaluation and some operational niches which were identified by the health programmers. So we set out to find out why the community offered resistance or was slow in acceptance of modern scientific health technology which was actually advocated as beneficial to them.

The health and development programmes and schemes are designed to suit the supervisor who could control and monitor the programme from his chamber, with the help of records. As the labour-room table is to suit the obstretician and not the patient, according to some senior obstetricians, the programme is designed for supervision of inputs and statistically measurable outcomes, sometimes of dubious validity and reliability. I was told by top executive in Health Ministry, when I told him that they were paying lip sympathy to health education, and they had no adequate budgetary provision for it, that the impact of health education was not measurable. If we could show how to measure the qualitative data quantitatively, they could possibly go all out for it. Another health bureaucrat suggested to us "Don't do too much health education—we have no adequate supplies of drugs if people ask for it."

It also follows that the behavioural scientist must have the knowledge of technical issues in plural medical systems, in order to think independently of health personnel and to engage in effective dialogue with them. The epidemiology needs to be understood. It is a sad commentary that leprosy projects submitted to ICSSR continue to be the ethnographic studies of leprosy colonies as villages, which are on the way out. Happily leprosy has risen above the divine compassion and is now subjected to behavioural science domain.

We are aware that social sciences got better deal in health research with people oriented primary health care approach of *Alma-Ata* in 1978. Emphasis on inter-sectoral co-ordination, community participation, appropriate technology, indigenous systems of medicine, all go in for meaningful roles for social scientists. Those who talk of totality of culture, integration of culture, culture and personality, social system, structural functional approaches could not get a better opportunity for health research. There is much to do to build bridges between techno-managerial systems and primary health care approach, under the wider umbrella of behavioural and social sciences.

What role can social scientists play in medical research? It starts with a meaningful dialogue, both parties demystifying knowledge by giving up the jargon. If social scientists speak in common language, it is branded as common sense. If they write like Talcot Parsons, making it unintelligible, it becomes mystifying, but not usable.

There are genuine concerns of the health scientists which we can share even in blue print models. Let these niches be identified by health programmes, but better if identified by social scientists. It would be meaningful to critically work into blue print models and suggest alternative models with more share of responsibility for the community, going in for participatory approaches in action and research. Social sciences must go in for intervention research, even to get funding and get involved in social action as a facilitator, if not as an administrator. We have role in public health care where plural medical systems are operating. It would be desirable to have networking with the voluntary sector and the governments to understand the macro issues as they are applied in micro situations.

Extending the definition of holism, to include the use and impact of technology, macro level decisions and micro level implementation of programmes, as also the public administrative system, has to be understood to analyse the gaps in addressing people's concern. Techno-managerial paradigm of top-down planning and implementation has to be understood, identifying the limitations in meeting the goals.

Anthropological paradigm of holistic understanding of an issue focusing on people's concerns and perspectives, evolved through field experience, and becoming a hard core of culture pattern is useful for sustainability.

A. PUBLIC HEALTH CARE SYSTEM

"Constitutionally, the Indian state is committed to improving the state of public health of the population (Directive Principles, Section 47), and several Supreme Court judgments in India have established the Right to Health as an extension of the Fundamental Right to Life. The Government of India is signatory to various international conventions that obligate it to ensure the Right to Health." (Planning Commission of India, 2011: 50)

Background

All people hold some opinion about health and it correlates. However, there has been no uniform strategy about ensuring health of the people. In different regions, in various cultures and at differing periods of time, health care strategies have varied. Primary Health Care approach is being advocated as a magical key to health problems of the people.

In India, an 'appropriate' strategy has been presented by a study group jointly set up by the Indian Council of Social Science Research and the Indian Council of Medical Research. Comprehensive health projects linking health care with total rural development involving people's participation are already in operation in various regions of India. These projects are designed to develop models for primary health care.

In anthropology, health is discussed as an aspect of culture thereby conceding that health attitudes, beliefs and practices are built in the sustainable, traditional way of life of a group or community. It could be described the way people assign importance to food, metabolism, rest, exercise, and medical help at various levels from various persons. It also indicates the ideas about deviant behaviour which could upset the body and mind, that would lead to imbalance and affect functioning, as required as per our status, ascribed or achieved and the roles to be performed accordingly.

However, when more people got affected due to similar ailment which is branded as an epidemic, there was no individual oriented medical solution. There have been epidemics of plague, influenza, malaria, cholera etc. which led to mortality and morbidity at mass level. In tribal communities, temporary or permanent migrations or isolation outside the village have been commonly observed to ward of the evil spirit. Isolation of individuals or families have been recommended in case of epidemics such as plague in the late nineteenth and early twentieth century.

Plague in Pune which prompted an energetic plague officer Mr. Rand administering coercion to vacate their respective places of residence and shift out of town in camps became a political issue since Bal Gangadhar Tilak had to criticize such efforts which violoated the norms of treating women and desecrating the deities in the house. The plague officer was subsequently murdered and the two brothers who did that were hanged. There have been gossips that there was shortage of firewood and cow-dung cakes to cremate the bodies who died in influenza epidemic, at Pune in 1920s.

The stabilization of population till the Census of 1931 in India indicates balance of high fertility and high mortality. The discovery of anti-biotics starting with penniciline reduced mortality. The immunizations by way of vaccines further reduced or prevented mortality due to communicable diseases. This led to the growth in population since there was no mechanism to reduce fertility. Family Planning programme had to be launched. But due to targeted programmes which led to irregularities, it led to ouster of ruling political party which administered the programme, without adequately taking the people into confidence.

Health care was considered an individual or a family issue. If not manageable by home remedies, professional help was sought from the traditional herbalist or *Dai* who possessed indigenous knowledge about herbal therapies. There were hardly any institutionally trained *Vaidyas* or *Hakims* and those were only in urban centres for referrals by the ruralites.

Bhore Committee

After India gained political independence, health care was considered the responsibility of the State. Following the Bhore Committee report (1946), rural health care became a part of community development movement initiated in 1952. Every community development block has a primary health centre with a MBBS doctor and some sub-centres looked after by an auxiliary nurse-midwife (ANM). As per the 'three million plan', three million being the population of a districts, primary and secondary health centres were to be established with links with hospitals at district headquarters and wherever feasible, with a medical college also.

It, therefore, becomes pertinent to understand the philosophy and recommendations of the Bhore Committee as it is relevant for any discussion pertaining to health planning.

The Bhore Committee had gone into the details of administrative set-up required for these health centres such as staffing pattern, financial commitments and the like. While the health administration paid closer attention to organizational aspects, the ideology behind the working of primary health centres was lost sight of.

Basic philosophy underlying the recommendations of the Bhore Committee:

> "The ferment of ideas arising out of world has resulted in an increasing awareness, on the part of governments and peoples, of the need of measures which will ensure social security, and health protection is becoming recognized as an essential part of social security. The idea that the State should assume full responsibility for all measures, curative and preventive, which are necessary for safeguarding the health of the nation is developing as logical sequence." (1946:7)

> "Health is one of the goals of life to which man has a right. Wherever this concept prevails the logical sequence is to make all measures for the protection and restoration of health accessible to all, free of charge. Medicine like education is no longer a trade, it becomes a public function of the State." (1946: 10)

> "In our view preventive and curative health work should be dovetailed with each other in order to produce maxium results. It is with this idea that the organization for the primary health unit has been dsired."

To elaborate this aspect, the Committee has stated further:

> "We consider that a combination of curative and preventive health work is in the best interest of the community and of the professional efficiency of medical staff employed. In fact the two branches cannot be separated without detriment to the health of the community. For instance, our primary health centre doctor treating a typhoid patient in his house, should, in addition to the medical attention he gives him, ensure that such precautions are taken as are necessary to prevent the spread of the infection to the other members of the household. Nor should his responsibility end there. In the interest of the community it is necessary that the source of infection should, if possible, be discovered in order to prevent the further spread of the disease." (1946: 40).

Finally, the committee refers to the statement of Prof. H.E. Sigerist on the physician of tomorrow:

> "Scientist and social worker, ready to cooperate in team work, in close touch with the people he disinterestedly serves, a friend and leader, he directs all the efforts towards the prevention of disease, and becomes a therapist when prevention is broken down, the social physician protecting the people, and guiding them to a healthier life." (1946:18).

The role of primary health centre has been summarized aptly by a public health philosopher:

> "We associate courthouse with justice, a school with education, a temple or church with religion, medicine has no symbol."
>
> "Let our primary health centres be symbols of health, where people should go to seek advice to remain healthy and when necessary to get cured for any ailment."

The Bhore Committee has raised very crucial issues with regard to health care and role of primary health centres.

The Bhore committee has identified health problem with wastage of human material and lowering of human efficiency through malnutrition and preventable morbidity.

The comprehensive and totalistic view of health problem has been comprehended by Bhore Committee by recommending various schemes of development aimed at elimination of unemployment, improvement in agriculture and industrial production and development of village roads and rural communication as distinct from national highways, as various facets of a single problem.

The philosophy of health enunciated by Bhore Committee, therefore, takes into account the health programme for people, considering health to signify state of well-being in which mind and body are able to function to their fullest capacity.

Disease control programmes were launched in diseases with high prevalence and incidence, such as malaria, leprosy, TB etc. The malaria control programme was wound up and to rehabilitate the malaria workers, multi-purpose-workers (MPW) were assigned to sub-centres along with ANM.

To popularize family planning programme, several knowledge, attitude, practice (KAP) surveys were undertaken. Similarly, several growth and nutrition surveys involving anthropometry were launched in order to address the malnutrition and stunted growth of Indian population. Anthropologists were involved in undertaking such surveys. Mother and Child Health programmes were launched mainly to provide anti-natal care (ANC) to pregnant women and immunization of the pregnant women and babies.

So, what was totally absent in India under British Rule was established, i.e. the primary health care facilities. Gradually referral hospitals at the District level were established. Every district had a District Health Officer supervising public health services. In Maharashtra, it was made obligatory for every DHO or DHO aspirant to acquire post-graduate diploma or degree in preventive and social medicine or referred to as community medicine at some places.

There have been two Directors relating to health in some States, Director of Medical Education and Research, and Director of Health Services. Since the health services had to deal with the people and community, an anthropologist like me was invited to lecture at the post-graduate programmes in PSM to orient the candidates about community life, and to talk about such concepts as culture, society, community, groups and about traditions and behavioural issues. In disease control programmes also, to ensure community participation, our help was sought in designing programme, such as health education or Information, Education and Communication (IEC) and now termed as Behavioural Change

Communication (BCC). We were also enlisted to undertake evaluations of programmes and make recommendations towards their improvements.

'Balwadi' as children's play school were started after the idea of Kindergarten was mooted to get children and parents interested in education. They were turned into *'Anganwadi'* (*'Angan'* as an open space inside the house specially used by women and children) combining the play school and providing nutrition to children. *Anganwadi* as a unit of Integrated Child Development Scheme (ICDS) was developed as a centre whereby the *anganwadi* worker who was considered as a paid volunteer, not an employee, looked after immunization of pregnant women and children and monitored growth of children. So, *anganwadi* worker became a partial health worker networking with the sub-centre and PHC. Since the doctor at the PHC was busy in running the OPD, providing clinical services to patients, the public health functions at the village level have been performed by the ANM and *anganwadi* worker. Now a social worker ASHA (Accredited Social Health Assistant), who is a citizen of the village has been added to the list of volunteer workers in the public sector, at village level. Before ASHA, a voluntary worker, Community Health Volunteer (CHV) or health guide were appointed to assist PHC system.

All this public health infrastructure is patterned according to allopathic system of medicine. In a State like Maharashtra, doctors trained in Indian Systems of Medicine, mainly Ayurved, are employed in the PHC, particularly in tribal belts where MBBS doctors are not available. Without the adequate and assured supply of ayurvedic drugs, they prescribe allopathic drugs to patients. In some States like Chhattisgarh, Madhya Pradesh, Himachal Pradesh, Rajasthan, there are Ayurvedic Health Centres (AHC) in the public sector with referral hospitals at district level supervised by District Ayurved (now AYUSH) Officer. So, the PHC and AHC run as parallel institutions. The AHC have no equivalent sub-centres resulting in AHC running only as OPD centres. So AYUSH is not discharging any public health functions although majority of the people follow traditional health care practices during pregnancy and maternity and child care.

Health Systems Research becomes an important research agenda in anthropology who claim to have acquired expertise in qualitative research at the community level. The traditional health care para-professionals such as herbalists, who are called by different names across the country, such as *Vaidu, Baiga, Gunia* etc. and *Dai or 'Suin'* have been performing public health functions.

Attempts have been made to bring all health care plural systems under one roof under the scheme of National Rural Health Mission (NRHM). But this idea of co-location has not been successfully implemented, it is alleged, due to non-cooperation of the allopathic system which is believed to be remote controlled or directed by market forces of pharmaceutical industry, which is a global economic power by way of multi-national pharma industry.

The private sector in health care has been increasing with the proliferation of medical colleges in all systems of medicine, particularly in Indian Systems of Medicine and Homoeopathy (ISM&H) now brought together with an acronym AYUSH with a distinct AYUSH Ministry. Till recently, up to 2017, there were two National Health Policies in India approved by the Parliament. The 2017 single national health policy does not seem to provide space to Indian Medical Systems to use their strengths in health care.

Health being a State subject according to Constitution of India, the State governments have freedom to follow their own pattern of health care in the public sector. Public Health in the tribal belts which have a difficult geographical terrain continue to be deficient. It appears, the immunization of children is done sufficiently well. However, due to land-forest relations and despite the Forest Rights Act, the access to forest which has been recognized as their traditional right is denied to tribals resulting in issues of food security and malnutrition.

Anthropologists have been doing ethnography of traditional health care in tribal communities, what is usually referred as ethno-medicine. However, operational research is needed in regard to public health with the use of plural systems of medicine, combining the traditional health care followed in homes and the functioning of public health in the public sector.

It is well known that institutional medical education in all systems of medicine is focused on diagnosis of illness and symptomatic treatment, not focusing on preventive or promotive health. Concept of public health research which is not possible without good grounding in epidemiology is a new area. Anthropology as an equidistant discipline from plural systems of medicine has a great scope in training and research in public health.

Public Health gets divided into primary health care and disease control programmes, such as in regard to leprosy, TB, HIV-AIDS, Cancer etc. Disease control programmes are usually referred to as vertical programmes whereby a distinct cadre is created from micro level to national level to focus on a particular disease. Ideally PHC framework need also to incorporate epidemiologically identified disease control activity as their responsibility. The Panchayats with 50 per cent of members being women as also CBOs need to be involved. New public health issues about non-communicable diseases, allegedly due to life style changes and mobility-migration patterns keep on emerging.

These are all areas of Health Systems Research. Knowing the reality that in the entire Public Health Sector, the para-medics or para-professionals are in close contact with the people, anthropologists could orient them to the standard methods of confidence building and capacity building about public health. The traditional healers and *Dais* with indigenous knowledge could be empowered with knowledge about textual Indian systems and skills, to address the contemporary health and disease issues.

The concept of social medicine developed very late i.e. around 1950-52 in India. The ICMR National Institute of Epidemiology at Chennai (NIE) was also established very late in India (1999). In the training of para-medics and in public health, anthropologists have an important role to play. There is a large component of social sciences in the curricula of public health and epidemiology at NIE.

Study of health behaviour of rural population in India undertaken by D. Banerji was aimed to understand 'the nature of interaction between the health services that are introduced through the primary health centres and the pre-existing culture of rural populations in India.' Some of the basic findings are reproduced as under:

> "But the surprising finding is that the response to the major medical care problems is very much in favour of Western (Allopathic) system of medicine, irrespective of social, economic, occupational considerations. Availability of such services and capacity of patients to meet the expenses, are the two major constraining factors. On the whole, the dispensary of the PHC projects a very unflattering image."

According to the study, people accepted healing practices, offered by practitioners of different Indian systems of medicine and homoeopathy, and combined these with home remedies,

(i) "Side by side with Western medicine"
(ii) "After Western medicine fails to give benefit"

(iii) "When Western medical services are not available or accessible to them due to various reasons", and

(iv) "Most frequently, when the illness is of minor nature."

The crux of the finding of Banerji's study clearly brings out that "there is no significant cultural resistance to acceptance of modern medicine as long as they are efficacious and they are available and accessible to them."

Banerji's study indicates that people are willing to use the facilities provided by dispensaries catering modern (Allopathic) medicine. It is also felt that people are eager to use the skills of ANM. However, the facilities are either not available or are beyond the purse of common man. Wherever physical facilities are present, health staff is unwilling to be available due to strong distaste for rural culture. According to Banerji, therefore, the problem is that of cultural adjustment for the health staff, while for the people, the problem is more financial than cultural.

Case Studies of Rural Health in Pune District

We undertook health ethnography in two rural centres in Pune district, the salient points of which are:

A. Health Management in Nira

Nira is a multi-caste village of 8000 people located in Purandhar tehsil of Pune district. It is located on Pune-Satara road at a distance of 85 kms from Pune. The tehsil place Saswad, which is also the headquarters of primary health centre is 32 kms and another tehsil headquarters Baramati, is at a distance of 30 kms from Nira.

There are 2 primary schools, 2 high schools and 3 pre-primary schools in the village. About 870 students and 1450 students are enrolled in the primary and high schools respectively. The village is divided into 5 wards by gram panchayat for administrative purposes. Each ward includes about 200 houses. There is tap water supply in the village from Nira river. The water is sufficiently polluted due to bathing and washing and due to effluence from sugar factory. However, the water is chlorinated before supplying to the people. The village is known to get epidemics of cholera, typhoid, hepatitis, diarrhoea and dysentery.

At least 70 per cent of the people go to the fields not too far from their houses for defecation. About 10 per cent of the houses have septic tanks and 20 per cent are having latrines with soak pits.

Personal Hygiene

People use charcoal powder, burnt tobacco or twig of a tree for brushing the teeth every morning.

People are more concerned about their bath for ritual cleanliness than for body cleanliness.

The child is massaged with coconut oil up to the age of 2 years, before bath. He is cleaned with mixture of gram flour, turmeric powder and milk, instead of with soap. Women and children apply *'kajal'* to their eyes for health of the eyes as also for aesthetic purposes. People clean their teeth and wash their faces in the morning in front of their houses.

Health and Disease

According to villagers, health means absence of disease. Healthy person is one who has muscular body and enough strength for hard work.

Diseases are believed to be caused due to various supernatural or secular reasons, like:

1. Breach of taboo
2. Breaking oath
3. Sorcery
4. Spirit intrusion
5. Evil eye
6. Wrath of Gods
7. Sins of past birth
8. Sleeping with feet towards south
9. Worshipping during menstruation
10. Illicit sex relations
11. Having sex on 4th day of menstruation
12. Mixing of hot and cold food
13. Catching infection due to contact.

Small pox, chicken pox, measles are caused due to wrath of Godess. The entire family follows certain taboos during the illness, such as not eating onions, garlic and mutton; on the 9th day Goddess is worshipped. Patient is given a holy bath with milk, *ghee*, and *neem* leaves. With new clothes on, the patient is ceremoniously taken to the temple. Presents are given to girls who are in the pre-menarche stage.

Sorcery and ghost intrusion affect children and women easily. Children are afflicted by disease of wasting leading to death. Evil eye is most common, affecting children. Wearing of charms, amulets and burning of *dhoop*, as also performing ritual to ward off evil eye with mustard seeds and salt are taken as preventive and remedial measures against black magic.

Many diseases are caused due to wrongful combination of hot and cold foods. Meat, fish, eggs, jaggery are hot foods while curd, lemon are cold foods. Diarrhoea, dysentery, typhoid and cholera are supposed to be caused with such combinations. Skin diseases are caused by impure blood. Leprosy is also associated with impurity of blood. It is believed that if a woman has coitus on the fourth day of her menstruation, then the child may suffer from leprosy in adulthood.

B. Data from the Villages in Junnar Taluk

Data from the villages in Junnar taluk bring out the following salient points:

1. When people decide that they are ill, they take care of their sickness by following various therapies singly or in combination, e.g.
   (a) By undertaking fasts on a particular week day, that is every Monday, Tuesday or Thursday etc. depending upon the nature of illness. Number of fasts, that is, 12 or 16 may be fixed by tradition.
   (b) By using home remedies as taking milk, turmeric etc.
   (c) By visiting temples located inside or outside the village.
   (d) Going to *Bhagat*, local medicine man, who prescribes a ritual to ward off the influence of evil spirits.
   (e) Taking treatment from an herbalist who has knowledge of medicinal herbs and its use.

It is thus clear that people continue to follow traditional methods of health care in regard to preventive and promotional aspects of health. They take the help of modern medical practitioners only after exhausting the traditional modes of disease cure. The doctors are aware of the fact that they are not the first persons contacted by people. The awareness that people visit them as a last resort, is exploited commercially by private medical profession, as stated by some doctors.

Data clearly substantiate the commonly known fact about the existence of plural systems of disease care in developing countries. People not only try multiple cures in successive order but may do so simultaneously. They undertake sacred fast, visit temples and continue to take modern drugs for cure of an ailment. People have got their own ideas as to the diseases for which they should go to a *Bhagat*, a herbalist or to a modern practitioner. It depends upon their ideas of disease causation or any pathological state. When they feel that they have been affected by a spirit or a ghost, they go to a *Bhagat*. The concept of infection is not widely believed amongst people. For disease conditions persisting over a considerable period, they take medical help. However, the decisions about the nature of sickness, probable channels of cure, causative factors of disease are taken by the patient, his family and neighbours or kin-group.

In regard to preventive and promotional aspects of health, no advice is sought nor offered in modern system. There is no lack of knowledge in modern medicine regarding preventive or promotive aspects of health but the curative aspects far outweigh the other aspects. The preventive and promotional aspects such as in case of infant care or maternal care, as given in traditional medicine, is known to people through cultural traditions.

Discussion

Medical profession has always been associated with healing. Healing is also considered sacred and divine. Lay people understand health in terms of absence or presence of disease. As a result, curative aspects assume importance in health organization. In fact, curative aspects are situational and people accept any therapy which is effective, cheap and readily available. The preventive and promotional aspects are built in the cultural system represented by food prescription and ideas of personal hygiene, maternal care etc.

The objective of primary health care as enunciated in the *Alma Ata* document "is essential health care based on practical, scientifically sound and socially acceptable methods and technology made universally accessible to individuals and families in the community through their full participation and at a cost that the community and the country can afford to maintain at every stage of their development in the spirit of self-reliance and self-determination."

"Primary Health Care addresses the main health problems in the community providing promotive, preventive curative and rehabilitative services accordingly." It also includes the development in other sectors such as economic, education, housing, communication etc. (Declaration of *Alma-Ata*, WHO, 1978).

The concept of health care as related to other aspects of social and economic development has also been spelt out in great details in the Bhore Committee report. At a conceptual level, in Anthropology, health is considered as one aspect of culture like other aspects such as economic, social and religious. The concept of integration of culture spells out the integral relation of health with other aspects of culture thereby making that changes in one aspect affect other aspects also.

The pertinent question is, as to whether the medical personnel as are trained in medical schools today are properly equipped, intellectually and technically, to cope up with preventive and promotional aspects of health? Are they equipped to take initiative in inter-sectoral coordination for total development? According to Halfdan Mahler, Director General of the World Health Organisation, "Most of the world's medical schools prepare doctors not to care for the health of the people but to engage in a medical practice that is blind to anything but disease and the technology for dealing with it." (World Health Forum, Geneva, 1981: Vol. II: No. 1: 15)

A word about health training may not be out of place. Candidates are admitted to medical colleges at an age of 17 or 18 years. In the college, a student is exposed to scientific facts about the working of the human body and disease system. The knowledge is imparted in the hospital set up. The ideals of medical practices which are presented to him by his teachers and practicing medical specialists are from his worldview and value system. Preventive and promotional aspects have no place in this worldview. Is it pragmatic to expect a young medical graduate in-charge of primary health centre to be an effective manager organizing priorities in preventive aspects of health as visualized by Bhore Committee and again reiterated in strategies for Health for All? Is the doctor being asked to deliver for what he is neither trained nor oriented? To what extent a doctor changes his own cultural practices with regard to preventive and promotional aspects of health? To what extent the knowledge of scientific facts reorients his cultural philosophy and basic personality configuration which is determined by culture in early years of life influenced by child rearing practices ?

Among the preventive health programmes, except for immunization, other programmes such as popularization of latrines, soakage pits, piped water supply and housing have not met with significant success. In fact, many preventive health or public health programmes are also social programmes. Social blockades may hamper the implementation of programmes.

Health planning has to be micro-level, i.e. village based planning. Each village is a unit of life and social action. Each village is a distinct entity in social, economic, religious, historical and geographical terms. Different villages may have different health and development problems depending upon the economic and social levels of the people. It is, therefore, necessary to do health planning in preventive aspects for each village in such fields as environmental sanitation.

The central problem may be to identify the preventive and promotional aspects of health which need to be adopted by the people. How can these become a part of the cultural system? Since primary health centres are not the health temples for villagers, which agency would play the role of delivering primary health care, which involves coordinated development in various sectors of society?

At an operational level, this may be achieved by pursuing basic research about village health or through participatory research, about changing the health attitudes and practices of rural folk.

1. Village Health Monograph: A detailed study of health behaviour and attitude in a representative village. All illness episodes and their management to be recorded for a period of one year. Other aspects of health to be studied. People's perception of health and disease, local health professionals—their training and their interaction with patients and people.

Para-medical staff and their interaction with people.

The study would include the knowledge about economic, social and religious culture of the village. The study should reflect the impact of developmental efforts in other sectors on health.

Illness episodes would be recorded on the basis of symptoms told by people and as perceived by those who would treat them. The study team would not offer treatment.

2. Participatory research in villages: Programmes of health education should be undertaken from the standpoint of modern medicine and ayurvedic medicine in two villages and people's action be studied for three years.

The CHV, MPW, ANM and other local health professionals and extension workers be given orientation for participating in health education work.

3. Studies of the para-medical and local health professionals to assess their perception of preventive, promotive and curative aspects of health.

Anthropology discussing health as an agenda, as a part of ethnography has described the health related beliefs, practices, including the role of traditional healers who may combine the herbal remedies with spiritual faith remedies. Anthropology considers health as an aspect of culture, which is a public issue. However, the public health as institutionalized in medical education and health services, are patterned as per modern medicine, which is believed to provide quick relief from the ailment. Major emphasis is given on disease control programmes based on chemotherapy. Gradually, traditional medical systems institutionalized on the pattern of modern medicine have become a subsidiary, alternative or complementary systems. When it comes to birthing, child rearing, people make a judicious mix of preventive care such as immunization and promotive health practices by way of mixing herbs with healthy dietary practices.

It needs to be emphasized that face-to-face interaction of people with health services is with the para-medics and para-professionals, such as ANM, *Anganwadi sevika*, ASHA, herbalist, *dai* etc. who enter the houses of the people and culturally belong to the same socio-economic-cultural stock as the people. Anthropologists who are comfortable with micro-level studies in the rural and tribal areas need to undertake the focused ethnography about how people negotiate the preventive, promotive and curative aspects of health and ailments with the use of home remedies, dietary patterns and use of plural systems of medicine, simultaneously or sequentially. Anthropologists are capable of showing the distinction between public health and health services limiting to disease causation and treatment.

Since public health deals with Public and Health and not with a patient with a disease for treatment, anthropology has to deal proactively with the hard aspects of health culture such as faith, beliefs, spiritual healing, rituals, pilgrimage for health and healing, and use of plural systems of medicine for treatment of various kinds of diseases, as classified by the community-vide its experience. Such documentation could devise strategic planning by integrating the plural systems of medicine with or without drugs, and assigning different roles to health personnel, including the indigenous healers, with appropriate accreditation in the public health system.

The strength of anthropology lies in the fact that the discipline is equidistant from all systems of medicine. However, since health is an aspect of culture and there are technical advances in medicine, public health has to be operationalised to offer maximum benefits to the people by integrating the strengths of plural systems. The drug-focussed therapies are curative in nature and get linked to pharmaceuticals, while drugless therapies should focus on preventive and promotive aspects, in tune with the cultural beliefs and practices and addressing to the changing life styles. Public health on the ground is delivered by the paramedics. Health systems, therefore, need to train the formal paramedics and indigenous healers, such as herbalists and *Dai* about the essentials of plural systems of medicine. Newer techniques do not have to replace or ignore the traditions, but have to build on them, upscale them, which would be acceptable to the people. Science does not know to what extent mind-body interaction takes place and influence each other, and the role of faith in maintenance of health and treatment of disease. Anthropology as a holistic science has to take a lead in coordinating and integrating the plural streams for the benefit of the people.

B. TRADITIONAL MEDICINE AND AYUSH

AYUSH (Initiation)

I was introduced to the world of traditional medicine through the international symposium on Medical Anthropology which we hosted at the Department of Anthropology, University of Pune as a post plenary session of the International Anthropology Congress held at Delhi in December 1978. Prof. Charles Leslie, who edited '*Asian Medical Systems*' advised me as co-chairperson of the Pune symposium to invite Pandit Shiv Sharma, doyen of Ayurved in post-Independent India and well known Ayurvedic clinician, and organize a plenary session on Ayurved. Prof. A.L. Basham, the well known Indologist and author of the classic '*The Wonder that was India*' was present on all the three days to discuss and invite about 50 western anthropology scholars at the scheduled International Congress on Traditional Asian Medicine (ICTAM) in September 1979 at Australian National University, Canberra.

The International Association for the Study of Traditional Asian Medicine (IASTAM) was formed during ICTAM. The Indian Chapter of IASTAM was discussed on 31st January, 1980 at Mumbai in the presence of Prof. Basham designating Pandit Shiv Sharma as the President of IASTAM-India. As per Panditji's directive, I organized a meeting at Pune University on 20th April, 1980 to adopt the Constitution for registration as a charitable trust. I was designated as General Secretary of IASTAM-India. Later, we organized an Asian Congress in 1983 and 3rd ICTAM at

Mumbai in 1990. I was the third President of IASTAM-India after Dr. K.N. Udupa's sad demise.

For the first time, a working group on 'AYUSH in Public Health' was formed under Steering Committee on AYUSH for the drafting of Eleventh Five Year Plan under my Chairmanship. Subsequently, two study projects were offered to us by AYUSH Ministry, which are documented (AYUSH in Public Health: Vol. I & II: 2016).

Introduction

Indian Systems of Medicine (ISM) are the health aspect of Indian culture, which includes beliefs and practices about causation and treatment of ailments, and ideas of normal health and its parameters. The health practices of common people are ignored as traditions, as if traditions are non-science in the context of laboratory testing, going through animal trials and industry sponsored clinical trials, ultimately resulting in withdrawal of drugs from the market after few years, all in the name of science as eternal truth and gospel. Traditions evolve out of experience, evidence and reflection by the teachers who generalise them as texts, whether it is Bible, Bhagvat-Geeta or Charak, Sushrut, Vagbhat. Fortunately, 'Reverse Pharmacology' is being advocated for those who blocked traditional knowledge in the name of laboratory science, while brazenly taking patents on medicinal herbs which are being used by millions of people as home remedies for common ailments, across the country.

People's Sector

Our studies about grassroots knowledge and health practices in rural-tribal homes in Himachal Pradesh, Chhattisgarh, Madhya Pradesh and Maharashtra, besides similar studies in 19 other States by NHSRC are documented in our book, 'AYUSH in Public Health—Vol. I (Concept Publishing Co., 2016). People continue to seek the first help from elders, traditional therapists, *dais*, before accessing the plural medical centres according to their affordability. However, the people's sector with age-old practices are totally ignored while formulating the health plans at the national level.

Public Health Care

Primary Health Centre model as health programme of Community

Development since 1952, under the leadership of an allopathic doctor, whose primary function has been to conduct an OPD, and to supervise the sub-centre activities carried by ANM, MPW about RCH and disease control activities. Anganwadi is not under PHC. CHV, Health Guides and now ASHA as a new nomenclature are attached to PHC. The community hospitals added later with some specialities like obstetrics, paediatrics and radiology remain largely non-functional due to vacant positions. Further referral is the district hospital at the district capital, linked upwards to medical college hospital. However, it is the paramedics who visit the families in their homes and huts and not the doctors.

In some states like Himachal Pradesh, Chhattisgarh, Madhya Pradesh, Rajasthan etc., there are parallel AYUSH (mostly ayurvedic) dispensaries, with referrals at subdivisional level and a district hospital managed by a medical superintendant and/or DAO. However, there is no maternity ward, except in teaching Ayurved hospital. There are no sub-centres, no para-medics, save a pharmacist and may be an attendant-*cum*-midwife.

NRHM with a lofty objective of co-location of plural systems largely remained inoperative due to apathy and non-co-operation from allopathic health system. In a state like Maharashtra, AYUSH doctors have been appointed in PHCs, mostly in tribal belt where MBBS were not available, branding them as co-location to claim NRHM grants. However, there has been a total miss-match between the posting of an AYUSH doctor and the supply of AYUSH drugs.

Chhattisgarh took the initiative in developing a concept of *Ayurved Gram* now accepted as *AYUSH gram* at national level, trying to link the AYUSH dispensary to the village community through PRI, under the leadership of the AYUSH doctor. To develop few ideal AYUSH gram models, is a challenge and an opportunity to AYUSH colleges and institutions, as an intervention research project.

It is now becoming increasingly evident that no single system of healthcare has the capacity to solve all of society's health needs. India has an immensely rich and mature indigenous medical heritage of its own, in addition to strong foundations in Western biomedical sciences.

The enhanced role of AYUSH requires substantial efforts and investments in core areas like education, research, industry, medicinal plants, public health and community based local health traditions.

AYUSH

All non-allopathic systems were put together in the erstwhile Department of Indian Systems of Medicine & Homoeopathy under Ministry of Health and Family Welfare. Now, it has been re-named as AYUSH (acronym) under a separate Ministry of AYUSH headed by a Minister of State, holding independent charge. Health being a State subject under Constitution of India, there are variations in health care in different States. There has been a distinct National ISM&H policy, apart from the National Health Policy. The two policies have been merged together in an integrated single policy in 2017. However, the attempts under NRHM to co-locate facilities of plural systems of medicine under a common roof, so as to allow people to access the strengths of respective systems have not met with success.

Plural systems of Medicine has been a gift to Indian people, bestowed by history. Although the planning process in Congress which was a single national party, out of which all the present parties have evolved, during 1920s, decided to opt Indian Systems as the mainstream health system after Independence, modern medicine was adopted as the official health care system after Independence. The Bhore Committee recommendations, in 1946-48 became the basis of primary health centres. There have been several committee reports on health after 1947, including related to ISM&H. In the princely states of India, Ayurved and Unani colleges were established, while under British Presidencies, allopathic colleges were established. The formally educated health facilities were available only in the urban centres which were used by the ruralites as referrals or when they visited grain markets in urban centres. In the villages, health and disease facilities and consultancies were available from the elders and from traditional herbalists and *Dai*. The prevalent situation has been documented by anthropologists as ethnomedicine.

Overview of AYUSH Sector

India's AYUSH sector has grown dramatically in the post-Independence period. Apart from China, there is no other country which has an educational infrastructure for under-graduate and post-graduate education in traditional medicine. The Indian educational, research and industrial infrastructure for the traditional health system is perhaps the largest in the world.

While there are a large number of AYUSH educational institutions imparting UG & PG education, many of them lack prescribed professional staff and clinical infrastructure due to sub-critical investments and, at times, poor vision compromising the standards of AYUSH medical education and affecting the quality of students being produced by the educational institutions. There is an urgent need for educational reforms due to the growing domestic and global demands for mainstreaming complementary healthcare in modern societies. It is therefore necessary to review the curriculum, infrastructure, staffing, systems for teacher's training, and standards prescribed for AYUSH education.

There is insufficient data on the quality and social impact of the health services provided by the government AYUSH institutions. In southern states like Kerala and Tamil Nadu and northern states like Himachal, the public acceptance for AYUSH services is believed to be high. Expectations from the sector are building up in many other states. However, policy makers at the Central and State level have so far not much engaged in the sector in national health programme. Hence, there is no macro-data available about the contribution of AYUSH to major national programmes for the management of communicable and non-communicable diseases. At the micro-level, however, there are reports of successful management of several communicable and non-communicable diseases.

The AYUSH health services largely focus on common and chronic diseases and on preventive and promotive health care. The preventive health aspect of AYUSH is of enormous contemporary value as health sector reforms in all developed countries are seeking to balance curative health practices with the introduction of viable preventive health care strategies.

In the last two decades, in urban areas, the private sector AYUSH services for health needs have significantly grown both in terms of size and reputation. There is, however, no reliable quantitative data on the size of the non-government health services at the primary, secondary or tertiary level.

Initially, Indian Council of Medical Research (ICMR) started trans-disciplinary research in 1964. Later (since the 1970s) the Central Council for Research in Ayurveda, Siddha, Unani, Yoga and Homoeopathy have been responsible for the officially sponsored research activities. One of the socially important outputs of research in the AYUSH sector has been setting up of the pharmacopoeias and formularies for the various systems of medicine. Whereas several dozens of important research projects have been undertaken in the last three decades across the various AYUSH Research Councils, there is no critical report on the quality or impact of these projects on the health sector in India. In the non-government sector, there are institutions carrying out pioneering research work.

In rural areas, apart from the health services delivered by licensed practitioners trained in various codified systems, there are around 1 million village-based and community supported traditional healers. The erosion in recent decades of local health cultures is a matter of concern as this affects the health security of millions of rural households. There is sociological and epistemological evidence to conclude that the folk healing traditions have a longstanding and symbiotic relationship with Ayurveda, Siddha and Unani.

For the first time, while formulating the Eleventh Five Year Plan, a working group on AYUSH in Public Health was constituted under my chairmanship by the Steering Committee on AYUSH. In a subsequent project, we were asked to document the ground realities in villages in Himachal Pradesh, Madhya Pradesh, Chhattisgarh and Maharashtra, in the context of NRHM. We conducted the studies with the help of anthropology students from the respective anthropology departments. In Himachal, Madhya Pradesh and Chhattisgarh, there are parallel AYUSH health centres/dispensaries, including district hospitals, along with PHCs and sub-centres. In Maharashtra, Ayurvedic doctors are placed in the PHCs with or without ayurvedic kit of medicines. At all places, traditional herbalists and *Dai* continue to provide services. Common people have good knowledge of herbal medicine which they use for management of common ailments, as the first defence, before approaching PHC or AHC.

Certain local health traditions constitute the community-health dimension of AYUSH. India has around a million village-based traditional healers in the form of birth attendants, bonesetters, and herbal healers and several million knowledgeable households who have useful nutritional knowledge of local grains, cereals, wild fruits and vegetables, and locally available medicinal plants. Pilot projects through NGOs and research institutes are required to document, assess and promote sound local health practices at the Taluka/Block level.

The second project offered to us was an intervention project to orient the AYUSH faculty and AYUSH Medical officers in the public sector, to public health and epidemiology. It was also meant to try out some case studies of epidemiological research in three states of Himachal Pradesh, Chhattisgarh and Maharashtra. Through Research Methods workshops at national, state and district level, the participants were exposed to qualitative and quantitative tools and techniques of research. Pilot intervention projects, such as prevalence of ano-rectal disorders and ANC-PNC care in Himachal, ideal *Ayurvedgram*, networking ayurvedic health centre with PRI and CBO in Chhattisgarh, health systems research about the AYUSH doctors working in allopathic PHCs, training of traditional herbalists in processing of medicinal herbal material into ayurvedic drugs etc. in Maharashtra were carried out. A notable pilot project related to maternity practices of lady doctors from all systems of medicine when they became mothers themselves revealed the universal cultural practices being followed by all women as a pan-Indian phenomena. This raises a policy question as to how, what was being followed by majority of women was not a part of public health maternity services. Why are we killing an age old institution of *Dai*, by promoting institutional delivery for which we offer incentives which breeds corruption and false register entries? In Scotland, labour is conducted invariably by a mid-wife in a hospital while an obstetrician is available in case of emergency. Dr. Rajanikant Arole and his wife Dr. Mabel trained village women as health workers as a model known as Jamkhed model which subsequently was accepted to have the lady CHV, ASHA etc. in the public sector. How is it that the para-medical persons such as ANM, MPW, ASHA, *Anganwadi* workers, who belonged to the community and visited the homes of villagers are not given basic training in the principles of AYUSH? We as anthropologists can understand these issues, since we interact with the people and have acquired an expertise to look at issues from people's perspectives. Anthropologists being equidistant from all systems of medicine, we appreciate the plurality of cultures and plurality of medical systems. The integrated national health policy of 2017 has to be properly implemented so as to make the strengths of plural systems accessible to the poorest of the poor people.

Medical Anthropology and AYUSH

Anthropology as a science of man in totality when applied to contemporary issues gets primarily linked with indigenous people, their knowledge systems and their culture systems. Although, health has not been documented in the ethnographic monographs, issues relating to health such as nutrition, traditional health care professionals and the rituals connected with treatment and cure have been documented under relevant chapters.

The acronym AYUSH which refers to Indian systems of medicine and homoeopathy is a natural subject matter of Medical Anthropology. The term Ethnomedicine should, therefore, refer to indigenous systems of medicine which are also termed as folk medicine or as local health traditions or as little tradition in the conceptual framework of little tradition—great tradition advocated by Robert Redfield. In that sense, the classical text like Charak, Sushrut and Vagbhat could be referred as great tradition. The term alternative medicine used for Ayush and Chinese Systems is totally wrong since, excluding Homoeopathy, the other systems are respectively the health aspects of Indian and Chinese culture. The knowledge of herbal medicine of the tribal communities or Caste-Hindu peasantry refers to the knowledge of medicinal properties of the environment around their localities. The home remedies so widely used all over the world as grandma therapy or kitchen medicine again refers to the little traditions which have universal coverage as well as local variations, depending upon the availability of herbal material. Charak has compiled these traditions after reflecting on the clinical evidence, as '*Charak Samhita*'.

Since food is medicine and food makes the body and is also considered to be affecting the mind, food is an important component of all medical systems. As culture is an integrated whole and functions in a state of equilibrium, particularly the hard aspects of culture, i.e. non-material aspects of culture, so is the body-mind equilibrium affecting each other about health and disease. The concept of Holism which is the main plank of Anthropology, also refers to the wholeness of human organism in the context of health and disease. It is now with the organ transplants being propagated widely, that integrative or organic nature of the human body is being challenged.

Ethnomedicine is people's medicine and is closely linked with the bio-diverse environment. Other animal species with their instinctive behaviour and closeness to nature take care of their health without the use of health professionals except in the case of domesticated pets like dogs whose life style we influence. The ethnography of health practices and behaviour could provide documentation of similarities and differences in the culture and health care systems. With industrialization and urbanization, which have led to occupational diversity, mobility and migration, culture and life style which used to be co-terminus are showing increasing variability. As a result, new disease patterns supposed to have been caused by new viruses have developed. Issues of immunity are yet a grey area in modern medical science, although given great importance in the traditional health systems.

In the book on '*Medical Anthropology*' by Foster and Andersen, Ayurved and Chinese medicine have been listed under Ethno-medicine. I asked George Foster in a meeting in Spain as to how could the Indian and Chinese Systems of medicine which were the textually great traditions be referred as ethno-medicine. With background of Anthropology, we initiated the term 'Plural Systems of Medicine' in preference to cosmopolitan medicine or alternative systems of medicine. Now, the term Plural Systems of Medicine has been accepted in common usage. Shri Darshan Shankar, currently Vice-Chancellor, Trans-disciplinary University, Bangaluru (Banglore) who had attended the Asian Congress on Traditional Asian Medicine in 1983 at Mumbai, while at the Academy of Development Sciences, established by him in a tribal belt at the foot-hills of Western ghat, popularized the term 'local health traditions' to which we usually refer in Anthropology as 'little tradition'. However, there is opposition to these terms from some leaders of Ayurved, who suspect that Ayurved as tradition, could get equated with herbalism, which in our terminology would mean ethno-medicine. Although, the local folk healers provide symptomatic treatment, it is not true that they do not have the concept of body, mind and its relationship with the forces and elements of nature or with the universe. Maybe, we have not gone in exploring these conceptual issues in our folk ethnography. We are aware that great and little tradition interaction has kept *Gita* and Bible useful even today. To maintain the great traditions of Charak, Sushrut, Vaghbhat alive, they need to be constantly reinterpreted and demystified.

Synthesizing Evidence on Acceptance and Utilisation of AYUSH Systems in India

In India, Department of Indian Systems of Medicine and Homoeopathy (ISM&H) was first created in March 1995 and re-named as Department of Ayurveda, Yoga & Naturopathy, Unani, Siddha and Homoeopathy (AYUSH) in November 2003 with a view to providing focused attention to development of education and research in AYUSH systems. Recognizing the strength of AYUSH system within its holistic and personalized system of health care, Government of India has initiated a number of steps for its propagation and promotion. In continuation with this, revitalization of local health traditions as well as mainstreaming of AYUSH has been envisaged as one of the important goals under the National Rural Health Mission (NRHM) launched by Government of India in the year 2005. The NRHM is committed to mainstreaming AYUSH and revitalizing local health traditions as a way of bringing about architectural correction in the system of health care delivery in the rural areas of the country. It has been assumed that integration of AYUSH and local health traditions has an important role to play in developing an integrated system of health care to provide better and accessible health care services to all, and especially to the rural population.

In policy planning circles, there are frequently questions raised regarding 'actual utilization' of AYUSH systems in the country. The national surveys such as NFHS, NSS and Census provide the quantitative data necessary for policy planning and budgeting. However, the micro level planning, implementation and logistics are not possible without supplementing it with qualitative data.

In consonance with these, some direct and indirect research efforts were undertaken to assess the utilization of AYUSH systems by the people. The National Family Health Survey (NFHS-II) conducted during 1998-99 recorded that only 8 per cent of reproductive illnesses were treated by private vaid/hakim/homeopath/traditional healers. In the same study, NFHS collected information on treatment of diarrhoea and reported that about 5 per cent of those who availed treatment used home remedies/herbal medicine (IIPS, 2000). In the year 2002-03 for the first time in India, realizing the need for systematic data on utilization of Indian systems of medicine (ISM), AYUSH Department, then called Department of Indian Systems of Medicine & Homoeopathy (ISMH), identified Institute for Research in Medical Statistics (IRMS, ICMR institutions) at New Delhi. This institution undertook a study on utilization of ISM in the country in 35 districts across nineteen States during 2002-03. The objective was to provide an all-India estimate of utilization of different ISM and to realize the reasons for preference and the cost of such treatments. The findings of the study were as follows:

- The study covered 33,666 households with at least one sick person during the reference period of the previous three months. The number of sick persons who had taken any treatment was 44,639, i.e. about 1.33 sick persons per household.
- On the basis of preference, ISM&H was preferred by about one third (95% Confidence Interval: 32.01% - 33.99%,) in case of normal ailments (18.7% for Ayurveda, 12.7% for Homoeopathy and 1% for Siddha/Unani).
- However, in case of serious ailments, preference for ISM&H was about 18 per cent (95% Confidence Interval: 17.2% - 18.8%) (11.4% for Homoeopathy, 5% for Ayurveda, 1% for Unani & 0.53% for Siddha).
- As for actual utilization about 14 per cent (95% Confidence Interval 13.4% - 14.6%) sick persons availed/used ISM&H

(7.1% Ayurveda, 6.3% Homoeopathy and less than 1% Siddha/ Unani).

- The reasons given for availing ISM&H treatment were no side effects (31%), cheap (30%), effective (25%) and doctor easily available (11%).
- Almost all of those who used allopathic treatment were aware of the Ayurveda and Homoeopathy.
- About half of the households preferred medical assistance from government health functionaries in case of common ailments whereas they preferred private health functionaries for serious ailments.
- The reasons for not using ISM&H were slow progress (28%), practitioners not available (27%), no faith (12%), medicines not available (5%) and others (28%).
- About 38 per cent of households reported to have visited traditional healers; 40 per cent in rural and about 30 per cent in urban areas.
- The illnesses for which traditional healers were visited included bone setting (30%), dog bite (16%), snake bite (19%), scorpio bite (10%), jaundice (15%), sciatica (3%) and measles (7%).
- The cost of allopathic treatment from private sources for three months was Rs. 258 (Rs. 219 for medicine and Rs. 39 for consultation); Rs. 252 in rural and Rs. 273 in urban area.
- The cost of treatment for those availing ISM&H was Rs. 160 (Rs. 131 for medicine and Rs. 29 for consultation); Rs. 146 in rural and Rs. 210 in urban area.
- The cost of treatment was little lower for ISM&H as compared to allopathy. The percentage of households preferring ISM&H showed increase with income and literacy level more for common ailments.

However, all the above-mentioned as well as several other (not mentioned here) research attempts followed bio-medical approach and mostly explored curative aspects concerning drug in-take in the community. Since, the theories and principles of AYUSH systems in India lay equal stress on promotion, prevention as well as cure, the enquiries in the utilization domain of these systems must give equal emphasis on promotive, preventive as well as curative aspects. In order to comprehensively assess the acceptance and utilization of AYUSH systems in India the following further important points about AYUSH should be taken into consideration.

There are also serious methodological issues in regard to such studies at the macro level by the exclusive use of statistical paradigm. The systems of medicine as we term them as Ayurved, Unani etc. are given terms. If we ask lay people as to which system do they follow to get the comfort back, they do not reply in terms of system. Some of them might say, '*videshi dawa*' or '*deshi dawa*' or '*gharelu dawa*'. If we ask them specifically as to what do they do when they have fever or stomach upset such as pain or diarrhoea or dysentery using the terms they use in their dialect, they would detail out the home remedies or sequence of referrals combining with dietary restrictions and prescriptions. They do not give a term of medicinal system. Do we collect our data, what we prefer to call the qualitative data, using the exact quotes used by the people? Or we follow the reductionist method of turning the data into our etic terms? Where is the objectivity of data and analysis?

When the lady doctors from all systems of medicine follow common practices like all other Indian women, when they become mothers themselves, what systems of medicine are they following ?If we term it as traditions, it becomes non-science. They are following the textual great traditions from Ayurved or Unani or equivalent system which have become the little or local health traditions.

To summarise:

- AYUSH is the health aspect of Indian culture and society.
- AYUSH is historically evolved and used by the people without external support, with the use of local health professionals, traditions and indigenous knowledge and wisdom.
- AYUSH is expressed as great tradition in ancient books like Charak and Sushrut which evolved by conceptualizing the folk and little traditions of the common people based on empirical experience.
- AYUSH being a part of Indian culture has inbuilt sustainability and coping mechanisms managed by lay people in their homes and with the help of traditional para-professionals, who abound in indigenous knowledge and wisdom.

We are aware that after Independence, modern medicine has become the national health system. Officially plural systems of medicine exist in India by way of medical colleges, research institutes, pharmaceutical industries, and Government departments in all systems under the umbrella of AYUSH, Central Council of Indian Medicine, Indian Council of Medical Research, Medical Council of India and the like. However, the budgetary provision and the infrastructure of public health care delivery system clearly indicates bias in favour of modern medicine.

AYUSH in Public Health: Perspectives for Implementation

Public Health in the Indian context has been equated with health care in the public sector, which started as a component of community development in 1952, following the Bhore Committee recommendations about PHC system. The people in rural and tribal areas were served by *vaidus* who had traditional knowledge of herbal medicine, mostly practicing symptomatic mono-therapy. In the urban centres, family or *Guru-Shishya* tradition trained *vaidyas* and *Hakims* were available who were also referrals for the ruralites. Only the epidemics of plague, influenza, cholera and pneumonia attracted government intervention, during British rule.

In India, Ayurvedic colleges were started in the princely states and Allopathic colleges in the British Presidencies. In Maharashtra, some Ayurvedic colleges were established in the spirit of freedom struggle. Now, Maharashtra has the largest number of AYUSH colleges, mostly in the private sector. Out of 116 AYUSH colleges, 63 are Ayurved colleges. Director of AYUSH (Medical Education) has the only function of supervising teaching institutions, nothing to do with health care. Himachal Pradesh has 1136 AYUSH dispensaries functioning as OPDs, with only couple of Ayurvedic colleges. There are parallel health systems in Rajasthan, Madhya Pradesh and Chhattisgarh, having no communication with PHC system and receiving no credit for mandatory participation in the national health programmes. A retired Director of Health Services of undivided Madhya Pradesh remarked, "MBBS and BAMS were equally good or bad for national programmes." All high powered Government committee reports welcome AYUSH doctors by their sheer numbers to contribute to implementation of national health programmes, without mentioning or soliciting their professional knowledge.

Why are we promoting AYUSH? We promote AYUSH because lay people, particularly in the villages are already following the principles and practices of AYUSH. They are using food as medicine, kitchen condiments as medicinal decoctions, plants and herbs, which are mentioned in AYUSH classics as of medicinal value. There are local indigenous herbalist professionals who treat people. They also supply herbal material to AYUSH professionals, and pharmaceutical industry. What people follow in their homes are the little or local traditions and what is given in the classic texts are the great traditions of the same health care phenomena. Great traditions were generalised by reflective scholars of those times, Acharyas, by studying and observing the little traditions. Academic debates like today's seminars, symposia, and conferences at academic centres like Kashi (Varanasi) led to confirmations and presented in the *Samhita* format. As we know, the religious or spiritual messages are presented in the poetic form of *Owi, Abhang, Shlok, Doha* etc. in the respective regional languages or dialects.

In the people's sector in Indian homes, more particularly in rural homes, home based herbal remedies are being practised as the first line of defence for common ailments. Kitchen condiments or flower-leaf offerings to deities at home in various climatic seasons are all of medicinal value known to elders in the family, as also prescribed in the medicinal texts. Such information is covered under ethnomedicine.

Even the lady doctors from all systems of medicine follow traditional health practices when they become mothers themselves. People are aware about the health and medicinal value of different food products and their mixtures in diet. Nutritious food is offered to deities on ritual and ceremonial occasions, as per people's perception about nutritious diet which need to be offered to the ancestors and family deities. With increased demand for vegetables during ritual period for ancestor worship, and such festivals as *Gauri-Ganpati*, the prices of vegetables sore high, due to supply-demand economic equations.

The Steering Committee on AYUSH for the Twelfth Five Year Plan has made some recommendations about research on folk healing practices as local health traditions or little traditions. On lines of *Ayurved Gram* concept in Chhattisgarh, *AYUSH gram* in the public sector has been recommended, as suggested by us, which could link the AYUSH health centres with Panchayati Raj Institutions (PRI), Community Based Organizations (CBO) and Self Help Groups (SHG).

Mainstreaming of AYUSH was to be achieved under NRHM by mainstreaming AYUSH infrastructure, including manpower and drugs to strengthen the public health system at all levels through co-location of AYUSH doctors and facilities in PHCs, CHCs and District hospitals. Important interventions aimed at inclusion of AYUSH medications in the village level kit of ASHA, inclusion of AYUSH formulations in the supply of generic drugs provided at SC, PHC, CHC levels, appointing AYUSH MOs at single doctor PHCs and providing place for AYUSH practitioner and pharmacist at CHCs as per IPHS model. Total functional integration between AYUSH dispensaries and hospitals and general health care facilities under allopathic system was envisaged so as to make available the entire spectrum of AYUSH and Allopathy systems of health care to the public so that people could exercise their choices for treatment. This could not be implemented due to resistance from the mainstream health services. Anthropologists have an opportunity to use focused ethnography to unravel the process which motivated or hindered the implementation of such lofty goals.

The first volume of the book 'AYUSH in Public Health' (2016) has documented the household practices of AYUSH studied by us, mainly in the four States of India, viz. Himachal Pradesh, Madhya Pradesh, Chhattisgarh and Maharashtra. Similar studies in Rajasthan and 18 other States in India (NHSRC) have also been referred which validate the little traditions (local health traditions) with the classical, textual great traditions. The annexures to Volume I detail out the home remedies practiced by people in their homes as also the prescriptions given by local indigenous healers and professionally trained AYUSH physicians. This brings out clearly the organic, historical link between the little traditions (local health traditions) and great textual tradition.

The AYUSH Mission has been set up to mainstream AYUSH at all levels in the health care system. The document provides implementation strategies by way of administrative and financial logistics, which fall in the area of bureaucracy.

There has been a reference to public health initiatives by way of operational research about the following agenda, which could be extended:

(i) Training material for AYUSH/Allopathic doctors and para-medics in public health.
(ii) Training of AYUSH/Allopathic doctors and para-medics in delivery of AYUSH interventions in public health.
(iii) Delivery of AYUSH public health interventions in one or more community blocks for developing AYUSH public health model, such as an AYUSH *gram*.
(iv) AYUSH schemes for adolescent girls, women of reproductive age group and geriatric care.
(v) Life Style disorders.
(vi) Nutrition and Anaemia.
(vii) IEC materials in AYUSH.

The proposals to be supported would be in the areas of:

(a) Mother-Child Care,
(b) Nutrition,
(c) Anemia,
(d) Epidemiological studies, and
(e) Training of AYSUH practitioners and paramedics.

The Steering Committee advocated a two-tiered research framework for AYUSH. First tier referred to the generation of 'ocean of knowledge' over the centuries as indigenous knowledge systems having their own distinct foundations, principles, worldviews, philosophical frameworks, theories of health and disease, therapies and concepts. It was necessary to conserve and revitalize these traditional knowledge systems.

Second tier refers to global communicability of the capabilities of AYUSH in dealing with contemporary problems of health care. Thus the standardization of drugs according to modern scientific parameters that are internationally accepted, and path-breaking health concepts and therapies related to pharmaco-genomics, drug delivery methods, human physiology, mental health, immunity, management of systemic disorders, geriatrics, maternity care and so on require inter-cultural and trans-disciplinary research.

As mentioned earlier, MAAS studies in four States of Himachal Pradesh, Madhya Pradesh, Chhattisgarh and Maharashtra brings out the widespread knowledge and use of home remedies for common ailments by the people. Services of local herbalists (*Baiga, Vaidu*) and *Dai* or senior ladies with dai experience are also widely accessed. The AYUSH system and PHC system for primary health care in the three states function as parallel rails with no convergence in sight. NRHM in terms of co-location has been functionally non-existent although the health personnel expressed the usefulness of such a system with proper orientation and CME. In Maharashtra, integration refers to employment of BAMS in the PHC system mostly in tribal belts where MBBS are not available, with a total mismatch between the postings and supplies of ayurvedic medicine.

The para-medics are using AYUSH in their homes, as members of community, which they have imbibed through socialization and enculturation, but not as part of the health care delivery system. They desire AYUSH training and kits. In Chhattisgarh, *Mitanin* (ASHA) programmes are fairly structured, with training modules on home remedies, but not about the textual great tradition concepts.

The concept of welfare state, the rise of international bodies under UN umbrella, global concerns about destroying natural environment, climate change and biodiversity has weighted in favour of public health in comparison to individual, clinically managed health care or treatment oriented system. Democratic governance presupposed active role of people in all aspects of governance. Constitution of India with the cardinal principles of equality and equity has recognized Right to Health and Right of Living.

Promotion of AYUSH through Paramedics

Having experience of community level health work and frequent and close contact with paramedics, the AMOs positioned in PHCs in Maharashtra reported that paramedics and local health functionaries working at village level had no knowledge or very little knowledge about AYUSH and they needed training and information about AYUSH strengths, for guiding appropriate treatment at community level for patient's benefit. Repeatedly, it has been pointed out that the paramedics as part of the larger community and in close contact with them, following AYUSH practices in their families, need to be formally oriented to AYUSH principles and practices about health and disease treatment.

Public Health

Public Health is a term which is totally unknown in the Ayush sector. As a result, the term Epidemiology is also unknown to Ayush graduates and Faculty. One of the greatest problems that our Centre of AYUSH in Public Health had, was to develop the vision of AYUSH administrators and doctors and college faculty about the concept of Public Health and importance of Epidemiology. While the people's sector is practicing AYUSH as home remedies and have cultural practices about nutrition and health, this knowledge is not getting into the IEC material of AYUSH. We are aware that the health care on the ground is actually provided by the paramedics and para-professionals like ANM, MPW, ASHA, AWW and traditional *Dai* and Herbalists like—*Vaidu, Baiga, Gunia, Bhagat, Devarshi* etc. In the training material of paramedics, there is no AYUSH component. In Chhattisgarh, the State Government has developed a concept of *Ayurved Gram*, whereby Ayurved Health Centre is expected to do networking with the local community and provide Ayush services to the people including the plantation of medicinal herbs. Some of these issues have now been recommended by the Steering Committee on AYUSH in the Twelfth Five Year Plan. Concept of AYUSH *gram* is a good subject matter for anthropological concept of holism with the micro planning possible by PRI and CBO, like *Mahila Mandals* and SHGs under the leadership of an AYUSH doctor. Why the AYUSH doctors are better communicators with lay people unless they mystify people with their Sanskrit terminology ? AYUSH, particularly Ayurved, Unani, Yoga or Siddha, except homoeopathy are culture friendly. The language of Ayurved and that of the lay people in terms of *panchamahabhootas*, *doshas* and about food prescriptions in terms of *dincharya* and *ritucharya*, hot and cold, light and heavy are same. AYUSH systems have strengths in preventive and promotive health care. AYUSH addresses the body-mind system, not only to symptoms, thus dealing with systemic causes of disease. Health being an aspect of culture is manageable at the individual, familial and national level as a control mechanism. Chemotherapy is not an answer to disease control programmes at national level. It would only enrich the multinational pharmaceutical industry. If consumption of drugs is taken as an indicator of utilization of a system, AYUSH would lose to modern medicine, in terms of attracting funds from the Planning Commission, linked to 'actual utilization of drugs'. We have to devise other methods to measure the utilization of AYUSH in the homes, not merely in the clinics and hospitals, as in allopathy. Allopathic drugs have essentially to be purchased from pharmacy shops, thus providing documentation unlike AYUSH products which could be made by respective practitioners and at home.

Naturopathy

Naturopathy as a system of medicine, as drugless therapy, is coupled with Yoga in AYUSH, 'Y' representing Yoga and Naturopathy. It is based on the principle of self-healing as is found among other animal beings in nature. Naturopathy shares *panchmahabhoota* concepts with Ayurved. Significant importance is given to diet in naturopathy, as that to be taken in as natural form as possible, such as seasonal fruits and sprouts. Diet is classified as eliminative diet, soothing diet and constructive diet. Diet is considered as medicine but not as a drug.

Mahatma Gandhi came to Pune to try naturopathy at a clinic run by Dr. Dinshaw Mehta. Gandhiji experimented naturopathy with himself. Subsequently, Nature-Cure Trust was formed with Gandhiji as life time Chairman. This Trust was taken over by Government of India in 1986 to establish 'National Institute of Naturopathy' at Pune. There are about 20 Naturopathy colleges in India offering Bachelor's degree. These are mostly located in southern states of India. In Tamil Nadu, orientation in naturopathy is being offered to para-medics. 18th November starting with 2018, every year is to be celebrated as National Naturopathy Day, that being the day when Mahatma Gandhi signed formation of Nature-Cure Trust as the Chairman of the Trust for life on 18th November, 1945.

Anthropology has to study the policy about Naturopathy since this system of medicine addresses to the whole person, not as a patient with some ailment. The concept of 'Holistic Man' is common to Anthropology and Naturopathy. Being a drugless therapy, other textual Indian systems of medicine do not consider naturopathy as a system of medicine. We have advised the researchers in naturopathy to do an ethnographic study of tribal villages and communities, particularly residing in the forests to document the people-nature relationship in totality. Anthropologists could form a team with naturopaths in undertaking such a study. Gandhiji's idea of propagating and practicing nature-cure for the poor people has yet to be developed as a public health programme. Our documentation of people using the herbs from the nature in four states of India has been detailed in the publication, 'AYUSH in Public Health' (Mutatkar, 2016)

Medical Anthropology being culture friendly and people friendly has a great scope in all aspects of training, in designing content of IEC; AYUSH *Gram* functioning and in epidemiology and public health research. Although, the bureaucrats demand and need statistical data, Anthropological qualitative methods such as ethnography, case studies, informal and key informant interviews, observation, genealogy, group discussions and life history, are very important to document the processes about the use of plural systems of medicine by the people. Anthropological knowledge about the hard and soft aspects of culture provide the insights about non-rational variance in behaviour and attitudes, about the causation of disease and treatment seeking behaviour. Mere ethnographic descriptions of traditions do not impress the planners unless it shows measurements of reducing national burden of morbidity and mortality. AYUSH is very strong in maternal and child health, in non-communicable, life style disorders. We have to document these strengths through epidemiological research. AYUSH medical institutions must concentrate on epidemiological research methods to mainstream their systems in national health care. All systems of medicine have their own strengths, and citizens have a right to get the benefits of these strengths. Currently, we know very little about the body-mind interaction and immunity.

Concept of Model AYUSH Gram

It can be an anaemia free *gram*, a village with 0 IMR and 0 MMR, has good environmental sanitation, i.e. there is 100 per cent use of latrines etc. It can also be a village where people know ayurved principles, have knowledge about medicinal plants, know processing of herbs to prepare *'kadha'* (medicinal decoction) for treating minor ailments, have kitchen garden of medicinal plants etc.

Which activities can be done to develop a model ? What are the subactivities ? Can we do all activities at a time? We will need activity planning preparing a schedule of activities with priorities. This will first need listing of activities and sub-activities to be done by the designated personnel, from the public and people's sector.

Common activities could be: (1) Growing medicinal plants on common land, (2) Water purification at source and home level, e.g. use of copper, munga (drumstick) seed plant powder, and 3 Use of latrines etc.

1. **Anaemia free village:** We will need Hb estimation, drugs for treatment, dietary advice.
2. **For 0 MMR**: We will have to give ANC, PNC care and ensure safe delivery: will need monitoring with ASHA's help, backup plan for referral, focus on adolescent girls.
3. **For 0 NNMR, IMR**: We will need ANC, PNC and delivery care, avoiding birth of low birth weight babies lactation and nutrition care of women and children, fortification of supplements, immunization coverage etc.
4. **For birth of normal weight babies**: We will need to work for nutrition of pregnant women, fortification of food with ayurved drugs for improving lactation etc.
5. **Community participation**: Dialogue with village community groups and their participation: Meetings of gram panchayat members, mahila mandals, self help groups, youth groups, senior citizens etc.
6. **Local Networking of Government Departments** (Inter-sectoral coordination):
   - (i) With Grampanchayat,
   - (ii) Education Department for school health,
   - (iii) ICDS for Anganbadis,
   - (iv) Yoga and Naturopathy,

(v) Government Public health system, and
(vi) NGOs and CBOs.

This will be required as an example for fortification of anganwadi nutrition supplement, mid-day meal fortification, yoga camp, health camp, adolescent health etc.

7. **Health education**: As per AYUSH principles and concepts about *Prakriti*, *Dincharya*, *Ritucharya* in the context of age groups, gender, occupation etc., we will have to prepare education material, for the people, for the doctors and for the para-medics.

What is the Contribution of Traditional Medicine in RCH?

Food habits of people get linked up with the socio-economic status of the families. What can people afford to eat although there is a concept of *Chauras Aahar*. There are definite post-delivery practices for improving the lactation, which also helps baby growth and aims at setting the internal organs to normality. There are also such customs as oil massage for the baby and mother for atleast 45 days, oil massage for baby could continue longer. In the paediatric ward of KEM Hospital, Pune, oil massage was given to low birth weight babies, which has shown good results (omega-3 fatty acids).

In the life cycle approach of RCH, adolescent health is also on the agenda. Concepts of male sexuality and sexual weakness are directly related to body metabolism given in Ayurved. Concept of '*Shukra*' and '*Ojas*' are also linked with immunity in relation to HIV-TB. In people's mind weak immunity as the causation of disease is considered more important than the bacteriological theory in modern medicine.

The main question is, can health care be delivered by paid low level health functionaries or should the people be motivated to strengthen health concepts and practices which are a part of the great tradition in traditional medicine.

Research

Public Health research could start with two kinds of issues in AYUSH sector.

1. What is the prevalence and incidence of a health or disease issue for which AYUSH has strengths or AYUSH interventions could be meaningful? Ex. Adolescent anaemia or anaemia in the reproductive stage. Anorectal disorders, Cultural practices of ANC-PNC.

2. Explore the areas where more people are likely to maintain health by promotional or preventive action. Ex. Geriatric age group whose population is increasing and who may be conscious about preventing disorder so as not to be a social or economic burden on the next generation family. People who have started practicing yoga as a therapy and for preventive and promotive uses. People who have taken to meditation consciously or undergo training in practices like *Vipashyana.*
3. Documentation of tribal therapy and diet practices in relation to natural environment.
4. What are the practices about care during reproductive stage and about maternity? What are the practices about neonatal or infant care, with what effect? What are these practices among various religious and ethnic groups, occupational or professional group including the practices among lady doctors and professionals when they became mothers themselves? What are the traditional preventive and promotive health care practices of the various ethnic group or social group populations including about nutrition and diet?

Public health and epidemiological research is aimed at identifying the health issues affecting large population groups in various categories such as age, gender, occupation, ethnic group, people with or without land, impacting migration etc. to be able to plan appropriate policies and their implementation for sustainability, promoting self help attitudes and practices. Whatever traditional patterns of attitudes and behaviour are found effective according to AYUSH need to be strengthened. If found contradicting the AYUSH principle, they need to be modified through various methods of communication without hurting the self-esteem and self-confidence of the people.

The crucial issue in research is to have a question or several questions in mind to find an answer to 'why' and 'how many' or 'how much', for which an answer has to be attempted with or without intervention.

Pilot Research Projects

Illustrative Pilot and Small Grant Projects could be:

1. Pilot operational projects at the sub-centre level linking ANM, ASHA, traditional *Dai*, AWW and Herbalist healer under the leadership of AYUSH doctor from AYUSH dispensary.

This would include training of all personnel in AYUSH by the Physician through interactive sessions.

2. Malnutrition: Supplementary foods fortified by AYUSH drugs to be given at the *Anganwadi,* schools where mid-day meals are served and in the residential *Ashram* schools.
3. AYUSH nutrition education to *Mahila Mandals*, SHGs, PRI with focus on women members, at AYUSH dispensary, sub-centre, *Anganwadi.*
4. ANC-PNC according to AYUSH at the sub-centre and AYUSH dispensaries. Deliveries to be conducted at the sub-centre/*Dai* hut *(Kuti)* in village, by a team of *Dai*-ANM-ASHA-Herbalist, with emergency management through referral pattern.
5. Water purification with herbal treatment at household and village level. AYUSH to take up this programme as nodal agency (e.g. Drumstick seeds, copper, alum).
6. Geriatric care: AYUSH health camps. *Rasayan Chikitsa*, yoga and meditation, *Dincharya, Ritucharya* as per *Prakriti.*
7. AYUSH as nodal agency for some national programmes in selected blocks/district.
   (a) Anaemia
   (b) Jaundice
   (c) Kshar-Sutra
   (d) Panchkarma
   (e) RCH
   (f) Geriatric Care
   (g) Adolescent Health
   (h) School Health
   (i) Cardio-vascular disorder
   (j) Respiratory disorder
   (k) Non-communicable ailments
   (l) Immuno-deficient disorders
   (m) Diabetes

   Strengths of AYUSH to be developed as national programmes: Intervention Research.
8. Propagation of kitchen gardens with medicinal plants in the households and at *anganwadi*, sub-centre, PHC, AYUSH dispensary, schools, *ashram schools* etc.
9. Concept of *ayurved gram* of Chhattisgarh government. *Gram Panchayat* to use common village lands for medicinal plants.
10. AYUSH medicinal kit processed by local herbalist to be

purchased for ASHA, *Dai*, ANM, AWW. Herbalist training in processing of locally available herbs.

11. Herbal nurseries under the supervision of traditional herbal healer in coordination with local forest department to be supervised by AYUSH physician of the dispensary.
12. AYUSH physician to supervise over two-three sub-centres around the dispensary to be developed according to AYUSH perspective.
13. Promote co-location and cross-referral services within AYUSH, in AYUSH dispensaries and in selected PHCs.
14. Providing maternity services including delivery at sub-centre and AYUSH dispensaries. Provide *Dai-huts* in big villages under sub-centre/AYUSH dispensaries, to be erected by the community/PRI.
15. Strengthen youth dormitories in tribal areas for adolescent health.
16. Surveys about home remedies for disease treatment and RCH (pregnancy, child birth, lactation and child rearing).
17. Health Systems Research: Integration at S.C., PHC, CHC and at district level. Common cadre of para-medical personnel.

Recommendations: Public Health

The existing Research-*cum*-Training Centre for Folk Medicine for revitalizing the AYUSH health practices of tribal communities in the North East need to have regional centres in other tribal areas.

Create a high power National Committee/Task Force on AYUSH and public health for selection, monitoring and evaluation of pilot projects.

Design pilot public health programmes related to eco-system specific herbal remedies, home and community herbal gardens, clean drinking water, non-specific diarrhoea, anaemia, MCH etc. for introduction into the National Rural Health Mission (NRHM).

Provide systematic, institutionalized and high quality short-term training to AYUSH medical practitioners and paramedics in public health at various levels before their deputation to the primary healthcare system across the country.

Install an AYUSH referral system at all levels from the village to the state level with equal salaries, promotional channels and supply of medicine and equipments on par with allopathy, sharing state-of-the-art diagnostic facilities.

Promote a comprehensive AYUSH Maternal and Child Health programme in select districts/tehsils/blocks.

Operationalize mainstreaming of AYUSH systems in Eleventh Five Year Plan in all the States of India.

Support under a coordinated programme, a network of AYUSH institutes and competent NGOs to carry out epidemiological research from an AYUSH perspective in selected districts.

Reform existing administrative structures for management of public health at the central, state and district levels so that they can be brought under an integrated management framework.

Introduce pilot projects in selected districts on preventive health for school children.

Review the Information, Education and Communication (IEC) scheme and suggest ways in which it can be expanded and professionally managed.

Develop AYUSH health awareness programmes and IEC materials for common people as well as for modern health professionals and para-professionals. Develop AYUSH initiatives in Water and Sanitation programmes.

Local Health Traditions

Support pharmacological studies and participatory community based clinical trials on selected local health practices relevant to public health.

Support coordinated projects *via* reputed NGOs and AYUSH institutions in selected blocks/districts for documentation of local traditions, assessment and based on scientific evidence, revitalization of traditional health practices related to primary health care, midwifery, bone setting and ethno-veterinary care in order to enhance health security of rural households.

It is a paradox that the para-medics who share AYUSH traditions with the people, in their own homes, do not get any orientation or training in AYUSH. The number of para-medical training centres is ridiculously low, while there is a clamouring for more medical colleges in all systems of medicine. Chhattisgarh in collaboration with State Health Resource Centre (SHRC) tried to bring out some AYUSH training material for the *Mitanins* (ASHA) and *Anganwadi* worker. However, the ANM, MPW and AWW workers are not the cadre of AYUSH department.

Nutrition

The supplementary food programmes in Anganwadi for children below

2 years, food supplements to pregnant and lactating women, as also to adolescent girls on the threshold of marriage, need to be based on AYUSH principles and fortified with AYUSH drugs. The traditional knowledge about good nutrition and diet exists in the communities by way of food offerings to deities on ceremonies and festivals and to the guests. Instead, food supplements and biscuits for *anganwadi* are recommended from the markets with obvious kick backs. The mid-day meals in the schools could easily be fortified with local greens, amla, drum-sticks, ragi etc. instead of potatoes coming from the contractor due to weekly bulk purchase and shelf life. All lady doctors during their own maternity followed the traditional food supplements useful for lactation, besides oil massage to self and new born babies.

Conclusion

Anthropologists have an important role to play to establish linkage between the ethno-medical, little/local traditional practices, with textual great traditions of AYUSH. Let us not feel shy of intervention research raising the colonial bogey of value neutrality in the name of pseudo-science. Silence and inaction, despite acceptance of universal values of life and human rights would make our knowledge of ethno-medicine irrelevant for human good. It would only help the commercial vested interests of those who proliferate pharma industry and 'nutritious' food products in the name of modern science using terms which are unintelligible to common people. As said, commercial products are sold having magical results when couched in scientific terminology. When traditionally time tested products are promoted, they are labelled as unscientific, lacking laboratory based evidence.

No research without deliverables for policy planning and implementation would be tolerated if it does not promote the spirit of the Constitution of India. Everything has to be good for 'We the People of India.'

C: LEPROSY: BIO-SOCIO-CULTURAL ISSUES

I

Initiation in Leprosy

At the recommendation of Prof. Irawati Karve I was invited as a guest faculty at the Armed Forces Medical College, Pune in 1963, at the PSM

Department followed immediately at B.J. Medical College, both colleges being affiliated to Poona University. In 1965, Gandhi Memorial Leprosy Foundation, Wardha had a month long orientation programme for their health education officers at B.J. Medical College with Dr. N.S. Deodhar, who was Head of the PSM department and also a member of GMLF executive committee. I was asked to speak on social aspects of leprosy while earlier I was asked to contribute a paper on the topic at the *Maharashtra Medical Journal* having a special number on leprosy. In 1967, I was inducted as a social science member of the executive committee of GMLF. I was asked to evaluate the health education programme of GMLF leading to a book "*Society and Leprosy*" published by GMLF. The Silver Jubilee volume of GMIF, 'Window on Leprosy' was my paper on 'Social Aspects of Leprosy', which caught the attention of WHO, Leprosy Division, Geneva. I was invited to write the first ever paper on 'Social and Economic Aspects of Leprosy' in 1981 as a working paper for an international meeting on the same subject. This followed continued participation at the WHO and GOI meetings about leprosy including the evaluations of NLEP of the government. I was asked to deliver a key-note speech at the plenary session of International Leprosy Congress at Delhi in 1984, followed by participating at the scientific meeting about various aspects of leprosy, representing social sciences, among the 12 scientists from the Western countries, at the Pontifical Academy of Sciences at Vatican. We had an hour-long audience with Pope John Paul II at his office at St. Peters Church.

A Centre for Social Science Research on Leprosy (CSSRL) was awarded to GMIF by WHO inviting me to head the centre, soliciting deputation from the University of Poona. The international NGOs also sought help in their research programmes. This has led to getting International Gandhi Award for Leprosy in 2015, recommended by Hon. Vice President of India as Chairman of International Jury.

Leprosy

Leprosy as one of the most ancient diseases afflicting human beings was considered untreatable in all systems of medicine, without divine intervention. The drug DDS (dapsone) was introduced in 1945. Multi-drug therapy (MDT) with a combination of Rifampicine, Clofazimine and DDS introduced in the control programme around 30 years ago has become the standard treatment for leprosy. Leprosy is a stigmatized disease leading to risk of social death, and the disease has been an enigma to medical sciences. Issues about the disease have been shuttled between branding it as a medical problem and a social problem, thus shying away from finding a holistic solution. The medical fraternity and social workers themselves have been the victims of social stigma like the afflicted. The humanity required divine intervention as from Jesus and his followers like Mother Teresa, or compassion of Mahatma Gandhi to address the issues, despite scientific advancement about the causation and curability of leprosy. This has been one medical problem, where it was considered necessary for the medical and social scientists to form joint teams in programme formulation, implementation and research. Anthropology with the strength of qualitative methods like life history and case study had a good chance of contributing to knowledge to decrease the disease burden at the individual and public health levels.

Motivated by biblical story, 'Jesus healed the leper,' the Christian church has taken to leprosy work with great commitment, having formed several associations and institutions all over the world towards leprosy control and cure. Mahatma Gandhi was also believed to be influenced by Bible about leprosy work, while in South Africa.

In India, non-Christian efforts have been visible in the Vidarbh region of Maharashtra. Leprosy has been an issue in Vidarbha with leprasoria at Warora established by Baba Amte and at Amravati by Shivajirao Patwardhan. Gandhi Memorial Leprosy Foundation was established at Wardha, since Gandhiji lived in Wardha, with a cottage in Sevagram ashram for the leprosy afflicted Parchureshastri, who was under the personal care of Gandhiji. The Leprosy Mission (TLM) also works in the neighbourhood at Champa, and Raipur. DANISH Leprosy Programme, DANLEP worked in MP, Chhattisgarh and Odisha. While I was drawn to leprosy at GMLF Wardha and later with all international, Christian Leprosy organizations, some of my colleagues in Anthropology complimented me with sympathy for doing good social work. I had to tell them that I was not cleaning the wounds of leprosy patients like Mother Teresa but was highlighting social science research issues which changed the objectives of leprosy control at WHO, and several international organizations modified their vision and mission documents, to extend their focus from patient to the family and community.

Leprosy was declared a non-public health issue recently by India and WHO, now again coming back with rising incidence of child leprosy and with grade 2 deformity at first reporting. Why? What is wrong? A vertical control programme was turned into a horizontal or integrated programme with general health services, by issuing a government order, without requisite preparation. Bacillus (mycobacterium laprae) as a causative agent was identified in 1873 by Hansen and accepted in 1897 by international leprosy organizations. In Latin American countries, leprosy is called as Hansen's disease, presumably to avoid the stigma associated with the term leprosy.

The demand for health behaviour research has been increasing since the acceptance of primary health care strategy to achieve 'Health for All' as per *Alma-Ata* declaration of 1978 by WHO. The inter-sectoral development approach fits very well in the anthropological theoretical concepts of integration of culture and culture change.

Health Programmers and Medical Scientists have been concerned with leprosy on two issues:

(1) Control of the disease as a public health issue within a reasonably short period.
(2) To understand the transmission process.

This has been sought to be achieved by technocratic approach, with the help of multiple drug therapy and vaccine. However, due to problems with animal experimentation, there still exist many gaps in medical knowledge about leprosy. Peoples' perception of the disease based on centuries old experiences and based on indigenous medical traditions make people believe that the disease is incurable and is identified with deformity. The threat of social death and communicability of deformity hamper peoples' participation in control programmes.

Help of behavioural researchers is sought by health programmers:

(i) To ensure community participation in diagnosis and treatment strategies by educating the people using appropriate communication media.
(ii) To understand socio-cultural and economic factors in transmission to have deeper understanding of the epidemiology of disease.

Problems of first order are expressed by using terms like case finding, case holding, stigma, community participation, cost effectiveness, dynamic interaction of health services, patients and community, and personal body image etc. Problems of second order are expressed in terms of life styles, contact with a patient, mobility, mating patterns, kinship, environmental sanitation, personal hygiene, nutrition etc.

In short, answers to the crucial question—why do people behave the way they do?—are sought from behavioural researchers.

Anthropology as a behavioural discipline is valued in international health forums due to qualitative research tools used in anthropology which provides holistic perception and depth of a problem. Anthropological approach of 'Going Native' help us to understand ethnographic details of health behaviour of people.

Just to take couple of examples about leprosy, which is a disease affecting the nerves:

(1) People identify leprosy with deformity; health programmers and medical personnel identify it with infection, with a patch, which is harmless, being anesthetic, not causing any discomfort to the afflicted.

While the priority of the programmers and the resultant strategies are drawn for controlling infection by medication, peoples' priorities are for controlling or if possible reversing deformities, i.e. nerve damage. Peoples' perception is based on cultural ideas of personal body image which are strengthened in indigenous medical systems. These differing paradigms among people and among the programmers result in peoples' apathy towards the programme.

(2) Most widely advertised health education slogan—'Leprosy is Curable' is unacceptable to people since curability in leprosy is a bacteriological concept, something which people have never experienced. Killing the bacilli with drugs does not reverse the anesthesia, nor reverses functional disability or visible deformity. If an anthropologist is asked about priorities in medical research in leprosy, the answer would be priority research in nerve damage since people are concerned with the effects of it affecting their lives.

We have carried out the evaluation of health education programme of Government of India in leprosy. The evaluation research clearly brings out peoples' perceptions as outlined above. (Mutatkar and Tare: *Evaluation of Impact of Health Education in SET Pattern*, ICMR report, 1988)

The varying research perspectives about leprosy could be analyzed around the key term "Identity." Man has an identity in his own self-esteem, in the family, community, work place with roles to play commensurate with the multiple statuses. A *Sanyasi* has no legal or social identity in terms of ownership and inheritance of property or in the social organization, but has social responsibility of helping the people at large. A *sanyasi* enjoys high social respect. On the other hand, once identified with affliction of leprosy by medical personnel or by community, identity crises for an afflicted emerge with prospect of rejection, isolation, and social death much abhorred than biological death. Although the terminological identity has been changed from 'Leper' to 'Leprosy patient', the stigma has not disappeared even after bacteriological 'cure', since the identity continues as 'ex-patient' even in leprosy institutions.

The English word 'Leprosy' which is identified as a chronic, communicable disease in modern medicine is now bacteriologically curable but community is not convinced due to potential danger and historical experience of deformity and disability. Programme is more concerned about reducing prevalence with the hypothesis that it would reduce incidence, ultimately achieving operationally defined 'Elimination'. In different languages and medical systems, the term 'leprosy' is perceived not in consonance with the English term. Debates about relapse, reaction, re-infection and nerve affliction among the scientific community is confusing to the lay medical fraternity, who share ignorance and stigma about scientific aspects with the community. This ignorance in the medical profession could be research documented instead of about the people and patients.

Researchers in Social Sciences including Anthropology continue to feel shy about health research since health is identified with restoration from illness with the use of drug treatment, which is the domain of health professionals in all systems of medicine. Hygiene renamed as Preventive and Social Medicine turning into Public Health is not yet a priority sector in health care system. Both the terms 'Public' and 'Health' are non-medical terms unlike 'Disease' and 'Treatment'. Leprosy programme also began with non-medical concepts like 'Case finding' and 'Case holding'. The key to success of the programme continues to be 'Voluntary reporting'. Leprosy is a queer disease, whereby the affliction and cure have to be pronounced by a third person, the signs and symptoms not identified by the afflicted. Solution to this problem was conceived by making people aware and knowledgeable about signs, symptoms and treatment of leprosy to modify their attitudes. Interestingly the programme of 'Health Education' got rechristened as 'Information, Education, Communication' to the present term 'Behavioural Change Communication'. ICMR research report in 1988 about studies in the States of Orissa and Andhra Pradesh done by Gandhi Memorial Leprosy Foundation concluded about the absence of 'E' in SET pattern. (Mutatkar and Tare: ICMR report on E in SET pattern)

Unlike medical research which has to be intervention research, social sciences and anthropology continued with the colonial bogey of 'value neutrality' which insulated them from initiating or participating in action for solution of a problem. Only Social Work discipline indulges into solutions, usually at individual levels as empathy, compassion, using the fire brigade strategies of extinguishing the problem after it has become serious, with no mechanism to prevent its causation. Anthropologists in spite of good grounding of theory and methodology to unravel the human behaviour, have not yet ventured in policy planning to find solutions appropriate to the communities and Nation-States.

It is disheartening that we are not willing to go beyond KAP studies after 60 years, which does not provide us with any new information worth translating which would provide instruments for action. Facilitating community intervention as an action research strategy has been tried by some leprosy NGOs like DANLEP and TLM with the help of behavioural scientists. Operational social science research evaluating the centrally designed vertical-horizontal strategies at macro level and the response of the people need to be prioritized. The bogey of stigma to cover up programme failures need to be research documented. From the social science perspective, medical research priority need to be nerve damage which is the crux of identity of leprosy, which shudders the community from shedding its age old attitudes preventing voluntary action. Best practices of successful community action need to be research documented. Social Scientists in medical institutions continue to work in isolation as service cadre to nurture the disease identity of health issues. Following the model of CME (Continuing Medical Education), ICMR-ICSSR joint programmes on health could devise capacity building and up-scaling programmes in social science theory and research methodology.

To conclude, contrasting paradigms of medical issues in reducing bacteriological prevalence and social issues of reducing deformity and disability prevalence and incidence, need to be merged to eradicate the fear of leprosy from the mind of the community so as to promote community action towards elimination of leprosy as a public health problem on lines of other communicable diseases.

II

The issue whether leprosy as a disease primarily caused by a bacillus can be eradicated or controlled is scientific in nature, since there is no irrefutable evidence about the transmission process. Bio-Medical scientists should have an answer to this issue.

From the social science point of view, the disease of leprosy can cease to be a psychological and social threat to an individual or the community if the programme takes into consideration the fears from which the community suffers on account of leprosy. People's perception of leprosy all over the world refers to ulcers, deformity, mutilation leading to social ostracism and resultant loss of social status or identity. People know death is unavoidable but prefer it without suffering. Leprosy is associated with physical and social suffering but not with death. It is, however, associated with social death which is worse than physical death for the social animal like man. People do understand infection on the basis of their experience with many other contagious diseases, while other diseases get cured or lead to mortality, people have no long experience of cure or death in leprosy.

How does the leprosy control programme, which aims to wipe out the disease by MDT, look at the problem? For the programme, it is basically a problem of controlling infection by reducing the pool of infection by treating the identified patients with drugs. Vaccine could possibly prevent infection but the vaccine trials have not been successful. The control programme is thus organized to identify the patients and persuade them to take drugs regularly. The programme conceptually recognizes the need to prevent deformities so that the disabled patients do not become a social and economic burden on the community.

The efficiency of such a programme would depend upon three factors:

(a) Motivation of the patients and their families to get diagnosed early and to take regular treatment.
(b) Committed health personnel who would maintain individual contacts with the patients and their families to prevent deformities, following a human, compassionate approach and to attend their work at regular hours.
(c) Fast acting drugs with an assured supply.

Fortunately, the fast acting drugs have been found and the MDT programme is based on the delivery of these drugs. However, the first two factors listed above are socio-cultural in nature. Why are people not motivated enough to participate in the activities of the control programme? Under what conditions would people participate in the programme? Is it true that there is more apathy on the part of medical personnel about leprosy? Is it true that social stigma associated with people is more of a bogey to cover up the inefficiency or apathy of health personnel ?

The people have experienced cure from other communicable diseases by taking drugs. But, they have not so far experienced cure from leprosy on a large scale. People are not yet aware about the concept or nature of cure in leprosy. Similarly, they continue to be ignorant about the evolution of the disease starting from non-itching patch or shiny, oily skin to nerve damage resulting in deformity. The health education in this regard has fallen short of communicating with the people about the concerns and issues they have experienced through centuries of non-curability and threat of social exclusion.

If the control programme is directed to prevention of deformity, people's cooperation is likely to be more active, since people are afraid of deformity in leprosy. As long as total prevention of leprosy is not possible, as long as large number of people are at risk in endemic areas, there is also the fear in the minds of the people about getting deformity. If people are assured that despite leprosy affliction, deformity was preventable, they could willingly cooperate with the programme strategies.

This change in the direction of the programme requires intense health education directed to the community, the families of the patients and the patients themselves. As soon as a patient is diagnosed, close monitoring has to be done by a health worker to ensure that the deformities do not occur or are corrected early. Voluntary action by the patient and his family is a utopian objective unmatched by the programme targeted to kill the bacilli only to reduce prevalence of disease. Similar problems persist in TB and HIV.

Mere sermonizing that regular treatment will prevent the onset of deformities will not motivate the patients to be regular about intake of drugs. It may be necessary to educate the patients and the community about the mechanism of nerve damage. This would require different kinds of health education which would need to be budgeted in the programme.

All health programmes are technical programmes aimed at technical solutions to human problems. Health education is given low priority by bureaucracy since its impact cannot be quantitatively measured easily or the programme cannot be targeted easily. Health education has to be measured as per qualitative rather than quantitative parameters.

Are our programmers willing to change the orientation of programme from eradication of infection to control or prevention of deformities? If not, the failures due to drug resistant bacilli would continue to require more potent drugs. From the anthropological and social science standpoint, deformity prevention programme has better chances of success and would prove cost effective, since people would readily volunteer to own such a programme if their capacities to identify and prevent deformities are enhanced through social action.

III

The scientists, administrators and fieldworkers in India have a perception of socio-economic determinants of leprosy in the country. However, available socio-economic data has not been computed with a view to present comprehensive picture in scientific terms. Socio-economic data available in control projects is used in epidemiological research but it is neither available as public document nor does it satisfy the social science research needs.

What is meant by 'socio-economic' and how is it perceived in leprosy work?

In social science research, the 'socio-economic' usually refers to assessment of social and economic status of a person, a family or a social group, under study. Data relating to age, sex, occupation, income, caste, religion, ethnic group, education, formal position in authority structure, composition of family, social contacts, material artifacts in the house, house type, cattle population, quality of land etc. is collected. The data reveals ascribed (at birth) status such as membership of a particular family, caste, traditional occupation and also achieved (acquired) status referring to education, new type of income or occupation etc. In an Indian village, even in a township, people of one ethnic group, such as a caste group, live together in one locality. Several such families are related to each other consanguineally or affinally. Such data is useful to understand the transmission process through contact survey. These data are used in epidemiological studies and are expected to help in identifying the causative factors in disease spread in the community.

Many leprosy workers understand socio-economic consequences of getting the disease, which are branded as social aspects of leprosy. The problems arising out of deformity, loss of ability to work and earn, economic dependence, social stigma and rehabilitation problems as also difficulty in getting a spouse, family estrangement are identified social problems related to leprosy. Such problems warrant the attention of social workers. These problems have a bearing on leprosy control programmes in regard to case finding, case holding, apathy of medical profession etc.

Thus, socio-economic factors may have a bearing on epidemiological picture on one hand and may manifest consequences of identification of disease in individuals, on the other hand.

In the perception of disease itself, there are variations. A disease may be a bacteriological, immunological or an epidemiological problem for a scientist, a public health problem for an administrator but for a common man, it may be discomfort at the physical and mental levels. Sense of ill-being, disorganisation in individual and family life about economic and social functions are identified with disease. Action for treating the disease is initiated according to the levels of sense of ill-being and disorganisation.

In leprosy, clinical manifestation changes the identity of a person and slowly leads him to social death, depending upon the degree of deformity and disability and prevalence of social stigma and other factors. Social stigma may itself vary according to prevalence and incidence rates, rural-urban differences, deformity rates and level of literacy. From societal stand-point, bacteriological condition of a disease in a patient makes no sense. If there is a sense of well-being, no visible signs of ill health, no loss of identity due to disfigurement, the person is considered healthy. People identify infective hepatitis by yellow pigmentation in the eyes and identify cure by its absence and normal appetite and physical vitality. Thus, people's concern about leprosy relates to efficiency of disease cure to make them functional in social and economic situations and does not relate to bacteriological consideration. A healthy person is one who is acceptable in his own group to perform social roles expected of him by virtue of his ascribed and achieved status.

What is important is that people should not be afraid of the disease and should shed off their prejudices. Quick relief from the exterior signs of leprosy and absence of deformity are enough indicators for social acceptability of the disease and the patient.

It would be worthwhile to find out the knowledge of people about successful vaccines of small pox or triple vaccine. People accept therapy or vaccine because therapy cures and vaccine prevents disease. People accept curative practices which are available, cheap, effective and do not disturb normal routine as far possible. However, this does not guarantee acceptance of causation theories put forth by therapists. They may continue to take medicines and yet harbour prejudices for a considerable time. In India, causation of leprosy continues to be associated with (a) sin, (b) sex, (c) heredity, (d) impure blood, (e) poor people, and (f) undesirable food mix.

Suggested study for contact transmission:

1. Usually range of marital ties in Indian villages do not go beyond a radius of 25 miles. In case of some caste groups, it may slightly vary on the positive or negative side.
2. There could be preferential cross-cousin or parallel cousin mating in some castes or religious groups.
3. Caste-wise genealogies need to be collected of all the people in one village including the patients. Almost all the villages within a radius of 25 miles or so are likely to be covered by these genealogies.
4. The recorded patients in these villages can be identified in the genealogies bringing out the picture of kin-contact, if any.
5. Nature, duration and extent of contact can be ascertained by interviewing the patients and their families.
6. If possible, genetic tests may also be taken.

IV

Health Education Evaluation

Health education is perceived as a tool of awareness programme. It is also perceived as a tool for empowering and enabling the people and the patients, to develop self-reliance. However, awareness does not ensure acceptance leading to positive action. In leprosy control programme, health education finds place in SET strategy. It aims to inform people about the signs and symptoms of leprosy as a disease, with a view to promote voluntary reporting and early case detection. The ICMR study has indicated that there is no well designed programme of health education in leprosy control. Leprosy programmes in the government and NGO sectors admit lack of will and vigour in health education programme. They attribute their apathy to helplessness in assessing the impact of health education on increasing the efficiency of leprosy control programme.

Health Education of the community and patients is recommended as an input to bring down prevalence in a cost-effective manner and to prevent deformities and disabilities. The real input that is considered desirable for bringing down prevalence is the intake of drugs by patients regularly, i.e. total compliance. Health education is expected to be a tool in ensuring compliance, as per leprosy programme Ideally, health education is expected to promote voluntary reporting once people are made aware of the early signs and symptoms of leprosy.

How to measure the impact of health education?

Since lowering prevalence is the prime objective of leprosy control and since that is dependent on identifying a case of leprosy and the case complying with the instructions about drug consumption, the impact of health education has to be measured in terms of voluntary reporting and regularity of treatment.

The recording system in leprosy control is geared to measure prevalence but not geared to measure the impact of health education. Even proper recording of health education inputs is not done which could favour evaluation.

Evaluation has been commonly done in health programmes by what is known as KAP, knowledge, attitude and practive studies. Usually KAP is assessed with the help of interview schedules before introducing a programme and again repeated when the programme is designed to be over. The differences, in the responses of people at two periods of time is perceived as the result of intervention strategies. KAP, however, based entirely on interview schedule went into disrepute due to idealized responses in the illiterate communities. Interviews conducted without proper initial contact with the participants are not likely to provide scientifically valid and reliable data. KAP was favoured in preference to anthropological methods of participant observation since it provided quantifiable indicators. However, recently the shift has again taken place in favour of qualitative techniques of data collection with the use of observation, informal interviews, focused group interviews and through presentation of case studies. Attempts are being made to devise methods to quantify the variables in qualitative analysis. It has now been accepted that a judicious mix of qualitative and quantitative tools for data collection and analysis have to be favoured.

Three examples of evaluation studies of health education in leprosy have been presented to bring out the relevant issues in evaluation.

1. Evaluation study of urban health education programme of Gandhi Memorial Leprosy Foundation: An urban health education unit of Pune identified as the best by the Chairman of GMLF was studied to assess the attitudes of urban people after the programme was administered for 10 years. A comparative assessment of the tools of health education was also sought to be studied which possibly changed the attitudes. A control study group was located in a town, Jalgaon, after eliminating the claims of many candidate towns in Maharashtra. The programme goals were identified through the interviews of Chairman, Director and Health Education Officer of the unit under study.

The main tool of collecting information from the people, the doctors and the teachers, has been the interview schedule. This was supplemented by an attitude scale. About six case studies were collected at Jalgaon and Pune. Observation notes at clinics and at health education programmes were maintained. The research hypothesis were spelt out for proper analysis. The results provided a contradictory panorama of peoples' perception. While people identified the signs and symptoms of leprosy and gave positive responses about infectivity and curability, they continued to nurture prejudices about hereditary nature of leprosy, association of deformity and leprosy and isolation or divorce of leprosy patients. The theoretical analytical frame of soft and hard core of culture in Anthropology was used to explain the contradictions in responses.

Actually evaluation is a soft term used in place of audit, which in India is commonly misunderstood as fault finding in the economic transactions in a department. Audit is performed at the end of the transaction or at the end of the financial year. Evaluation is also likewise recommended at the end of the programme or when fresh decisions are to be sought about the continuation or discontinuation of the programme. While 'Before and After' model is considered ideal model for measuring the impact of a programme, usually 'After only' is the model that is possible since evaluation is not built into the administration or design of the programme. As a result, no base line data is available for subsequent evaluation. 'After only' model essentially requires a control for comparison. Though, not ideal, there is no other method to evaluate, without a control.

It would, however, be difficult to measure the impact of health education in terms of voluntary reporting and regularity of treatment alone. The effectiveness of drugs, acceptance of diagnosis, and the duration of period for which the drugs have to be taken may be the variables affecting voluntary reporting and regularity of treatment. Marked behavioural change is expected from the period under DDS Monotherapy as compared to MDT. It would thus have to be determined as to what should be the objectives of health education in leprosy which need to be evaluated.

"Evaluation is the process of assessing the achievement of the stated objectives of a programme and it attempts to measure the adequacy, efficiency and acceptance of the programme by all parties concerned." (WHO:TRS: 409)

The basic goal of programme evaluation is to see whether a project or a programme is doing what it is intended to do, that is, whether it is meeting its goals. It is, therefore, necessary to know the programme goals, before setting and working on the goals of evaluation process (research goals). Sometimes the stated goals are not the real goals, the stated goals having entered the programme due to political or other vested interests. The goals as perceived by the Chairman of the organization, by the Director of the institution, by the field supervisors and by the fieldworkers actually implementing the programmes may be at variance with each other. In such a situation which goals are being evaluated ?

Health education programme could be evaluated at two levels: (1) Whether the programme has been successful in achieving the desired changes in peoples' health behaviour? (2) To what extent the desired change in peoples' behaviour has brought down morbidity and mortality in a given disease? While the disease control programmes would be interested in evaluation as per second level, the social scientists would be satisfied with the first level. Actually there can be no standard duration of time to reach the first level and from first level to second level.

Discussion

There are considerable methodological problems involved in undertaking such evaluation studies. Usually no benchmark data is collected before starting health education programme. Scientific data having bearing on prevalence and incidence is collected before studies on drug trials, vaccine trials or similar scientific studies are undertaken. As a result, scientific experimental model of evaluation research cannot be implemented in evaluation of health education. However, GMLF health education study in zone C has been done on scientific lines since base line data was collected. NLEP study is a classic example of 'after only with comparison group' model of evaluation.

Another problem is to get research staff trained in leprosy as well as in social science research methodology. This problem has been sorted out in NLEP study by having a team of two workers, one trained in leprosy and another trained in social science research. This creates another problem. Since leprosy worker is a programme activist, he does not appreciate the research role, resulting in role conflict. In GMLF study, evaluation research was done by programme workers themselves who had been assigned zones for research other than their zone of leprosy control. Most of these workers were involved in base line study. Role conflict was sought to be minimized by organizing a week long rigourous orientation workshop in social science research methodology.

The following methodological gains were expected from the studies:

1. Mix of quantitative and qualitative methods of data collection would bring out data relevant to medical aspects of control as also relevant to social aspects of control.
2. Two sets of research investigators in NELP and GMLF studies could provide insights for social science research in leprosy and to undertake multi-disciplinary team research. It could also provide leads in social science research training in leprosy.
3. Problems of role conflict, if the research is conducted by action team itself, would provide insights to improve participatory research. Understanding of objective research role would enhance the quality of programme role.
4. Studies could help to design strategies and tools for scientific measurement of impact of health education.

Implications to Leprosy Control Programme

While importance of health education is stressed, comparable inputs are not invested in health education on account of problems of measurement and lack of indicators to assess impact. Measurements are done in terms of reduction in pool of infection by lowering prevalence and incidence. However, people perceive leprosy by deformity and not by infection. As a result they do not co-operate in the control activities, unless social benefits accrue.

1. These evaluation studies could bring out patient's and people's perception of the cause and cure of leprosy and the role of health education programmes in this perception.
2. It could try to establish that the qualitative impact in turn manifests in qualitative results.
3. Studies could highlight the importance of collecting base line data of sociological or qualitative nature in addition to collecting scientific data even in medical studies, pertaining to drug trials and vaccination.
4. Human factors which impede people's response to control activities would be highlighted.

5. It could help scientific planning of health education programme. Before designing health education programme, evaluation strategies of impact analysis in a scientific manner could be built into the structure of the programme. Base line data could be collected before a programme was implemented if the impact of programme needed to be evaluated.
6. The importance of social science research inputs in leprosy control and particularly in health education could be highlighted.
7. The results could clearly indicate, whether there was a well designed health education programme in NLEP and if so, what was its impact on leprosy control. GMLF study would clearly indicate the nature and extent of health education impact. Leprosy control programme of SET model could be redesigned on the basis of results.

V

Discrimination and Stigma

We understand, Supreme Court of India has asked a question in regard to a public interest litigation that if leprosy was curable, why should there be social discrimination in public services or institutions, such as refusing admissions or jobs or other such issues? So discrimination becomes a legal and human rights issue.

Discrimination of groups on account of class, caste, religion, gender etc. have been widely prevalent. But within a group there is no discrimination between peers. People follow their social roles as obligated by traditional social norms, within their respective groups where they live their lives.

When a person is identified as having leprosy, he faces a threat of social exclusion from his own group and all groups. A separate caste or brotherhood of leprosy patients in leprosy colonies used to be formed. (Now there is no new recruitment to these colonies. Some of these have become general hospitals).

However, there is a wide divergence between the biomedical and people's paradigm about leprosy, between the agent and the host perspective.

Leprosy and Stigma have become synonymous terms. Stigma is a direct result of associated deformities and disabilities leading to exclusion and social death, through human history. Epidemiological paradigm focused on control of infection by early detection, voluntary reporting and effective treatment. Awareness and educational programmes are launched for community involvement. However, community concerns about social consequences of leprosy are not the first priority of medical paradigm. As reported earlier, at a WHO meeting on Epidemiology of leprosy in relation to control in November 1983, the third objective "To prevent the development of associated deformities "was added to the first two objectives about infection, treatment and cure (TRS 716–1985). A case of leprosy was defined by the WHO expert committee focusing on clinical signs of leprosy requiring chemotherapy. Mention has been made about rehabilitation needs due to disabilities. The control programme has not gone beyond teaching self-care and providing footware, thus emphasizing the consequences of the diseases. The discussion about disability prevention programme refers to sequential follow-up after reaching the objective of controlling prevalence and incidence.

The social paradigm refers to leprosy as it is perceived by the people and not by what leprosy is understood in medical sciences. The objective of leprosy control has to be the elimination of fear of leprosy, that is, fear about disability, deformity, leading to social exclusion. The programmes designed towards this goal addressing to the concerns of the people would ensure community involvement towards voluntary reporting and regularity of treatment including self-care. DANLEP programmes in Chhattisgarh focusing on community diagnosis, training in differential diagnosis and self-care in ulcer management at public places led to elimination of fear of leprosy and resultants stigma.

A paper on "Social and Economic Aspect of Leprosy "(Mutatkar, 1981) written for WHO recommended priority to nerve damage research, addressing the concerns of the people. Operational research is required in training the community not only about diagnosis of leprosy but also to suspect nerve involvement as early as possible. Since leprosy control is being integrated into primary health programme, this training is also required to be given to the health care staff. The community and several health care personnel have yet to get the conviction of the message that 'disability and deformity are not the consequences of leprosy infection but result due to neglect of leprosy'. Intervention research is, therefore, needed in following the 'experiment–control model' and 'before-after model' of the intervention programmes, about prevention of disability and deformity through community involvement.

Current scenario of leprosy in India refers to the goal of 'leprosy elimination achieved' but incidence of delayed detection, child cases and Grade 2 disabled cases are a cause of concern.

There was an agreed observation that stigma prevented voluntary reporting which identified 'Case Finding' and 'Case Holding' as the major proactive activity of leprosy programne. However, 'E' was reported absent in SET as per study by GMLF for ICMR. There has been confusion between the paradigms of reduction in (a) Prevalence of cases, (b) Prevalence and incidence of deformity-disability, and (c) Prevalence of Stigma.

All actions were to be initiated by 'We', the programme providers in the government or NGO sector. What about People's sector? No attempt was made to make it a people's programme for the community to own it, to solve it, in spite of gradual expansion of PRI, CBO, SHGs etc. in the development sector. There was a risk to bring stigma associated with visible deformity to an innocuous patch due to health education, since both conditions in bio-medical paradigm are branded as leprosy. No attempts were made to inform the people about the process by which patch developed into deformity, except the advice to undertake regular treatment. Health Education, IEC, BCC are meant for compliance, adherence, not for empowering the people with the existing knowledge and the gaps about transmission process.

There have been successful experiments such as by DANLEP in Rajnandgaon in Chhattisgarh or CARRELS Project of TLMI. P-Scale is a good tool of measurement.

My involvement in NLEP mid-term evaluation in Assam during November 2014 as a team leader brings out that there was no stigma to patches, but there continued ignorance about early signs and symptoms. The integrated programme with GHS was being managed by vertical programme left over NMA-NMS, and ASHA reporting to ANM. PRI when exposed to Health Education session demanded such sessions for *gram sabha*.

What needs to be done to ward off the fear of leprosy is to undertake intervention research as 'before and after model of evaluation', not the bio-medical experimental-control model, by identifying the causes of disability through in-depth qualitative case studies as retrospective studies. This could help to design larger multi-centric intervention research studies. The studies need to be participatory, to be undertaken by paramedics/ volunteers approved by *Gram Sabha*/PRI/CBOs.

The focus has to be brought down from quantitative prevalence paradigm to removal of fear of leprosy affliction by people-centric, not patient-centric programme, since the affliction affects the quality of life and lowers aspirations in the life of a person as a member of a family, kin-group, neighbourhood group, peer group. Epidemiological unit of action has to be the people's unit of social living and social action (a hamlet or a village), and not the revenue unit of tehsil, district; development unit of block and public health unit of primary health centre.

Have we been able to reduce Stigma?

We know that Stigma is a generic term associated with community response to a situation at the individual, family or group level. It restricts the freedom to function as per one's choice due to formal or informal controls by those in authority. A female foetus is not allowed to survive for which a scientific tool or technique of Sonography is now misused. But this is not true among tribal communities where a tribal woman is never ever molested by a tribal man. The British Raj stigmatized castes and communities as criminal groups to facilitate police administration. Many of them known to us now were freedom fighters. What we mean is stigma is social/political construct and culturally relative.

Historically, we have gradually understood leprosy as a bio-medical phenomena, the term referring to innocuous patches as well as disabilities and deformities. For the people, leprosy has been deformities which would change physical identity, incapacitate them and transmit these to others. The only coping mechanism was to sacrifice the few to protect the majority. Compassionate quarantine in leprosy colonies, later dignified as leprosy hospitals, provided institutionalized stigma, which affected leprosy workers also, since leprosy was untreatable for thousands of years. Even a casual visit to leprosy colony would be looked at with suspicion of a visitor, as a patient of leprosy. As a social science member of the governing boards of several leprosy organizations, I was asked by my academic peers, whether I was going for personal consultation or as a consultant to attend a meeting. When I went to a leprosy dispensary to inquire about a leprosy doctor, I was given a suspicious look by the receptionist, while I wanted to discuss the production of a documentary on leprosy health education. Things have changed remarkably for the leprosy workers, after MDT treatment regimen was initiated.

With the euphoria of DDS and later MDT, having identified the culprit bacillus way back in 1873, we set targets to decrease the load of infection on earth through case finding, case holding and SET with 'E' missing.

People never knew what we call leprosy. Even *Kushta* is a given term. People's term has been *Maharog* and *Kodh/Kodhi*. So even vitiligo was '*kodh*' and the vertical control programme was stigmatised within medical profession. Probably health education in its zeal to popularize patch and asking people to suspect every patch as leprosy unless otherwise proved, increased the fear, since patch and deformity became synonyms, one ending invariably in the other as HIV and AIDS written as HIV/AIDS are giving the message as synonyms. Earlier, people identified leprosy only by visible deformities, not by bacteriological patch.

It was thought that there was a technical solution and people did not accept it due to stigma. With great difficulty, WHO added 'Prevention of development of associated deformities' as the third objective of leprosy control in 1983 as a success of social science intervention. In my WHO working paper in 1981, I had recommended nerve damage research as priority research agenda from social science perspective. We are after quantitative reduction of prevalence, with the hypothesis of reducing incidence. People do not act or accept quantity at the district or state or national level. They go by their world of social action, by quality of life in their kin group or village or peer group. Many NGOs accepted that the focus had to change from patient to family to community, but the medicalised public health programme never sincerely translated it in action.

In the name of science, we want people to comply to our programme, whether vertical or integrated. What dialogue do we have with the people, for the people to own the programme? This is our programme, not people's programme; their concerns are different, and paradigms are different.

People learn by experience and by total information, not part information, about transmission, about nerve, about progression. We can win their confidence by telling them what was not leprosy, (differential diagnosis) instead of dangers of leprosy, putting the fears in mind.

There have been success stories of DANLEP in Rajnandgon in Chhattisgarh or CARRELS project of TLM. In TLM project, we walked on village roads and discussed issues with the people in front of the houses of identified patients. We did not call people to meet us at places where chairs were lined up for us. In Sevagram villages under the control programme of GMLF, Wardha, due to continuous interaction of Dr. Joshi with the people, even the street children could tell us the early signs and symptoms of leprosy, including about anesthetic patch.

CARRELS Case Studies: TLM Stigma Reduction Project in Three States

Village people visiting TLM hospitals to see leprosy and non-leprosy patient sharing the ward made the dialogue meaningful to remove the fear about instant communicability of the disease.

TLM project regarding transfer of ownership about stigma reduction to community in Purulia (West Bengal), Faizabad (Uttar Pradesh) and Champa/Jangir (Chhattisgarh) has been well documented.

Community based action research studies undertaken by the Leprosy Mission Trust, India in three States brought out that the community under the guidance and leadership of the village committees formed to focus on stigma reduction could own the issues in their respective villages and blocks and find solutions. The members of these committees were oriented to stigma issues through lectures, visit to leprosy hospitals of TLM and visiting the patients in the wards, visit to laboratory and through constant interaction with the community organizers appointed by TLM.

The village level committees reached out to the community by way of IEC activities such as banners, posters, hoardings, wall paintings, video shows, processions in the village, library in panchayat office and educational activities in the schools. Other activities included health camps, identifying suspect cases and referrals to TLM hospital, follow up of active cases, group discussions, family and patient counselling. The leprosy patients were invited to village level and committee meetings and invited to participate in local social, religious, cultural and sports events, including organizing village common meal with the leprosy afflicted. The villages were ranked for success by evaluation undertaken by the committee members in villages other than their own.

Towards the completion of the project, in the public meetings, when asked who would own the task of continuing the activities, the opinion leaders responded that they would continue with the work, now that they knew the issues about leprosy and stigma affecting the people.

The project was supervised by an anthropologist research scientist under the guidance of a senior biostatistian at the TLM and a senior medical anthropologist as consultant.

Community Ownership of Programme: Case Study from DANLEP Project in Rajnandgaon, Chhattisgarh

There were mixed group workshops to discuss the organization of leprosy programme. The participants were DANLEP medical and behavioural practitioners, District Leprosy Officer (DLO) and the non-medical supervisors in leprosy programme, cured persons, opinion leaders (*janbhagidars*) from some villages. The programme composed of skin camps, ulcer care camps in a village organized by village level panchayat covering 8-10 villages. There were also public meetings to discuss differential diagnosis. The camps were visited or inaugurated by high level district level government officials.

At one of the mixed group workshops, a village head Batu Patel told his story. "I had cough, cold and fever. I went to a nearby town and visited a government hospital. I was given medicine. Looking at my face, the doctor advised me to go to another room in the corridor. A 'doctor' there gave me a handful of tablets (probably DDS). There was some board on the room about '*Kusta*' which I did not understand. I took the tablets for few days. Once my fever and cough receded. I threw away the handful tablets given to me. After few months again, I had a bout of cough and fever. This time, my son-in-law who happened to have visited us took me to the same hospital. On this occasion, the 'doctor' in the '*Kusta*' room told my son-in-law that I had early signs of leprosy and advised to meet the PMW who used to visit our village occasionally. On all occasions, I used to bring snacks for my children while I visited the town. On that day, I did not purchase anything for then. On return to the house, I did not fondle my children nor did I speak to them, but went straight to my room and bolted the door.

The PMW confirmed leprosy and gave MDT to be taken regularly for six months. I kept the medicines above the door frame and told my wife, they were recommended for my cough. After the completion of treatment, I was declared cured by the PMW. On that day, I told my wife about the disease, since I had kept a distance from her and children all these days. My wife meekly responded, 'now, it is over, isn't it'? I prompted him to say that he had sex that night, to which he gave a nod in the affirmative in the group workshop."

All along he was also participating in the DANLEP programmes in the village as a village head. Later he told his story in a village meeting to advise the people to take medicine and not feel shy about it or be apathetic. When I asked, why did he not tell the villagers while he was on medication, he said the village politics could have forced him to give up headship of the village.

WHO, Global Leprosy Programme (GLP)

In Assam in November 2014 during NLEP mid-term evaluation, people who had not seen deformity did not fear patches of leprosy for which treatment was available, thanks to ASHA, ANM and left over vertical programme workers NMA-NMS. At the *Panchayat* meeting the lady president and lady vice president of 10 village group *gram panchayat* lamented that nobody ever went to them to tell them about facts and process of leprosy. They volunteered to tell this in the *gram sabha* every time, if some presenter was available.

So the challenge is to integrate the quantitative prevalence reduction paradigm, with paradigm of addressing people's fears and concerns. With Panchayati Raj, with 50 per cent ladies, with CBO like Mahila Madals, SHG, Youth groups and gradual increase in female literacy, with paramedics running the public health programmes in rural homes and not the PHC-OPD doctors, people can own and manage the control programme.

We have experience of village opinion leaders, formal and informal, in Purulia and Chhattisgarh who were willing to take the responsibility of case finding, case holding and deformity prevention and management. We have experience during P. Scale development fieldwork of women wanting to do social work. Young educated women in Chhattisgarh who had reduced their time management in kitchen with pressure cookers and mixers, look forward to work in the community.

There has never been an experience of social change in human history brought about by paid employees. Employees can be motivated if they received appreciation from community. Even our bio-medical evaluation of social issues like experiment-control model is impractical and unethical. Charismatic leaders in control area could excel your programme in an experimental area.

In short, bio-medical approach is concerned with agent in the epidemiological triangle, while social science approach is concerned with the host. How to put them together is a challenge of intervention research, which anthropologists should accept.

WHO added a third objective to leprosy control to prevent development of associated deformities in 1983 advocated by an anthropologist and supported by a leading epidemiologist. But no programmes, have been laid down until today towards meeting this objective. Expert committee on leprosy in 1987 widened the definition of the case of leprosy to include social issues to rehabilitation, but we continue to remain locked in the statistics of bacteriological prevalence.

Up to late 1970s, leprosy programme considered social consequences to be an agenda of Social Welfare Ministry and the Social Welfare Ministry thought leprosy to be a medical problem to be handled by Health Ministry. This was the line of thinking even at the WHO level. Even the reputed NGO, 'Rehabilitation International' did not consider leprosy rehabilitation as their agenda.

Inter-sectoral coordination is a prime issue, which the Primary Health Care approach in Health for All, *Alma-Ata* declaration, propagated but not followed in government vertical system of governance. The anthropological concept of holism and structural functional approach forms the basis of intersectoral coordination.

Leprosy is a community problem. The problem is felt within the groups of family, kin group neighbourhood and occupational groups. How do we interact at that level? Who will do it?

There are statutory village governance bodies, *Panchayat* in India with 50 per cent reservation for women as members, or as heads in municipal bodies of towns and cities.

There are CBOs—women's groups, self help group, youth groups formal like Scouts and Guides, National Cadet Core (NCC), National Social Service (NSS) which have been used for health education and community action.

Female literacy is on the increase and family size has shrunk. Young ladies want to undertake socially useful tasks which would raise their self-esteem, through social recognition outside homes. All public health programmes are implemented by paramedics, mostly women, who enter the houses of people. They need to be properly trained including about nerve damage. People continue to use the services of traditional healers and TBAs for health care. In all systems of medicine like Chinese, Ayurved, Unani etc. nerve and immune systems are important subjects. We have never used them in leprosy; we have not involved other systems in dealing with leprosy for complementing our efforts, although they are in public health. Plural systems of medicine need to be integrated to complement each other to address issues of infection, immunity and nerve damage.

People accept new things by experience through action, not by slogans and messages.

We have seen skin camps of people in Chhattisgarh orgainsed by DANLEP to discuss differential diagnosis. Instead of knowledge of what is leprosy; which skin patches are not leprosy will reduce fear of the people and will promote voluntary reporting. Formal and opinion leaders are willing to take up responsibility of individual patients for regularity of treatment, preventive care about nerve impairment. They do not want cash incentives but social/public recognition of their services, which promotes their social status in respective communities and groups. Aspirants for status positions, for political positions at village level want to implement the programmes to get votes of people. They seek information. Let us not treat them not be treated as our agents but as *janbhagidars* (community volunteers and opinion leaders).

We have to budget expenditure for community mobilization, reimburse local travel of people coming for meetings, provide tea and snacks etc. and provide untied funds to village level governance to undertake community activities.

The message "Educate and empower communities to end discrimination against leprosy" has to be turned into a programme with all logistic details, whereby the programme is owned by the community with technical assistance from us focusing the on nerve.

- Like the term Leper, banish the term, ex-Leprosy Patient.
- Define and use the term cure. Banish the terms, RFT/RFC.
- Banish deformity photos or pictures for fund raising.
- H.Ed, IEC for deformity/ ulcer prevention, not limiting to early diagnosis and regular treatment.
- Integrate leprosy disability/ulcer with other disabilities, as due to diabetes.
- All laws about leprosy to be repealed and publicized in all media.
- Propagate rights of leprosy afflicted using right approach.
- Earmarked funding for nerve damage programmes and research.

Summary

In leprosy, the control policies made theoretical or conceptual amends to address the deformity concerns with a potential threat of social death. Pilot projects about community at the micro level, becoming an active partner in management have been tried by NGOs, with anthropological paradigm. People's capacity to manage their lives as witnessed by history could be tried with formal and informal mechanisms such as the PRIs, CBOs and SHGs, now active in village social and political organization. The role of paid employees in governance, with revenue mind-set administration still following the British Raj regularity authority *versus* the role of community volunteers and electoral representatives, is an important area of research inquiry about democratic governance.

When we were designing a meeting on 'Social aspects and social action in leprosy' on behalf of IAL to be held at SLRTC, Karigiri, we social scientists emphasized that the discussion need not be within the framework of NLEP. There was nothing sacred about the blue print model of NLEP. We might like to suggest another model of NLEP or for that matter recommend several models in a vast country like India. (Srinivasan, H, ed.1991)

We have been crying hoarse that NLEP should address itself to the needs of the people, not only to killing the bacillii. People are afraid of deformity and its consequences, and the programme should try to address it. People pursue regularity in chemotherapy and the targets would be achieved. With the pursuance of social science argument, despite WHO extending the objectives of leprosy control to include prevention of associated disabilities as the third objective, the appropriate programmes have not yet been formulated.

The definition of a case of leprosy now includes a person needing chemotherapy, for calculation of prevalence as also a person needing rehabilitation. Now that the prevalence is going down the leprosy institutions are facing funding crunch and are turning their attention to disability prevention and management. We had not recommended this sequential order of chemotherapy and disability prevention. We wanted the order to be reversed. DANLEP under the leadership of a behavioural scientist reversed that order in Madhya Pradesh and Chhattisgarh and achieved tremendous success. Several non-technical tasks of leprosy workers could be shifted to people. The people and opinion leaders through interactive communication could learn differential diagnosis and gain confidence to suspect leprosy, to manage ulcers and take preventive measures against the onslaught of deformity of limbs.

Leprosy as a disease in bio-medical terms shows so many ramifications in all natural and applied sciences, social sciences and humanities which warrants the attention of the holistic discipline like anthropology to unravel all these variables for designing people-centred and inclusive control policies, and implement them by giving ownership of the programme to the people. Leprosy is a challenging subject for anthropological research linking bio-medical and social science aspects.

D. SEXUALITY AND SEXUAL BEHAVIOUR

Initiation

I was drifted from leprosy to sexuality research by participating at a UNICEF meeting on STD at Chennai, when the first cases of HIV positive women in India were identified at Chennai. I was possibly invited because the keyword 'stigma' was common to leprosy and HIV-AIDS.

I was invited as the only Indian resource person at the first research methodology workshop for the participants from the NGOs working in the field of RCH/MCH, funded by Ford Foundation, held at Delhi in early 1990. One such workshop was also held at Tata Institute of Social Sciences in 1995. Subsequently the working group was formed to design the research programmes on sexuality and sex behaviour. The first such meeting was held at Bangalore in December 1995, the second one being hosted by us in August 1996 at Poona University. One meeting was also organized by FRHS at Ahmedabad. A research project on adolescent sexuality was undertaken by the KEMHRC, Pune with me as the principal investigator and Dr. Hemant Apte, alumni of Anthropology Department of Pune University, as co-investigator.

Ford Foundation offered funding at the Inter-disciplinary School of Health Sciences, Poona University in 2003, as a capacity building programme, through small research grants and Ph.D. fellowships, and for organising seminars and workshops about sexuality and sexual behaviour. We were offered this capacity building programme in view of our association with earlier programmes of the Ford Foundation in regard to building social science research capacity for studies regarding women's reproductive health.

I

Introduction

Human beings share the biological instinct of sex with other animals and more so with the primates. To a large extent, sexual behaviour is acquired behaviour, which is supposed to channelise sexuality. In human society, sex is institutionalized in marriage and is governed by rules of endogamy, exogamy, monogamy, polygamy, hypergamy and such other coping mechanisms as levirate and sororate. Endogamy ensures group solidarity by institutionalising sex through marriage. Exogamy rules out competition among the members of a group on account of sex. Sexuality is thus socially constructed. A majority of human societies are patriarchal, giving rise to issues of gender. In the evolution of human society, man-woman relationships have been conceptualized differently in pastoral and agricultural communities. In *Mahabharata* times, society would permit insemination of a woman, if she could not conceive from her husband, a practice called "*Niyog*." Choice of male was an issue since seed was considered more important than the field.

Hindu mythology is full of sex episodes involving the sages and *Deo-lok* (heavenly) kings like Indra. There have been celestial sex workers who are called '*Apsara*'. In Indian mythology and ancient history, there are several references to sexuality and sexual behaviour. '*Kamsutra*' by Vatsayan is probably meant for urban, middle class and high society. We have erotic sculpture at Khajurao and Konark and we have an erotic and romantic poetry '*Geet Govind*' of Jaydeo and plays by Kalidasa. Both epics *Ramayana* and *Mahabharata* are focused on women, Sita and Draupadi, who were subjected to evil designs about intimate relationships. We have also the story of seduction of Ahilya by Indra. Incidentally all these three women are part of '*Panchkanya*' who are idealized women in the Hindu scriptures. The same theme of suffering of women continues in the modern day Indian movies. Similarly, there are stories about seduction of Vishwamitra by the celestial sex worker Menaka after whose grandson's name is our country called in the Constitution of India, i.e. Bharat. We also have celestial sex worker Urvashi, the mistress *apsara* of Indra, who was biological father of Arjuna. She cursed Arjuna to become impotent all through his life, since he declined to accept her sexual favours with the argument that she was having motherly kinship ties, being connected with his biological father Indra. Indra's intervention reduced his impotency period to one year as 'Brahannala', as a dance and music teacher to the princess, in the kingdom of Virata, during incognito period of one year of the Pandavas.

The example of sage Vishwamitra's seduction is rooted in the fear that Indra had about the spiritual powers Vishwamitra attained by sublimating his sexual energy to arouse '*Kundlini*' situated in the cerebral region, which is believed to bestow the immense intellectual and spiritual powers to the person. Menaka was successful in lowering Vishwamitra's spiritual powers as a result of consumption of 'seminal fluid' with a daughter, Shakuntala, born out of liason. It is this Indian psyche, which is enshrined in Ayurved and Yoga that makes 'vasectomy' unsuccessful and the cardinal reason for the defeat of Indira Gandhi in elections. (Election slogan against Indira Gandhi was—remove Indira and save India, and male sex organ—*Indira hatao, India/Indriya bachao).* Shri Choudhary Charan Singh, later Prime Minister of India for few weeks and Shri Raj Narayan, later Health Minister of India, told women's meetings that the women would virtually become 'widows' if their husbands were vasectomised *(Nasbandi se tum randuwa ho jaogi).*

We have books like '*Kamsutra*' in Indian literature. We have 'aphrodisiacs'. Viagra is a recent invention but we have in our literature, in Ayurved and Unani, various food products classified according to 'Viagra' effects. In our concepts of body metabolism, '*Shukra*' is a distilled form, which is a source of potency, virility and energy to a person. It is not a matter of chance that 'Vasectomy' programme has been a total failure in India. It is also not a chance that Indira Gandhi and her Congress party lost elections in north India due to vasectomy campaigns. Vasectomy continues to be compared with castration resulting in loss of physical power and energy bringing in overall weakness. The illiterate rural women could be persuaded to vote against Indira Gandhi with the argument that they would become *de facto* widows after their husbands underwent vasectomy operation for family planning. Widowhood is considered the worst curse for traditional Indian woman. There is pre-occupation of Indian man about semen in its relationship with virility and muscle power of a man. To but it briefly, ideas about sexuality and sex behaviour are cultural or social construct. Male and female sex may be biological realities but gender again is a social construct. Now, there is public and statutory recognition of third gender.

The sexual urges among the male and female would follow the biological instincts and would be age specific, and may be manifested in variations in sex related activities and behaviour. Sexual relations outside marriage also tend to follow the limits set by these norms of behaviour. Premarital and marital sex may be guided by class, caste, *gotra* regulations as also extramarital relations, guided by rules of hypergamy. Sex relations violating these rules would be labelled as deviant behaviour and may be punishable by society. Murders and violence on account of deviant liaisons are not rare in Indian rural and urban life. There are permissible liaisons guided by rules of levirate and sorrorate whereby the joking relations between a woman and young brother of her husband, and between a man and younger sister of his wife could lead to marriage and/or sex relationship. Levirate marriages have been commonly and publicly approved to rehabilitate young war widows in the family. Several case studies are available in literature, and oral narratives whereby *Bhabhi* educates *Devar* about negotiating sex-play on the first night after marriage.

The most frequently asked questions by adolescent males in the course of research on adolescent sexuality bring out their concerns about loss of semen and the resultant weakness or possible impotence in case of masturbation. Recently, there has been a full length commercial Hindi movie discussing erectile dysfunction in a comic presentation. The IEC material of the government dismissing such concerns as psychic issue and masturbation or involuntary discharge of seminal fluid in sleep or dream, as natural body function, does not convince the adolescent boys. Ayurveda recognizes the dominant sex drive but advises to channelize it in legitimate sex relations with the spouse, and to restrain or control it according to age and other conditions as pregnancy, menstruation and early days after child birth.

There has been a clear distinction between CSW and dancing girls. During the feudal rule of princes and *jagirdars-zamindars*, even during British rule in India, the dancing girls or nautch girls were not commercial sex workers. They were invited on some occasions as birth or marriage ceremonies to perform with their team of instrumental musicians, to entertain the audience. In Maharashtra, *Lavni* dance and *Nautanki* in Hindi belt, are performed by such dancers who are quite famous for their art. In my village study in Gwalior in 1958, people would say, if the engagement cash present was Rs. 1000, there would surely be a dancing girl performing at the marriage ceremony. During the period of field trip, on the night of *kojagiri purnima* (first full moon after monsoon), I was invited at a police station by the in-charge police officer in a neighbourhood town, to enjoy the customary ritual of drinking milk with other local government functionaries such as *tehsildar*, BDO etc. The police station is located in a *garhi* (small fortress). I was shocked with the performance of a dancing girl on the occasion. One could see the classic example of feudal behaviour which was normally limited to the festivals in the *zamindar's* mansions. Dance performances were accompanied by classical instrumental and classical music, thus providing feudal patronage to these arts.

A dancing girl could develop a lasting relationship with one of the clients and could beget a child but not as commercial sex. Having a mistress or a live-in relationship was considered a status symbol of power and money. As a result, female actors were not available to play female roles in drama or film. A *marathi* actor Balgandharv became famous due to his playing excellent female roles in *marathi* theatre.

Now, with the potential risk of Tsunamic dimension of AIDS epidemic, sex is directly linked with disease, with chronic morbidity and mortality. The variations in sexual behaviour are all within the risk behaviour of AIDS. Sex has thus become a bio-medical concern. Sexuality is getting medicalised with research on therapy and vaccines. In the absence of effective treatment, and preventive vaccine, the emphasis is on behavioural change which calls for documentation of behavioural variability.

As a result, there have been surveys to find out the groups at risk of getting HIV infection like the truckers or CSWs. The need has also been felt to identify the risk behaviour in which some people indulge. The migrant youth including the hotel workers who are not subjected to family controls but are exposed to opportunities of sex in a metropolitan area could indulge in risk behaviour. It has been found necessary to understand the perceptions and knowledge of young about sexual activities and the behaviour which could be labeled as risk behaviour.

In summary, we have to admit that sex research by way of documentation by anthropologists on sexuality and sex behaviour in their ethnographic monographs to complete the holistic picture of respective cultures, has been different than what is required now in view of its implication for AIDS. The quantitative epidemiological surveys are no doubt required by policy planners to plan and implement the policies based on numerical and geographical spread of the issues. However, in order to understand the contextual reasons for behaviour in the dynamic and changing societies in the days of globalized economic, political and health systems, it is necessary to follow the qualitative methods which has been appropriately modified to study issue specific focused ethnography.

It is believed that Sonagachi brothels in Kolkata and Kamathipura brothels in Mumbai were initiated by the British to comfort their troops. At Pune, brothels were catering to the affluent decadence of Brahmin rulers, not very far from the seat of power at 'Shaniwarwada'. The decadence has been portrayed in a famous play, '*Ghasiram Kotwal*'.

However, there was a marked difference between the entertainers, such as dancing girls or nautch girls as the British addressed them and the commercial sex workers referred to as prostitutes. The dancing girls and singing girls would give entertainment performances at the festive occasions of birth and marriage. Customers could also visit their places (*Kotha*) to watch dance and enjoy music, as people visit dance-drama theatres. Such scenes are commonly depicted in the Hindi movies in the 1950s and early 1960s. The dancing girl could be adopted as a mistress with a live-in relationship with a client-patron, giving birth to a child and looked after whole life by the biological father.

The abolition of feudal institutions like princely states and *zamindari*, incongruous with electoral democracy, took away the feudal patronage to dance and music as an entertainment profession, which incidentally got embedded in Bollywood. The kind of traditional dancing labelled as *Nautanki* or *Lavani* has become 'Item Song' in Bollywood. However, these traditional dance performances continue at the village fairs.

Currently in the market, there are brothels without the art performances of dance and music. The mobility which enforced absence from family for a long duration, such as by truckers, opened the avenues of *Dhaba* (road-side food joints on the highways) culture which satisfied the dual biological urges of hunger and sex, at a reasonable price. The young sales representatives of commercial companies, who are mobile and reside in lodges, also indulge in risk behaviour. At the Dockyard area at Mumbai, in the vicinity of Dockyard Road railway station, there are hotels where rooms could be hired on an hourly basis.

Since culture and lifestyle which were traditionally co-terminus, got separated due to multiplicity of occupations necessitating mobility and migration, risky sex behaviour received a spurt in growth. It was thus necessary to document the variety of risky sexual behaviour for different ethnic and occupational groups. Sexual behaviour which has been protected for centuries by 'culture of silence' being intensely personal, could be unfolded only with the use of qualitative research tools and techniques, to unravel the socio-psychological processes. Anthropologists who claim to have fine tuned qualitative methods were not so far going beyond ethnography of culture of isolated communities, focusing on religion and kinship.

The Ford Foundation in India took initiative to enhance the capacity building of researchers in the universities and NGOs to undertake research on Sexuality, Sexual Behaviour and Reproductive Health. Some of the books edited by research-administrators like Saroj Pachauri (1999), Joel Gitteisohn *et al.* (1994), Radhika Ramasubban and Shireen Jejeebhoy (2000), deal with reproductive health issues and sexual behaviour. The book, "*Sexuality in the time of AIDS*" edited by Ravi Verma and others (2004), deals with case studies primarily on sexual behaviour in the context of developing strategies to prevent AIDS. The book has been the result of Ford Foundation support for network, to promote social science research on sexuality issues. A recently edited book, "*Sexuality and Sexual Behaviour: Social Science Perspective*" (2019) has put together 18 completed projects funded by Ford Foundation as a capacity development programme, presented as research papers. There are papers on commercial sex workers, their morbidity patterns and their clients; we have also the papers on adolescent girls and boys. The adolescent slum girls are greatly influenced by Bollywood projection of love which results in risky behaviour. We have a paper on Nat community from Rajasthan amongst whom sex work is a traditional occupation as amongst the Kolhati in Maharashtra. There is a conceptual paper on construction of sexuality among college going male youth. The *adi*, as dance and music teachervasi or the tribals do not consider female breast as a sex object but as the one meant for feeding the babies as in other mammals or primates. The tribal college boys, although exposed to Bollywood films, continue to echo the same cultural attitudes. There is also a paper on gender construction and its impact on health amongst rural women. We have also presented the reproductive health issues of sex workers as well as high caste urban women. The concerns of parents in rural areas about the behaviour of their wards migrated to urban areas for living, are discussed in one of the Ph.D. dissertation paper. Hotel and restaurant boys who have migrated in the town have been studied, particularly the restaurants in the red light area. Similarly, there is a study of stigma among those affected by HIV transmission. We have tried to conceptualize these studies giving anthropological interpretation of sex behaviour within cultural framework and to bring out how sexuality is constructed socially.

The change in emphasis in India, from family planning to controlling the risk of HIV has meant a 'paradigm shift' in the research agenda.

I had a shocking revelation from anthropology trained student couple settled in New York. On inquiry about the source of their livelihood, my male student, who apparently received training in Psychology after Anthropology at Pune said, he was counselling the 'same sex partners' to resolve their 'partnership discord'.

II

One of the significant fall out of social science research regarding sexuality, sexual behaviour and reproductive health in the context of HIV, is the discussion of private issues in the public domain, in the media, in the judicial courts, giving inputs to the government to take executive and legislative action, when necessary.

Recently the Supreme Court of India struck down century old law about adultery as a criminal offence and dismissing the criminality clause of homo-sexual relationships. The debates have not been in the context of HIV infections but about private behaviour being labelled as criminal behaviour in law, for over a century, subjected to prison punishment by the government.

The issues about 'Lesbian, Gay, Bisexual and Third Gender' (LGBT) require bio-medical and bio-social research about the prevalence and incidence. The cases of sex change are being freely reported and discussed in the media, and the relevant surgeries in public hospitals are being advertised about offering reduced rates, as compared to private sector.

Verrier Elwin romanticized sexuality and sexual behaviour in his tribal monograph, 'Muria and their Ghotul'. Youth dormitories are a part of tribal life in several tribal communities. These are kind of traditional educational institutions through peer education. The youth do play an important role in community life and support the elderly. In Odisha, it has been seen that share of food from Podu cultivatation (forest land used after burning the shrubs for cultivation) is equally distributed to all residents including the old and infirm citizens. When we resided in Laheri, an interior Maria village in Gadchiroli district in December 1963, for field training of the first batch of Anthropology students from Pune University, we found all women topless and could barely cover their thighs with a white cloth, while all men were with langoties only to cover their groins. As reported in several studies, the tribal people considered female breasts as mammary glands to feed the babies and not as sex objects. They did not milch the cows since the milk was meant for the calves as mother's milk was meant for the child. In tribal communities where pre-marital sexual relations are not uncommon and are permitted, the pregnancy consequences are not denied or disowned, and could culminate in socially approved marriage. The idea about sex in tribal societies differs from that of the caste peasant society. In tribal society, adultery is frowned upon since the divorce and re-marriage are relatively easy and approved with social and economic procedures.

Why is it that in tribal communities, a tribal woman is never raped or molested by a tribal man and why is it, in the so called civilized urban and industrial society, she is a saleable item in the market as advertised for all merchandise? There is no advertisement without figuring women.

During the wars, land and women are grabbed and raped. Both have productive value. In labour intensive tribal economy, woman is a labour and also as a producer of labour. Her father is compensated for losing his working hands, by paying the bride price, while we do exactly the opposite. We marry a girl and the father of the bride has to shell out the dowry, which has led to dowry deaths and female foeticide. There is no female foeticide in tribal society.

In the male dominated northern Hindi belt, sometimes, the wives are purchased, since sex ratio has become adverse. While I revisited Jaurasi, a village I had studied, located on Gwalior-Jhansi road after about 23 years in 1981, I inquired with the villagers in a gossip session as to from where they got the brides since they committed female foeticide, as reported in the media. After meekly denying the charge of female foeticide, they showed me two women in the field, from the window of *choupal* where we were sitting, whom they had purchased from Bhusaval in north

Maharashtra for Rs. 300 each. This was the time when a journalist from Dholpur (Gwalior-Agra road) had allegedly purchased a girl, reported her name as Kamla in media, for Rs. 1500 and became a matter of hot debate in Parliament.

We keep on raising the issue of HIV-AIDS written as HIV/AIDS. Why Slash? Are we not giving a message to people that HIV and AIDS are synonymous, while trying to assure HIV^{+ve} on the other hand, that with a particular life style and proper treatment, terminal condition could be postponed for a very long period. I once asked Prof. Ramalingswamy, the reputed DG of ICMR as to how come the condom which was promoted for contraception was now being promoted on the hoardings for safe sex only, and contraception was forgotten. How come that Congress party and personally Indira Gandhi lost elections in Hindi belt on vasectomy issue in 1977? What are the beliefs of people about seminal fluid and masculine physical—intellectual power in a patriarchal society, which has a base in Ayurved? How do we analyse the concepts of immunity in plural medical systems? An anthropologist with his comparative method, objectivity and understanding of people's perception, and culture systems, can immediately decipher these issues. With the large scale mobility and migration, for making a living, and the phenomena of urbanization whereby the metropolitan areas are devouring the villages around 50-100 km radius, the risk of HIV infection has become a reality.

The technical interventions either to prevent conception or to prevent morbidity in the context of STD and HIV infection have raised other behavioural issues. It is a cultural practice to provide for privacy in sex to young married couples, to promote fertility as early as possible after marriage. Even in the hard core Hindi speaking patriarchal belt, six months of privacy is provided by the parental generation whatever may be the housing patterns and gender specific locations of sleeping. Enough information is available about the non-use of condoms among emotionally or socially accepted hetero-sexual partnerships. Even relationships between CSWs and their frequent clients preclude the use of condoms in the relationships. In the patriarchal societies there are double standards of permitted and tolerated sex behaviour for men and women. If a woman uses any method for preventing fertility or morbidity, such as microbicides promoted in recent times, without the knowledge of the male partner, a needle of suspicion is directed to woman about infidelity. The use of condoms continues to be associated with deviant sexual relationship. A migrant rural youth to a city visiting CSW occasionally and trying to use condom in his relationship with his wife to protect her from infection, would arouse suspicion of deviant behaviour on his part in the city.

One of the dark areas in legitimate relationships between husband and wife relates to locations of sleeping, which would prohibit privacy of sex. The only privacy women could have could be a bathing place or a place where she could ease out. The more complicated issue pertains to knowledge and approval of the husband. One of the crucial issue pertains to free and frank communication between husband and wife about sex, and risk involved in case of opportunistic deviant behaviour. It has been seen that self help groups of women in India have facilitated better inter-spouse communication in general.

There have been discussions on the platform of ICMR about the use of microbicides by women as a gel within their control to use it without the knowledge or permission of the man. The issue about contraception has been, as to whether the methods have been male-centred or female-centred. Male-centred vasectomy having failed, tubectomy was promoted. Tubectomy raises male doubts as to whether a woman would be free to entertain extra-marital sex, having been freed from the risk of pregnancy. The issues of consent in such surgical procedures have been reported by such NGOs as Family Planning Association of India.

The best suitable methods for microbicides studies would be the in-depth interviews of women of various age groups, class groups from tribal, rural and urban communities. The insistence by CSWs of the use of condom by clients is fairly successful since the clients are now aware about the potential risks. For the same reason, the use of condoms is not favoured between married couples. The migrant youth from rural areas around Pune who work at Pune as rickshaw drivers, hotel workers and as labour have started using condoms in relation to CSWs, but would not use them in their relationship with village girls.

The information about microbicide trials would require knowledge about the logistics of sexual contact in the general population in the rural and urban setting. In view of the absence of concept of bedroom privacy and well demarcated bathroom privacy for the women, it is necessary to get the emic information about the use of gels. Although women are aware about the double standards of men in sexual behaviour and even tolerate it in a patrilocal setting, the matters could be discussed openly between the spouses. The community and in some cases the parents do perceive the risk in certain occupational groups which keep the men away from homes for long duration and in the urban setting where there are temptations, peer group pressure and easy available money to indulge in risky sex behaviour. However, it has been possible to unravel the behavioural patterns of these groups through informal open ended in-depth interviews by developing a good rapport with the subjects. Multicentric studies are required in India to understand the emic perspectives about sexual behaviour and practices.

The issue is about understanding the cultural and opportunistic context in which sexual interactions formally take place. The quantitative methods of data collection such as survey methods provide the information about 'how many' and 'how much' prevalence. The qualitative methods can provide the information in the context and provide explanations about the variety of behavioural patterns. Administration of intervention programmes usually take into account the requirements for success of technology and would strive to promote the acceptance of technology by the people. Peoples' response to the technology is based on their attitudes or personalities which are shaped by the process of enculturation and socialization and by their experience.

To transform the awareness of new technology into acceptance at the individual level depends upon social acceptance and approval of the use of technology.

At a meeting at the Pennsylvania Medical School about collaboration with the School of Health Sciences, Pune University, a presentation was made by the Professor of Obstetrics and Gynaecology about his research on a gel which could act as a contraceptive as also would protect from HIV infection. We pointed out that we did not have a concept of bedroom providing privacy to couples in rural India as also in the small houses in the cities, particularly in the slums.

As we know, rural-urban mobility and migration, earlier to the pre-industrial cities and now to the post-industrial metropolitan and mega cities for whatever reasons have resulted into various kinds of problems affecting sexual behaviour. In traditional pre-agricultural, pastoral and agricultural society, culture and lifestyles were coterminous. Now in industrial cities, heterogeneous lifestyles tend to conflict with culture patterns. Cultures do try to control lifestyle behaviour by asserting kinship controls and through rituals at birth, puberty, marriage, pregnancy, death and ancestor worship. The empirical studies have brought out various change resistant practices as also the dynamic processes affecting the reproductive and sexual behaviour. Age at marriage, fear of sex security for women, fertility practices to attain the desired sex composition of family, lack of knowledge about physiological processes regarding sex and reproduction, do not seem to change despite development efforts.

Awareness of contraceptive technology is perceived but not its acceptance. Blue films and yellow books are more readily available even in rural areas. However, the kinship pressures including that of the mother-in-law are still pre-dominant affecting decision making regarding fertility and reproduction.

The question is, since how long sex research has been on the social science academic agenda? We are aware that hunger and sex as biological instincts for the survival of any species, have been institutionalized in the process of cultural evolution. We are also aware that both hunger and sex are valued in commerce, markets, social organization, politics and power. Capturing land, cattle, women and now visible and invisible assets, have been the issues in politics and war. Pleasure seeking appears to be instinctive behaviour which is sought to be curtailed by religious values. In traditional systems of health and medicine, sex has been linked with health and disease, although HIV connection is a recent phenomena. Relationship of sex and body immunity leading to such chronic diseases like TB is well known in the minds of lay people. Relationship of the biological fact of the sex with the sociological category of gender is a matter of recent studies. Although sex has not been on the agenda of the society, gender has been on the agenda of the social reformers for a long time.

The then Director General of Health Services, Government of India, while opening the earlier referred Chennai meeting on STD had two opening sentences, "Prostitution was most ancient profession in human society. We should scare the people to death so that they behave properly." We doubt whether disease control programmes could be successful with scare, or with providing full knowledge to the people. We know that awareness campaigns in leprosy, family planning and now HIV do not ensure acceptance of the biomedical concerns. Our campaigns are addressed to people to change their behaviour so that they accept the diagnostic and cure technology in malaria, TB, leprosy and such other diseases. The questions are asked by the administrators, policy planners, technocrats, successful entrepreneurs and we do-gooders, as to why people don't change their behaviour, as per our wishes and accept scientific technology of prevention and cure ungrudgingly.

The whole dichotomy of 'we' and 'they' including we researchers and they common people, create methodological problems. How can we collect the scientifically valid, reliable and objective data on such issues as sex behaviour? Actually, in several meetings on sexuality and sexual behaviour, the main concerns of deliberations have been about appropriate social science research methodology.

I personally feel that we need not be limited in our deliberations about the groups or behaviour at risk in relation to HIV-AIDS. We have to go beyond sex workers and their clients like truck drivers. Socio-economic political dynamics which has forced several behavioural changes as a result of lifestyles making dents, in the stability and equilibrium of culture, need to be the context in which we can understand sexuality and sexual behaviour. Relationship of sex and gender through historical times in the social context and the changes therein, if any, have yet to be understood adequately. This might sound too much academic but we are discussing sexuality and sexual behaviour in the context of academic and knowledge discipline of anthropology, to develop our research capabilities to make it applicable nationally.

In a country of the size of India, there is wide variety of gender behaviour, both male and female, which we have to understand in the socio-cultural context by using appropriate research methods. Towards this end, we bring sexuality research on the academic agenda and as a first step, we have to strive to arrive at research agenda and research priorities.

What is sexuality? It refers to sexual personality, i.e. attitudes, behaviour and practices about sex. Desmond Morris has discussed the comparison of human being with other primates, namely the monkeys and apes like chimpanzees and gorilla in his two books "Human Zoo" and "Naked Ape." How does sexual personality develops? Although sex is biological phenomenon, sexuality is a cultural and social construct like gender.

This varied scenario brings out a question as to why sexuality has become an academic agenda and a very important international programme agenda. This is obviously a result of potential risk of HIV and AIDs which has forced the humanity to systemically think about sexuality. More so, because there is no technical solution to the problem by way of preventive vaccine or curative treatment. In the contemporary world, we have the film like 'Fire' on lesbian relationship and now the stories of IT couples not engaged in sex relations due to overwork and career development issues. Recently, there has been an international media wave about "Me Too" exploitation reported by celebrity women, mostly from the film world about celebrity males occupying power positions in public life.

Sexuality and Sexual behaviour in all its socio-cultural, economic and medical ramifications is an area where anthropological research could make a very important contribution in basic knowledge as would be useful to control HIV-AIDS pandemic. The focused ethnography about sexuality in tribal communities where women are not reportedly molested by tribal men would add to the knowledge about biological instincts, and social constructs about sexuality and sexual behaviour.

7

Anthropology and Voluntary Sector

Initiation

I was introduced to voluntary sector, when I was invited to lecture to health education officers of Gandhi Memorial Leprosy Foundation at B.J. Medical College. Pune. Subsequently, I was inducted as a social science member of the executive body of GMLF. In later years, I was invited to be member of scientific bodies, governing boards and ethics committees of several leprosy and medical institutions in the voluntary sector. However, at the University, when a desire was expressed by social science teachers to form an academic organization, while they were invited to participate at the Research Methodology workshop in November 1975, the 'Maharashtra Association of Anthropological Sciences' (MAAS) was established as a registered voluntary organization. This facilitated a partnership with the university departments, with the government and with other voluntary associations for undertaking joint training and research assignments. The facility for action/intervention anthropology became feasible which could not be possible under the conventions of a university. Although, University Grants Commision mandates the duties of faculty as teaching, research and extension, extension probably meaning reaching the knowledge and its use for the people at large, has never been credited for promotional channels. Networking of voluntary sector and university social science departments is important for extension activities for the faculty and for application of knowledge for social good. We have experienced this in undertaking intervention research in tribal areas.

Introduction

Ethnography of isolated communities generally referred to as primitive or tribal communities describes the self-governance monitored by elders headed by a chief (*Mukhiya*), usually a hereditary position. In India, this mechanism has been traditionally functioning even in a mutti-caste peasant village called as *Panchayat* headed by a *Sarpanch (Patel, Patil)*. The ideal democratic governance is referred as *Ram Rajya*. Currently, this system of governance as democratic decentralization has put in place statutory panchayats, the elected bodies providing affirmative reservation to marginalized groups such as SC, ST, OBC etc and women, as per 73rd and 74th Amendments Constitution of India.

The conscience keepers of governance, values and morals have been the ordained *Sanyasis* who have no social and familial identity. Saint-poets, not necessarily *Sanyasis*, belonging to different castes or tribal ethnic groups are treated as demi-gods by the masses. An exemplary case is of Saint Dnyaneshwar in Maharashtra who is referred as '*Mauli*' that is mother, by the masses. The word *'Mauli'* has become a synonym of Dnyaneshwar. The legend is that Shivaji had bestowed his kingdom at the feet of Saint Ramdas, which he declined, but as a symbol of blessing, gave a saffron coloured piece of cloth which Shivaji turned into the flag of his kingdom. This has been reportedly narrated by Shri Rabindranath Tagore also.

Anthropology as history of civilization and culture, studies formal and informal governance of groups, communities and political states, by way of documenting the interactions of government sector, voluntary sector and people's sector.

During foreign rule, the people rallied around the voluntary sector by way of caste councils, religious councils etc. The preventive and protective mechanisms of traditional village panchayat *(Gram panchayat)* and caste councils (*Jati panchayat*) sometimes led to inhuman treatment to 'marginalized groups' and to women, within these 'marginalized groups'.

Social reform movements have deprecated such exploitation. In all regions of India, besides saint-poets, familiar names of social reformers have been Dayanand Saraswati, Raja Ram Mohun Roy, Ishwarhchandra Vidyasagar, Vivekanand, Justice Ranade, Agarkar, Jyotiba Phule, Dhondo Keshav Karve from Bengal and Maharashtra, and several others, in the late nineteenth and early twentieth century who initiated social reform movements focusing on caste inequalities, untouchability and plight of women, particularly the widows. Some kind of voluntary organizations with distinct identity developed with a provision to become their members, such as Arya Samaj, Prarthana Samaj, Brahmo Samaj, Satyashodhak Samaj etc. Indian National Congress may have been the first political voluntary organization and Asiatic Society of Bengal as the first academic voluntary organizations in British India.

Mahatma Gandhi could integrate the social transformation ideas and movement for political freedom, into a unitary movement, in the wake of the debate, particularly in Maharashtra, as to whether social reforms should precede political freedom movement.

Political Independence from colonial rule in 1947, led to incorporating social reform ideas in the Constitution, which led to social legislation and formation of Ministry such as Social Welfare Ministry, now called as Ministry of Social Justice.

During British Rule in late nineteenth century, having tested the enlightenment through English language, even complimenting it as 'milk of tigress' in Maharashtra, there was an urge to start colleges in the voluntary sector. Fergusson College at Pune established in 1885 has been one such example. The British Government had already established the Universities at Calcutta, Madras and Bombay. Lord Macaulay in his address to British Parliament on 2nd February, 1835 had advocated that the best way to break the nerve of India was to introduce British education so that the Indians would lose their self-esteem and praise everything foreign.

There was also a need to have English educated Indians at middle and lower level management levels to implement British revenue and police administration, as also transport and communication networks. The schools were also established by voluntary organizations. Voluntary efforts were not largely directed in health sector except some medical colleges in Indian Systems of Medicine were established. Allopathic medical colleges were established in the government sector in British Presidencies while Ayurved and Unani medical colleges were established in the states ruled by the Princes. However, there was nothing for public health sector in rural areas, which was serviced by traditional healers and *Dais*, trained as family occupation.

Social workers like Dhondo Keshav Karve, Jyotiba Phule and his wife Savitribai took initiatives in women's education in Maharashtra. University of Poona has been recently renamed as 'Savitribai Phule Pune University'. When I was a school going student at Gwalior, ruled by a Maratha king, during early 1940s and in college in 1950s, we had hardly four girl students from high caste groups such as Brahmins in a class with 40 boys. They would remain absent for four days in a month, during the menstrual cycle.

The international voluntary organizations like Rockefeller and Ford Foundation had opened their India offices to function as partner with the Government.

During political freedom struggle, the comprehensive political party, Congress, used to deliberate on the vision of transformation of India after Independence. There were planning units within Congress party which would table resolutions at national conventions. Actually the provincial government according to Government of India Act, 1935 was formed in Bombay Presidency, the elections having been won by Congress party with Shri B.G. Kher as the Chief Minister (then called Prime Minister or Premier) of Bombay Province. He again became the first Chief Minister of Bombay State after Independence.

It is common knowledge that the Planning Commission was established with an aim to plan to transform India into a modern State on socialist principles, following the principle of equity as enshrined in the Constitution. Every five year plan henceforth had set some goals in that direction to be pursued by the governments, towards directed socio-economic and culture change. One of the first major national programme was Community Development for rural transformation initiated on October 2, 1952. Gradually the development administration, parallel to revenue administration, was in place with democratic decentralization up to village level. However, some of the intellectuals got disenchanted with the slow speed and misdirection of government administration. Immediately after Independence the voluntary programmes such as the Constructive Programmes of Gandhiji became government schemes. The government also realized that it was not possible to administer the programmes with required speed for want of finance and personnel without community participation. They, therefore, invited the voluntary organizations to be partners with government with some financial aid from the government. The concept of NGO, non-government organization was thus born whereby the NGOs would administer some of the government schemes as per government pattern in a given geographical area. Health and education were the social sector areas where NGOs could function effectively. The governments engaged such organizations as Family Planning Association of India (FPAI). The Leprosy Mission and many other in developing partnership.

Some of the committed doctors in Maharashtra such as Dr. Rajnikant and Dr. Mabel Arole, Dr. N.H. Antia, Dr. Banoo Coyaji, and disciples of Mahatma Gandhi such as Manibhai Desai, Acharya Bhise, Tarabai Modak established their NGOs (voluntary organizations) to work in the field of health, education, livelihood and development in rural and tribal areas. Comprehensive Rural Health Project (CRHP), Jamkhed; Foundation for Research in Community Health (FRCH), Mumbai-Pune; KEM Hospital Research Centre (KEMHRC), Pune, with projects in the rural area; Bhartiya Agro-Industries Foundation (BAIF); Adiwasi Satpuda Shikshan Prasarak Mandal, Dhadgaon (Nandurbar); Sarvodaya Seva Mandal, Kosbad-Bordi (Palghar District) etc. were established in Maharashtra. BAIF had a spread of their livelihood related activities in several states in India. Such voluntary associations were established in several states in India. The well known doctors as Dr. Arole couple, Dr. Antia, Dr. Banoo Coyaji wanted to offer curative services in the villages. However, they soon realized that curative treatment would not address the health issues of people. So, they initiated the preventive services. They experienced that unless they worked with the community towards comprehensive holistic development, they could not achieve any goals conceived internationally or contribute to the livable lives of the people. They trained the local people, focusing on marginalized women such as widows or deserted women to become the volunteers in the health and development programmes.

In the field of leprosy, international Christian organizations taking the message from Bible, first took care of socially rejected leprosy patients giving them place in leprosy colonies and later as cured persons, in the diagnosis and drug delivery programmes. Institutions like Gandhi Memorial Leprosy Foundation established in memory of Gandhiji's work and commitment to the cause of leprosy, developed models of leprosy control programme co-opted by the government as National Programme.

Establishment of residential Ashram Schools in tribal area in the voluntary sector became the government programme of ashram schools in the government sector. In Maharashtra, the proportion of government ashram schools and ashram schools from the voluntary sector are almost equal.

With democratic decentralization, the national political parties reached out to the people to get elected to the statutory bodies from village, taluka, district levels to capture political authority at the state and national level. The process of elections require the potential candidates to be visible to the people constantly and to help people at the individual and collective level addressing their needs, concerns and aspirations. Expansion of the government sector due to development agenda and expansion of service sector due to industrialization and urbanizations opened up salaried jobs which required minimum educational qualifications. Expansion of educational enrolment required expansion of educational institutions which was taken up by leaders with political aspirations.

Some young educated persons desirous of doing social work also established their own voluntary organizations commonly branded with the international nomenclature as NGOs.

The expansion of voluntary/NGO sector took a boost about a decade after the Community Development Programme was launched in 1952. Some doctors also established hospitals as 'charitable organizations and research institutions' taking the advantage of tax exemptions for health research approved by the government. The government realized that it was not possible to establish such institutions in the public sector. So they encouraged the private/voluntary sector to establish such institutions and to give fillip to research, by providing tax exemptions for research work.

All these institutions, big and small, required community participation for their sustenance. Some organizations who had realized the necessity of addressing holistic and comprehensive development programmes turned to social science faculty in the universities for conceptual clarity and mechanisms of getting community participation. Sociology, Psychology, Anthropology and Social work disciplines were perceived useful for such collaboration and consultation. Some leaders of big NGOs preferred anthropology trained personnel who were field oriented and thus could directly communicate with the people. More than others, anthropology exhibited holistic approach to deal with an issue. The voluntary sector, whose entry point with the community was health care, education or livelihood, and the small NGOs who took up advocacy and rights of people as their agenda, had to address all issues subsequently, although focusing on their initial agenda at the entry point. Whether initiating health care, education or livelihood issues, they had to understand that no single issue could be addressed in a vertical fashion, since they were all linked up functionally and structurally to the holistic ground reality. They had to function with multiple tasks to be addressed with few employees or volunteers, with limited budgets, unlike the line departments of the governments.

I was thus involved with helping several voluntary/NGO bodies in the training of their personnel about concepts and methodology which would provide them the knowledge of techniques and tools of interacting with the community to understand community concerns. Some NGOs wanted to undertake baseline surveys before launching a programme or a mid-term evaluation or evaluation of the programme at the end, mainly to give impact reports to funding agencies.

Third party evaluation was a requirement for the funding agencies. The NGOs had the quantitative data about services provided to the people linked with the expenditure data. But that would not explain the impact, since quantitative measurement of impact required more time to exhibit itself. Qualitative evaluation proved useful to unravel the process of change through case studies and spontaneous quotes of the people about change as they perceived it.

Dr. Manibhai Desai, disciple of Mahatma Gandhi, Founder of BAIF had initiated livelihood interventions at Vansda in tribal area on the border of Maharashtra and Gujarat. Asking the tribals as to why they were drinking alcohol and getting the response that they had no food to eat, Manibhai offered them mango horticultural 'Wadi'. Five families volunteered to plant mango saplings, being paid for labour, with the undertaking that they would give up drinking alcohol. 'Wadi' Project of BAIF became the flagship programme with about 5000 tribal families opting for it in Maharashtra and Gujarat. After several years, he asked me to evaluate the programme with a suspicion as to whether the tribals with 'Wadi' had resorted back to alcoholism with affluence. I went to Vansda, visited one of the first five families who had accepted the 'Wadi' concept. I talked to all members of the family. They were using their surplus money to enhance their status in the community by way of constructing a large house, with factory roof tiles, in preference to indigenous tiles, better clothes, motor cycle for the son and a wrist watch for the educated daughter-in-law, who kept the 'wadi' account; inviting villagers for ceremonies, offering good food etc. I talked to women in other villages who were involved in BAIF's nursery development programmes earning good amount of money which they spent on better clothes and books for school going daughters, and enhancing the common facilities at the village level by way of purchasing cooking utensils and *Daris* (Carpets) for large number of people to sit in a hall on such occasions, as marriage or village meetings.

We also offered training in research methods to BAIF staff to improve the documentation and in-house evaluation. We conducted base line surveys, when BAIF started a new programme in a new geographical tribal area.

Women Empowerment

As mentioned earlier, there have been three prominent medical doctors in Maharashtra who floated NGOs, in mid-70s, probably disenchanted with government programmes of health care. Dr. Mrs. Banoo Coyaji, an obstetrician-gynaecologist; Dr. N.H. Antia, a plastic surgeon and Dr. Rajnikant and Dr. Mabel Arole, a doctor couple as general practitioners, started work to provide affordable curative services to villagers. They evolved their work to preventive issues, going in for general development through their experience. All were working mainly through women workers whom they trained. Dr. Arole and Dr. Coyaji gave preference to marginalised women, who were deserted or widows.

We offered research methods training to the staff of FRCH, KEMHRC, CRHP and evaluated their programmes. Most of these evaluations were 'after only' evaluations since the base-line survey was not undertaken when the programmes were implemented, which were not planned according to a protocol, but had evolved in response to the emic needs and etic perceptions of the programmers. Since leprosy NGOs participated in national and international conferences and had to submit research papers, more structured workshops about social science research were organized across the country.

KEMHRC's women empowerment programme in the villages located about 50 km from Pune, focusing on marginalized women such as widows, or deserted by their husbands was evaluated in the 'after only' mode. The measurable data was visible as houses constructed by themselves, daughter's getting married and may be some consumable durables in the house.

Dr. Coyaji gave sheep to women which had an urban market. I was asked to evaluate the women empowerment programme which had no baseline data. Usually, we are asked to undertake evaluation of programmes, where 'After Only' evaluation model has to be used, which is achievable with the use of anthropological qualitative methods. We do not use the bio-medical model of control group, since in some cases, control group may have done better than the experimental group, due to dynamic leadership at the local level.

While the data about women's earnings and expenditure on such items as house construction and daughter's wedding was collected which indicated their achievements and gave them self-confidence, which was visible in the group meetings, usually referred to as FGD, the real insights came from qualitative quotes. An all men closed door meeting was convened to get spontaneous assessment of men about women's empowerment, among them also the men who ridiculed and mocked these women in the past. The original quotes are in Marathi, which translated in Hindi are, "*Unki nazare saf hogai*" (Bright, clear eyes), "*Unka boz halka ho gaya*" (Mental pressure/tension has reduced). "They have become self-confident. Their self-esteem is visible in their sparkling eyes.

They can hold their neck high. They can look into your eyes without fear." An example from a man about his wife. "Earlier, if I asked for a cup of tea for a guest, my wife would keep the cup in a saucer on the threshold of door and I would give it to the guest. Now, she comes into the room, in front of the guest, looks into his eyes and hands over tea to him." While this evaluation was presented to a group of three dignitaries, as trustees of KEM hospital and Research Centre, viz. retired Cabinet Secretary, GOI; D.G., CSIR and D.G., ICMR; they said, the spontaneous, cultural quotes conveyed empowerment more effectively than the statistics.

There have been more interactions with the leprosy organizations. Gandhi Memorial Leprosy Foundation asked for evaluation of their Health Education Programme, followed by ICMR who wanted evaluation of 'E' (education) in their SET (Survey, Education, Treatment) Programme. DANLEP wanted documentation of their '*Janbhagidari*' (Community Involvement) programme in Chhattisgarh. In all these exercises, qualitative methods proved very useful for analyzing the process of change. The Leprosy Mission requested participation in their intervention programme to reduce stigma by involving the community in Chhattisgarh, Uttar Pradesh and West Bengal in their hospital outreach area in Champa, Faizpur and Purulia respectively. The anthropological method of visiting the people in their homes, instead of calling them at our office or hospital paid dividends. Confidence building and rapport are essential steps for people to open out without reservations. Listening to them provides emic perspectives.

During National Leprosy Elimination Programme mid-term evaluation in December 2014, I as team leader for Assam convened the *gram sabha* supervised by lady President and lady Vice-President of 10 village group gram panchayats, in panchayat hall. Nowhere else in India, this happened, as an activity of mid-term evaluation, where mostly the interaction took place with health and leprosy personnel at various levels of health administration and in the hospitals.

In all such exercises, academics from the universities are invited by governments or NGOs to evaluate the programmes, train their staff about research and documentation and advise about meaningful community participation.

The medical scientists for undertaking clinical research have to undertake intervention research by giving a drug to a patient. Then they follow the experiment-control model for research. There is no paradigm of such kind of intervention research in social sciences including social anthropology. Interventions are administered by governments by designing schemes. NGOs either implement government schemes as their agents or design their own models of interventions.

Maharashtra Association of Anthropological Sciences (MAAS)

The anthropology department of Savitribai Phule Pune University (earlier called Poona University) in 1975-76 formed an academic NGO, The Maharashtra Association of Anthropological Sciences (MAAS), in response to the desire expressed by social science college teachers from across the State of Maharashtra to have an association in the absence of any social science association in the State. The teachers were the participants at the Research Methodology workshop as hands-on training about data collection, data analysis and report writing, first at the university in November 1975, followed by field training in the tribal area in Thane (now Palghar) district in Western Maharashtra, in November 1976. The workshop and field training supported by WRC, ICSSR, Mumbai, in both the years were of fortnight duration. Although MAAS was registered at Pune University, it moved out of campus after few years. The commitment or support from the teaching faculty of anthropology was lukewarm. But the social, a-political activists working in tribal areas took initiatives to join the organization in large numbers.

Several seminars were organized about tribal issues on the university campus jointly by MAAS and Department of Anthropology. Being an academic platform, government officers from Tribal Development Department and Forest Department, specifically from Forest Development Corporation attended these seminars. As recommended by the social activists, working in tribal areas, a quarterly magazine-*cum*-journal—'*Hakara*' (clarion call) in Marathi, exclusively devoted to tribal issues was started on 1 January, 1980. The magazine provided a forum for tribal litterateurs, particularly the poets, to publish their literary work. MAAS even organized a state level conference of tribal litterateurs, presided over by Prof. G.B. Sardar, teaching in Marathi Department in a university and unanimously elected as President of the apex body of the state level Marathi literary body, Marathi Sahitya Sammelan. He was the President of MAAS. He was preferred in view of his social sensitivity about *dalits*, more particularly the tribals, since he was born in a tribal town. The other Presidents have been Prof. A.R. Kulkarni who was Chairman, Indian Council of Historical Research, Prof. P.V. Sukhatme, pioneer agricultural statistician and Director, FAO, Rome, and Janardan Maharaj Valvi, a Bhil pioneer educationist from the hilly terrain of Nandurbar district. I opted to be General Secretary since the inception of MAAS for about 25 years, before becoming President for the next twelve years. I was followed by Prof. Pandit Vidyasagar, a physicist with social commitment and Vice-Chancellor of Swami Ramanand Teerth University, Nanded. The immediate past president has been Prof. S. Parasuraman, anthropologist-demographer and erstwhile Director/Vice-Chancellor of Tata Institute of Social Sciences, Mumbai, for a decade and half. He has been succeeded by Dr. M.D. Gupte who was the first Director, National Institute of Epidemiology (ICMR), Chennai.

MAAS has been an Asian partner of London School of Hygiene and Tropical Medicine for a decade, to conduct operational research, focusing on HIV and TB. MAAS in partnership with CRHP, Jamkhed administered an intervention project about Tribal malnutrition across all ethnic tribal communities in Maharashtra in nine tribe dominant taluks (Book: *Tribal Health and Malnutrition*, 2018). Besides, MAAS has had projects from Ministry of AYUSH about 'AYUSH in Public Health' in four States, Himachal Pradesh, Madhya Pradesh, Chhattisgarh and Maharashtra (Book: *AYUSH in Public Health*, 2 Volumes, 2016). MAAS is now recognized as a research centre of the Savitribai Phule Pune University.

The wider term 'anthropological sciences' has been used to denote the classical, holistic model of anthropology to encourage open door policy. "The term Anthropological Sciences encompasses all the disciplines, which deal with Man and His works in holistic and historical perspective in relation to environmental, biological, behavioural, economic, social, political and cultural aspects. Anthropological Sciences thus include all social sciences and humanities and all the ethno-sciences such as ethno-botany, ethno-biology, etc. and biomedical sciences." The Motto of MAAS has been, "People Centred Comprehensive and Sustainable Development for Human Dignity."

The international apex organization of anthropology is called 'International Union of Anthropological and Ethnological Sciences' (IUAES). Thus, through close networking of the Department of Anthropology at the University and academic NGO, MAAS, opportunities could be created to complement each other, both being rooted in the field, with the people, to create and use knowledge for the good of the people.

There has been voluntary sector in anthropological research organizations providing platform for the peers to come together to exchange research finding which could lead to publications.

There have been journals like '*Man in India*' or '*Eastern Anthropologist*' in India. Anthropological Society of Kolkata or Anthropological Association at Delhi also published journals. The primacy of Anthropological Society in founding the apex body, Indian National Confederation and Academy of Anthropologists (INCAA) cannot be underestimated. INCAA has also initiated the '*Indian Journal of Anthropology*'. INCAA is regularly organizing Anthropology Congress every year across the country with a publication of Round Table discussions. There are specialized associations like Society for Indian Medical Anthropology (SIMA) which links ethno-medicine with mainstream AYUSH.

The academic voluntary sector has an advantage of taking academic initiatives not regulated by public sector academic bodies like the University Grants Commission (UGC). The academic voluntary sector can keep its platform open and take up intervention research projects, networking with university departments as also the general voluntary sector involved in social action. The voluntary sector welcomes such interaction to strengthen the conceptual base of their work with the people, and we stand to gain experience of the real life situations and processes of social change, without doing rigorous field research ourselves.

Normally, science departments in a university could have a tie up with industry, while social sciences could have a complementary tie up with the NGOs, for intervention research.

While descriptive ethnography provides the ground reality of culture and life styles, focused ethnography about the issues provide insights about the dynamics of change through understanding the interplay of emic-etic, micro-macro, involving various stake holders. The politics and economics of etic and macro level policies of development and their implementation through paid-employees, provides space to anthropologists to undertake policy research and make pro-people and doable recommendations. This is not wholly possible as a university based academic discipline. The ground realities of the concerns of the people through their perspectives are understandable if a partnership is forged between the university based academic discipline and the voluntary sector, who also have to interact with the public and private sector.

We have experienced success in medical anthropology, particularly in regard to leprosy control. The establishment of Social-Behavioural Research Division at the ICMR is one such instance. In leprosy, the WHO modified its objectives of leprosy control and expanded the definition of the case of leprosy. International leprosy NGOs modified their mission by expanding their activities from patient, to his family and the community. In AYUSH, public health agenda has been added which was totally absent in the public sector.

Indian Association for the Study of Traditional Asian Medicine (IASTAM)

An academic voluntary organization in traditional medicine at the international and national levels were established as a result of interaction of Medical Anthropology, Indology and Asian Medical Systems. The initiatives taken by famous Indologist Prof. A.L. Basham in consultation with the Medical Anthropologist Prof. Charles Leslie and leader of Ayurved, Pandit Shiv Sharma, gave a fillip for organizing the first International Congress on Traditional Asian Medicine (ICTAM) held at Australian National University, Canberra in September 1979. The discussions were structured at the International Post-Plenary Symposium on Medical Anthropology following the International Anthropology Congress at Delhi in December 1978, which was hosted by Department of Anthropology at Pune University. The Indian chapter (IASTAM-India) of the international body, 'International Association of the Study of Traditional Asian Medicine' (IASTAM) which was constituted at ICTAM, at Canberra, was formalized at Pune University in April 1980.

The Indian Association adopted the objectives of the International Association which are given in the preamble to the Constitution as under:

> "In every Ethnic group there exists a traditional health care system which is culturally patterned. In traditional societies, this is the first line of defence in health care. The contribution of traditional health care has gained the full recognition of the World Health Organisation. It is in the interest of the people that traditional medicine should be fully exposed in its Ethno-Historical, Social, Cultural and Scientific context. In a country like India, there exists great tradition of Health System enshrined in various scriptures and texts. There also exists folk medicine practised in tribal and rural homes. Constant interaction between the great tradition which is taught and transmitted in traditional and institutionlised medical schools, and the local traditions of the simple folk, needs to be studied. It may be necessary to develop a distinct methodology for research in Traditional Asian Medicine since the methodology of cosmopolitan medicine may not be found wholly suitable for the purpose. A national forum is, therefore, needed where the traditional health care systems express their constituent components and communicate across linguistic and territorial barriers. Besides traditional therapies, the allied disciplines, and

> other techniques and languages connected with tradition such as Sanskrit, Urdu, Tamil, History, Botany, Anthropology Indology, Yoga etc. would have to play an important role in the study of Traditional Asian Medicine." (IASTAM-India website)

While the IASTAM at the international level has been dominated by Western Scholars of History, Sanskrit, Medical Anthropology etc. IASTAM-India is dominated by clinicians, pharmacists and researchers of Indian medicine. The organization holds seminars, conferences and have instituted several memorial awards. However, no research projects or training programmes have been initiated so far.

The voluntary sector has further extended to the people, after the micro-finance concept in Bangladesh became visible as '*grameen bank*' established by Muhammad Yunus and has became popular. Self Help Groups (SHG) of women as Community Based Organization (CBO) have proliferated in India with linkage to banking sector provided by the Government. This has led to empowerment of women strengthened by 50 per cent reservation for women representation at the institutions of democratic decentralization. Focused ethnography of such processes and the working of CBOs is needed.

The governments are alive to the bureaucratization in all public sector undertakings including the research organizations. The escape route has been to bestow autonomous status to such organizations as TRTI, registering it under the Charitable Societies Act. However, the total funding comes from State exchequer putting limitations. The heads of such institutions are also drawn from the civil services, irrespective of their training in focused issues of the organizations, dealing with the tribals or *dalits* or other historically marginalized groups, such as denotified or nomadic groups.

Nation's governance, vision, planning process and logistics of implementation has to be understood in terms of the roles of people's elected representatives, bureaucracy, judiciary, media, academics, and voluntary sector etc. Briefly, it could be referred as public sector, private sector, people's sector and voluntary sector. However, people's sector such as CBOs and academics have yet to make their mark, impacting the policy planning and implementation.

Unless anthropology takes proactive interest in the affairs of such organizations as expert members of governing or advisory bodies, the knowledge base of the academic discipline would not develop to become meaningful to the affairs of the nation and the people.

8

Ethical Issues in Research

Ethical Issues in anthropology have to be discussed at two levels. When an anthropologist studies 'other people' using a methodology to understand the people and their culture and society, they try to take up the role of objective investigator. Even while doing participant observation or non-participant observation, by going 'native', he is trying to be sympathetic to understand the meaning of behaviour or events that is followed by 'other people', what is termed as functionalist approach.

For eliciting information which is not observable, relating to hard core of culture, the strategy which is also ethical, enjoins the investigator to share the values and practices followed in his own community, to motivate the respondent to open up what is thought or followed in his community. We know from some ethnographic literature that if a married tribal woman wants to divorce a man, she may have to return a part of the bride price she had received. In case she takes another lover, he may have to pay back proportionate consideration to her first husband as per customary regulatory mechanism, such as directed by the *Mukhiya* or *Panchayat.* My point of inquiry was directed to a Madia tribal in a village in Gadchiroli district of Maharashtra, as to what happens if he does not follow this practice. What punishment would he receive and who would inflict or administer that punishment. While this was a hypothetical inquiry beyond his comprehension, he could respond when I said, we had a judicial system to which we could refer our disputes. They also have their *panchayats.* Besides, he said he would play black magic on the person not following the norm and on further probe said, that would work since he was morally or ethically right and the other person was wrong, violating the social norms.

There are issues of research ethics. There are anecdotes that a particular community after reading the book about them which had used fictitious names, took out a procession hanging their real names around the neck and burnt the book. A book about Poona University, focusing on academic politics, using the conceptual model of primitive society "Contradictions and Conflict" by Donald Kurtz, a political anthropologist (1994) was reviewed by an eminent professor of political science with a full page article in a Marathi newspaper. The real names which were given fictitious identity in the book were revealed in the article since the reviewer was familiar with the University. This greatly embarrassed the academic politicians in authority, and was not refuted, since the investigator-author had objectively documented the happenings as case studies.

Anthropological knowledge of ethnography could be objective. But the rulers, colonial or country governments could use it for their own purpose. Intelligence agencies would like anthropologists to do ethnography of communities in the neighbouring countries. The data could be used for positive purpose such as designing the foreign policy or negatively for defence purposes. Ethnography of diaspora could be useful as addition to knowledge as also its application.

What Nehru said about tribal development, that let the development take place or be planned according to their own genius, meant along the line of culture, which would make it acceptable and sustainable. However, it presupposes that we should have the objective data about people's culture, their attitudes and faith and their concerns in the context of increasing contact, and interaction with the governance system, technology and aspirations of the young.

The ethnography, and now focused ethnography, has proved the test of time about objectivity depending upon our residence or time spent with the people whom we want to study. This helps in such applied aspects as to adjudicate about the pseudo-tribal claims to get ST status. Our practice is to go to the field instead of only listening to the delegations and reading memoranda. Entering their houses and kitchens, visiting their shrines and temples, piligrimage centres, looking at the nature of deities and the material used for their composition, the food served to them at rituals etc., life-cycle rituals and listening to women, provide us the objective data about the authenticity of claims.

There are more ethical issues in medical anthropology, in research, as also due to bacteriological or medical paradigms. According to Helsinki Declaration, medical research is justified if there is likelihood that it will benefit the majority of people from the results of research. Informed consent appears to be the only ethics mechanism to undertake clinical trials. There have been several deaths due to clinical trials, about which the Supreme Court of India had to take notice. In case of foreign funded public health or drug trial research projects, which are multi-national or multi-centric within country, issue of language for communicating with the people becomes a prime issue. The documents which are originally in English have to be translated in the language of investigation. The foreign funding agencies or the principal investigator insist that the correctness of translation could be verified by rendering back translation of the investigation tools such as questionnaire into English.

This expresses lack of confidence in the required research partners. Language has cultural expression which makes it difficult to back-translate the tool into English. There are also ethical issues relating to objectivity. As an example, in HIV related research, the medical scientists or doctors could freely discuss the details of sex acts etc. without inhibitions due to their professional training and interest in diseases caused due to sex act. They treat a disease, not a person afflicted with a disease. In real life, sex is a subject of silence for public discussion, but there are cultural expressions which convey the meaning without appearing shameless. A village woman to a querry about sex act, may say that "when we talk (*batchit*) to each other (i.e. between husband and wife), it hurts." This cannot be translated or understood in English. However, this is culturally perfect polite and effective communication. So, ethics is also a cultural issue. There have been issues about tabling a bill in Parliament by individual member about sterilization of leprosy afflicted as if it was a hereditary disease or a genetic disorder. There are ethical issues about organ transplants or 'renting out the uterus'.

Academic NGOs may take up intervention projects to prepare models of development or to address a public issue, such as tribal malnutrition. In evaluation research about such issues, the medical model of experiment-control is recommended. Apart from the fact that such model is being questioned since the control group is denied or withheld from giving facilities to experimental group, in dealing with human communities, the control group may do better than the experimental group depending upon the accessibility to facilities which are open to all, and in case the dynamic leadership at the control site, may push forward innovative, out-of-the-box enterprises. Interventions could be designed as per government schemes, or according to religious faith or practicing a conceptual framework. Anthropological preference for holistic understanding, analysis and intervention could be different. Community participation or involvement in an issue which is of their concern is morally or ethically more appropriate.

A research training workshop for two weeks in a tribal area for college teachers of social sciences about educational issues held in November 1976 led to data collection and analysis in the field. In a town, Jawhar, in the neighbourhood of field area, a seminar was organized with participation of senior scholars from Pune, Mumbai, Surat whereby the data and findings were presented to a group of citizens of the villages from where the data was collected. On another occasion, anthropology students during their field training collected ethnographic details living in a Korku village. At the end of fieldwork, data was presented in the study village whereby the district level officials such as in education, health, agriculture etc were invited, to relate the village data with their district level perception.

Participatory research is evolving with active participation and training of the local people, to analyze their issues objectively so as to undertake micro-planning about their area. It is understood that law regulates external behaviour but right and wrong behaviour is regulated by moral code of conduct which could be culturally patterned as normative or deviant behaviour.

Research ethics has to be standardized as a norm. In different cultures, norms could be different. While the legal age of marriage for girls in India could be 18, in African countries it could be different. In such cases, muti-national research studies would face difficult situations for sex or microbicide research. If a multi-national intervention study is planned to try acceptability of a microbicide among the adolescent girls at risk of HIV, due to pre-marital sex, the legal age of consent in the respective countries has to be taken into account. To undertake such a study in India involving girls below the age of 18 years would require consent of the parents, while in some countries, it may not be required for the girls of 15 years of age. The studies, however, show that in India, the girls particularly in urban slums are vulnerable to have pre-marital sex below the age of 18 years (Joshi, Maushmi, 2019: 186-208). In such cases, law supercedes ground reality. Many adolescents charged with rape try to argue their age as that of minor to escape the provisions of criminal proceedings. Law, morality and ethics become the subject of controvertial debates.

In *Mahabharat* epic, Kunti, a princess, was given a boon by a sage Durvas to possess power to invoke any celestial deity. As unmarried adolescent, she invoked Sun-God and begot a son, called Karna (ear) believed to be delivered from the ear, not violating the virginity of Kunti. Being an illegitimate child according to social norms, the baby was abandoned in a basket put in the river and reared by a charioteer of the

Kaurava kings. Irawati Karve has analysed this personality in her book '*Yugant*' (end of an epoch) about anthropological analysis of the epic, '*Mahabharat*', acclaimed as a piece of literature and won highest national award for literature. From anthropological perspective, the book is about 'culture and personality' studies in a pastoral society.

Ethical issues are important. Only that we have to make a distinction between research ethics and the issues about imperial powers, very visible during Second World War. We know that academicians could be funded by intelligence agencies to undertake studies in other countries. However, academicians/scientists argue that the purpose for which scientific data was used could not be their primary concern. Nuclear science could be used for peaceful purposes as also for destruction.

It is well known that the whole process of research ethics in medical sciences assumed significance since the German concentration camps of POWS (Prisoners of War) were misused for drug trials (1946) which led to Nuremberg Code (1947) and discussion about Human Rights, and Helsinki Declaration (1964). ICMR policy statement about ethical consideration regarding research on human subjects was issued in 1980. Every institution now has to have a research ethics committee. There are even animal ethics committees to discuss as to how minimum number of animals could be used for undertaking research trials.

Anthropologists may not deflect from their objectivity in ethnography. It is for the governments to use the information for their ends. We cannot shy away from making people-centric recommendations on such issues as tribal malnutrition or bringing in people's perspectives in disease control programmes. We know how Indira Gandhi personally lost elections on family planning, since the opposition could exploit the ignorance of people about vasectomy as synonym of castration and impotence, which they had observed among farm animals. As anthropologists, we can analyse such results, knowing people's ideas about body metabolism, about semen getting transmigrated to empower '*kundalini*' and about Vishwamitra-Menaka storey, and the role and machinations of Indra, in destroying the spiritual and intellectual powers of the sage Viswamitra by breaking his continence, through mating with the celestial nymph, Menaka.

Prof. H.K. Bhat has discussed the issue of ethics and objectivity in his presentation at INCAA Congress-2019, at Pune University.

> "Ethical and objectivity dimensions are very rarely discussed in Indian Anthropology. A thorough review of the works of the British administrator-anthropologists is desired as well as the works of the Indian disciples of the foreign anthropologists.

> Although there are many issues, concepts and approaches which need to be discussed, the following shall be subjected for scrutiny and critical evaluation in this paper:
>
> - The neglect of the historical and civilizational dimensions of Indian society and culture by anthropologists.
> - Use of terms like tribe, primitive, criminal, backward etc. in describing communities in India.
> - The correctness of treating Indian communities as the "other" culture by Indian anthropologists.
> - Research priorities of Indian anthropologists. Were they blind followers of their Western masters in selecting the research areas?
> - Under the ethical practices to be made mandatory for all anthropologists, the following may be considered:
>   a. Maintaining cordial relationship with the subjects.
>   b. Maintaining confidentiality of data.
>   c. Contribution to nation building or international understanding.
>   d. Maintaining loyalty to the discipline.
>   e. To include felt-needs of the people in the research agenda.
>   f. To avoid any clash of interest with the researched subjects, with reference to any personal material benefits.
>   g. To avoid acting as servants of foreign anthropologists and work against the interest of the nation."

Prof. P.K. Misra has made observations in the similar vein at this Congress.

> "North-East India had been on boil during the entire British regime, where a good number of anthropological studies too were conducted. That itself raises the question as to why there was so much anthropological focus on North-East India in the context of unfolding of the history of that area. Now we know that on the eve of Indian independence some famous British Anthropologists were part of the proposed Crown Colony Plan which envisaged carving out an eastern tribal belt and putting the same under the protective care of the British administrators since it was believed that the hill tribes had nothing in common

with mainland India and Indians. Beside, there are examples when human settlements in North-East India were being raided and demolished, still anthropological enquiries were going on that were recognized in the Western world as illustrations of academic excellence." (Misra P.K., 2019: 3, INCAA Newsletter, Indian Anthropology Congress.)

Ethical Issues in Medical Anthropology

Another new area that open up anthropological insights relate to ethical issues which have assumed significance in medical and biological research. At least an attempt is made to involve the participation of subjects of research in research investigations. Informed consent forms (at the moment, many of them are documents in drug trials in clinical research) are being designed or evaluated by anthropologists and other social scientists.

Anthropological concepts of culture, integration of culture and cultural relativism bestow equal status to all ethnic groups and communities without any superiority or inferiority. Emic perspectives presuppose looking at things through the spectacles of subjects under study, in contrast with etic perspectives. Interventions are justified within the purview of universal values for humanity. Anthropology thus respects plurality and variability and advocates tolerance and co-existence.

Medical Anthropology respects all formal medical systems, and those practices based on indigenous knowledge, as health aspects of respective culture systems and those based on modern biology and science.

Conflicting situations arise when laboratory tested solutions are transformed into public programmes globally, seeking behavioural change among the people. Informed consent is being used as a single instrument to conduct research on human subjects. There are varying issues in communicable and non-communicable disease management programmes. Clinical trials of pharmaceutical products seem to undermine variable genetic composition of people. Cultural practices regarding endogamy, exogamy and preferential kin marriages seem to be linked with genetic disorders.

While Ayurvedic time-tested drugs are questioned for efficacy and safety, several modern drugs having gone through animal trials and clinical trials are subsequently withdrawn as unsafe or with bad side effects. Supreme Court of India has made observations about deaths of 'subjects' during clinical trials of drugs. Applied Science appears to be used for commerce.

The ethical issues in social science research have not yet taken roots. Anthropologists undertaking field research, residing for long duration with the people had to win the confidence of the people, through constant dialogue. Field residence provides opportunity for the people being studied to observe the researchers and their life, bringing them close to each other, even establishing an emotional bond. The constant difference between research ethics and ethical issues in action anthropology have to be appreciated and followed, using the principle of cultural relativism on one hand and following the universal values of humanism and human rights, on the other, balancing each other, with the spirit of benevolence.

The ethics issues while the studies were/are directed to 'other' people and while they are directed to our own people would appear different, although both would be done objectively. The research studies or intervention programmes or recommendations to better the lives of common people need not be abandoned by anthropologists in the garb of 'value neutrality', as long as the research process observes the criteria of objectivity. Universal values and human rights are the internationally accepted guidelines for action. Nationally, Constitution of India is the guiding principle, although not sacrosanct, since it may need amendments with changing times. Anthropology as holistic study of Man and having experience of cross-cultural plurality and variability is conceptually well equipped to guide research ethics.

9

Epilogue

Indian Anthropology

Pandit Madan Mohan Malviya who established Banares Hindu University in 1916 and was the Vice-Chancellor in 1936, when he asked Prof. P.V. Sukhatme, the pioneer agricultural statistician in India as to what difference the knowledge of statistics made to the lives of poor people. Prof. Sukhatme had gone with an idea to establish Statistics Department at the University. Prof. Sukhatme later worked with FAO at Rome as Director of Statistics. He established Indira Community Kitchen at Pune, after his retirement with the motto of poor helping the poor. He was President of Maharashtra Association of Anthropological Sciences when he passed away in 1997.

Introduction

What is anthropology, as a knowledge discipline and as an academic discipline functioning in the university system as departments and in the research institutes in the public sector and voluntary sector? What is the public image of anthropology and its visibility to the political leadership and to the governing bureaucracy? Are we considered viable to address the national issues of development, poverty, health, foreign relations and national security, including global perspective to complement international interactions?

Is anthropology only ethnography of isolated, 'Primitive' people extending to rural settlements and urban slums or has a capacity to analyse civilizations with textual history, value systems having roots in the mythology and scriptures?

In this book, attempts have been made to discuss these issues not theoretically but with the use of concrete examples based on subjective experience as objective evidence.

Anthropology developed as a knowledge discipline claiming to be holistic study of Man without any time dimension but putting up an image as past oriented with stress on stability and equilibrium. Study of geographically isolated communities became a special focus which later turned into a conceptual design of study, being easier to undertake methodologically and for analysis. It may have started with curiosity about 'queer customs' turned into imperialist design, for prosletysation, further used for indirect rule to administer large populations with their distinctive and diverse cultures, history and geographical spread; not losing sight of exploiting the natural resources of the colonies.

The study of 'primitive' or isolated communities was branded as studies in evolution and diffusion to understand the diversities, universals, pluralities across the world, developing concepts of Culture in all the ramifications including cultural relativism, basic cultural personality, status and role. For communities with oral history, structural-functional concepts proved helpful for analysis addressing the needs doctrine. For large, plural communities as in India and China, with textual history, mythology, philosophical values as guiding principles of behaviour, with monuments, art forms related to mythological stories, personal and place names, pilgrimage or sacred geography, anthropological analysis of civilization in place of culture has been done as we get from scholars like Irawati Karve.

Indian culture diffused to South-East regions not through military conquests but through poetic narrations of mythology and history as non-violent processes. India itself, however, was subjected to military conquests through north-west or through west coast trade voyages. The Mughals settled down as rulers and citizens of 'Hindosthan', the Portuguese and French occupying some territories as small colonies. The East India Company took possession of the whole country of India with extended adjacent territories such as Burma (Mynmar) and Ceylone (Sri Lanka). With the process of transculturation among Hindu and Muslim, Indian culture developed in new integrated forms visible in art and architecture, music, cuisine, apparel etc. Overwhelmed by British technological, administrative and management supremacy, British education impressed the Indian intellectual class through which the concepts of democracy, equality, welfare state became the cherished goals. Freedom struggle for self-rule was required to reach these goals by controlling the resources of the country owned and exploited by the British.

As we have discussed in earlier chapters, the intellectuals and leaders in India were deliberating since the late nineteenth century and twentieth century till the political independence was in sight, about the vision of Indian's social and economic transformation under self-rule. Several Committees were formed by the then universal political party Congress, to deliberate on these issues. Provincial governments were also formed under the 1935 Act which also appointed such committees. Mahatma Gandhi's constructive programmes were available for implementation at the national level. The debates in the constituent assembly deliberated about the structure of the Constitution to address the concerns, vision and welfare of the people debated since the 1880s. Socialist model of directed and planned development were largely acceptable to the leadership.

Anthropology as an academic discipline started at Calcutta University in 1920 and the seeds of it earlier in Asiatic Society of Bengal were following the Western model of ethnology and ethnography.

The development of technology coinciding with Second World War in different fields including medicine as also the establishment of economic organisations at the global level, such as World Bank and International Monetary Fund facilitated the rise of global economy impacting the new de-colonised countries, in all aspects of life such as education, health and industry. USA became the global leader with capitalist model of development while the Soviet Union as socialist model provided an anti-dote as a world power in defence supremacy. The so-called Third World countries had to balance between the two powers. India was striving to be a model for the Third World, providing the label as non-aligned countries.

Post-independence model of development focused on public participation by way of adult franchise at all levels from village, taluka/ tehsil/ block to district, state and national level. Principle of equity was implemented by way of affirmative action, i.e. reservation for the historically deprived and isolated communities in elective bodies, and in educational institutions and public sector jobs. Community development incorporating health at primary and secondary level was initiated. Special Tribal Sub-Plan was also initiated as a result of several committees and commissions of which anthropologists were members. TRTIs were established. Tribal ministers were selected to monitor tribal development programmes. Governors were provided special constitutional authority about tribal issues over and above the state governments.

In this whole process, there have been debates about the meaning of development. Normally development is understood in terms of GNP and GDP or in terms of infrastructure of transport, communication, energy, technically trained man power and health indicators. Several indices at national and international levels have been used to rank the countries on scales of development.

Anthropology used to be a compulsory subject at ICS examination during British rule. What role did anthropology trained bureaucrates play, except administering 'indirect rule' so as not to confront the people at all levels, with British face and not to interfere with people's rituals and customs, unless they turned into law and order issues or flared into disease epidemics?

With de-colonisation, UN agencies became larger and more effective with the third world countries becoming the member-states of UN bodies such as WHO, FAO, UNICEF, UNESO, ILO etc. with their regional offices in such countries. These bodies deliberated on developing policies and guidelines for member states to reach out to the masses. *Alma Ata* declaration about Health for All in 1978, emphasised inter-sectoral co-ordination advocating the contribution of non-health sectors towards attainment of health and about universalization of primary health care. Disease control programmes became international programmes. Importance of indigenous medicine and traditional medicine was formally recognised. These systems were studied and documented by Western medical anthropologists. Debates about protein deficiency *versus* calorie deficiencies were raised by an Indian bio-statistician Prof. P.V. Sukhatme on the FAO forum. Issues of women empowerment were formalised through concepts like Grameen Bank coming from Bangla Desh leading to formation of self-help group. In India 50 per cent of seats in elective bodies at the village, district and municipal levels have been reserved for women. Anthropologists extended their ethnography about health, to what is called as ethno-medicine. Community development in India was propagated as man-centred programme although the bureaucracy always implemented it as financial and physical target oriented programme.

All these processes required participation of communities in disease control programmes, grow more food programmes, enrolment in education programmes etc. The slogan 'Think Globally, Act Locally' or inter-sectoral coordination for health, use the anthropological insights about integrative nature of culture and the etic-emic perspectives.

As discussed earlier, the community development programme based on extension approach which was later formally introduced in agriculture university education curriculum, had American anthropologists as consultants. Indeed, after my Masters degree in Anthropology from Saugar University, I had an offer to be a faculty member in Extension at the Agricultural University at Jabalpur.

However, the economists replaced anthropologists in issues of rural development, due to the utility of measurable output in terms of physical targets of production and other such variables, required for budgeting, and expenditure by 31st March, which continues to be the end of financial year in India. We achieved green revolution and white revolution while facing farmer's suicides in increasing numbers in recent years.

Realising the grave human and social problems in the affluent West as also the facts about increasing wide disparities between the rich and the poor in India, despite Indian economy being branded as the 'fastest growing economy', the concept of development has undergone a change.

The term Human Development originating in development economics has given rise to Human Development reports published since 1990. Amartya Sen has discussed 'development as capability expansion'. HDR 1990 has remarked, "People do not isolate the different aspects of their lives. Instead, they have an overall sense of well-being."

"The idea of human development has great intuitive appeal. Articulating development as a widening of choices, an expansion of freedoms and a fulfilment of human rights gives it a distinct edge over the more narrow perception of development as economic expansion alone. By bringing into sharp focus issues of deprivation and inequality, human development puts people—and among them, the most deprived, at the centre of development interventions. Embedded in the concept is a firm commitment to democracy, human rights, participation and a deep respect for the environment."

"Progress can be judged only if we see marked improvements in the lives of people, in their health, in their levels of education and in their sense of security. Ultimately, development is about improving the quality of people's lives and advancing human dignity." (Brown Mark: 2005: v, (ed.) Sakiko Fukuda-parr, A.K. Shiv Kumar: Readings in Human Development)

"Viewing human development as an expansion of people's capabilities, an enlargement of choices and the assurance of human rights has several policy implications. To begin with, this approach offers a people-centred analytical framework for designing and assessing public policy interventions. Outcomes are to be judged not in terms of how much production has increased or incomes have grown, but rather in terms of improvements in the quality and security of people's lives." (Fukuda-Parr, Shiva Kumar: 2005: xxvii: Readings in Human Development, Oxford Publication)

To put it briefly, "The human development paradigm covers all aspects of development..... On some aspects of human development paradigm, there is fairly broad agreement:

- "Development must put people at the centre of its concerns.
- The purpose of development is to enlarge all human choices, not just income.
- The human development paradigm is concerned both with building up human capabilities (through investment in people) and with using those human capabilities fully (through an enabling framework for growth and employment).
- Human development has four essential pillars: equality, sustainability, productivity, and empowerment. It regards economic growth as essential but emphasizes the need to pay attention to its quality and distribution, analyses at length its link with human lives and questions its link with human lives and questions its long-term sustainability.
- The human development paradigm defines the ends of development and analyses sensible options for achieving them." (Haq, Mahbub ul 2005:19) (ed) Sakiko Fukuda-parr, A.K. Shiv Kumar: Readings in Human Development)

So human development approach is an anthropological approach, a holistic approach, highlighting the emic perspective of life. A tribal community where a woman is never molested by a tribal man and our urban communities where women are always under the threat of sexual attack, which amongst these is more developed community? The tribal problem of food security or economic deprivation, are the direct consequence of our policies and programmes of greedy acquisition of the natural resources, located in tribal belts, to multiply national growth and income in the global perspective.

What is the role of anthropology as a knowledge discipline in the present day India where political parties talk of development as an agenda of democratic governance? How do we translate that knowledge into an academic discipline to undertake studies, undertake intervention research, develop models for policy planning and implementation, and to raise a sizeable cadre to undertake this work objectively, and to guide those who want to administer people-centric schemes of well-being and empowerment of self-esteem and dignity?

II

It is being argued that anthropology as a knowledge system may appear to have originated in the West, out of the pioneers coming from various academic disciplines undertaking voyages and witnessing the queer customs of natives or others. The anthropological thought of understanding Man and his philosophy, his works in a civilization like that of India, has been in existence in the texts of antiquity. We have the discussions in '*Arthshastra*' by Chanakya, Charvak, Vatsayan's *Kamsutra*, even Kalidas; Charak, Susrut and Vagbhat about human behaviour, not limited to medicine. During Golden Jubilee celebrations in 2011, Anthropological Society discussed Vivekanand, Bankim Chandra Chatterjee, Tagore, Gandhi, Ambedkar and Jyotiba Phule as alternative voices in anthropology. Gandhiji's attire from three piece suit to a loin cloth and living style in Sevagram Ashram is how we identify ourselves when we live in a tribal hut, with a tribal family and their cattle. We 'go native' to understand their perspectives as Gandhiji tried to understand *Daridranarayan*, which culminated into his famous talisman about the philosophy of working for the people.

Anthropology in India is ridiculed by some ideologues as 'colonial anthropology'. We have also started debating it as pre- and post-colonial anthropology, as we usually talk of pre and post-Independent India. It is not just a matter of time-frame but an attitude about governance, inheriting the British revenue administrative mindset, although paradoxically speaking all the time about development and democratic decentralization, or community involvement as an inclusive policy, symbolized by adult franchise.

INCAA publication "*Anthropology in India: Current Epistemology and Future Challenges*" (2010), which presents the Round Table discussions at Hyderabad Congress 2009, has discussed these issues.

Kamal K. Misra in this book has said, "Many anthropologists believe that the subject matter of Indian anthropology began with the writings of British scholar-administrators, missionaries and travellers.".... To trace the colonial origin of Indian Anthropology, Mahapatra (2006) writes, "As early as 1807, the Court of Directors of The East India Company made a formal decision to acquire anthropological information on India, as 'such knowledge would be of great use in the future administration of the country' (Roy, 1921)"...... "In pursuit of this policy of The East India Company, the British Government of India sponsored many anthropological/ethnographic regional studies. E.T. Dalton (1872), Sir

H.H. Risley (1891), Edgar Thurston (1909), R.V. Russell (1916) and others undertook regional studies in eastern and north-eastern India, Bengal Presidency, Madras Presidency (which covered the major part of South India), and Central Provinces of India." (2010: 3-4)

Amitabha Basu and Suhas Biswas have referred to Vidyarthi in this book. "That colonial interests provided the major motivation for social anthropology is evident from the presidential address to the 1st International Congress of Anthropological and Ethnological Sciences, London, 1934, which emphasized that the discipline should be used "in diplomacy and colonial administration in dealing with the races of alien civilization." (Vidyarthi, 1978 in 2010: 187)

Ajit Danda in a concluding chapter in the book, titled "Anthropology in India: Current Epistemology and Future Challenges" has said, "Published accounts on anthropology in India appear more or less unanimous in their view that anthropology, being the product of colonial constructs, grew in this country particularly under the British colonial patronage."....."Even prior to 1920, around which anthropology became a part of the university curriculum, a good deal of ethnographic literature were produced, mostly by the British administrators in India, demonstrating further the colonial influence of anthropology in India." (2010: 208).....He has quoted N.K. Bose about the pressures of application. "Indian anthropology has of late been very much under the stress of the need of application. All over our country there are various organizations which are concerned with the welfare of the people, with the welfare of cities even, and anthropologists, therefore, are being harnessed for the purpose of suggesting ways and means" (1962:175 in 2010, 219).....Danda has bemoaned about the tribal expertise slipping away from the anthropologists, which was also voiced by Yogesh Atal in the first S.C. Dube Memorial Lecture at Anthropology Congress at Lucknow. "It is pathetic that anthropologists have lost more or less their exclusive domain of expertise on tribal matters. It is rather precarious that they have not been able to identify any other new area yet where they could have easily browsed without facing any major threat or challenge. Opportunities, particularly in the background of continuing developmental programmes, were obviously in plenty. Anthropologists could have concentrated their attention to the weaker sections of the Indian population in general and analyze reasons for their existence in poverty in the midst of apparent affluence. They also could have drawn attention to the ills of industrialization, particularly in creating disharmonies and imbalances and suggested measures for their possible remedy. Problem of ethnicity in the nation building process is another major area where anthropological knowledge could have been of such advantage for exploding the calculatively created myths and providing clarity in understanding the situation. Such areas are many and the said few are mere illustrations." (2010, 224)

Further, Danda has concluded, "For ex-colonial powers, the discipline of Anthropology has lost a great deal of its utilitarian value. The discipline, in fact, is not considered that essential for them any more. In contrast, Anthropologists in India appear to be on the threshold of a major breakthrough to demonstrate how even without making war machines, this specific branch of knowledge can meaningfully serve a society as well as the humanity, by suggesting innumerable alternatives of life-styles that in turn have the potential to transform the whole world." (Danda, Ajit, K., 2017: Vol. 52, No. 1 & 2, pp. 15)

There has been discussion about indigenization of Indian Anthropology. K.K. Misra has proposed. "I am of the opinion that there should be an urgent paradigm shift in the research agenda of Indian anthropology. So far, Indian anthropology is more or less obsessed with microcosmic approach, which is in line with the positivist-empiricist approach of the West, with the assumption that by studying a part of the society, one can understand the macrocosm or the whole. As a result, textual analysis is unfortunately left to the domain of Indologists or Sanskritists." (2010: 13-14). Irawati Karve was one acknowledged anthropologist who subjected textual material and even mythology to anthropological analysis. However, such attempts are more recognised under humanities rather than in anthropology.

It is quite clear that the ethnographic notes about the various communities in various parts of the country compiled by British civil servants, conceived by us as model ethnography was actually meant for application by the civil servants for administration, that would not step on the cultural toes of Indians. When British Government took over India from East India Company after 1857 rebellion, Queen Victoria assured Indian people that the government would not interfere with the religious feelings and customs of the people. So, documentation of cultural and religions customs and practices was necessary for guidance of the administrators. What has been ethnography for us, was data for application by the British rulers.

What is theory and application, and are they mutually exclusive of each other? Malinowski as one of the pioneer anthropologist, a functionalist, was a promoter of applied anthropology. Malinowski memorial orations are organized by 'Society for Applied Anthropology' and the compilation of these lectures are worth studying.

"Applied anthropology, as I understand it, is a science concerned with the transformation of human society through the knowledge of social sciences....The question is, for whose benefit and for what purpose should social anthropology be used ? If it is for the good of the people, for the common security and prosperity of the great majority, and hopefully even for humanity as whole, if it is used for meeting their growing need for an ever-better material and social life, then, and only then, can science be made to play its proper role in human history." (Xiaotong Fei, 2002:141)

Issues of applications have been debated in terms of ethics and objectivity of science, citing the concept of cultural relativism. But, there are also universal values of humanity and charter of human rights at the global and as per the Constitution of India. Value neutrality also means potential support to the establishment which may be anti-people.

"Malinowski held that ethnographers who have studied culture contact and assessed its potential and dangers have the right and duty to formulate their conclusions in a way in which they can be seriously considered by those who frame policy and carry it out. They also have the duty to speak as the natives' advocate." (Firth, 1981:195).

It is not an issue of only academic discussion whether an anthropologist should address his knowledge or enhance his knowledge by using it to analyse the contemporary regional or national issues and if called upon to do so, make recommendations following the spirit of universal values, human rights and objectivity. Several anthropologists or anthropology associations in India are commissioned to undertake such work by the government or even by the judiciary. Anthropologists are called upon to be expert members of committees to adjudicate the claims of pseudo-tribals to be included in the ST or some such reserved category as backward communities. As a result of *suo-moto* injunction by the High Court, intervention projects are offered to develop a model, addressing the issue of widespread malnutrition of tribal children. We are asked to review the Tribal Sub-Plan strategy and implementation and make recommendations for its proper utilisation. The tribal cell in *Rajbhavan* may consult you formally or informally before they use their constitutional authority to direct the state government about implementation of PESA, FRA, about tribal employment at local level or about regional development imbalances.

We are asked to advise in our capacity as experts on tribal issues. How can we shy away from taking up such responsibilities as citizens with the label of academic objectivity that is associated with autonomous university system, which is also formally headed by the Governor as Chancellor, who is also the Head of the State? As medical anthropologist, we are called upon to undertake studies about the functioning of AYUSH or to analyse the behavioural issues in regard to chronic ailments such as leprosy, TB or HIV and AIDS. We are offered funding for undertaking research studies which have to be translated into action programmes. Several questions are raised about tribal education, from drop-outs, to utility of *ashram* schools to the scope of universities in tribal belts addressing special requirements or about training of tribal youth. Do we need to have a separate curriculum in these universities in the tribal belt or even in the *ashram* schools?

Development has become synonymous with displacement of people. What human factors are to be addressed in the rehabilitation of such displaced people? Is poverty only an economic issue? How do people address such issues? Do we have ethnography of how people struggle for life from early morning till late at night working all the time? In the extending urban areas and cities, not only there are pavement dwellers but several food joints on the pavements catering to the needs of floating workers who are migrants or those like male and female municipal workers who have to start their work for living early morning. The mobile toilets for such female workers have been visible in some towns. Good qualitative case studies or life histories could provide insights for organising their need satisfaction.

Some subjective experiences of interacting with various organisations and issues have been discussed in the relevant chapters of the book. The so-called objectivity raising the bogey of value neutrality and ethical issues connected with interventions and recommendations leads to total inactivity glorified in the name of science. Many people misunderstand the term *'sthitpradnya'* in *Gita* as inactivity, since destiny would decide the course of action and its result. Lokmanya Tilak in his interpretation of *Gita* presents the scenario as to what kind of dialogue was possible while the two armies were facing each other in battle formation about to strike each other. The term 'war footing' conveys action par excellence with a concrete result in a short time, What is *Karma*, that is, nothing but focused action in a battle? So according to Tilak, *Karma-yoga* is the essence of *Gita*. The objectivity in *Gita* refers to ambivalence between victory and death, which could not be the guiding force of activity or inactivity. The legitimate action on the battlefield is to kill the enemy or get killed (*Dushman-ko-maro* is the war slogan).

So knowledge has to be used for the good of the people, for human development. Judiciary is supposed to be objective in pronouncing justice. Media has to be objective in giving information and in projecting different views, opinions about an issue without any bias. What are academics supposed to do while they have been provided with autonomy to promote objectivity. Do they have no social responsibility?

These issues are discussed on the platform of INCAA, but not carried forward to make an impact on Anthropology as an academic discipline as is taught in the university system. It does not show visibility in the research projects undertaken by the faculty or in the M.Phil. and Ph.D. topics of research students. With our experience of undertaking an intervention project to develop a model to reduce tribal malnutrition as partners of state government (action anthropology) as a fall out of *suo moto* injunction of Bombay High Court, I would agree with Kamal K. Misra, "This leads me to think that some limited degree of activism within the permissible boundary of the law of the land is not all that bad for an anthropologist to make a dent in public policy, instead of remaining a mute spectator of injustice and exclusion of the marginalized....Anthropological knowledge and perspectives have undergone a sea change in recent times. For example, development agencies working on poverty, inequality, corruption, social fragmentation, violence and ethnic tensions, and rights-based approaches require deep socio-cultural analysis and policy inputs from anthropologists for policy making. There is no room in today's anthropology to create a watershed between theory and practice." (INCAA Anthropology Congress, Bhubaneswar: February 2015).

It is in this spirit, that *Rajbhavan*, TRTI and tribal activists would discuss, the issues about PESA, FRA and the like with us as academicians having field experience. The Indian Anthropology Congress held by INCAA at Pune University in 2007 and 2019 have addressed such issue. In 2007, Pune Declaration about 'Vision for Indian Anthropology and Role of INCAA' was adopted, the salient points of which are reproduced here "Pune Declaration at INCAA Congress 2007."

"This Declaration adopted at Second INCAA Congress at Pune on 23rd February, 2007 on the Vision for Indian Anthropology, provides the direction for INCAA and through INCAA, to the professional World of Anthropology in India, about using and further developing theory and methodology, in all aspects of Anthropology, towards policy planning and implementation for human welfare development and dignity. Anthropology as the only holistic science of Man, studies human origins, human variation, human nature and human creations as evolved historically, blending the biological and cultural facts and perspectives. The holistic perspectives of mankind at all periods of time encompassing the dynamic triological relationship of Man-Environment- Supernatural is the heritage of Anthropology which anchors the civil society for peace and harmony."

"Anthropology contributed to the body of knowledge by studying the cultural and biological variability which got enshrined in UN Charter of Human Rights respecting the principle of cultural relativism. Studies also led to policies abolishing racial discrimination. It is not recognized that Human Genetics, Ethnography and Qualitative research methods and many other methods, concepts, tools and techniques are the gift of anthropology which are being used and marketed by other disciplines."

"The post-colonial era has shifted the focus of humanity to egalitarian order, poverty elimination and development issues encompassing health and education. Human Development is the key term used for measurement, as well as an approach, which is essentially anthropological, since it signals comprehensive and sustainable development flowing from culture theories. New dimensions are added due to desegregation of culture and life style, and due to global technological effects."

"Indian Anthropology is broadly visible in the University Departments, Tribal Research Institutes, Anthropological Survey of India, Research Institutes of ICMR, ICSSR etc. committees and commissions dealing with backward communities and in the NGO sector undertaking health and development action research. Responding to the local requirement, anthropologists have tried to constitute academic associations. INCAA has evolved as a national platform to confederate networking of these regional bodies. As an Academy, it has a vision to address national issues without interfering or jeopardising the local interest organisitions. On the other hand the regional associations would gain strength from national linkage and by participating in national endeavour."

"While Anthropology is the only discipline which primarily focuses on the people, describing the cultural, social and economic framework that leads to the poverty and deprivation, including dehabilitation, due to development of the "mainstream", it has not addressed these issues at policy level. INCAA has to play the facilitator role at the micro (such as micro-planning) as also at the macro policy planning level, by using the network of anthropologists."

"While other disciplines including bio-medical applied disciplines, form their attention on the outcomes, labelling them as problems, and use curative symptomatic methods to solve them, Anthropology is equipped to study the processes resulting in the outcome problems, providing preventive solutions; such as farmers' suicides, infant mortality, health and disease issues, intergroup disparities, increasing gap between the rich and poor, displacement etc."

"Applied Anthropology would not only provide professional employment to students trained in Anthropology, but would develop new theories about the dynamics of change. A new paradigm of Holism has to be developed analyzing the micro-macro interaction or by incorporating the perspectives of various actors and stakeholders." (INCAA website)

In the same spirit as of this declaration, theme of the Indian Anthropology Congress: 2019, organised second time after 2007, under the auspices of INCAA, at Savitribai Phule Pune University (SPPU) in February 2019 was chosen as "Anthropology for Developing India: Policy Planning and Implementation."

The concept note about the theme published in INCAA newsletter Vol. 13, January 2019 reads as under:

> "Developing India is understood in terms of development governance of Indian Republic as per the Constitution, through the mechanism of Electoral Democracy, Electoral politics, Constitutional amendments and Public Interest Litigations, including *suo motu* injunctions by the judiciary in matters of public policy and implementation. Policy planning of Socialist pattern of Five Year Plans, gave boost to Rural Transformation by way of Dam irrigation projects and Community Development Programmes, and industrial infrastructure by way of Steel Plants, National Science Laboratories and Research Councils. However, India's branding as fastest growing economy, has not made any appreciable dent on economic and social deprivation, nor has it improved India's global ranking in Human Development Index, despite phenomenal growth of banking sector and service sector indicating the oscillating pendulum of vibrancy. The introduction of GST as economic freedom was symbolized like the midnight session on 14 August, 1947 to formalize transfer of power from the British."

> "The academic discussions and participation in the policy formulation at the Macro level has become the exclusive preserve of economists. The implementation is administered by the British

legacy of Bureaucratic steel frame, despite distinct democratic decentralization (Zila Parishad) to promote rural development. Government means the Secretariat, although in some States like Maharashtra, the seat of governance has been renamed as Mantralaya. What is the role of people-centric Anthropology with its expertise of understanding micro-level and emic perspectives in a people-centric electoral democracy?"

"Anthropological Thought is not the hegemony of Colonial period, nor can it be limited to concepts of biological and socio-cultural evolution attributed to Darwin's ideas of evolution. The Universities of Takshshila and Nalanda created a scholar-statesman-administrator, Kautilya, whose *Arthshastra* is a classic about governance. Man in relation to nature has been discussed in several ancient scriptures, as also in the writings and preaching of saint-poets."

"The classic ethnographic monographs about culture and society of isolated communities have led to concepts of Cultural Relativism and Universal Values of humanity, respecting plurality and diversity, becoming the sheet anchor of Human Rights at the UN and at national levels. The concepts of Great and Little Traditions have helped to analyse the rise of civilizations and their sustenance, despite foreign rule for centuries, commonly expressed as :'Unity in Diversity' in the Indian context."

"Indian Anthropological Society, Kolkata during its Golden Jubilee celebrations organized a Symposium about Alternative Voices of Anthropology (2011-12) discussing the contributions of Swami Vivekanand, Mahatma Gandhi, Rabindranath Tagore, Bankimchandra Chatterjee, Dr. B.R. Ambedkar and Mahatma Jyotiba Phule, as examples."

"Anthropological Survey of India as an apex academic institution of anthropologists did come out with a tool of socio-cultural impact assessment since the environment impact assessment was falling short of addressing human issues. Draft legislation was also prepared for addressing the issues of IVF, stem cells and relevant issues. Restudies of Villages undertaken by AnSI are expected to document the dynamics of rural transformation leading to useful recommendations for policy planning and implementation, as also issues such as farmers' suicides. Our expertise is already being used to address the issues of pseudo-tribalism. These are few examples."

"Anthropologists as a part of Humanity, also as the citizens of a nation-state, are bound by our Constitution to perform fundamental duties. Anthropology as a people-centric discipline has to contribute towards nation-building, addressing the bio-cultural issues of health and disease, education, poverty, inequality, deprivation, displacement etc. focusing on the marginalized people. Due to our understanding of emic perspectives, qualitative methods and micro level studies, we understand the practical issues of implementation of development schemes among the people, engrossed in the struggles of day-to-day living. Due to holistic perspectives, we understand the issues of policy planning at the macro level and the divergent perspectives of various stakeholders."

"For a considerable period, voices are being raised about the relevance of Anthropology in the contemporary 'our world', not the 'other cultures'. Indian Anthropology has to shed off the allegation made by some sections, as 'Colonial Anthropology'. Anthropology as an academic discipline has the strength to become a professional discipline, with the combination of liberal philosophy and the skills, to address the concerns of common man, by mentoring the policy planning and implementation. Occasionally, we have to conceptualize, implement and create intervention models, in partnership with the government or voluntary sector, without compromising the scientific objectivity. The scholars involved in research studies in all sub-disciplines of Anthropology should strive to present the policy implications of their respective studies at the Anthropology Congress." (INCAA Anthropology Congress, 2019)

Conclusion

Anthropology has been and continues to be a holistic study of Man and his culture, at all times of history. However, in public image, Anthropology is connected with the past, as a synonym of ethnology. Culture in common

English usage continues to be associated with art, music, drama and literature, which provides a unique entity and identity. This culture is to be preserved and protected since it signifies the identity and provides self-esteem. Ministry of Culture is driven to preservation in museums for future generations. The dynamic aspects and planned development cherishing the universal values and human rights are neglected. Democracy as a value by itself is the spirit of Indian Constitution. Principle of equity is invoked to bring about equality of opportunity to develop one's capabilities and extend the alternative choices, according to one's talent and desire. We keep on hearing about development of infrastructure, possibly to develop economic opportunities for growth. But, the emphasis is now being shifted to Human Development approach, as discussed by Amartya Sen and Mahbub ul Haq. Human Development index is being used to measure development in preference to GNP or GDP, which does not reduce the poverty gaps among ethnic groups or between geographical areas.

Constitution provides a road map for development of the people of India, within the limits and strategic approach of democracy. Ideally, democracy signifies self-governance which is institutionalised in representative democracy. Anna Hazare has been advocating supremacy of *gram sabha* over other elected bodies, since *gram sabha* is not an elected body, but a natural body of all eligible voters. *Gram Sabha* has also been recognised as a unit of action under PESA. *Gram Sabha* functions effectively in Mendha Lekha in Gadchiroli district of Maharashtra which has successfully implemented community forest-rights under FRA.

Who decides what is development, for whom? Do the decisions flow from top to down or flow upwards? We are good at understanding the micro situations. But the macro seems to rule the micro. The global macro seems to function in the mind-set of economic imperialism, dominating the bodies like IMF and World Bank. Development from the Western perspectives limits itself to aid, coming from international NGOs, like Rockefeller or Ford Foundation, in the immediate past. Even visual media and digital instruments are owned and controlled by the West. Country is represented and functional through common currency. One decision of nationalisation of banks as also about demonetisation affected all citizens of the nation. Policy may be a strategy, a blue-print to guide action in a given direction. Policy when implemented necessitates rules and regulations which may not provide equal facility to all. Paradigm is a model, a pattern based on concepts. We say, disease control has a bio-medical paradigm while we want a people-centric paradigm which we think will ensure results. Our field experience with the people tells us, that nothing succeeds about people without the active involvement of the people. Country is made and sustained by the people, through historical times and through nurturing of the basic values which are the hard aspects, emotional aspects of culture. So, public policy has to have a say of the public, what universally accepted definition of democracy by Lincoln means. Anthropology as a holistic discipline understands people in totality, through their eyes, spectacles. But, we have to shed off our descriptive ethnography of the microcosm as an end point, and use focused ethnography as a technique to analyse the factors influencing policies. This requires changing our concept of Holism to include the perceptions of all stakeholders, to build bridges between the micro and macro, and emic-etic interaction. We have to act in the name of universal values of humanism, expressed through Right's approach to human development. Anthropology is a people-friendly, humanistic science, which has to develop as a professional discipline for effectively studying and contributing to policy planning and implementation towards human development.

Our dream is to turn the useful 'hobby' of Anthropology as practised by the pioneers in Anthropology, into a professional discipline in India, which it so richly deserves, with the strength of methodology and emerging plural sub-disciplines, like medical anthropology and development anthropology. This results into widening of holistic concept useful for contribution to public policy and implementation at the micro-level with emic perspectives. Actually the slogan 'Think globally and act locally' is an anthropological concept of linking the macro and micro, and putting the etic and emic in a single integrated totality for human development. We have to go beyond ethnography as an end product or outcome of research. Focused ethnography is a useful technique to understand, analyze microcosm; it has to be linked to policy planning and implementation at the micro level.

Anthropological Survey of India has to be the policy planning arm of the Government of India on all issues about human development. Since the University Grants Commission (UGC), abandoned academic discipline based panels or committees to monitor and make recommendations about the quality of teaching and research of the respective academic disciplines in the University system, the Anthropological Survey of India, in collaboration with Indian National Confederation and Academy of Anthropologists (INCAA), has to provide academic leadership in

Anthropology. The International School of Anthropology of the AnSI need to take proactive role in modifying the curricula and introduce Certificate and Diploma Courses in various branches of Anthropology, continuing to promote the holistic nature and fieldwork tradition of Anthropology.

Anthropologists stop at describing "What is" by way of ethnographic monographs of the people and their groups and communities. People, their representatives from village to national level constantly think about 'What ought to be' and how to achieve within the directives of the Constitution of India, if possible; if not, by amending the relevant articles in the Constitution to meet the aspiration of people, majority of whom are deprived. Could anthropologists be the mute spectators of all these happenings around them and keep on bemoaning about dwindling number of students opting for Anthropology in the university departments? Or be satisfied that there is student enrolment only to study anthropology to opt the course at the competitive State and Union Public Service examinations for Civil Services. Since proactive participation by anthropologists in public affairs is not visible, economists, with the secondary quantitative data at their command guide the policies and politicians which are not implementable at the grassroots level, lacking the micro-level emic understanding. Anthropology as a people–centric discipline, continuing the knowledge of grassroots level realities are unable to translate their field level knowledge gained through incisive qualitative methods into doable policies. The need for policy research or research providing data for policy framework and implementation is desired from social scientists. There is need of intervention research which may be feasible, if academic institutions develop networks and partnerships with the government and NGOs.

Ideally participatory research would be useful for understanding the behavioural variables, which in the process also empowers the participants, by analyzing the contexts, with objectivity. Such researches addressed to people's behaviour and their concerns, could provide insights for giving solutions, and could lead to conceptualization about the social and economic dynamics about social and cultural change, and about values of morality. The judiciary and media have emerged as the powerful arms of democracy. When would the academic research become significant arm, to contribute to policy framework and implementation, to address the issues of normative and deviant behaviour, as impacting the health and disease, in the scenario of plural medical systems?

Irawati Karve said, she was paying her debt to the society through her research. We also have to pay our debt to the society as anthropologists by presenting the holistic analysis of ground realities to help formulate implementable policies at the micro level to make the life livable of all people focusing on marginalized people, since we get our bread and salt from the society. We cannot comprehend the whole, hence we talk of parts. But the reality and truth and life are whole. Anthropology understands this. Only that macro is not the only whole. Macro-Micro together form the whole which is politically a Nation guided by the Constitution.

I subscribe to the dream of anthropology developing as a professional discipline which has all the potentials in theory and methodology to become one. Only if on one hand we continue to hold Gandhi's talisman of thinking about the last man who is a tribal and on the other, aim at policy research which is sought after by some enlightened bureaucrats and some well meaning politicians.

I consider myself fortunate as a student of Anthropology which takes me to the poorest of the poor and provide me with insights which are ploughed back in the processes that are meant to help the poor and disadvantaged. We get our bread and salt from anthropology. Gandhiji understood the value of salt as common man's food and used it as an effective weapon against the British. We received a package of bread and salt from a Leprosy funding agency from Munich, Germany as a symbol of solidarity and best wishes on the day we started functioning as a WHO sponsored 'Centre for Social Science Research on Leprosy' (CSSRL) at Gandhi Memorial Leprosy Foundation, Wardha in 1985. Let us be true to the salt of 'Anthropology as the holistic study of Man', which is our living, and we will be satisfied with our lives and those of others, whom we can help with our knowledge.

The policy is meant for human development as spelt out with the beginning of community development programme in 1952 for rural and tribal transformation. The bureaucratic practice, however, was aimed at completing the physical targets, such as infrastructure development, measurable in quantity, and meeting the financial targets. The result has been the widening gaps between the rich and the poor, between ethnic groups and regions, rural to urban migration for survival; continuing with the economic hypothesis of trickledown effect of growing economy, which is now being branded as 'crony capitalism' by those who initiated liberal economy, and growing farmer distress. Anthropologists have not even documented this dynamic process with focused ethnography, identifying the different variables, in the context of holistic ground reality. We have some analysis of health and disease control policies in the context of plural systems of medicine. The integrated single Health Policy of 2017 has yet to be seen in its implementation. The traditional expertise about tribals by anthropologists has yet to be used for analysing the tribal development policies and practice. The anthropological paradigm has to be demonstrated through holistic analysis with the field data generated through focused ethnography about issues, through intervention and action research, by networking, and by forging partnerships viable for such exercise.

Indian Anthropology has to use field based knowledge of the ground reality in India, to address the concerns of the people, and make recommendations, which is possible with the theoretical and methodological strengths of the discipline, towards policy planning and implementation for human development.

References

Anthropological Survey of India (1961). "Proceedings of the summer school in anthropology, Kodaikanal", as *Bulletin of the Anthropological Survey of India*, Vol. X, Number 2, Calcutta (Kolkata).

Anthropological Survey of India (2011). "Module-Social impact assessment", In *Journal of the Anthropological Survey of India* 60. 2: 216-244.

Aiyar, S.P. (1973). *Modernization of Traditional Society*, Madras.

Atal, Yogesh, (1981). "The call for indigenization", In *International Social Science Journal*. XXXIII, No. 1, 189-197.

Atal, Yogesh (ed.) (1983). *On Crisis and Commitment in India*, (Papers of Prof. S.C. Dube), New Delhi: Abhinav Publications.

Atal, Yogesh (2012). *Anthropology Today and Tomorrow*, Kolkata: INCAA.

Adiseshiah, Malcolm (1973). *Review of the Indian Council of Social Science Research*", New Delhi: ICSSR.

Bhattacharya, D.K. (ed.). (1978). *Anthropologists in India-Directory of Professional Anthropologists*, Delhi: Indian Anthropological Association.

Basham, A.L. (1954). *The Wonder That Was India*, New York: Grove Press.

Bidney, David (1953). "The concept of value in modern Anthropology", In Kroeber, A.L. (ed.). "*Anthropology Today*", The University of Chicago Press.

Bhat, H.K., Joshi, P.C. Vijayendra, B.R. (eds.) (2013). *Explorations in Indian Medical Anthropology*, (Essays in Honour of Prof. R.K. Mutatkar), Vol. I and II, New Delhi: Concept Publishing Co. Pvt. Ltd.

Bhat, H.K. (2019). "Ethics and Objectivity in Anthropology", at Round Table, Indian Anthropology Congress", Pune.

Bhanage, N.P. (ed.), (1993). *Tribal Commissions and Committees in India*, Bombay: Himalaya Publishing House.

Biraj Swain and Sethi Vani, (2014). "Mind the gap", In *Seminar: The Malnourished Tribal*, No. 661, New Delhi.

Brown, M.M. (2003). "Preface", In Fukuda-Parr, Sakiko and Shiva Kumar, (eds.), *Readings in Human Development*. Oxford University Press.

Cernea, Michael M. (ed.) (1985)/(1991). *Putting People First: Sociological Variables in Development*, Oxford University Press.

Cernea, Michael, M. (2002). "Social organization and development anthropology", In Weaver, T. (ed.) *The Dynamics of Applied Anthropology in the Twentieth Century: The Malinowski Award Papers*", Society for Applied Anthropology, Oklahoma City.

Crewe, Emma and Axelby Richard (2013). *Anthropology and Development*, Cambridge University Press.

Caudill, William (1953). "Applied anthropology in medicine", In Kroeber, A.L. (ed.), *Anthropology Today*. The University of Chicago Press.

Danda, Ajit and Dipali (eds.). (2010). *Anthropology in India: Current Epistemology and Future Challenges*, INCAA.

Danda, Ajit K. (2010). "Anthropology in India: Current epistemology and future challenges", In Danda and Danda (ed.). *Anthropology in India: Current Epistemology and Future Challenges*, INCAA.

Danda, Ajit K. *et al.* (eds.) (2013). *Contested identities in the Globalized World*, INCAA.

Danda, Ajit K. *et al.* (eds.) (2014). *Anthropology and the Future of Humankind*, INCAA.

Danda, Ajit K. (2014). "Maladies of anthropology in India", In *Journal of the Indian Anthropological Society*, 49:227-236.

Danda, Ajit K. (ed.) (2017). *Identities, Ethnic Boundaries, and the State*, INCAA.

Danda, Ajit K. (2017). "Anthropology in contemporary India", In *Journal of the Indian Anthropological Society*, 52, 1 and 2, 4-16.

Das, Pradipta (2013). "Anthropology in Eastern India", In *The Indian Journal of Anthropology*, INCAA: Vol. 1: No. 1: 191-202.

Dey, S.K. (1955). "The Story of Our Programme", In *Kurukshetra: A Symposium on Community Development in India*, Delhi: The Publications Division, GoI.

Dube, S.C. (1958). "The Study of Indian Village Communities", Presidential Address "Social Anthropology Section", Indian Sociological Conference, Agra.

Dube, S.C. (1971). *Explanation and Management of Change*, New Delhi.

Dube, S.C. (1974). *Contemporary India and its Modernization*, New Delhi.

Dube, S.C. (1983). "Anthropology and the challenge of development", In *On Crisis and Commitment in Social Sciences*, (ed.) Yogesh Atal, New Delhi: Abhinav Publications.

Dreze, Jean (2002). "On research and action", In *Economic and Political Weekly*, Vol. 37-9, 817-819, Mumbai.

Eisenstadt, S.N. (1969). *Modernization: Protest and Change*, New Delhi.

Eisenstadt, S.N. (1973). *Tradition, Change and Modernity*, New York.

Firth, Raymond (1981). "Engagement and detachment: Reflections on applying social anthropology to social affairs", In *Human Organization*, 40, 3:193 201.

Foster, George (1952). "Relationship between theoretical and applied anthropology", In *Human Organization*, 11-3, pp. 5-16).

Foster, G.M. (1962). *Traditional Culture and the Impact of Technological Change*, New York.

Foster, George and Anderson, B. (1978). *Medical Anthropology*, New York: John Wiley & Sons.

Foster, George M. (1982). "*Community Development and Primary Health Care: Their Conceptual Similarities*", In *Medical Anthropology*, 6: 183-195, Redgrave Publishing Company.

Fukuda-Parr, Sakiko and Shiva Kumar (2003). (Ed): "*Readings in Human Development*", Oxford University Press.

Government of Bombay (1938). *Report on the Aboriginal and Hill Tribes of the Partially Excluded Areas in the Bombay Presidency*, (Symington Report), Bombay.

Government of Maharashtra (1985). *Report of the Expert Committee on the Halba/Halba Koshti Problem in the State of Maharashtra*, Tribal Development Department, Mumbai.

Government of Maharashtra (1993). *Report of the Banjara-Vanjari Expert Committee*, Department of Social Welfare, Pune.

Government of Maharashtra (1993). *Report of the Expert Committee on Inclusion of Communities in the list of Scheduled Castes, Vimukta Jati, Nomadic Tribes and Other Backward Classes, in the State of Maharashtra*, (Mutatkar Committee), Department of Social Welfare, Pune.

Government of Maharashtra (1999). *The Report of the Expert Committee for the Verification of the Entries in the Annexure of the Government Resolution No. CBC (1684)/(309)/D-11, Dated 24.4.1985*, Tribal Development Department.

Government of Maharashtra (2000). "*Socio-Economic Information of Tribals in Tribal Area of Maharashtra State*", Tribal Research and Training Institute, Pune.

Government of Maharashtra (2002). *Maharashtra Human Development Report*, Mumbai.

Government of India (2006). *Report of the Prime Minister's High Level Committee on the Social, Economic and Educational Status of the Muslim Community of India*, New Delhi.

Government of Maharashtra (2012), *Maharashtra Human Development Report*, New Delhi: Sage Publications.

Government of Maharashtra, Planning Department (2013). "High Level Committee on Balanced Regional Development Issues in Maharashtra", (Kelkar Committee), Mumbai.

Government of India, Ministry of Tribal Affairs (2014). *Report of the High Level Committee on Socio-Economic, Health and Educational Status of Tribal Communities of India*, New Delhi.

Ghosh, Abhik (2013). "Anthropology in Northern India", In *The Indian Journal of Anthropology*, 1: 1: 153-166.

Gopalan, C. (1989). "Nutritive Value of Indian Foods", National Institute of Nutrition (ICMR).

Gough, Kathleen (1967). "New proposals for anthropologists", In *Economic and Political Weekly*, II, 36: 1653-1658.

Haq, Mahbub Uu. (2003). "The Human Development Paradigm", In Fukuda-Parr, Sakiko and Shiva Kumar, (ed.). *Readings in Human Development*, Oxford University Press.

Haimendorf, C. Von Furer (1956). "Culture History and Cultural Development", In Thomas, W.L. (ed.) *Current Anthropology*, The University of Chicago Press.

Haldipur, R.N. (1974). "Sociology of community development and Panchayat Raj", In ICSSR-Volume II. *A Survey of Research in Sociology and Social Anthropology*, New Delhi: ICSSR.

Herskovits, Melville (1948). *Man and His Works*, Alfred A. Knopf, New York.

INCAA, (2007). "*Human Development: Evolution and Vision*", An Abstract Book of Second Anthropology Congress, Pune.

ICSSR. (1972). *A Survey of Research in Sociology and Social Anthropology*, Vol. III, New Delhi.

ICSSR (1973). "Social and cultural anthropology", In *A Report on Social Sciences in India: Retrospective and Prospective*, Vol. II, New Delhi.

ICSSR (1973). "Anthropology", In *A Report on Social Sciences in India: Retrospective and Prospective*, Vol. I., New Delhi.

Joshi, Maushmi (2019). "Perspectives of sexuality among adolescent girls", In Mutatkar, R.K. and Nagarkar, Aarti (eds.) *Sexuality, Sexual Behaviour and Reproductive Health*, Delhi: Concept Publishing Co. Pvt. Ltd.

Kulkarni, Sumati (1990). "Demographic aspects of poverty", In Tarlok Singh (ed.), *Social Science Research and Problem of Poverty*, New Delhi: Concept Publishing Co.

Kulirani, B. Francis (2013). "Anthropology in Southern India", In *The Indian Journal of Anthropology*, 1:1, 203-228. INCAA.

Kuper, Adam (2010). "Social Anthropology", In Backhouse, R. and Fontaine, P., (eds.) *The History of the Social Sciences Since 1945*, Cambridge University Press.

Kroeber, A.L. (ed.) (1953). *Anthropology Today*, University of Chicago Press.

Karve, Irawati (1953). *Kinship Organization in India*, Deccan College Postgraduate Research Institute, Poona.

Karve, Irawati (1961). *Hindu Society: An Interpretation*, Deccan College Post Graduate and Research Institute, Poona.

Karve, Irawati (1968). *Maharashtra—Land and its People*, Maharashtra State Gazetteer, Government of Maharashtra, Bombay.

Kluckhohn, Clyde (1959). *Mirror for Man*, McGraw Hill (premier edition, second print).

Katy Gardner and David Lewis (2015). *Anthropology and Development*, London: Pluto Press.

Kurtz Donald (1994). *Contradictions and Conflict*, E.J. Brill, Leiden, The Netherlands.

Kroebar. (1948). *Anthropology*, Harcourt, New York: Brace and Co.

Kroebar, A.L. (1953). "Introduction", In Kroebar, A.L. (ed.) *Anthropology Today*, The University of Chicago Press.

Leslie, Charles (ed.). (1980). "Medical Pluralism", (Special Issue on Pune Medical Anthropology Symposium) *Social Science and Medicine* 14 B, 4, Pergamon Press.

Malinowski, B. (1945)/(1961). *The Dynamics of Culture Change*, Yale University Press.

Malinowski, Bronislaw (2002). In Cernea, M. "Social organization and development anthropology", In Weaver, T. (ed.) *The Dynamics of Applied Anthropology in the Twentieth Century*, The Malinowski Award Papers. Society for Applied Anthropology, Oklahoma City.

Mandelbaum, David G. (1963). "The transmission of anthropological culture", In Mandelbaum, *et al.* (ed.) *The Teaching of Anthropology*, American Anthropological Association.

McElroy, Ann and Townsend, Patricia. (1979). *Medical Anthropology in Ecological Prospective*, Duxbury Press.

Mead, Margaret (ed.) (1955). *Cultural Patterns and Technical Change*, UNESCO, New York, (Mentor Book, Fifth reprint, 1960).

Mehta, Shalina (2007). *What Ails Anthropology in India: Need for a Paradigm Shift in Research and Teaching*, Indian Anthropology Congress 2007, Pune.

Misra, K.K. (2010). "Academic colonialism, indigenization and production of knowledge in Indian Anthropology", In Danda (ed.) *Anthropology in India: Current Epistemology and Future Challenges*, INCAA.

Misra, P.K. (2019). "Ethics and objectivity in anthropology", *Newsletter*, INCAA, Indian Anthropology Congress, Pune.

Mutatkar, R.K. (1961). "Changes in the caste system in a village near Gwalior, M.P", In *Proceedings of the Summer School in Anthropology, Kodaikanal* as Bulletin of the Anthropological Survey of India, Vol. X, Number 2, Calcutta (Kolkata).

Mutatkar, R.K. (1974). "Social structure, change and modernization", In Sirsikar, V.M. (ed.), *Modernization process in India*, University of Poona.

Mutatkar, R.K. (1978). *Caste Dimensions in a Village*, Shubhada Saraswat, Poona.

Mutatkar, R.K. (1978). "Social aspects of leprosy", In Chatterjee, B.R., *A Window on Leprosy*", Gandhi Memorial Leprosy Foundation, Wardha.

Mutatkar, R.K. (1979). "Society and Leprosy", Gandhi Memorial Leprosy Foundation, Wardha.

Mutatkar, R.K. (1981). *Social and Economic Aspects of Leprosy*, (Working Paper), WHO, Geneva.

Mutatkar, R.K. (1984). "Leprosy, A Challenge to Social Sciences", (Key Note Address), XIIth International Leprosy Congress, New Delhi, Gandhi Memorial Leprosy Foundation, Wardha.

Mutatkar, R.K. and Tare, S.P. (1988). "ICMR Report on Evaluation of Impact of Education in SET pattern of NLCP", Gandhi Memorial Leprosy Foundation, Wardha.

Mutatkar, R.K. and Patankar, Pandit (1991). "Social sciences and social action for leprosy control", In Srinivas, H. (ed.) *Social Science Research and Social Action for Better Leprosy Control*, Indian Association of Leprologists, Madras.

Mutatkar, R.K. (1991). "Social science research on leprosy: A review", In Srinivas, H. (ed.), *Social Science Research and Social Action for Better Leprosy Control*, Indian Association of Leprologists, Madras.

Mutatkar, R.K. (1994). "The social responsibility of social scientists", In *Social Science and Medicine* (Editorial), 39:6, 755-756, Pergamon Press.

Mutatkar, R.K. Apte Hemant, (1999). "Sexual behaviour amongst adolescents in rural Maharashtra", In *AIDS Research and Review*, National AIDS Research Institute, Pune.

Mutatkar, R.K. (2004). *Action Strategies for Health and Education in Tribal Nandurbar: Maharashtra Human Development Action Research Study*, Indira Gandhi Institute of Development Research, Mumbai.

Mutatkar, R.K. *et al.* (ed.) (2004). *Towards Community Participation for Leprosy Elimination*, Alert India, Mumbai.

Mutatkar, R.K. (2005). "Understanding EMIC perspectives," In *Socio-Behavioural Aspects of Microbicide Trials for HIV Prevention*, ICMR, New Delhi.

Mutatkar, R.K. (2007). "Nation building and development, role of social anthropology: Interdisciplinary dialogues with partners in development", In Roy, Sanjay and Danda, Ajit, (eds.) *Methodological Questions in Social Anthropology*, INCAA.

Mutatkar, R.K. (2010). "Practicing anthropology for human dignity", In "*Journal of the Asiatic Society*", Vol. LII, No. 2, 21-40.

Mutatkar, R.K. (2010). "Emerging paradigms: Anthropology and social realities", In Danda, Ajit and Dipali (eds.) (2010). *Anthropology in India: Current Epistemology and Future Challenges*, INCAA.

Mutatkar, R.K. *et al.* (eds.). (2010). "*Studies on Bio-Medical Anthropology*", INCAA, New Delhi: Aryan Books International.

Mutatkar, R.K. (2010). "On medical anthropology", In Mutatkar, R.K. *et al.* (eds.), *Studies on Bio-Medical Anthropology*, INCAA, New Delhi: Aryan Books International.

Mutatkar, R.K. (2012). "Anthropological perspectives of health care", In Danda, Ajit *et al.* (eds.), *Plural Nature of Anthropology*, Indian Anthropological Society, Kolkata.

Mutatkar, R.K. (2012). Understanding Mahatma Gandhi: An anthropological perspective", In Danda, Ajit and Das, Rajat K. (eds.) *Alternative Voices in Anthropology*, Indian Anthropological Society, Kolkata.

Mutatkar, R.K. (2013). "Threat to identity of anthropology", In Danda, Ajit *et al.* (eds.) *The Globalized World*, INCAA.

Mutatkar, R.K. (2013). "Anthropology in Western India", In *The Indian Journal of Anthropology*, 1:1: 185-190, INCAA.

Mutatkar, R.K. (2014). "Anthropology and the future of Humankind: Research issues", In Danda, *et al.* (eds.) *Anthropology and the Future of Humankind*, INCAA.

Mutatkar, R.K. (2016). "*AYUSH in Public Health*", Vol. I and II, New Delhi: Concept Publishing Co. Pvt. Ltd.

Mutatkar, R.K. (2017). "Practicing medical anthropology for policy shifts", In Sharma, B.V. (ed.) *Medical Anthropology, Tradition and Change*, New Delhi: Concept Publishing Co. Pvt. Ltd.

Mutatkar, R.K. (2018). "*Tribal Health and Malnutrition*", New Delhi: Concept Publishing Co. Pvt. Ltd.

Mutatkar, R.K. and Nagarkar, Aarti (ed.). (2019). "*Sexuality, Sexual Behaviour and Reproductive Health*", New Delhi: Concept Publishing Co. Pvt. Ltd.

Mutatkar, R.K. (2019). "Anthropology and sexuality", In Mutatkar, R.K. and Nagarkar, Aarti (ed.). (2019). *Sexuality, Sexual Behaviour and Reproductive Health*, New Delhi: Concept Publishing Co. Pvt. Ltd.

Mutatkar, Rohit (2007). *Social Group Disparities, Ethnicity and Poverty in India*, Ph.D. Thesis. (unpublished), Indira Gandhi Institute of Development Research, Mumbai.

Mutatkar, Rohit (2014). *Backward Communities in Maharashtra, Background Paper for the Maharashtra Human Development Report*, Government of Maharashtra, YASHADA, Pune.

Mutatkar, Rohit (2017). "Poverty and deprivation among the Katkari", In *Economic and Political Weekly*, LII:13:27-29.

Mutatkar, Kalpana (2013). "Practicing medical anthropology: Addressing malnutrition among tribal children", In Bhat, H.K. *et al.* (eds.) *Explorations in Indian Medical Anthropology*, Vol. I and II, New Delhi: Concept Publishing Co. Pvt. Ltd.

Mukerji, B. (1961). *Community Development in India*, Orient Longmans, Bombay.

Naik, T.B. (1972). "Applied anthropology in India", In ICSSR *A Survey of Research in Sociology and Social Anthropology*, Vol. III. ICSSR, New Delhi.

Nehru, Jawaharlal (1955). "Kurukshetra", In *Kurukshetra: A Symposium on Community Development in India*, The Publications Division, GoI., Delhi.

Parasuraman, S. (2013). *Development Anthropology: Defining Values and Methodologies to Facilitate Creation of a Better World*, INCAA, Kolkata.

Patwardhan, P.H. (1955). "Success or Failure?", In *Kurukshetra: A Symposium on Community Development in India*, The Publications Division, GoI., Delhi.

Pandit, C.G. (1982). *My World of Preventive Medicine*, New Delhi: ICMR.

Paul, Benjamin (ed.). (1955). *Health, Culture and Community*, Russell Sage Foundation, New York.

Planning Commission, (2006). *Report of the Steering Committee on AYUSH in Public Health*, New Delhi.

Pontifical Academy of Sciences, (1984). *Immunology, Epidemiology and Social Aspects of Leprosy*, Vatican.

Priya, Ritu and Shweta, A.S. (2010). *Status and Role of AYUSH and Local Health Traditions under NRHM*, New Delhi: NHSRC.

Prasad, Rajendra (1955). "Yajna", In *Kurukshetra; Symposium on Community Development in India,* The Publications Division, GoI, Delhi.

Radhakrishnan, R. (2007). *Report of the Expert Group on Agricultural Indebtedness*, Ministry of Finance, GoI., New Delhi.

Raju, M.S. Rao, P.S.S., Mutatkar, R.K. (ed.), (2014). *Eliminating Leprosy Stigma: A Manual for Community Action*, The Leprosy Mission Trust, India, New Delhi.

Redfield, Robert (1953). "Relations of anthropology to the social sciences and to the humanities", In Kroebar, A.L. (ed.) *Anthropology Today*, The University of Chicago Press.

Redfield, Robert (1962). "Cultural role of cities", In Redfield, Margaret (ed.) *Human Nature and the Study of Society,* The University of Chicago Press.

Redfield, Robert (1962). "The natural history of folk society", In Redfield, Margaret (ed.), *Human Nature and the study of Society,* The University of Chicago Press.

Redfield, Robert (2018). *Peasant Society and Culture*, Rawat Publications (Indian reprint for sale in India).

Roy Burman, B.K. (1990). "Development and poverty among the tribals", In Tarlok Singh (ed.), *Social Science Research and Problem of Poverty,* New Delhi: Concept Publishing Co.

Saxena, N.C. (2014). "Children of a lesser god", In *Seminar: The Malnourished Tribal*, No. 661, New Delhi.

Sethi, Vani, (2014). "The Problem", In *Seminar: The Malnourished Tribal*, No. 661, New Delhi.

Sinha, Dharani (1991). "Anthropology in the 21st Century: Issues and Challenges", 78th Indian Science Congress: Sectional Presidential Address, Indian Science Congress Association, Kolkata.

Srinivasan, H, (1991). Ed. *Social Science Research and Social Action for better Leprosy Control*, IAL, Madras.

Srinivas, M.N. (1966). *Social Change in Modern India*, Berkeley.

Symington, D. (1938). *Report on Partially Excluded Areas: Measures for improvement of conditions of Bhils and other aboriginal hill tribes in Bombay Presidency*, Government of Bombay.

Spicer, Edward (ed.) (1957). *Human Problems in Technological Change*, Ithaca: Cornell University Press, N.Y.

Spicer, Edward (ed.) (1977). *Ethnic Medicine in the Southwest*, University of Arizona.

Sukhatme, P.V. (1982). *Newer Concepts in Nutrition and Their Implications for Policy*, Maharashtra Association for the Cultivation of Science, Pune.

Sukhatme, P.V. (1990). *Relationship between Poverty and Malnutrition*, In Tarlok Singh (ed.), *Social Science Research and Problem of Poverty*, New Delhi: Concept Publishing Co.

Sengupta, Sarthak (2013): "Anthropological Studies on the People of North-East India", In *The Indian Journal of Anthropology*: 1: 1:167-184, INCAA.

Tax, Sol. "The setting of the science ofman", as "Anthropology Series 1", The Voice of America Forum Lectures.

Tata Institute of Social Sciences (2006). *High Court Judgement about the Farmers Suicide in Maharashtra*, Mumbai.

Tata Institute of Social Sciences (2015). *Tribal Sub-plan in Maharashtra: A Diagnostic Study*, Mumbai.

Tata Institute of Social Sciences (2015). *A Tribal Atlas for Maharashtra*, Mumbai.

Tarlok Singh (ed.) (1990). *Social Science Research and Problem of Poverty*, New Delhi: Concept Publishing Co.

Taylor, Carl C. (1955). "Questions and Answers", In *Kurukshetra,* Publications Division, GoI, Delhi.

Trostle, J. (2005). *Epidemiology and Culture*, Cambridge University Press.

University Grants Commission, (2001), *UGC Model Curriculum: Anthropology*, UGC, New Delhi.

Valiathan, M.S. (2003). *The Legacy of Caraka*, Chennai: Orient Longmans.

Vidyarthi, L.P. (1972). "Tribal ethnography in India", In ICSSR (ed.) *A Survey of Research in Sociology and Social Anthropology,* Vol. III. New Delhi.

Vidyarthi, L.P. (1978). "Foreword", In Bhattacharya, D.K. (ed.). *Anthropologists in India*, Indian Anthropological Association, Delhi.

Vogel, Virgil J. (1970). *American Indian Medicine*, University of Oklahoma Press.

WHO (1985). *Epidemiology of Leprosy in Relation to Control*, TRS–716, Geneva.

Weaver, Thomas (ed.) (2002). "The Dynamics of Applied Anthropology in the Twentieth Century: The Malinowski Award Papers", Society for Applied Anthropology, Oklahoma City.

Xiaotong Fei. (2002). "Towards a people's anthropology", In Weaver, T. (ed.) *The Dynamics of Applied Anthropology in the Twentieth Century: The Malinowski Award Papers*, Society for Applied Anthropology, Oklahoma City.

Index